THE THEORY AND PRACTICE
OF ONLINE LEARNING

THE THEORY AND PRACTICE OF ONLINE LEARNING

Second Edition

edited by
TERRY ANDERSON

AU PRESS

© 2008 AU Press
Fourth printing 2010

First edition published 2004

Published by AU Press, Athabasca University
1200, 10011 – 109 Street
Edmonton, AB T5J 3S8

Library and Archives Canada Cataloguing in Publication
Theory and practice of online learning / edited by Terry Anderson. –
  2nd ed.

Includes bibliographical references and index.
Issued also in electronic format.
ISBN 978-1-897425-08-4

1. Computer-assisted instruction. 2. Internet in education.
3. Distance education. I. Anderson, Terry, 1950-

LB1044.87.T54 2008   371.33'4   C2008-902587-3

Printed and bound in Canada by Marquis Book Printing

Please contact AU Press, Athabasca University at
aupress@athabascau.ca for permission beyond the usage
outlined in the Creative Commons license.

Today, online learning is the most accessible pathway to the new knowledge economy and related jobs for the majority of working people. To be effective for the next generation, online learning has to include mobile learning, e-gaming, online communities, and learning management systems that engage each user. Athabasca University is a leading institution in the design, testing, and application of new e-learning environments. The authors of this second edition of the Theory and Practice of Online Learning *illustrate that leadership. With this book Athabasca University, its faculty, and staff share their expertise, knowledge, and enthusiasm for the learning tools and techniques that promise to extend access, while retaining high quality learning opportunities.*

Frits Pannekoek
President, Athabasca University

TABLE OF CONTENTS

FOREWORD TO
THE SECOND EDITION

The revised version of the *Theory and Practice of Online Learning*, edited by Terry Anderson, brings together recent developments in both the practice and our understanding of online learning.

Five years have since passed between this new edition and the first version. Five years is certainly a long time in this business as this second edition illustrates. The improvement in versatility and sophistication of the technologies that have been coming into common use has been so significant that a revisit of our knowledge of learning technologies and their application was becoming increasingly necessary. Anderson and the other authors of this text have responded to the need and have done the higher education community a great service by bringing it out in the electronic open access format under a Creative Commons License. Those of us from the other world are beneficiaries of this generosity and intellectual benevolence.

Online learning has begun to embed itself as a part of our educational environment, especially in the higher education and training sectors. The practice is not widespread yet but the growing number of institutions and individuals resorting to this innovation seems to be increasing exponentially. This increase is not limited to the developed world; colleagues in the developing world are equally enthusiastic about mediated learning for any number of reasons, including expanding access and providing flexibility to populations hungry for learning and training.

This revised publication with new knowledge and additional chapters is a great help for many of us who are still very much on the learning curve in our understanding of online learning.

Raj Dhanarajan
Vice Chancellor
Wawasan Open University
Penang, Malaysia
4 April 2008

INTRODUCTION

TERRY ANDERSON

This second edition of the *Theory and Practice of Online Learning* is an updated version of the highly successful 2004 first edition. Each of the chapters has been revised to reflect current theory and practice, and four new chapters have been added.

The first edition was a landmark experiment: it was both produced in paper copy and made available for free download under a Creative Commons license. The 400 paper copies sold rapidly and over 80,000 copies of the full text have been downloaded, in addition to thousands of copies of individual chapters. A number of the chapters have also been translated into five languages and reprinted regionally. The text and individual chapters have also been widely cited by other scholars. A December 2007 search of *Google Scholar* shows that the full text has been cited 65 times and the individual chapters a further 243 times. Finally, each of the authors has received positive feedback, both for the quality of the work and for its availability.

As with the first edition, this is a collection of works by practitioners and scholars actively working in the field of distance education. The text has been written at a time when the field is undergoing fundamental change. Although not an old discipline by academic standards, distance education practice and theory has evolved through five generations in its 150 years of existence (Taylor, 2001).

For most of this time, distance education was an individual pursuit defined by infrequent postal communication between student and teacher. The last half of the twentieth century has witnessed rapid developments and the emergence of three additional generations, one supported by the mass media of television and radio, another by the synchronous tools of video and audio teleconferencing, and yet another based on computer conferencing.

The early twenty-first century has produced the first visions of a fifth generation – based on autonomous agents and intelligent, database-assisted learning – that has been referred to as the educational Semantic Web (Anderson, 2004) and Web 2.0. Note that each of these generations has followed more quickly upon its predecessor than the previous ones. Moreover, none of these generations has completely displaced previous ones, so that we are left with diverse yet viable systems of distance education that use all five generations in combination. Thus, the field can accurately be described as complex, diverse, and rapidly evolving.

Acknowledging complexity does not excuse inaction. Distance educators, students, administrators, and parents are daily forced to make choices regarding the pedagogical, economic, systemic, and political characteristics of the distance education systems within which they participate. To provide information, knowledge, and, we hope, a measure of wisdom, the authors of this text have shared their expertise, their vision, their concerns, and their solutions to distance education practice in these disruptive times.

Each chapter is written as a jumping-off point for further reflection, for discussion, and, most importantly, for action. Never in the history of life on our planet has the need for informed and wisdom-filled action been greater than it is today. We are convinced that education – in its many forms – is the most hopeful antidote to the errors of greed, of ignorance, and of life-threatening aggression that menace our civilization and our planet.

Distance education (of which online learning is a major subset) is a discipline that subsumes the knowledge and practice of pedagogy, of psychology and sociology, of economics and business, of production and technology. We attempt to address each of these perspectives through the words of those trained to view their work through a particular disciplinary lens. Thus, each of the chapters represents the specialized expertise of individual authors who address that component piece of the whole with which they have a unique familiarity. This expertise is defined by a disciplinary background, a set of formal training skills, and a practice within one component of the distance education system. It is hardly surprising, then, that some of the chapters are more academic, reflecting their authors' primary role as scholar, while others are grounded in the more practical application focus of their authors.

In sum, the book is neither an academic tome nor a prescriptive "how to" guide. Like the university itself, the book represents a blending of scholarship and of research; practical attention to the details of teaching and of provision for learning opportunity; dissemination of research results; and mindful attention to the economics of the business of education.

In many ways, the chapters represent the best of what makes for a university community. According to the Allwords English Dictionary (2008), the word *university* comes from the Latin *universitas* (totality or wholeness), which itself contains two simpler roots, *unus* (one or singular) and *versere* (to turn). Thus, a university reflects a singleness or sense of all-encompassing wholeness, implying a study of all that is relevant and an acceptance of all types of pursuit of knowledge. The word also retains the sense of evolution and growth implied by the action embedded in the verb to turn. In our progress through the first part of the twenty-first century, the world is in the midst of a great turning as we adopt and adapt to the technological capabilities that allow information and communication to be distributed anywhere, anytime.

The ubiquity and multiplicity of human and agent communication, coupled with tremendous increases in information production and retrieval, are the most compelling characteristics of the Net-based culture and economy in which we now function. The famous quote from Oracle Corporation, "The Net changes everything," applies directly to the formal provision of education. Institutions that formerly relied on students gathering in campus-based classrooms are suddenly able (and many seem eager) to offer their programming on the Internet. Similarly, institutions accustomed to large-scale distance delivery via print or television are now being asked to provide more flexible, interactive, and responsive Net-based alternatives. Each of the chapters in the book reflects the often disruptive effect of the Net on particular components of a distance education system.

This book is written in large part by authors from a single university – Athabasca University – which has branded itself "Canada's Open University." As an open university, we are pleased to be the first such institution to provide a text like this one as an open and free gift to others. The book is published by Athabasca University's AU Press, one of the world's first open-access presses. It is published under a Creative Commons license (see http://creativecommons.org) to allow for free use by all, yet the copyright is retained by the university (see the copyright page for license details).

This open-access license format was chosen for a number of reasons. First, it is true to the original spirit of a university, and especially of an open university. We believe that knowledge is meant to be shared, and further, that such sharing does not diminish its value to its creator. Thomas Jefferson eloquently expressed these ideas in 1813 when he wrote,

> He who receives an idea from me, receives instruction himself without lessening mine; as he who lights his taper at mine, receives light without darkening me. That ideas should freely spread from one to another over the globe, for the moral and mutual instruction of man, and improvement of his condition, seems to have been peculiarly and benevolently designed by nature, when she made them, like fire, expansible over all space, without lessening their density in any point, and like the air in which we breathe, move, and have our physical being, incapable of confinement or exclusive appropriation. (1854, pp. 180–181)

As you will see from the quotations and references that augment the text in most chapters, we have learned much from the works of others, and thus feel bound to return this gift of knowledge to the wider community.

Second, we believe that education is one of the few sustainable means to equip humans around the globe with the skills and resources to confront the challenges of ignorance, poverty, war, and environmental degradation. Distance education is perhaps the most powerful means of extending this resource and making it accessible to all. Thus, we contribute to the elimination of human suffering by making as freely available as we can the knowledge that we have gained from developing distance education alternatives.

Third, the Creative Commons license provides our book as a form of "gift culture." Gift giving has been a component of many cultures;

witness, for example, the famed Potlatch ceremonies of Canadian West Coast First Nations peoples. More recently, gift giving has been a major motivation of hackers developing many of the most widely used open-source products on the Internet (Raymond, 2001). Distributing this text as an open-access gift serves many of the same functions that gift giving has done through millennia. The gift weaves bonds within our community and empowers those who benefit from it to create new knowledge that they can then share with others and with us. Interestingly, research on neuro-economics is showing that freely giving and sharing is a behaviour that has had important survival functions for humans groups since earliest times (Grimes 2003). David Bollier (2002) argues that gift cultures are surprisingly resilient and effective at creating and distributing goods, while protecting both long-term capacity for sustained production and growing cultural assets. Bollier also decries the private plunder of our common wealth, and discusses the obligation of those employed in the public sector to ensure that the results of publicly-funded efforts are not exploited for personal gain.

Open-access gifts also provide those from wealthy countries with some small way to redress many economic inequalities and to share more equitably the gifts we receive from our planet home. We hope especially that this text will be incorporated as an open educational resource into the syllabi of the growing number of programs of distance education study that are being offered by both campus and distance education universities throughout the world. In the words of Sir John Daniel, President and CEO of the Commonwealth of Learning, sharing offers a viable means to "increase the quality and quantity of electronic courseware as materials are refined, versioned and adapted by academics around the world and made freely available in these new formats" (Daniel, 2001, p. viii). We believe that the free sharing of course content is a powerful tool to encourage the growth of public education institutions. We also think that such sharing will not result in a net value loss for the delivering institution. Rather, its reputation will be enhanced and its saleable services will increase in value.

Fourth, providing this book as open access frees us from potentially acrimonious debates over ownership, return for value, and distribution of any profit. Educational books rarely make large profits for their authors, and most of us have personally witnessed the old aphorism that "acrimony in academic arguments runs so high because the stakes are so low." Open-access licensing allows us to go beyond financial arguments that are likely to have little consequence in any case.

Finally, our experience with the first edition has proven that open access allows the work to be more widely distributed and read. Through this dissemination, the ideas proposed are exposed to critical dialogue and reflection. We hope that much of this commentary will make its way back to the authors or flow into the discussion forums associated with the text's web site. Through review within the community of practice, ideas are honed, developed, and sometimes even refuted. Such discourse not only improves the field as a whole, but also directly benefits our work at Athabasca University, and thus handsomely repays our efforts.

In summary, we license the use of this book to all – not so much with a sense of naïve idealism, but with a realism that has been developed through our life work – to increase access to and opportunity for all to quality learning opportunities.

BOOK ORGANIZATION AND
INTRODUCTION TO THE CHAPTERS

In the following pages, we briefly review the main themes covered in this book and its chapters. Part I serves as a foundational and theoretical base for the full book. In Part II, we describe the essential infrastructure with particular focus on media and technology – critical carriers of distance education programming. In Part III, we examine issues related to course development and instructional design. In Part III, the structures, tools, and resource centres necessary to support students are reviewed.

Part I: Role and Function of Theory in Online Education Development and Delivery

The opening section provides the theoretical foundations for this volume. Chapter 1 presents the foundation of education theory for online learning. It opens the debate by discussing the contributions of behaviorist, cognitivist, constructivist, and connectivist theories to the design of online materials, noting that behaviorist strategies can be used to teach the facts (what), cognitivist strategies the principles and processes (how), and constructivist strategies the real-life and personal applications that contextualize learning. This edition of the chapter introduces connectivism, with its capacity to exploit the connections to knowledge and to people afforded by the now ubiquitous Internet and its applications. The chapter notes a shift toward constructive learning, in which learners are given the opportunity to construct their own meaning from the information presented during online sessions. Learning objects will be used to promote flexibility and the reuse of online materials to meet the needs of individual learners. And online learning materials will be created in such a way that they can be redesigned for different learners and different contexts. Finally, online learning will become increasingly diverse to allow it to respond to diverse learning cultures, styles, and motivations.

Chapter 2 presents a general assessment of how people learn, including the unique characteristics of the Web to enhance these generalized learning contexts, and discusses the six forms of interaction and their critical role in engaging and supporting both learners and teachers. The author presents a model of online learning, a first step toward a theory in which the two predominant forms of online learning – collaborative and independent study – are considered, along with a brief discussion of the advantages and disadvantages of each. Finally, the chapter discusses the emerging tools of the Semantic Web and the way they will affect future developments of the theory and practice of online learning.

In this first new chapter in the second edition, Chapter 3 details the important role of Prior Learning Assessment and Recognition (PLAR) in open education. Recognizing, in a formal structure, the knowledge that learners have garnered, both within and outside of formal education, is a challenge for educational institutions. We need to control the quality of the credential awarded but at the same time we need to value learners' time and ensure that they are not needlessly completing courses with knowledge they already own, solely to earn credits. The means by which Athabasca University has developed and implemented systems and tools that effectively measure an individual's knowledge, cost, and time are outlined in the chapter. In particular, the role of portfolios, composed by learners and assessed by faculty, is highlighted.

Chapter 4 is also new to this edition and adds a philosophical dimension to the text. It focuses first on the importance of understanding our philosophy of practice-in-practice. It then overviews commonly held philosophies of technology and of teaching. This chapter helps us, as individuals and as institutional decision makers, to make sound pedagogical and technological decisions that will then be reflected in the nature, quality, cost, and effectiveness of our distance education programming.

Part II: Infrastructure and Support for Content Development

This section covers the necessary infrastructure to produce and delivery quality distance online learning. Chapter 5 discusses the various factors that must be considered in developing the infrastructure for online learning, including planning, structural and organizational issues, the components of a system and the interfaces among them, and various related issues, such as human resources, decision-making, and training. The authors explain why any designed online learning infrastructure must also be able to evolve and work in a context of constant and accelerating change to accommodate changing student needs, technologies, and curricula.

Chapter 6 examines some available and potential technologies and features used in online instruction. Rather than continue to focus on how technology has helped or can help the instructor, teacher, or tutor, this chapter concludes with a look at how technologies – existing and emerging – can aid this first generation of online learners. This chapter has been updated to explore some of the technologies, including blogs and wikis, that have become prominent in online learning since the date of the first edition.

Chapter 7 discusses attributes of media, and of the modes of teaching presentation and learning performance they support, in relation to some influential learning models. It also clarifies some of the implications in the choice of any specific delivery or presentation medium. The author notes that the decision to adopt online technology is always complex and can be risky, especially if the adopting organization lacks structural, cultural, or financial prerequisites, and concludes that, while education has a responsibility to keep pace with technological change, educational institutions can reduce the costs and uncertainties of invention by following the technological lead of the corporate sector.

Chapter 8 is another new chapter for this edition that focuses on the use of mobile technologies to support teaching, learning, and research. The drastic reduction in the cost of portable electronic devices, coupled with increasing access to mobile connectivity, allows online learning to begin to situate online education anywhere. This chapter overviews the affordances and restrictions of this technology and provides examples of products developed at Athabasca University.

Chapter 9 was added as a suggestion from an anonymous learner who suggested (quite correctly) that new social software and Web 2.0 tools are being used very extensively, and that a discussion on the opportunities and challenges they afford for online learning was missing from the first draft. While still in the future for mainstream use, this chapter documents the development of a social software suite (http://me2u.athabascau.ca) and explains why we believe this type of student and community tool work in an online environment. In describing aspects of teaching and applying team dynamics online, the authors highlight the unique values and capabilities of an online learning environment.

REFERENCES

Anderson, T. (2004). The educational semantic web: A vision for the next phase of educational computing. *Educational Technology, 44*(5), 5–9.

Allwords Dictionary. University. Retrieved Feb. 2008, from http://www. allwords.com/word-unisersity.html

Bollier, D. (2002). *Private theft: The private plunder of our common wealth.* New York: Routledge.

Daniel, J. (2001, May 18). Evolution not an e-revolution in global learning. *Times Higher Education Supplement,* p. VIII.

Grimes, K. (2003). To trust is human. *New Scientist, 178,* 32–37.

Jefferson, T. (1854). Letter to Isaac McPherson. In H. A. Washington (Ed.), *Writings of Thomas Jefferson* (Vol. 6, pp. 180–181). Philadelphia: Lippincott.

Raymond, E. (2001). *The cathedral and the bazaar.* Cambridge, MA: O'Reilly.

Taylor, J. (2001). The future of learning – learning for the future: Shaping the transition. *Proceedings of the 20th ICDE World Congress.* Retrieved Dec. 2007 from http://www.fernuni-hagen.de/ICDE/D-2001/final/keynote_speeches/wednesday/taylor_keynote.pdf

PART I

ROLE AND FUNCTION OF THEORY IN ONLINE EDUCATION DEVELOPMENT AND DELIVERY

CHAPTER 1

Foundations of Educational Theory for Online Learning

Mohamed Ally
Athabasca University

INTRODUCTION

There is ongoing debate about whether using a particular delivery technology improves the learning (Beynon, 2007; Clark, 2001; Kozma, 2001). It has long been recognized that specialized delivery technologies can provide efficient and timely access to learning materials; however, Clark (1983) claims that technologies are merely vehicles that deliver instruction, and do not themselves influence student achievement. As Clark notes, meta-analysis studies on media research show that students gain significant learning benefits from audiovisual or computer media, as opposed to conventional instruction; however, the same studies also suggest that the reason for those benefits is not the medium of instruction, but the instructional strategies built into the learning materials. Similarly, Schramm (1977) suggests that learning is influenced more by the content and instructional strategy in the learning materials than by the type of technology used to deliver instruction.

According to Bonk and Reynolds (1997), to promote higher-order thinking on the Web, online learning must create challenging activities that enable learners to link new information to old; acquire meaningful knowledge; and use their metacognitive abilities; hence, it is the instructional strategy, not the technology, that influences the quality of learning. Kozma (2001), on the other hand, argues that the particular attributes of the computer are needed to bring real-life models and simulations to the learner; thus, according to Kozma, the medium does influence learning. Kozma claims that it is not the computer per se that makes students learn, but the design of the real-life models and simulations, and the students' interaction with those models and simulations. The computer is merely the vehicle that provides the processing capability and delivers the instruction to learners (Clark, 2001).

Online learning allows participants to collapse time and space (Cole, 2000); however, the learning materials must be designed properly to engage the learner and promote learning. The delivery method allows for flexibility of access, from anywhere and usually anytime, but the learning must use sound instructional design principles. According to Rossett (2002), online learning has many promises, but it takes commitment and resources, and must be done right. Doing it right means that online learning materials must be designed properly, with the learners and learning in focus, and that adequate support must be provided. Ring and Mathieux (2002) suggest that online learning should have high authenticity (i.e., students should learn in the context of the workplace), high interactivity, and high collaboration. This chapter discusses the foundation of educational theory for the design of effective online learning materials, and suggests a model for developing online instruction based on appropriate educational theory.

Different terminologies have been used for online learning, which makes it difficult to develop a generic definition. Terms commonly used for online learning include e-learning, Internet learning, distributed learning, networked learning, tele-learning, virtual learning, computer-assisted learning, web-based learning, and distance learning. All of these terms imply that the learner is at a distance from the tutor or instructor, that the learner uses some form of technology (usually a computer) to access the learning materials, that the learner uses technology to interact with the tutor or instructor and with other learners, and that some form of support is provided to learners. This paper will use the term online learning throughout. There are many definitions of online learning in the literature, reflecting the diversity of practice and associated technologies.

Carliner (1999) defines online learning as educational material that is presented on a computer. Khan (1997) defines online instruction as an innovative approach for delivering instruction to a remote audience, using the Web as the medium. Online learning, however, involves more than just the presentation and delivery of materials using the Web: the learner and the learning process should be the focus of online learning. As a result, the author defines online learning as

> [t]he use of the Internet to access learning materials; to interact with the content, instructor, and other learners; and to obtain support during the learning process, in order to acquire knowledge, to construct personal meaning, and to grow from the learning experience. (Ally, p. 7)

BENEFITS OF ONLINE LEARNING

Increasingly, organizations are adopting online learning as the main delivery method to train employees (Simmons, 2002). At the same time, educational institutions are moving toward the use of the Internet for delivery, both on campus and at a distance. For organizations and institutions to make this often expensive move, there must be a perception that using online learning provides major benefits. Some of the benefits for learners and instructors are detailed below.

For learners, online learning knows no time zones, and location and distance are not issues. In asynchronous online learning, students can access the online materials anytime, while synchronous online learning allows for real-time interaction between students and instructors. Learners can use the Internet to access up-to-date and relevant learning materials, and can communicate with experts in the field which they are studying. Situated learning, or the application of knowledge and skills in specific contexts, is facilitated, since learners can complete online courses while working on the job or in their own space, and can contextualize the learning.

For instructors, tutoring can be done anytime, anywhere. Online materials can be updated, and learners can see the changes immediately. When learners are able to access materials on the Internet, it is easier for instructors to direct them to appropriate information based on their needs. If designed properly, online learning systems can be used to determine learners' needs and current level of expertise, and to assign appropriate materials for learners to select from, to achieve their desired learning outcomes.

DESIGNING ONLINE LEARNING MATERIALS

The goal of any instructional system is to promote learning. Therefore, before any learning materials are developed, educators must tacitly or explicitly know the principles of learning and how students learn. This is especially true for online learning, where instructors and learners are separated. The development of effective online learning materials should be based on proven and sound learning theories. As discussed above, the delivery medium is not the determining factor in the quality of learning per se; rather, course design determines the effectiveness of the learning (Rovai, 2002).

There are many schools of thought on learning, and no one school is used exclusively to design online learning materials. As there is no single learning theory to follow, we can use a combination of theories to develop online learning materials. In addition, as research progresses, new theories that should be used are emerging and evolving. A recent example is connectivist theory, which is needed for the emerging age of distributed and network learning. Some may question the need for a new learning theory, however, especially when there are already well-established theories used successfully to design instruction. Also, past learning theories have been adapted to address new and changing learning contexts. These existing learning theories, however, were developed before distributed and networked learning was used widely by educators. According to Siemens (2004), we now need a theory for the digital age to guide the development of learning materials for the networked world. Educators should be able to adapt existing learning theories for the digital age, while at the same time using the principles of connectivism to guide the development of effective learning materials. What is needed is not a new stand-alone theory for the digital age, but a model that integrates the different theories to guide the design of online learning materials.

To select the most appropriate instructional strategies, the online developer must know the different approaches to learning. Strategies should be selected to motivate learners, facilitate deep processing, build the whole person, cater to individual differences, promote meaningful learning, encourage interaction, provide relevant feedback, facilitate contextual learning, and provide support during the learning process. The remaining sections of this chapter present the different schools of thought on learning and suggest how these different schools of thought can be used to develop effective online materials.

SCHOOLS OF LEARNING

Early computer learning systems were designed based on a behaviorist approach to learning. The behaviorist school of thought, influenced by Thorndike (1913), Pavlov (1927), and Skinner (1974), postulates that learning is a change in observable behaviour caused by external stimuli in the environment (Skinner, 1974). Behaviorists claim that observable behaviour indicates whether or not the learner has learned something, and not what is going on in the learner's head. In response, some educators claim that not all learning is observable and there is more to learning than a change in behaviour. As a result, there has been a shift away from behaviorist to cognitive learning theories.

Cognitive psychology claims that learning involves the use of memory, motivation, and thinking, and that reflection plays an important part in learning. Cognitive theorists see learning as an internal process, and contend that the amount learned depends on the processing capacity of the learner, the amount of effort expended during the learning process, the depth of the processing (Craik & Lockhart, 1972; Craik & Tulving, 1975), and the learner's existing knowledge structure (Ausubel, 1974).

Recently, there has been a move towards constructivism. Constructivist theorists claim that learners interpret the information and the world according to their personal reality, that they learn by observation, processing, and interpretation, and then personalize the information into personal knowledge (Cooper, 1993; Wilson, 1997). Learners learn best when they can contextualize what they learn for immediate application and personal meaning.

A recently proposed theory under discussion is connectivism (Downes, 2006; Siemens, 2004). According to Siemens, connectivism is the integration of principles explored by chaos, network, complexity and self-organization theories. Due to the information explosion in the current age, learning is not under the control of the learner. Changing environments, innovations, changes in the discipline and in related disciplines all suggest that learners have to unlearn what they have learned in the past, and learn how to learn and evaluate new information. What must be learned is determined by others and is continually changing. And since machines are becoming smart with the use of intelligent agents, Siemens also asks whether, in fact, learning may reside in machines. Some knowledge will reside in machines while some will reside in humans. The challenge for educators, therefore, is how to design instruction for both machines and humans, and how the two can interact with each other. For example, if there is a change in a procedure on how to use a machine, the wireless capability in the machine will allow the updated procedure to be downloaded into the machine's memory. When a learner goes to interact with the recently updated machine, that learner will be informed that the procedure has changed and that the machine will guide them through the procedure (Siemens 2004).

Under a close analysis of the behaviorist, cognitivist, and constructivist schools of thought, many overlaps in the ideas and principles become apparent. The design of online learning materials can include principles from all three schools of thought. According to Ertmer and Newby (1993), the three schools of thought can, in fact, be used as a taxonomy for learning. Behaviorists' strategies can be used to teach the *what* (facts); cognitive strategies can be used to teach the *how* (processes and principles); and constructivist strategies can be used to teach the *why* (higher-level thinking that promotes personal meaning, and situated and contextual learning). Janicki and Liegle (2001) analyzed different instructional design models to identify the components that support quality design of web-based instruction. They identify components from each of the behaviorist, cognitivist, and constructivist schools of learning, and explore connectivist theory to help designers use it to guide the design of learning materials.

Behaviorist School of Learning

The behaviorist school sees the mind as a black box, in the sense that a response to a stimulus can be observed quantitatively, thereby ignoring the effect of thought processes occurring in the mind. This school, therefore, looks at overt behaviours that can be observed and measured as indicators of learning (Good & Brophy, 1990).

Implications for Online Learning

1. Learners should be told the explicit outcomes of the learning so they can set expectations and judge for themselves whether or not they have achieved the outcome of the online lesson.

2. Learners must be tested to determine whether or not they have achieved the learning outcome. Online testing or other forms of testing and assessment should be integrated into the learning sequence to check individual learner's achievement level and provide appropriate feedback.
3. The learning materials must be sequenced appropriately to promote learning. The sequencing could take the form of simple to complex, known to unknown, and knowledge to application.
4. Learners must be provided with feedback so that they can monitor how they are doing and take corrective action if required.

COGNITIVIST SCHOOL OF LEARNING

Cognitivists see learning as an internal process that involves memory, thinking, reflection, abstraction, motivation, and metacognition. Cognitive psychology looks at learning from an information processing point of view, where the learner uses different types of memory during learning (Figure 1). Sensations are received through the senses into the

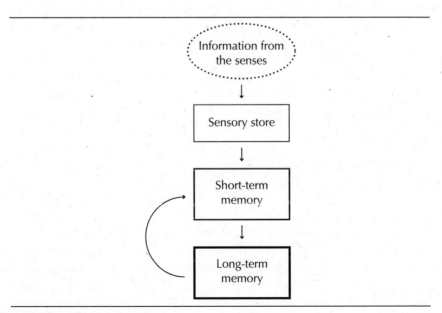

FIGURE 1. Types of memory

sensory store before processing occurs. The information persists in the sensory store for less than one second (Kalat, 2007), and if it is not transferred to working memory immediately, it is lost. Online instruction must use strategies to allow learners to attend to the learning materials so they can be transferred from the senses to the sensory store and then to working memory. The amount of information transferred to working memory depends on the amount of attention that was paid to the incoming information and whether cognitive structures are in place to make sense of the information. The duration in working memory is approximately 20 seconds, and if information in working memory is not processed efficiently, it is not transferred to long-term memory for storage (Kalat, 2007). So, designers must check to see if the appropriate existing cognitive structure is present to enable the learner to process the information. If the relevant cognitive structure is not present, pre-instructional strategies, such as advance organizers, should be included as part of the learning process (Ausubel, 1960).

Online learning strategies must present the materials and use strategies that enable students to process the materials efficiently. Since working memory has limited capacity, information should be organized or chunked in pieces of appropriate size to facilitate processing. According to Miller (1956), because humans have limited short-term memory capacity, information should be grouped into meaningful sequences, such as five to nine (i.e., 7 ± 2), meaningful units.

After the information is processed in working memory, it is stored in long-term memory. The amount transferred to long-term memory is determined by the quality and depth of processing in working memory. The deeper the processing, the more associations the acquired new information forms in memory. Information transferred from short-term memory to long-term memory is either assimilated or accommodated in long-term memory. During assimilation, the information is changed to fit into existing cognitive structures. Accommodation occurs when an existing cognitive structure is changed to incorporate the new information.

Cognitive psychology postulates that information is stored in long-term memory in the form of nodes which connect to form relationships; that is, in networks. So, information maps that show the major concepts in a topic, and the relationships between those concepts, should be included in the online learning materials. According to Stoyanova and Kommers (2002), information-map generation requires critical reflection and is a method for externalizing the cognitive structure of learners. To facilitate deeper processing, learners should be encouraged to generate their own information maps.

Implications for Online Learning

1. Strategies used should allow learners to perceive and attend to the information so that it can be transferred to working memory. Learners use their sensory systems to register the information in the form of sensations. Strategies to facilitate maximum sensation should be used. Examples include the proper location of the information on the screen, the attributes of the screen (e.g., colour, graphics, size of text), the pacing of the information, and the mode of delivery (audio, visuals, animations, or video). Learners must receive the information in the form of sensations before perception and processing can occur; however, the learner must not be overloaded with sensations, which could be counter-productive to the learning process. Non-essential sensations should be avoided, to allow learners to attend to the important information. Strategies to promote perception and attention for online learning include the following:

   • Important information should be placed in the centre of the screen for reading, and learners must be able to read from left to right.

   • Information critical for learning should be highlighted to focus learners' attention. For example, in an online lesson, headings should be used to organize the details, and formatted to allow learners to attend to and process the information they contain.

   • Learners should be told why they should take the lesson, so that they can attend to the information throughout the lesson.

   • The difficulty level of the material must match the cognitive level of the learner, so that the learner can both attend to and relate to the material. Links to both simpler and more complicated materials can be used to accommodate learners at different knowledge levels.

2. Strategies used should allow learners to retrieve existing information from long-term memory to help make sense of the new information. Learners must construct a memory link between the new information and some related information already stored in long-term memory. Strategies to facilitate the use of existing schema are the following:

- Use advance organizers to activate existing cognitive structure or to provide the information to incorporate the details of the lesson. A comparative advance organizer can be used to help learners recall prior knowledge to help in processing, and an expository advance organizer can be used to help incorporate the details of the lesson (Ausubel, 1960). Mayer (1979) conducted a meta-analysis of advance organizer studies, and found that these strategies are effective when students are learning from text that is presented in an unfamiliar form. Since most courses contain materials that are new to learners, advance organizers should be used to provide the framework for learning.
- Provide conceptual models that learners can use to retrieve existing mental models or to store the structure they will need to use to learn the details of the lesson.
- Use pre-instructional questions to set expectations and to activate the learners' existing knowledge structure. Questions presented before the lesson facilitate the recall of existing knowledge, help learners to learn the materials, and motivate them to find additional resources to achieve the lesson outcome.
- Use prerequisite test questions to activate the prerequisite knowledge structure required for learning the new materials. With the flexibility of online learning, students with diverse background and knowledge can choose the most appropriate path to review previous or prerequisite learning before new information is presented.

3. Information should be chunked to prevent overload during processing in working memory (Miller, 1956). To facilitate efficient processing in working memory, online learning materials should present between five and nine items on a screen. If there are many items in a lesson, their organization should be shown in the form of information maps. A generalized information map is provided as an overview for the online lesson, and can be linear, hierarchical, or spider-shaped, as illustrated in Figures 2 to 4 (Holley, Dansereau, McDonald, Garland, & Collins 1979; Smith & Ragan, 1999). As the lesson progresses, each item in the generalized information map is presented and broken down into sub-items. At the end of the lesson, the generalized map is shown again, but with the relationships among the items illustrated.

To facilitate deep processing, learners should be asked to generate the information maps during the learning process or as

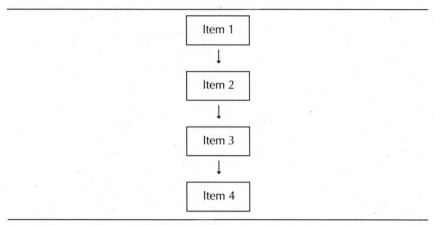

FIGURE 2. Linear information map

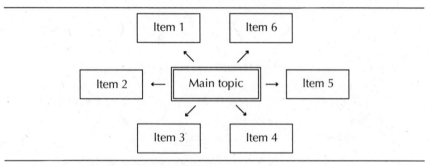

FIGURE 3. Spider-shaped information map

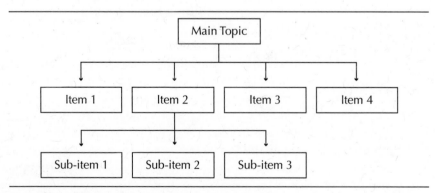

FIGURE 4. Hierarchical information map

a summary activity after the lesson (Bonk & Reynolds, 1997). In addition to facilitating deep processing, information maps can provide the big picture, to help learners to comprehend the details of a lesson. Online learning can capitalize on the processing and visual capabilities of the computer to present information maps to learners, or to ask learners to generate information maps using map-making software.

4. Other strategies that promote deep processing should be used to help transfer information to long-term storage. To make the transfer to long-term memory more effective, strategies should be used that require learners to apply, analyze, synthesize, and evaluate promote higher-level learning. Online strategies to allow learners to apply the information in real life should also be included, to contextualize the learning and to facilitate deep processing.

5. A variety of learning strategies should be included in online instruction to accommodate individual differences and *learning styles* (Cassidy, 2004). Learning style refers to how a learner perceives, interacts with, and responds to the learning environment; it measures individual differences. Different learning style instruments are used to determine students' learning styles. The Kolb Learning Style Inventory (LSI) looks at how learners perceive and process information (Kolb, 1984), whereas the Myers-Briggs Type Indicator uses dichotomous scales to measure extroversion versus introversion, sensing versus intuition, thinking versus feeling, and judging versus perception (Myers, 1978). In the following discussion, we consider the Kolb Learning Style Inventory.

Kolb suggests that two components make up our learning experience: perceiving and processing. Perceiving refers to the way learners sense and absorb the information around them, from concrete experience to reflective observation. Concrete experience relates to learners' desire to learn things that have personal meaning. During reflective observation, learners like to take the time to think about and reflect on the learning materials. The second component, processing, refers to how learners understand and process the information that is absorbed after perceiving. Processing ranges from abstract conceptualization to active experimentation. Learners who have a preference for abstract conceptualization like to learn facts and figures and research new information on different topics. Learners who have a preference for active experimentation like to apply what they learn to real-life situations and to go beyond what was presented. They like to try things and learn from their experience. Online learning can cater for individual differences by determining a learner's preference and providing appropriate learning activities based on that learner's style.

Online learning materials should include activities for the different styles, so that learners can select appropriate activities based on their preferred learning style. Concrete-experience learners prefer specific examples in which they can be involved, and they relate to peers more than to people in authority. They like group work and peer feedback, and they see the instructor as a coach or helper. These learners prefer support methods that allow them to interact with peers and obtain coaching from the instructor. Reflective-observation learners like to observe carefully before taking any action. They prefer that all the information be available for learning, and see the instructor as the expert. They tend to avoid interaction with others. Abstract-conceptualization learners like to work more with things and symbols and less with people. They like to work with theory and to conduct systematic analyses. Active-experimentation learners prefer to learn by doing practical projects and participating in group discussions. They prefer active learning methods and interact with peers for feedback and information. They tend to establish their own criteria for evaluating situations. Adequate supports should be provided for students with different learning styles. Ally and Fahy (2002) found that students with different learning styles have different preferences for support. For example, the assimilator learning style prefers high instructor presence, while the accommodator learning style prefers low instructor presence.

Cognitive style refers to a learner's preferred way of processing information; that is, the person's typical mode of thinking, remembering, or problem solving. Thus, cognitive style is another individual difference indicator. Cognitive style is considered to be a personality dimension that influences attitudes, values, and social interaction. One of the dimensions of cognitive style that has implications for online learning is the distinction between field-dependent and field-independent personalities (Witkin, Moore, Goodenough, & Cox, 1977). Field-independent personalities approach the environment in an analytical manner; for example, they distinguish figures as discrete from their backgrounds.

Field-independent individuals experience events in a more global, less differentiated way. Field-dependent individuals have a greater social orientation compared to field-independent personalities. Field-independent individuals are likely to learn more effectively under conditions of intrinsic motivation, such as self-study, and are influenced less by social reinforcement.

6. Information should be presented in different modes to facilitate processing and transferring it to long-term memory. Where possible, textual, verbal, and visual information should be presented to encourage encoding. According to dual-coding theory (Paivio, 1986), information received in different modes (textual and visual) will be processed better than that presented in a single mode (text). Dual-coded information is processed in different parts of the brain, resulting in more encoding. Presenting information in different modes also accommodates individual differences in processing.

7. Learners should be motivated to learn. It does not matter how effective the online materials are, if learners are not motivated, they will not learn. The issue is whether to use intrinsic motivation (driven from within the learner) or extrinsic motivation (instructor- and performance-driven). Designers of online learning materials should use intrinsic motivation strategies to motivate learners (Malone, 1981); however, extrinsic motivation should also be used since some learners are motivated by externally driven methods. Keller proposes the ARCS model (*Attention, Relevance, Confidence, Satisfaction*) for motivating learners during learning (Keller, 1983; Keller & Suzuki, 1988):

    - *Attention:* Capture the learners' attention at the start of the lesson and maintain it throughout the lesson. The online learning materials must include an activity at the start of the learning session to connect with the learners.
    - *Relevance:* Inform learners of the importance of the lesson and how taking the lesson could benefit them. Strategies could include describing how learners will benefit from taking the lesson, and how they can use what they learn in real-life situations. This strategy helps to contextualize the learning and make it more meaningful, thereby maintaining learners' interest throughout the learning session.
    - *Confidence:* Use strategies such as designing for success and informing learners of the lesson expectations. Design for success

by sequencing from simple to complex, or from known to unknown, and use a competency-based approach where learners are given the opportunity to use different strategies to complete the lesson. Inform learners of the lesson outcome and provide ongoing encouragement to complete the lesson.

- *Satisfaction:* Provide feedback on learners' performance and allow them to apply what they learn in real-life situations. Learners like to know how they are doing, and they like to contextualize what they are learning by applying the information in real life.

8. Encourage learners to use their metacognitive skills to help in the learning process (Mayer, 1998; Sternberg, 1998; Yorke & Knight, 2004). *Metacognition* is a learner's ability to be aware of his or her cognitive capabilities and use these capabilities to learn. When learning online, learners should be given the opportunity to reflect on what they are learning, collaborate with other learners, and check their progress. Self-check questions and exercises with feedback throughout a lesson are good strategies to allow learners to check how they are doing, so they can use their metacognitive skills to adjust their learning approach if necessary.

9. Online strategies that facilitate the transfer of learning should be used to encourage application in different and real-life situations. Simulation of the real situation, using real-life cases, should be part of the lesson. Also, learners should be given the opportunity to complete assignments and projects that use real-life applications and information. Transfer to real-life situations could assist the learners to develop personal meaning and contextualize the information.

Cognitive psychology suggests that learners receive and process information to be transferred into long-term memory for storage. The amount of information processed depends on the amount that is perceived, and the amount stored in long-term memory depends on the quality of the processing in working memory. Effective online lessons must use techniques to allow learners to sense and perceive the information, and must include strategies to facilitate high-level processing for transfer of information to long-term memory. After learners acquire the information, they create personal knowledge to make the materials meaningful. The constructivist school of learning, which is discussed below, suggests that learners construct personal knowledge from the learning experience.

CONSTRUCTIVIST SCHOOL OF LEARNING

Constructivists see learners as active rather than passive. Knowledge is not received from the outside or from someone else; rather, the individual learner interprets and processes what is received through the senses to create knowledge. The learner is the centre of the learning, with the instructor playing an advising and facilitating role. Learners should be allowed to construct knowledge rather than being given knowledge through instruction (Duffy & Cunningham, 1996). The construction of knowledge includes both physical and intellectual learning activities (Phillips, 2005). A major emphasis of constructivists is *situated learning*, which sees learning as contextual (Hung, Looi, & Koh, 2004). Learning activities that allow learners to contextualize the information should be used in online instruction. If the information has to be applied in many contexts, then learning strategies that promote multi-contextual learning should be used to make sure that learners can indeed apply the information broadly. Learning is moving away from one-way instruction to construction and discovery of knowledge (Tapscott, 1998).

In his transformation theory, Mezirow (1991) uses both constructivism and cognitivism to explain how people learn. He sees learning as "the process of using a prior interpretation to construe a new or revised interpretation of the meaning of one's experience in order to guide future action" (p. 12). Transformative learning involves "reflectively transforming the beliefs, attitudes, opinions, and emotional reactions that constitute our meaning schemes or transforming our meaning perspectives" (p. 223). Mezirow claims that learning involves five interacting contexts: the frame of reference or meaning perspective in which the learning is embedded; the conditions of communication; the line of action (process) in which the learning occurs; the self-image of the learner; and the situation encountered during the learning process (p. 13).

Implications for Online Learning

1. Learning should be an active process. Keeping learners active doing meaningful activities results in high-level processing, which facilitates the creation of personalized meaning. Asking learners to apply the information in a practical situation is an active process, and facilitates personal interpretation and relevance.
2. Learners should construct their own knowledge, rather than accepting that given by the instructor. Knowledge construction is facilitated by good interactive online instruction, since the students

have to take the initiative to learn and to interact with other students and the instructor, and because the learning agenda is controlled by the student (Murphy & Cifuentes, 2001). In an online environment, students experience the information first-hand, rather than receiving filtered information from an instructor whose style or background may differ from theirs. In a traditional lecture, instructors contextualize and personalize the information to meet their own needs, which may not be appropriate for all learners. In online instruction, learners experience the information first-hand, which gives them the opportunity to contextualize and personalize the information themselves.

3. Collaborative and cooperative learning should be encouraged to facilitate constructivist learning (Hooper & Hannafin, 1991; Johnson & Johnson, 1996; Palloff & Pratt, 1999). Working with other learners gives learners real-life experience of working in a group and allows them to use their metacognitive skills. Learners will also be able to use the strengths of other learners, and learn from others. When assigning group work, membership should be based on the expertise level and learning style of individual group members, so that individual team members can benefit from one another's strengths.

4. Learners should be given control of the learning process. There should be a form of guided discovery where learners are allowed to made decisions about learning goals, with some guidance from the instructor.

5. Learners should be given time and the opportunity to reflect. When learning online, students need the time to reflect and internalize the information. Embedded questions about the content can be used throughout the lesson to encourage learners to reflect on and process the information in a relevant and meaningful manner; or learners can be asked to generate a learning journal during the learning process, to encourage reflection and processing.

6. Learning should be made meaningful. Learning materials should include examples that relate to the learners so that they can make sense of the information. Assignments and projects should allow learners to choose meaningful activities to help them apply and personalize the information.

7. Learning should be interactive to promote higher-level learning and social presence, and to help develop personal meaning. According to Heinich, Molenda, Russell, and Smaldino (2002),

learning is the development of new knowledge, skills, and attitudes as the learner interacts with information and the environment. Interaction is critical to creating a sense of presence and a sense of community for online learners, and to promoting transformational learning (Murphy & Cifuentes, 2001). Learners receive the learning materials through the technology, process the information, and then personalize and contextualize the information. In the transformation process, learners interact with the content, with other learners, and with instructors to test and confirm ideas and to apply what they learn. Garrison (1999) claims that the design of the educational experience includes the transactional nature of the relationship between instructor, learners, and content that is of significance to the learning experience.

Different kinds of interaction will promote learning at different levels. Figure 5 shows interactive strategies to promote higher-level

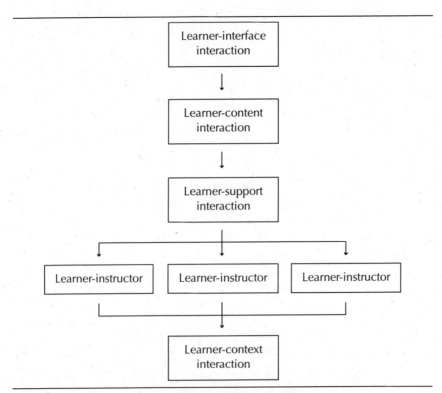

FIGURE 5. Levels of Interaction in online learning

learning (Berge, 1999; Gilbert & Moore, 1998; Schwier & Misanchuk, 1993). Hirumi (2002) proposes a framework of interaction in online learning that consists of three levels. Level one is learner-self interaction, which occurs within learners to help monitor and regulate their own learning. Level two is learner-human and learner-non-human interactions, where the learner interacts with human and non-human resources. Level three is learner-instruction interaction, which consists of activities to achieve a learning outcome. This chapter goes one step further and proposes interactions that go from lower-level to higher-level interactions, based on behaviorist, cognitivist, and constructivist schools of learning.

At the lowest level of interaction, there must be learner-interface interaction to allow the learner to access and sense the information. The interface is where learners use their senses to register the information in sensory storage. In online learning, the interface is with the computer, to access the content and to interact with others. Once learners access the online materials, there must be learner-content interaction to process the information. Learners navigate through the content to access the components of the lesson, which could take the form of pre-learning, learning, and post-learning activities. These activities could access reusable learning objects from a repository to present to learners (McGreal, 2002; Wiley, 2002), or they could use content custom-created by the designer or instructor. Students should be given the ability to choose their own sequence of learning, or should be given one or more suggested sequences. As online learners interact with the content, they should be encouraged to apply, assess, analyze, synthesize, evaluate, and reflect on what they learn (Berge, 2002). During the learner-content interaction, learners process the information to transform it from short-term to long-term memory. The higher the level of processing, the more associations are made in the learners' long-term memory, which results in higher-level learning.

As learners work through the content, they will find the need for learner support, which could take the form of learner-to-learner, learner-to-instructor, instructor-to-learner, and learner-to-expert interactions (Moore, 1989; Rourke, Anderson, Garrison, & Archer, 2001; Thiessen, 2001). There should be strategies to promote learner-context interaction, to allow learners to apply what they learn in real life so that they can contextualize the information. Learner-context interaction allows learners to develop personal knowledge and construct personal meaning from the information.

CONNECTIVIST THEORY FOR ONLINE LEARNING

According to Siemens (2004), connectivist theory is for the digital age, where individuals learn and work in a networked environment. As a result, we do not have control over what we learn since others in the network continually change information, and that requires new learning, unlearning old information, and/or learning current information. Siemens proposes some guidelines for designing learning materials for the learner, based on connectivist theory. Below is an elaboration of these guidelines for the development of online learning materials.

- Because of the information explosion, learners should be allowed to explore and research current information. Learners of the future need to be autonomous and independent learners so that they can acquire current information to build a valid and accurate knowledge base. Appropriate use of the Internet is an ideal learning strategy in a networked world.

- Some information and procedures become obsolete because of changes in the field and innovation; learners must therefore be able to unlearn old information and mental models and learn current information and mental models. The information that is valid today may not be valid tomorrow.

- The rapid increase of information available from a variety of sources means that some information is not as important or genuine as other information. As a result, the learner must be able to identify important information from unimportant information.

- Learners must have the ability to recognize what knowledge is no longer valid so they can acquire the new knowledge for a discipline. This requires that learners keep up-to-date in the field and be active participants in the network of learning.

- Because of globalization, information is not location-specific, and with the increasing use of telecommunication, technologies experts and learners from around the world can share and review information. Learning and knowledge rests in a diversity of opinions. As a result, learners must be allowed to connect with others around the world to examine others' opinions and to share their thinking with the world. Mobile learning promises to help learners function in a networked world where they can learn at any time and from anywhere (Ally, 2005).

- The world is connected by telecommunication technology. Hence, information for learning should not be taken from one source but should be assembled from many sources to reflect the networked world and the diversity of thinking. Learning should be delivered in a multi-channel system where different communication technologies are used to deliver the learning materials to facilitate optimal learning (Mukhopadhyay & Parhar, 2001).
- The field of computer systems is altering the learning process. The intelligent agents that are being built into devices and appliances will affect how students learn and where they obtain their learning materials. For example, devices and appliances will have built-in learning materials. When learners interact with the equipment, the training will be provided to them. Or, if the learner makes a mistake while using the equipment, the system will detect the mistake and provide the correct information. Hence, what learners need to learn depends on the type of equipment they use and their prior knowledge.
- Because of the information explosion, learners of the future must be willing to acquire new knowledge on an ongoing basis. Online teaching strategies must give learners the opportunity to research and locate new information in a discipline so that they can keep up-to-date in the field. In addition to using the Internet to deliver flexibility, instruction must be designed for experiential and authentic learning (Schmidt & Werner, 2007).
- The Internet is expanding education into a global classroom, with learners, teachers, and experts from around the world. As a result, learners must network with other students and experts to make sure that they are continually learning and updating their knowledge.
- Because of innovation and our increasing use of technology, learning is becoming more multidisciplinary. Learners must be exposed to different fields so that they can see the connections between the information in the fields. For example, learning about learning theories requires that learners be exposed to what the research says in psychology and information technology.

Siemens (2004) suggests that because of the networked society, globalization, and the constant changes to information and new information, educators need to look at new ways to design learning materials. He proposes a theory based on connectivism to prepare learners to function in the digital and networked age; however, further work needs to be done on how this theory can be used by educators to design and develop learning materials.

CONCLUSION

This chapter concludes by proposing a model, based on educational theory, that shows the important learning components that should be used when designing online materials. Neither placing information on the Web nor linking to other digital resources on the Web constitutes online instruction. Online instruction occurs when learners use the Web to go through the a sequence of instruction, to complete the learning activities, and to achieve learning outcomes and objectives (Ally, 2002; Ritchie & Hoffman, 1997). A variety of learning activities should be used to accommodate the different learning styles. Learners will choose the appropriate strategy to meet their learning needs. Refer to Figure 6 for key components that should be considered when designing online learning materials.

Learner Preparation

A variety of pre-learning activities can prepare learners for the details of the lesson, and to connect and motivate them to learn the online lesson. A rationale should be provided to inform learners of the importance of taking the online lesson and to show how it will benefit them. A concept map is provided to establish the existing cognitive structure, to incorporate the details of the online lesson, and to activate learners' existing structures to help them learn the details in the lesson. The lesson concept map also gives learners the big picture.

Learners should be informed of the learning outcomes of the lesson, so they know what is expected of them and will be able to gauge when they have achieved the lesson outcomes. An advance organizer should be provided to establish a structure, to organize the details in the online lesson, or to bridge between what learners already know and need to know. Learners must be told the prerequisite requirements so that they can check whether they are ready for the lesson. Providing the prerequisites to learners also activates the required cognitive structure to help them learn the materials.

A self-assessment should be provided at the start of the lesson to allow learners to check whether they already have the knowledge and

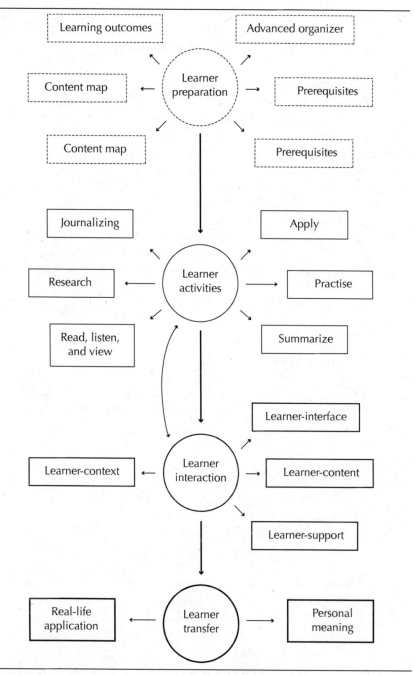

FIGURE 6. Components of effective online learning

skills taught in the online lesson. If learners think they have the knowledge and skills, they should be allowed to take that lesson's final test. The self-assessment also helps learners to organize the lesson materials and to recognize the important materials in the lesson. Once learners are prepared for the details of the lesson, they can go on to complete the online learning activities and to learn the details of the lesson.

Learner Activities

Online learning should include a variety of learning activities to help students achieve the lesson's learning outcome and to cater for their individual needs. Examples of learning activities include reading textual materials, listening to audio materials, and viewing visuals or video materials. Learners can conduct research on the Internet or link to online information and libraries to acquire further information. Having learners prepare a learning journal will allow them to reflect on what they have learned and provide the information with personal meaning. Appropriate application exercises should be embedded throughout the online lesson to establish the relevance of the materials. Practice activities, with feedback, should be included to allow learners to monitor how they are performing, so that they can adjust their learning method if necessary. To promote higher-level processing and to bring closure to the lesson, a summary should be provided, or learners should be required to generate a lesson summary. Opportunities should be provided for learners to transfer what they learned to real-life applications, so that they can be creative and go beyond what was presented in the online lesson.

Learner Interaction

As learners complete the learning activities, they will be involved with a variety of interactions. Learners need to interact with the interface to access the online materials. The interface should not overload learners, and should make it as easy as possible for learners to sense the information, for transfer to sensory store and then into short-term memory for processing. Learners need to interact with the content to acquire the information needed and to form the knowledge base. There should be interaction between the learner and other learners, between the learner and the instructor, and between the learner and experts to collaborate, participate in shared cognition, form social networks, and establish social presence. Learners should be able to interact within their context to personalize information and construct their own meaning.

LOOKING AHEAD

Behaviorist, cognitivist, and constructivist theories have contributed in different ways to the design of online materials, and they will continue to be used to develop learning materials for online learning. Behaviorist strategies can be used to teach the facts (what); cognitivist strategies, the principles and processes (how); and constructivist strategies to teach the real-life and personal applications and contextual learning. There is a shift toward constructive learning, in which learners are given the opportunity to construct their own meaning from the information presented during the online sessions. In addition to the existing learning theories, connectivism should be used to guide the development of online learning, since the other learning theories were developed before we became a networked world. Globalization has also affected what students learn and how they learn. The use of learning objects to promote flexibility, and reuse of online materials to meet the needs of individual learners, will become more common in the future. Online learning materials will be designed in small coherent segments, so that they can be redesigned for different learners and different contexts. The integration of 3D interactive graphics and web technologies (Web3D) will allow educators to develop highly interactive and realistic learning environments to enhance online learning (Chittaro & Ranon, 2007). Finally, online learning will be increasingly diverse in response to different learning cultures, styles, and motivations.

REFERENCES

Ally, M. (2002, August). Designing and managing successful online distance education courses. Workshop presented at the *2002 World Computer Congress*, Montreal, Canada.

Ally, M. (2005). Using learning theories to design instruction for mobile learning devices. In J. Attwell and C. Savill-Smith (Eds.), *Mobile learning anytime everywhere* (pp. 5–8). Proceedings of the Third World Conference on Mobile Learning, Rome.

Ally, M., and Fahy, P. (2002, August). Using students' learning styles to provide support in distance education. *Proceedings of the Eighteenth Annual Conference on Distance Teaching and Learning*, Madison, WI.

Ausubel, D. P. (1960). The use of advance organizers in the learning and retention of meaningful verbal material. *Journal of Educational Psychology, 51,* 267–272.

Ausubel, D. P. (1974). *Educational psychology: A cognitive view.* New York: Holt, Rinehart & Winston.

Berge, Z. L. (1999). Interaction in post-secondary web-based learning. *Educational Technology, 39*(1), 5–11.

Berge, Z. L. (2002). Active, interactive, and reflective learning. *The Quarterly Review of Distance Education, 3*(2), 181–190.

Beynon, M. (2007). Computing technology for learning – in need of a radical new conception. *Educational Technology & Society, 10*(1), 94–106.

Bonk, C. J., & Reynolds, T. H. (1997). Learner-centered web instruction for higher-order thinking, teamwork, and apprenticeship. In B. H. Khan (Ed.), *Web-based instruction* (pp. 167–178). Englewood Cliffs, NJ: Educational Technology Publications.

Carliner, S. (1999). *Overview of online learning.* Amherst, MA: Human Resource Development Press.

Cassidy, S. (2004). Learning Styles: An overview of theories, models, and measures. *Educational Psychology, 24*(4), 419–444.

Chittaro, L., & Ranon, R. (2007). Web3D technologies in learning, education, and training: Motivation, issues, and opportunities. *Computers and Education, 49*(1), 3–18.

Clark, R. E. (1983). Reconsidering research on learning from media. *Review of Educational Research, 53*(4), 445–459.

Clark, R. E. (2001). A summary of disagreements with the 'mere vehicles' argument. In R. E. Clark (Ed.), *Learning from media: Arguments, analysis, and evidence* (pp. 125–136). Greenwich, CT: Information Age Publishing.

Cole, R. A. (2000). *Issues in web-based pedagogy: A critical primer.* Westport, CT: Greenwood Press.

Cooper, P. A. (1993). Paradigm shifts in designing instruction: From behaviorism to cognitivism to constructivism. *Educational Technology, 33*(5), 12–19.

Craik, F. I. M., & Lockhart, R. S. (1972). Levels of processing: A framework for memory research. *Journal of Verbal Learning and Verbal Behavior, 11,* 671–684.

Craik, F. I. M., & Tulving, E. (1975). Depth of processing and the retention of words in episodic memory. *Journal of Experimental Psychology: General, 104,* 268–294.

Downes, S. (2006). *An introduction to connective knowledge.* Retrieved March 26, 2007, from http://www.downes.ca/post/33034

Duffy, T. M., & Cunningham, D. J. (1996). Constructivism: Implications for the design and delivery of instruction. In D. H. Jonassen (Ed.), *Handbook of research for educational communications and technology* (pp. 170–198). New York: Simon & Schuster Macmillan.

Ertmer, P. A., & Newby, T. J. (1993). Behaviorism, cognitivism, constructivism: Comparing critical features from an instructional design perspective. *Performance Improvement Quarterly, 6*(4), 50–70.

Garrison, D. R. (1999). Will distance disappear in distance studies? A reaction. *Journal of Distance Education, 13*(2), 10–13.

Gilbert, L., & Moore, D .L. (1998). Building interactivity into web courses: Tools for social and instructional interaction. *Educational Technology, 38*(3), 29–35.

Good, T. L., & Brophy, J. E. (1990). *Educational psychology: A realistic approach* (4th ed.).White Plains, NY: Longman.

Heinich, R., Molenda, M., Russell, J. D., & Smaldino, S. E. (2002). *Instructional media and technologies for learning.* NJ: Pearson Education.

Hirumi, A. (2002). A framework for analyzing, designing, and sequencing planned e-learning interactions. *The Quarterly Review of Distance Education, 3*(2), 141–160.

Holley, C. D., Dansereau, D. F., McDonald, B. A., Garland, J. C., & Collins, K. W. (1979). Evaluation of a hierarchical mapping technique as an aid to prose processing. *Contemporary Educational Psychology, 4,* 227–237.

Hooper, S., & Hannafin, M. J. (1991). The effects of group composition on achievement, interaction, and learning efficiency during computer-based cooperative instruction. *Educational Technology Research and Development, 39*(3), 27–40.

Hung, D., Looi,, C. K., & Koh, T. S. (2004). Situated cognition and communities of practice: First-person 'lived experiences' vs. third-person perspectives. *Educational Technology & Society, 7*(4), 193–200.

Janicki, T., & Liegle, J. O. (2001). Development and evaluation of a framework for creating web-based learning modules: A pedagogical and systems approach. *Journal of Asynchronous Learning Networks, 5*(1). Retrieved June 10, 2007, from http://www.sloan-c.org/publications/jaln/v5n1/pdf/v5n1_janicki.pdf

Johnson, D. W., & Johnson, R. T. (1996). Cooperation and the use of technology. In D. H. Jonassen (Ed.), *Handbook of research for educational communications and technology* (pp. 170–198). New York: Simon & Schuster Macmillan.

Kalat, J. W. (2007). *Introduction to psychology.* Pacific Grove, CA: Wadsworth-Thompson Learning.

Keller, J. M. (1983). Motivational design of instruction. In C. M. Reigeluth (Ed.), *Instructional design theories and instruction: An overview of their current status* (pp. 383–429). Hillsdale, NJ: Lawrence Erlbaum.

Keller, J. M., & Suzuki, K. (1988). Use of the ARCS motivation model in courseware design. In D. H. Jonassen (Ed.), *Instructional design for microcomputer courseware* (pp. 401–434). Hillsdale, NJ: Lawrence Erlbaum.

Khan, B. (1997). Web-based instruction: What is it and why is it? In B. H. Khan (Ed.), *Web-based instruction* (pp. 5–18). Englewood Cliffs, NJ: Educational Technology Publications.

Kolb, D. A. (1984). *Experiential learning: Experience as the source of learning and development.* Englewood Cliffs, NJ: Prentice-Hall.

Kozma, R. B. (2001). Counterpoint theory of 'learning with media'. In R. E. Clark (Ed.), *Learning from media: Arguments, analysis, and evidence* (pp. 137–178). Greenwich, CT: Information Age Publishing Inc.

Malone, T. W. (1981). Towards a theory of intrinsically motivating instruction. *Cognitive Science, 5*(4), 333–369.

Mayer, R. E. (1979). Twenty years of research on advance organizers: Assimilation theory is still the best predictor of results. *Instructional Science, 8*(2), 133–167.

Mayer, R. E. (1998). Cognitive, meta-cognitive, and motivational aspects of problem solving. *Instructional Science, 26*(1–2), 49–63.

McGreal, R. (2002, February). *A primer on meta-data standards.* Session presented at Athabasca University.

Mezirow, J. (1991). *Transformative dimensions of adult learning.* San Francisco, CA: Jossey-Bass.

Miller, G. A. (1956). The magical number seven, plus or minus two: Some limits on our capacity for processing information. *Psychological Review, 63,* 81–97.

Moore, M. G. (1989). Three types of interaction. *The American Journal of Distance Education, 3*(2), 1–6.

Mukhopadhyay, M., & Parhar, M. (2001). Instructional design in multi-channel learning system. *British Journal of Education Technology, 32*(5), 543–556.

Murphy, K. L., & Cifuentes, L. (2001). Using web tools, collaborating, and learning online. *Distance Education, 22*(2), 285–305.

Myers, I. (1978). *Myers-Briggs type indicator.* Palo Alto, CA: Consulting Psychologists Press.

Paivio, A. (1986). *Mental representations: A dual coding approach.* Oxford: Oxford University Press.

Palloff, R. M., & Pratt, K. (1999). *Building learning communities in cyberspace.* San Francisco, CA: Jossey-Bass.

Pavlov, I. P. (1927). *Conditioned reflexes.* London: Clarendon Press.

Phillips, D. C. (2005). Theories of teaching and learning. In *A companion to the philosophy of Education.* Blackwell Synergy: Online Journals for Learning, Research, and Professional Practice. Retrieved March 26, 2007, from http://www.blackwellreference.com/subscriber/tocnode?id=g9781405140515_chunk_g978140514051519

Ring, G. & Mathieux, G. (2002, February). The key components of quality learning. Paper presented at the *ASTD Techknowledge 2002 Conference,* Las Vegas.

Ritchie, D. C., & Hoffman, B. (1997). Incorporating instructional design principles with the World Wide Web. In B. H. Khan (Ed.), *Web-based instruction* (pp. 135–138). Englewood Cliffs, NJ: Educational Technology Publications.

Rossett, A. (2002). Waking in the night and thinking about e-learning. In A. Rossett (Ed.), *The ASTD e-learning handbook* (pp. 3–18). New York: McGraw-Hill.

Rourke, L., Anderson, T., Garrison, D. R., & Archer, W. (2001). Assessing social presence in asynchronous text-based computer conferencing. *Journal of Distance Education, 14*(2). Retrieved June 10, 2007 from http://cade.athabascau.ca/ vol14.2/rourke_et_al.html

Rovai, A. (2002). Building sense of community at a distance. *International Review of Research in Open and Distance Learning, 3*(1). Retrieved June 10, 2007, from http://www.irrodl.org/index .php/irrodl/article/view/79/152

Schmidt, J. T., & Werner, C. H. (2007). Designing online instruction for success: Future oriented motivation and self-regulation. *Electronic Journal of e-Learning, 5*(1), 69–78.

Schramm, W. (1977). *Big media, little media.* Beverly Hills, CA: Sage.

Schwier, R. A., & Misanchuk, E. (1993). *Interactive multimedia instruction.* Englewood Cliffs, NJ: Educational Technology Publications.

Siemens, G. (2004). *A learning theory for the digital age.* Retrieved March 26, 2007 from http://www.elearnspace.org/Articles/connectivism.htm

Simmons, D. E. (2002). The forum report: E-learning adoption rates and barriers. In A. Rossett (Ed.), *The ASTD e-learning handbook* (pp. 19–23). New York: McGraw-Hill.

Skinner, B. F. (1974). *About behaviorism.* New York: Knopf.

Smith, P. L., & Ragan, T. J. (1999). *Instructional design.* New York: John Wiley & Sons.

Sternberg, R. J. (1998). Meta-cognition, abilities, and developing expertise: What makes an expert student? *Instructional Science, 26*(1-2), 127–140.

Stoyanova, N., & Kommers, P. (2002). Concept mapping as a medium of shared cognition in computer-supported collaborative problem-solving. *Journal of Interactive Learning Research, 13*(1,2), 111–133.

Tapscott, D. (1998). *Growing up digital: The rise of the Net generation.* New York: McGraw-Hill.

Thiessen, J. (2001). *Faculty attitudes in delivering undergraduate distance education.* Unpublished master's thesis, Athabasca University, Athabasca, Alberta.

Thorndike, E. L. (1913). *Educational psychology: The psychology of learning.* New York: Teachers College Press.

Wiley, D. (2002). Learning objects need instructional design theory. In A. Rossett (Ed.), *The ASTD e-Learning Handbook* (pp. 115–126). New York: McGraw-Hill.

Wilson, B. G. (1997). Reflections on constructivism and instructional design. In C. R. Dills & A. J. Romiszowski (Eds.), *Instructional development paradigms* (pp. 63–80). Englewood Cliffs, NJ: Educational Technology Publications.

Witkin, H. A., Moore, C. A., Goodenough, D. R., & Cox, P. W. (1977). Field-dependent and field-independent cognitive styles and their educational implications. *Review of Educational Research, 47,* 1–64.

Yorke, M., & Knight, P. (2004). Self-theories: Some implications for teaching and learning in higher education. *Studies in Higher Education, 29*(1), 25–37.

ABOUT THE AUTHOR

Mohamed Ally is an associate professor for the Centre for Distance Education at Athabasca University. Dr. Ally teaches courses in distance education and is involved with research on improving design, development, delivery, and support in distance education.

CHAPTER 2

TOWARDS A THEORY
OF ONLINE LEARNING

TERRY ANDERSON
Athabasca University

It is the theory that decides what we can observe.
– Albert Einstein

There is nothing more practical than a good theory.
– Lewin, K., Field Theory in Social Science

INTRODUCTION

Theory has been both celebrated and condemned in educational practice and research. Many proponents have argued that theory allows and even forces us to see the big picture and makes it possible for us to view our practice and our research from a broader perspective than envisioned from the murky trenches of our practice. This broader perspective helps us make connections with the work of others, facilitates coherent frameworks and deeper understanding of our actions, and perhaps most importantly, allows us to transfer the experience gained in one context to new experiences and contexts. Critics of theory (McCormick & McCormick, 1992) have argued that too strict adherence to any particular theoretical viewpoint often filters our perceptions and thus blinds us to important lessons of reality. The intent of this chapter is to look at learning theory generally, and then to focus in on those attributes of the online learning context that allow us to focus and develop deeper and more useful theories of online learning.

Wilson (1997) has described three functions of a good educational theory. First, it helps us to envision new worlds. Few of us need help envisioning new worlds in the midst of the hype and exuberance of online learning proponents that flood the popular press. We do need theory, however, to help us envision how education can best take advantage of the enhanced communication, information retrieval, creative tools, and management capability provided by the Net. It is all too easy to consider new innovations in a horseless-carriage manner, and attempt to develop new actions based on old adaptations to now obsolete contexts.

Second, a good theory helps us to make things. We need theories of online learning that help us to invest our time and limited resources most effectively. There are many opportunities, but always critical shortages of resources – time being perhaps the scarcest of these – demanding that we maximize the efficiency of our development and educational delivery efforts. This book has a number of chapters with particular recommendations and suggestions for online course development and teaching. Hopefully, this chapter provides a theoretical big picture to make sense of these specific recommendations. Third, Wilson argues that a good theory keeps us honest. Good theory builds upon what is already known, and helps us to interpret and plan for the unknown. It also forces us to look beyond day-to-day contingencies and ensure that our knowledge and practice of online learning is robust, considered, and ever expanding.

This chapter begins with a general assessment of how people learn, based on Bransford, Brown, and Cocking's (1999) work. It then assesses the unique characteristics or affordances of the Web to enhance these generalized learning contexts. The chapter then discusses the six forms of interaction and their critical role in engaging and supporting both learners and teachers. It then presents a model of e-learning, a first step towards a theory, in which the two predominate forms of e-learning – collaborative and independent study modes – are presented with a brief discussion of the advantages and disadvantages of each. The chapter ends with a discussion of the emerging tools of the Semantic Web, and the way they will affect future developments of theory and practice of online learning.

ATTRIBUTES OF LEARNING

As many theorists have argued (Herrington & Oliver, 1999) and practitioners have experienced for themselves, online learning is but a subset of learning in general – thus, we can expect issues relevant to how adults learn generally to also be relevant in an online learning context. Bransford, Brown and Cocking (1999), in an insightful book on the new science of learning, provide evidence that effective learning environments are framed within the convergence of four overlapping lenses. They argue that effective learning is community-centred, knowledge-centred, learner-centred, and assessment-centred. Discussing each of these lenses helps us to define learning in a general sense before we apply this analysis framework to the unique characteristics of online learning.

Learner-Centred

A learner-centred context is not one in which the whims and peculiarities of each individual learner are slavishly catered to. In fact, we must be careful to recognize that learner-centred contexts must also meet the needs of the teacher, the institution, and of the larger society that provides support for the student, the institution, and often for a group or class of students, as well as for the particular needs of individual learners. For this reason, I have argued earlier (Anderson 2005) that this attribute may be more accurately labelled learning-centred, as opposed to learner-centred.

Learner-centred, according to Bransford and colleagues (1999), includes awareness of the unique cognitive structures and understandings that learners bring to the learning context. Thus, a teacher makes efforts to gain an understanding of students' prerequisite knowledge, including any misconceptions that the learner starts with in their construction of new knowledge. Further, the learning environment respects and accommodates the particular cultural attributes, especially the language and particular forms of expression that the learner uses to interpret and build knowledge. Learner-centred activities make extensive use of diagnostic tools and activities to make visible these pre-existing knowledge structures to both the teacher and the students themselves.

Online learning can present challenges to educators, as the tools and opportunities to discover students' preconceptions and cultural perspectives are often limited by bandwidth constraints, which limit the users' view of body language and paralinguistic clues. Some researchers argue that these restrictions negatively affect communication efficacy (Short, Williams, & Christie,1976). Others argue that the unique characteristics that define online learning (appropriate combinations of asynchronous and synchronous voice, text, and video) can actually lead to enhanced or hyper communications (Richardson, 2000). For example, we have found evidence of significant social presence in text-based computer conferencing contexts (Eggins & Slade, 1997a; Smolensky, Carmondy, & Halcomb, 1990). Nonetheless, it is fair to say that assessing student preconditions and cultural prerequisites is often more challenging in an online learning context, because teachers are less able to interact transparently with students – especially in the critical early stages of learning community formation. It is for this reason that experienced online learning teachers must make time at the commencement of their learning interactions to provide incentive and opportunity for students to share their understandings, their culture, and the unique aspects of themselves. This can be done formally through electronically administered surveys and questionnaires, but is often more effectively accomplished by virtual icebreakers (Dixon, 2007) and providing opportunities for students to introduce themselves and express any issues or concerns to the teacher and the class.

The online learning environment is also a unique cultural context in itself. Benedikt (1991) argues that cyberspace "has a geography, a physics, a nature, and a rule of human law" (pp. 123). Increasingly, students come to online learning with preconceptions gathered from both formal and informal experience in virtual environments. They exercise their mastery of communication norms and tools, some of which are not be appropriate to an educational online context. Researchers have attempted to quantify students' proficiency and comfort with online environments through use of survey instruments that measure learners' Internet efficacy (Kirby & Boak, 1987). They argue that it is not Internet skills alone which determine competency, but the users' strong sense of Internet efficacy that enables them to effectively adapt to the requirements of working in this environment. Thus, the effective online teacher is constantly probing for learner comfort and competence with the intervening technology, and providing safe environments for learners to increase their sense of Internet efficacy. Learner-centred online learning contexts thus are sensitive to this cultural overlay that interacts with the technical affordances and skill sets acquired in offline contexts.

Knowledge-Centred

Effective learning does not happen in a content vacuum. John McPeck (2000) and other critical thinking theorists argue that teaching general thinking skills and techniques is useless outside of a particular knowledge domain in which they can be grounded. Similarly, Bransford et al. (1999)

argue that effective learning is both defined and bounded by the epistemology, language, and context of disciplinary thought. Each discipline or field of study contains a world view that provides unique ways of understanding and talking about knowledge. Students need opportunities to experience this discourse and the knowledge structures that undergird discipline thinking. They also need opportunities to reflect upon their own thinking; automacy is a useful and necessary skill for expert thinking, but automacy without reflective capacity greatly limits learners' capacity to transfer their knowledge to unfamiliar contexts or to develop new knowledge structures.

Online learning neither advantages or disadvantages knowledge-centred learning in comparison to campus-based learning. As I discuss below, however, the Net provides expanded opportunities for learners to plunge ever deeper into knowledge resources, providing a near limitless means for them to grow their knowledge and find their own way around the knowledge of the discipline, benefitting from its expression in thousands of formats and contexts. This provision of resources, however, can be overwhelming, and the skillful e-teacher needs to provide the big-picture scaffolding upon which students can grow their own knowledge and discipline-centred discoveries. The recent emergence of theories of learning that are based on networked contexts, such as "heutagogy" (Phelps, Hase, & Ellis, 2005) and "connectivism" (Siemens, 2005), helps us to understand that learning is about making connections with ideas, facts, people, and communities. Obviously the Net excels at allowing users to both find and utilize these connections.

Assessment-Centred

Bransford et al. (1999) present the necessity for effective learning environments to be assessment-centred. By this term, they do not give unqualified support for summative assessments (especially those supposedly used for high stakes accountability), but they look at formative evaluation and summative assessment that serve to motivate, inform, and provide feedback to both learners and teachers.

Quality online learning provides many opportunities for assessment – opportunities that involve the teacher, but also ones that exploit the influence and expertise of peers and external experts, others that use simple and complex machine algorithms to assess student learning, and perhaps most importantly, those that encourage learners to reflectively assess their own learning. Understanding what is most usefully – rather than most easily – assessed is a challenge for online learning designers.

Development in cognitive learning theories and their application to assessment design are helping us to develop assessments that are aligned with the subject content and assess cognitive processes, in addition to end results. For example, Baxter, Elder, and Glaser (1996) find that competent students should be able to provide coherent explanations; generate plans for problem solution; implement solution strategies; and monitor and adjust their activities. However, when reviewing assessments that my own children are subjected to in school and at university, I am continually disappointed to note the very high percentage of recall questions and the lack of strategies that effectively measure the four sets of competencies identified by Baxter and others.

Can we do any better in online learning? The diminution of opportunities for immediate interaction between learners and teachers may reduce opportunities for process assessment. The enhanced communication capacity of online learning, as well as the focus of most adult online learning in the real world of work, however, provide good opportunities to create assessment activities that are project- and workplace-based, that are constructed collaboratively, that benefit from peer and expert review, and that are infused with opportunity and requirement for self-assessment.

A danger of assessment-centred learning systems is the potential increase in workload demanded of busy online learning teachers. Strategies that are designed to provide formative and summative assessment with minimal direct impact on teacher workload are most needed. A growing list of tools provide such assessment without increased teacher participation. These tools include

- the use of online computer-marked assessments that extend beyond quizzes to simulation exercises, virtual labs, and other automated assessments of active student learning;
- collaborative learning environments that students create to document and assess their own learning in virtual groups;
- mechanisms such as online automated tutors that support and scaffold students' evaluation of their own work and that of their peers;
- student agents who facilitate and monitor peer activities to allow students to informally assess and aide each other;
- the development of project-based and product-based assessment in which artefacts are created and their value is attested to by users within the formal learning class or program, as well as those lifelong learners spread out on the long tail of the Net (Anderson, 2004);

- use of sophisticated software tools, such as LSA (see http://lsa. colorado.edu/), or neural networks to machine score even complicated tasks, such as students' essays (Lee, 2006);
- informal social networks wherein students can post and reflect upon the ideas of others enrolled in the course and beyond (Farmer, 2005).

Thus, the challenge of online learning is to provide very high quantity and quality of assessment, while maintaining student interest and commitment – something that is often best done by developing a learning community, to which we turn next.

Community-Centred

The community-centred lens allows us to include the critical social component of learning in our online learning designs. Here we find Vygotsky's (2000) popular notions of "social cognition" relevant, as we consider how students can work together in an online learning context to collaboratively create new knowledge. These ideas have been expanded in Lipman's (1991) "community of inquiry," and Etienne Wenger's (2002) ideas of "community of practice," to show how members of a learning community both support and challenge each other, leading to effective and relevant knowledge construction. Wilson (1997) has described the characteristics of participants in online communities as having a shared sense of belonging, trust, expectation of learning, and commitment to participate in and contribute to the community.

Although many online learning researchers celebrate the capacity to create learning communities at a distance (Byrne, Flood, & Willis, 1999), others note problems associated with lack of attention and participation (Morris & Ogan, 1996), economic restraints (Annand, 1999), and an inbuilt resistance among many faculty and institutions to threatening competition from virtual learning environments (Cutler, 1995). Ethnographic studies of the Net (Jonassen & Carr, 2000) illustrate how the lack of "placedness" and the complications of anonymity attenuate different components of community when located in virtual space. In short, it may be more challenging than we think to create and sustain these communities, and the differences may be more fundamental – differences that are linked to lack of placedness and synchronicity in time and place, the mere absence of body language, and the development of social presence.

I have been struck by the wide variation in expectation of learners towards participation in a community of learners. Traditionally, the independent modes of distance education have attracted students who value the freedom and independence of time and place. Contrary to popular belief, the major motivation for enrolment in distance education is not physical access per se, but the temporal freedom that allows students to move through a course of studies at a time and pace of their choice. Participation in a community of learners almost inevitably places constraints upon this independence – even when the pressure of synchronous connection is eliminated by use of asynchronous communications tools. The demands of a learning-centred context at times may force us to modify the proscriptive participation in communities of learning, even though we may have evidence that such participation will likely advance knowledge creation and attention. The flexibility of virtual communities allows for more universal participation, but a single environment that responds to all students' needs does not exist. Thus, the need for variations that accommodate the diverse needs of learners and teachers at different stages of their life cycles is necessary. Finally, we are seeing the proliferation of new types of communities and networks that exist far from the formal constraints of educational communities. These social software networks, such as *mySpace, flickr, SecondLife,* and *Facebook,* support millions of participants in the creation of friendship and sharing networks. We are only beginning to understand how these environments can be useful for formal education, or if they truly are "myspaces" and not institutional or school spaces.

All of these potential barriers and opportunities argue for a theory of online learning that accommodates but does not prescribe any particular format of time and place "boundedness," and that allows for appropriate substitution of independent and community-centred learning. To this requirement, we add the need for a theory of e-learning to be learning-centred, provide a wide variety of authentic assessment opportunities, and be attuned to – and grounded in – existing knowledge contexts.

AFFORDANCES OF THE NET

Effective educational theory must address the affordances and the limitations of the context for which it is designed (McDonald, 1998). The World Wide Web is an extremely multifaceted technology that provides a large – and seemingly ever-growing – set of communication and information management tools which can be harnessed for education provision. Similarly, it suffers from a set of constraints that are also briefly overviewed in this section.

Online learning, as a subset of all distance education, has always been concerned with provision of access to educational experience that is, at the least, more flexible in time and in space than campus-based education. Access to the Web is now nearly ubiquitous in developed countries. In Canada, 2005 data shows that 68% of the population are regular Internet users – figures that are undoubtedly higher today, and much higher again among younger users and students. This high percentage of users would likely include well over 95% of those interested in taking a formal education course. Access to the Web is primarily through home or workplace machines, followed by computer placements in public libraries, Internet cafes, and by personal wireless devices. In sum, access is non-problematic for the vast majority living in developed countries. Access is also faster and more convenient, as demonstrated by annual increases of 33% in broadband connectivity in the thirty-member Organisation for Economic and Cooperative Development countries between 2005 and 2006 (OECD, 2006). I have also been surprised by access availability in developing countries, as exemplified by numerous Internet cafes in nearly every major city of the world. Access is still problematic for those with a variety of physical handicaps. However, in comparison to books or video media, the Web provides much greater quality and quantity of access to nearly all citizens – with or without physical disabilities.

Not only is access to technology increasing, but access to an ever-growing body of content is also increasing. The number of open-access scholarly journals (see http://www.doaj .org/); educational objects (see www.merlot.org); educational discussion lists and communities (see http://lists.topica.com/dir/?cid=4); online courses and educational resources (see http://www.oercommons.org/); and general references to millions of pages of commercial, educational, and cultural content (see www.google.com) is large and increasing at an exponential rate. Thus, online learning theory must acknowledge the change from an era of shortage and restriction to an era of abundant content; content resources are now so large that filtering and reducing choice is as important as provision of sufficient content itself.

The Web is quickly changing from a context defined by text content and interactions to one in which all forms of media are supported. Much of the early work on instructional use of the Internet (Smith, Feld, & Franz, 1992) assumed that asynchronous text-based interaction defined the medium (Short, Williams, & Christie, 1976), thus techniques were developed to maximize interaction using this relatively lean media. We are now entering an era, however, where streaming video, video, and audio-conferencing, pod and videocasts, and immersive worlds are readily available for educational use. Thus, online learning theory needs to help educators decide which of the numerous technological options is best suited for their application.

The Web's inbuilt capacity for hyperlinking has been associated with the way in which human knowledge is stored in mental schema and the subsequent development of mental structures (Jonassen, 1992). Further, the capacity for students to create their own learning paths through content that is formatted with hypertexts links is congruent with constructivist instructional design theory, which stresses individual discovery and construction of knowledge (Shank, 1993).

Finally, the growing ease with which content can be updated and revised, both manually and through use of autonomous agent technology, is making online learning content much more responsive and potentially more current than content developed for any other media. The explosion of web blogs (Richardson, 2006) and user-friendly course content management systems built into web delivery systems, such as *Blackboard®* and *Moodle*, are creating environments in which teachers and learners can easily create and update their course contents without the aide of programmers or designers. Naturally, this ease of creation and revision leads to potential for error and less than professional standard output; however, educators who are anxious to retain control of their educational content and context welcome this openness and freedom.

Education, however, is not only about access to content. The greatest affordance of the Web for education use is the profound and multifaceted increase in communication and interaction capability. The next section discusses this affordance in greater detail.

ROLE OF INTERACTION IN ONLINE LEARNING

Interaction has long been a defining and critical component of the educational process and context (Anderson, 2003b). However, the term itself is used in many ways to describe many different types of exchanges between different actors and objects associated with teaching and learning.

DEFINING AND VALUING INTERACTION IN ONLINE LEARNING

It is surprisingly difficult to find a clear and precise definition of this multifaceted concept in the education literature. In popular culture, the use of this term to describe everything from toasters to video games to holiday resorts further confuses precise definition. I have discussed these varying definitions at greater length in an earlier document (Anderson 2003a), and so I will confine discussion here to an acceptance of Wagner's (2001) definition as "reciprocal events that require at least two objects and two actions. Interactions occur when these objects and events mutually influence one another" (p. 8).

Interaction – or its derivative term *interactivity* – serves a variety of functions in the educational transaction. Sims (1999) lists these functions as allowing for learner control, facilitating program adaptation based on learner input, allowing various forms of participation and communication, and aiding meaningful learning. In addition, interactivity is fundamental to creating the learning communities espoused by Lipman (1991), Wenger (2002), and other influential educational theorists who focus on the critical role of community in learning. Finally, the value of another person's perspective, usually gained through interaction, is a key learning component in constructivist learning theories (Shank, 1993), and in inducing mindfulness in learners (Visser, 2000).

Interaction has always been valued in distance education – even in its most traditional, independent study format. Holmberg (1981) argues for the superiority of individualized interaction between student and tutor when supported by written postal correspondence or via real-time telephone tutoring. Holmberg also introduces us to the idea of simulated interaction, which defines the writing style appropriate for independent study models of distance education programming, and that he refers to as "guided didactic interaction." Garrison and Shale (1990) define all forms of education – including that delivered at a distance – as essentially interactions between content, students, and teachers. Laurillard (1997) constructs a conversational model of learning in which interaction between students and teachers plays the critical role.

As long ago as 1916, John Dewey's writings refer to interaction as the defining component of the educational process that occurs when students transform the inert information passed to them from another and construct it into knowledge with personal application and value (Esposito, 2003). Bates (1991) argues that interactivity should be the primary criteria for selecting media for educational delivery. Thus, there is a long history of study and recognition of the critical role of interaction in supporting and even defining education.

The Web affords interaction in many modalities. In Figure 1, we see the common forms of interaction media used in distance education charted against their capacity to support independence (of time and place) and interaction. The higher and richer the form of communication, the more restrictions are placed upon independence. Figure 2 shows the capability of the Web to support these modalities. As can be seen, nearly all forms of mediated educational interaction are now supported, and if one adds the use of the Web to enhance classroom-based education, the Web supports them all. Thus, describing the characteristics of online learning in general is usually too large a domain for meaningful discussion until one specifies the particular modality of interaction in use.

Interaction can also be delineated in terms of the actors participating in the interaction. Michael Moore first discussed the three most common forms of interaction in distance education – student-student; student-teacher and student-content (Christenson & Menzel, 1998). These interactions were expanded by Anderson and Garrison (1988) to include teacher-teacher, teacher-content, and content-content interaction. In 2002, I developed an equivalency theorem describing the capacity to substitute one form of interaction for another, based upon cost

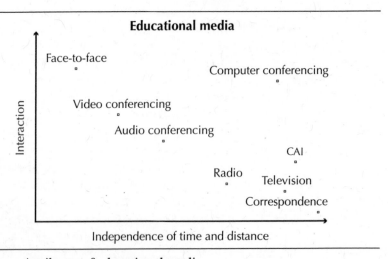

FIGURE 1. Attributes of educational media

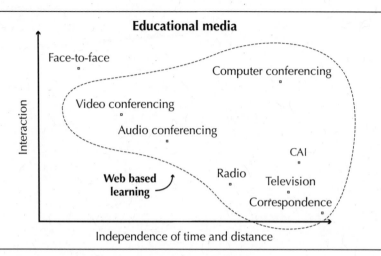

FIGURE 2. Educational media subsumed by the Web

and accessibility factors (Anderson, 2003b). Figure 3 illustrates these six types of educational interaction; they are also briefly described below.

Student-Student Interaction

Student-student interaction has traditionally been downplayed as a requirement of distance education, due to constraints on availability of technology and an earlier bias amongst distance education theorists towards individualized learning (Andersen et al., 1981). Modern constructivist and connectivist theorists stress the value of peer-to-peer interaction in investigating and developing multiple perspectives. Work on collaborative learning illustrates potential gains in cognitive learning tasks, as well as increasing completion rates and acquisition of critical social skills in education (Kirby & Boak, 1987). Work related to peer tutoring, by Resnick (1996) and others, illustrates the benefits that can result for both tutor and learner from a variety of forms of "reciprocal teaching." In our work, we found that student-led teams can result in higher levels of cognitive, social, and even teaching presence, than those led by teachers (Rourke & Anderson, 2002). Finally, peer interaction is critical to the development of communities of learning (Rumble, 1999; Wenger, McDermott, & Snyder, 2002), that allow learners to develop interpersonal skills and investigate tacit bodies of knowledge shared by community members as well as the formal curriculum of studies (Seely, Brown, & Hagel, 2005).

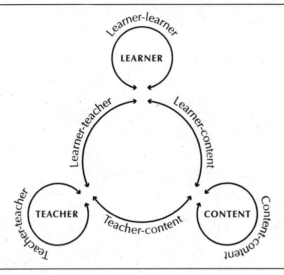

FIGURE 3. Educational interactions

Student-Content Interaction

Student-content interaction has always been a major component of formal education, even in the forms of library study or reading textbooks in face-to-face instruction. The Web supports these more passive forms of student-content interaction, but also provides a host of new opportunities, such as immersion in micro-environments, exercises in virtual labs, and online computer-assisted learning tutorials. The development of interactive content that responds to student behaviour and attributes (often referred to as a student model) allows for customization of content in unprecedented ways to support the individual needs of each unique learner. Eklund (1995) lists some potential advantages of such approaches to

- provide an online help facility, or an intelligent help, if the user is modelled and their path is traced through the information space;
- use an adaptive interface, based on several stereotypical user classes, that modifies the environment to suit the individual user;
- provide adaptive advice and model users' acquisition of knowledge through their use of the environment (including navigational use,

answers to questions, help requested), to intelligently suggest a preferred individualized path through the knowledge base.

To these must be added the capacity for immediate feedback: not only formal learning guidance, but also just-in-time learning assistance provided by job aides and other forms of performance support tools.

Student-Teacher Interaction

Student-teacher interaction is supported in online learning in a large number of varieties and formats that include asynchronous and synchronous communication in text, audio, and video communications. The volume of such communication often overwhelms many new teachers. Moreover, students often hold unrealistic expectations for immediate responses from their teachers. Emerging best practices now recognize the flow of communication in online courses to be much less "teacher-centric" than in traditional classroom discourse; teachers do not have to respond immediately to every student question and comment, and playing a less dominant role in class discourse can actually support the emergence of greater learner commitment and participation.

Teacher-Content Interaction

Teacher-content interaction focuses on the teacher's creation of content: learning objects as well as units of study, complete courses, and associated learning activities. Teacher-content interaction allows teachers to continuously monitor, construct, and update course content resources and activities.

Teacher-Teacher Interaction

Teacher-teacher interaction creates the opportunity to sustain teachers with professional development and support through supportive communities. These interactions encourage teachers to take advantage of knowledge growth and discovery, in their own subject area and within the scholarly community of teachers.

Content-Content Interaction

Content-content interaction is a new and developing mode of educational interaction wherein content is programmed to interact with other automated information sources to constantly refresh itself and acquire new capabilities, through updates and interaction with other content sources. For example, a weather tutorial may take its data from current meteorological servers, creating a learning context that is up to date and relevant to the students' learning context. Content-content interaction also provides a means to assert control of rights and facilitate tracking content use by diverse groups of learners and teachers. The recent development of tagging (both "folksonomie" and formal ontological systems) and syndication tools, such as RSS Atom, allow for automated machine harvesting, distribution, and selection of content. Such automation allows for the effective harvesting and selection of content-by-content.

Having exhausted all the pair-wise permeations of student/content/teacher above, I thought I had covered all the bases. I was wrong. I was surprised to read Jon Dron's (2007) paper, in which he argues that the group itself is an educational resource with characteristics that are different than the bounded interaction among two or more learners registered in a course. Dron's groups include responses from strangers retrieved from services like *Google Answers*, referrals from networks of friends and friends of friends, such as those supported in *MySpace* and other social software sites, and discussions in communities of avatars clustered in virtual spaces in immersive environments. These groups support far more diverse and often less reliable interactions. Nonetheless, they are far more generative than the discourse that typically merges from interaction among a bounded class of students and teachers. Thus, learner-group and teacher-group interaction opens the online classroom door to viewpoints, resources, and insights gathered from throughout the Net.

A MODEL OF E-LEARNING

A first step in theory building often consists of model building, in which the major variables are displayed and the relationships between the variables schematized. In Figure 4, the two major modes of online learning (collaborative, community-of-inquiry models, and community-of-learning models) are illustrated.

The model illustrates the two major human actors: learners and teachers, and their interactions with each other and with the content. Learners can, of course, interact directly and spontaneously with any content that they find, in multiple formats and especially on the Web; however, many choose to have their learning sequenced, directed, and credentialed through the assistance of a teacher in a formal education system. This interaction can take place within a community of inquiry, using a variety of net-based synchronous and asynchronous (video, audio,

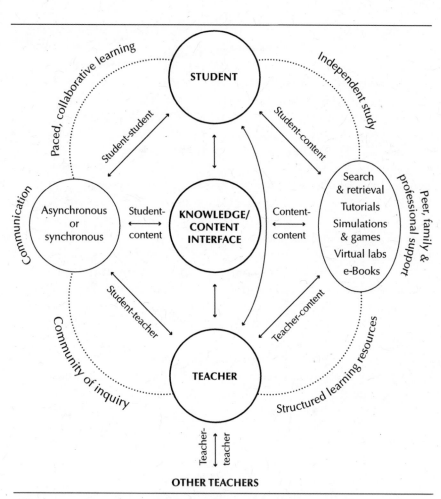

FIGURE 4. A model of online learning

computer conferencing, chats, or virtual world) interactions. These environments are particularly rich and allow for the learning of social skills, collaboration, and the development of personal relationships among participants. The community, however, binds learners in time, and thus forces regular sessions – or at least group-paced learning. Community models are also generally more expensive simply because they cannot scale up to serve larger numbers of students. The second model of learning (on the right) illustrates the structured learning tools associated with independent learning.

Common tools used in this mode include computer-assisted learning tutorials, drills, and simulations. Virtual labs, where students complete simulations of lab experiments and have access to sophisticated search and retrieval tools, are also becoming common tools. Texts in print – and now distributed and read online – have long served as the basis for conveying teacher interpretations, insights, and knowledge in independent study. It should also be emphasized, however, that although engaged in independent study, the student is not alone. Often colleagues in the workplace, peers located locally or distributed across the Net, formal and informal groups, and family members, have been significant sources of support and assistance to independent study learners (Potter, 1998). Emerging social software solutions also allow students to meet and develop common interests, such as forming study-buddy or study-group relationships or engaging in cooperative course-related activities – even while engaged in independent study programs (Anderson, 2005). Finally, as noted earlier, Dron (2007) argues that knowledge can be created through many knowledge networks and through collective activities – the wisdom of crowds – that are supported and aggregated on the Net.

Using this online model then requires decision making on the part of teachers and designers. A key deciding factor is based on the nature of the learning that is prescribed. Marc Prensky (2001) argues that different learning outcomes are best learned through particular learning activities. Prensky asks not *how students learn*, but more specifically *how do they learn what?*

Prensky postulates that in general, we all learn
- behaviours through imitation, feedback, and practice
- creativity through playing
- facts through association, drill, memory, and questions
- judgment through reviewing cases, asking questions, making choices, receiving feedback, and coaching
- language through imitation, practice, and immersion
- observation through viewing examples and feedback
- procedures through imitation and practice
- processes through system analysis, deconstruction, and practice
- systems through discovering principles and graduated tasks
- reasoning through puzzles, problems, and examples
- skills (physical or mental) through imitation, feedback, continuous practice, and increasing challenge

- speeches or performance roles by memorization, practice, and coaching
- theories through logic, explanation, and questioning (156)[1]

Prensky also argues that forms and styles of games can be used online or off-line to effectively facilitate learning each of these skills.

I would argue that each of these activities can be accomplished through e-learning, using some combination of online community activities and computer-supported independent study activities. By tracing the interactions expected and provided for learners through the model (see Figure 4), one can plan for and ensure that an appropriate mix of student, teacher, and content interaction is uniquely designed for each learning outcome.

ONLINE LEARNING AND THE SEMANTIC WEB

We have entered an era in which the Web has expanded from a medium to display content created by professional designers and publishers, to one where commercial content is augmented, annotated, enhanced, and, in some cases, displaced by content created by the end users themselves. Increasingly, ways are being developed to have content harvested, filtered, repurposed, and transformed, through the manipulation of both human and automated processes. This enhanced capacity is based on two emerging network technologies. The first is the set of formal technologies prominently championed by the original designer of the Web, Tim Berners-Lee, and named the Semantic Web (Berners-Lee, 1999). This technology is used to annotate information using formal taxonomies so that the information becomes aware of itself. For example, a data heading might be "author's telephone number," rather than simply information about the font size and colour in which the information is to be displayed – this is what once defined the HTML capacity of the original World Wide Web. The Semantic Web, on the other hand, allows the defining of the label in taxonomy such that autonomous agents and humans could determine that this set of numbers corresponded to a telephone number, and that in turn, this telephone number is related to an individual or an organization. Given this additional information, autonomous agent programs can then sort, query, format, and even make calculations and inferences based upon the additional information.

The second technology is the development of social technologies that add a self-organizational capacity to the Net, through explicit tagging by users and through the tracking of usage. This data is then used to search, retrieve, reconfigure, and filter information on the Net, a capability that has application for many educational, entertainment, and commercial applications. For example, the CiteULike site (see http://www.citeulike.org/) allows users to upload, annotate, and rate scholarly articles they have read. The resulting database can be used by the individual contributor as an aide in their scholarly production, but more importantly, the database of articles can be searched (and further annotated and evaluated) by others to generate a collective assessment of the article.

In the first edition of this chapter, I perhaps over-optimistically championed the emergence of the Semantic Web. Though work continues in the formal classification and annotation of content, there have been significant problems noted with the near impossible challenges of formally describing all data on the Web using standardized terminology and language (McCool, 2006). In response, advocates of the Semantic Web are turning to a second technology of user-tagged content, informally described by emergent folksonomies to proclaim a Semantic Web 2.0 (Spivack, 2007).

The vision of the Semantic Web includes extensive use of autonomous agents to support and facilitate learning. *Student-alert agents* are used for intelligent searching of relevant content (see *Google Alerts* at http://www.google.com/alerts): secretaries booking and arranging for collaborative meetings (see http://meetingwizard.com); reminding students of deadlines (see http://www.calendarhub.com); and negotiating with the agents of other students for assistance, collaboration, or socialization (see http://ihelp.usask.ca/). *Teacher agents* are used to provide remedial tuition, to assist with record keeping and monitoring of student progress, and even to mark and respond to student communications. The content itself can be augmented with agents that control rights to its use, automatically update content, and track means by which the content is used by students (Yu, Brown, & Billett, 2007; Feng, Shaw, Kim, & Hovy, 2006; Clements & Nastassi, 1988).

The Semantic Web also supports the reuse and adaptation of content through support for the construction, distribution, and retrieval of digitized content that is formatted and formally described, using semantic web technologies (Eggins & Slade, 1997b). The emergence of educational modelling languages (Koper, 2001) allow educators to formally describe, in the language accessible on the Semantic Web, not

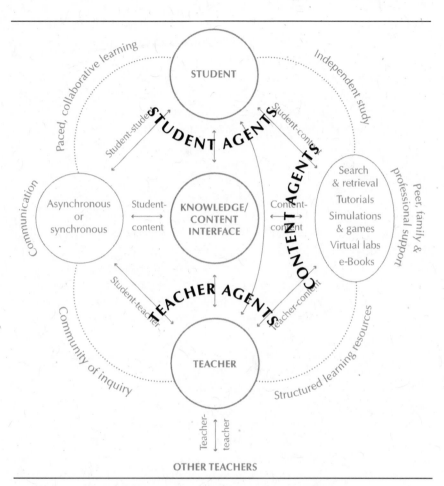

FIGURE 5. Educational interactions on the Semantic Web

only the content but also the activities and context or environment of learning experiences. Together, these affordances of the Semantic Web allow us to envision an e-learning environment that is rich with student-student, student-content, and student-teacher interactions that are affordable, reusable, and facilitated by active agents (see Figure 5).

TOWARDS A THEORY OF ONLINE LEARNING

The Web offers a host of very powerful affordances to educators. Existing and older education provision have been defined by the techniques and tools designed to overcome limitations and exploit the affordances of earlier media. For example, the earliest universities were built around medieval libraries that afforded access to rare handwritten books and manuscripts. Early forms of distance education were constructed using text and the delayed forms of asynchronous communications afforded by mail services. Campus-based education systems are constructed around physical buildings that afford meeting and lecture spaces for teachers and groups of students. The Web now provides near-ubiquitous access to quantities of content that are many orders of magnitude larger than that provided in any other medium.

From earlier discussions, we see that the Web affords a vast potential for education delivery that generally subsumes almost all the modes and means of education delivery previously used – with, perhaps, the exception of rich face-to-face interaction in formal classrooms, though even its supremacy is now being challenged by immersive environments such as *Activeworlds* (see http://www.activeworlds.com) and *SecondLife* (see http://secondlife.com/). We have also seen that the most critical component of formal education consists of interaction between and among multiple actors – human and agents included.

Thus, I conclude this chapter with an overview of a theory of online learning interaction which suggests that the various forms of student interaction can be substituted for each other, depending upon costs, content, learning objectives, convenience, technology used, and time availability. The substitutions do not decrease the quality of learning that results. More formally: Sufficient levels of deep and meaningful learning can be developed as long as one of the three forms of interaction (student–teacher; student-student; student-content) is at very high levels. The other two may be offered at minimal levels or even eliminated without degrading the educational experience. (Anderson 2003b)

The challenge for teachers and course developers working in an online learning context, therefore, is to construct a learning environment that is simultaneously learner-centred, content-centred, community-centred, and assessment-centred. There is no single best media of online learning, nor is there a formulaic specification that dictates the type of interaction most conducive to learning in all domains and with all learners. Rather, teachers must learn to develop their skills so that they can respond to both existing and emergent student and curriculum needs. Teacher can do this by developing a repertoire of online learning activities that are adaptable to diverse contextual and student needs. Table 1 illustrates how the affordances of these emerging technologies

How People Learn Framework (Bransford et al.)	Affordances of the Current Web	Affordances of the Semantic Web 2.0
Learner-Centred	Capacity to support individualized and community-centred learning activities	Content that changes in response to individualized and group learner models. Content that is created, augmented and annotated through student and teacher use
Knowledge-Centred	Direct access to vast libraries of content and learning activities organized from a variety of discipline perspectives	Agents and user referrals for selecting, personalizing, and reusing content. Social augmentation and book marking by communities of experts, practitioners, and other students filter and qualify information so as to transform to knowledge
Community-Centred	Asynchronous and synchronous; collaborative and individual interactions in many formats	Agents and content management systems for translating, reformatting, time shifting, monitoring, and summarizing community interactions. Communities tagging content and issue of interest and value
Assessment-Centred	Multiple time and place shifted opportunities for formative and summative assessment by self, peers, and teachers	Agents for assessing, critiquing, providing 'just-in-time feedback'

TABLE 1. Affordances of Network environment and the attributes of the "way people learn."

can be directed to create the environment most supportive of how people learn.

CONCLUSION

This discussion highlights the wide and diverse forms of teaching and learning that can be supported on the Web today, and the realization that the educational Semantic Web 2.0 will further enhance the possibilities and affordances of the Web, thus making it premature to define a particular theory of online learning. What we can expect, however, is that online learning – like all forms of quality learning – will be knowledge-, community-, assessment-, and learner-centred. Online learning will enhance the critical function of interaction in education, in multiple formats and styles, among all the participants. These interactions will be supported by autonomous agents and the aggregated contribution of other users. The task of the online course designer and teacher now, therefore, is to choose, adapt, and perfect, through feedback, assessment, and reflection, educational activities that maximize the affordances of the Web. In doing so, they will create learning-, knowledge-, assessment-, and community-centred educational experiences that will result in high levels of learning by all participants. Integration of the new tools and affordances of the educational Semantic Web and emerging social software solutions will further enhance and make more accessible and affordable quality online learning experiences.

Our challenge as theory builders and online practitioners, therefore, is to delineate which modes, methods, activities, and actors are most cost- and learning-effective in creating and distributing quality e-learning programs. The creation of a model is often the first step towards theory creation. The model presented illustrates most of the key variables that interact to create online educational experiences and contexts. Our next step is to theorize and measure the direction and magnitude of the effect of each variable on relevant outcome variables, including learning, cost, completion, and satisfaction. The models presented in this chapter do not yet constitute a theory of online learning per se, but hopefully they will help us to deepen our understanding of this complex educational context, and lead us to hypotheses, predictions, and most importantly, improvements in our professional practice. Hopefully, the model and discussion in this and other chapters in this book will lead us towards a robust and comprehensive theory of online learning.

NOTES

1. I am grateful to Joo Khim Tan (email JooKhim@np.edu.sg) for making this link between the model and the work of Marc Prensky in a discussion on ITForum in September, 2002.

REFERENCES

Anderson, T. (2003a). Modes of interaction in distance education: Recent developments and research questions. In M. Moore & W. Anderson (Eds.), *Handbook of distance education.* (pp. 129–144). Mahwah, NJ: Lawrence Erlbaum.

Anderson, T. (2003b). Getting the mix right: An updated and theoretical rational for interaction. *International Review of Research in Open and Distance Learning,* 4(2). Retrieved August 27, 2007, from http://www. irrodl.org/index.php/irrodl/article/view/149/230

Anderson, T. (2004). Student services in a networked world. In J. Brindley, C. Walti, & O. Zawacki-Richter (Eds.), *Learner support in open, distance and online learning environments.* Oldenburg, Germany: Bibliotheks-und Informationssystem der Universität Oldenburg.

Anderson, T. (2005). Distance Learning – Social software's killer app? *Proceedings of the Open & Distance Learning Association (ODLAA) of Australia.* Adelaide: ODLAA. Retrieved August 27, 2007, from http:// www.unisa.edu.au/odlaaconference/PPDF2s/13%20odlaa%20-%20 Anderson.pdf

Anderson, T., & Garrison, D.R. (1998). Learning in a networked world: New roles and responsibilities. In C. Gibson (Ed.), *Distance learners in higher education* (pp. 97–112). Madison, WI: Atwood.

Andersen, T., Norton, J.R., & Nussbaum, J. (1981). Three investigations exploring relationships between perceived teacher communication behaviours and student learning. *Communication Education, 30,* 377–392.

Annand, D. (1999). The problem of computer conferencing for distance-based universities. *Open Learning, 14*(3), 47–52.

Bates, A. (1991). Interactivity as a criterion for media selection in distance education. *Never Too Far, 16,* 5–9.

Baxter, G. P., Elder, A. D., & Glaser, R. (1996). Knowledge-based cognition and performance assessment in the science classroom. *Educational Psychologist, 31*(2), 133–140.

Benedikt, M. (1991). Cyberspace: Some proposals. In M. Benedikt (Ed.), *Cyberspace: First steps* (pp. 119–224). Cambridge, MA: MIT Press.

Berners-Lee, T. (1999). *Weaving the Web: The original design and ultimate destiny of the World Wide Web by its inventor.* San Francisco: Harper.

Bransford, J., Brown, A., & Cocking, R. (1999). *How people learn: Brain, mind experience and school.* Washington, DC: National Research Council. Retrieved August 27, 2007, from http://www.nap.edu/html/howpeople1/

Byrne, M., Flood, B., & Willis, P. (1999). Approaches to learning of Irish students studying accounting. *Dublin City University Business School Research Paper Series, 34.* Retrieved August 27, 2007, http://www.dcu.ie/business/research_papers/no36.html

Christenson, L., & Menzel, K. (1998). The linear relationship between student reports of teacher immediacy behaviors and perceptions of state motivation, and of cognitive, affective, and behavioral learning. *Communication Education, 47*(1), 82–90.

CiteULike. (n.d.). *CiteULike homepage.* Retrieved August 28, 2007, from http://www.citeulike.org/

Clements, D., & Nastassi, B. (1988). Social and cognitive interactions in educational computer environments. *American Educational Research Journal, 25*(1), 87–106.

Cutler, R. (1995). Distributed presence and community in cyberspace. *Interpersonal Computing and Technology: An Electronic Journal for the 21st Century, 3*(2), 12–32. Retrieved August 27, 2007, from http://www.helsinki.fi/science/optek/1995/n2/cutler.txt

Dewey, J. (1916). *Democracy and Education.* New York: Macmillan.

Dixon, J. (2007). Breaking the ice: Supporting collaboration and the development of community online. *Canadian Journal of Learning and Technology, 32*(2). Retrieved August 27, 2007, from http://www.cjlt.ca/content/vol32.2/dixon.html

DOAJ. (n.d.). *Directory of Open Access Journals (DOAJ) web site.* Retrieved August 15, 2007, from http://www.doaj.org/

Dron, J. (2007). *Control and constraint in e-learning: Choosing when to choose.* Hershey, PA: Information Science Pub.

Eggins, S., & Slade, D. (1997a). *Analyzing casual conversation.* Washington, DC: Cassell.

Eggins, S., & Slade, D. (1997b). Approaches to analyzing casual conversation. In S. Eggins & D. Slade (Eds.), *Analyzing casual conversation* (pp. 23–66). Washington, DC: Cassell.

Eklund, J. (1995). *Cognitive models for structuring hypermedia and implications for learning from the World Wide Web.* Retrieved Feb. 2008, from http://ausweb.scu.edu.au/ aw95/hypertext/eklund/

Esposito, J. (2003). The processed book. *First Monday, 8*(3). Retrieved August 15, 2007, from http://firstmonday.org/issues/issue8_3/esposito/index.html

Farmer, J. (2005). Communication dynamics: Discussion boards, weblogs, and the development of communities of inquiry in online learning environments. *James Farmer's BlogSavvy blog.* Retrieved August 15, 2007, from http://www.commoncraft.com/james-farmers-blogsavvy

Feng, D., Shaw, E., Kim, J., & Hovy., E (2006). An intelligent discussion-bot for answering student queries in threaded discussions. Paper presented at the *International Conference on Intelligent User Interfaces (IUI-2006.* Sydney, Australia.

Garrison, D. R., & Shale, D. (1990). A new framework and perspective. In D. R. Garrison & D. Shale (Eds.), *Education at a distance: From issues to practice* (pp. 123–133). Malabar, FL: Robert E. Krieger.

Google. (n.d.). *Google search engine.* Retrieved August 15, 2007, from http://www.google.com

Google Answers. (n.d.). *Google Answers homepage.* Retrieved August 28, 2007, from http://answers.google.com/answers/

Herrington, J., & Oliver, R. (1999). Using situated learning and multimedia to investigate higher-order thinking. *Journal of Interactive Learning Research 10*(1), 3–24.

Holmberg, B. (1989). *Theory and practice of distance education.* London: Routledge.

Jonassen, D. (1992). Designing hypertext for learning. In E. Scanlon & T. O'Shea (Eds.), *New directions in educational technology* (pp. 123–130). Berlin: Springer-Verlag.

Jonassen, D., & Carr, C. (2000). Mindtools affording multiple knowledge representations for learning. In S. Lajoie (Ed.), *Computers as cognitive tools: No more walls* (pp. 65–96). Mahwah, NJ: Lawrence Erlbaum.

Kirby, D., & Boak, C. (1987). Developing a system for audio-teleconferencing analysis. *Journal of Distance Education, 2* (2), 31–42.

Koper, R. (2001). Modeling units of study from a pedagogical perspective: The pedagogical meta-model behind EML. In R. Koper (Ed.),

Modeling units of study from a pedagogical perspective: The pedagogical meta-model behind EML. Heerlen: Open University of the Netherlands. Retrieved August 28, 2007, from http://dspace.ou.nl/bitstream/1820/36/1/Pedagogical+metamodel +behind+EMLv2.pdf

Laurillard, D. (1997). *Rethinking university teaching: A framework for the effective use of educational technology.* London: Routledge.

Lee, A. (2006). Learning and transfer in two web-based and distance applications. *Web-based learning: Theory, research and practice.* In H. O'Neil & R. Perez (Eds.), Mahwah, NJ: Lawrence Erlbaum.

Lipman, M. (1991). *Thinking in Education.* Cambridge: Cambridge University Press.

McCool, R. (2006). Rethinking the Semantic Web. *IEEE Internet Computing, 10*(1), 93–96.

McCormick, N., &McCormick. J. (1992). Computer friends and foes: Content of undergraduates' electronic mail. *Computers in Human Behavior, 8*(4), 379–405.

McDonald, J. (1998). Interpersonal group dynamics and development in computer conferencing: The rest of the story. *American Journal of Distance Education, 12*(1), 7–25.

McPeck, J. (1990). *Teaching critical thinking.* New York: Routledge.

MERLOT. (n.d.). *Multimedia Educational Resource for Learning Online Technology (MERLOT) homepage.* Retrieved August 15, 2007, from http://www.merlot.org/merlot/index.htm

Morris, M., & Ogan, C. (1996). The Internet as mass medium. *Journal of Computer Mediated Communications, 4*(1), 39–50.

MySpace. (n.d.). *MySpace homepage.* Retrieved August 28, 2007, from http://www.myspace.com/

OECD. (2006). *Organisation for Economic and Cooperative Development 2006 factbook.* Retrieved August 15, 2007, from http://lysander.sourceoecd.org/vl=8150559/cl=19/nw=1/rpsv/fact2006/

Opencontent.org. (n.d.). *Opencontent.org homepage.* August 15, 2007, from http://opencontent.org/

Phelps, R., Hase, S., & Ellis, A. (2005). Competency, capability, complexity and computers: Exploring a new model for conceptualising end-user computer education. *British Journal of Educational Technology, 36*(1), 67–85.

Potter, J. (1998). Beyond access: Student perspective on support service needs in distance education. *The Canadian Journal of University Continuing Education, 24*(1), 59–82.

Prensky, M. (2001). *Digital game-based learning.* New York: McGraw-Hill.

Resnick, M. (1996). Distributed constructivism. *Proceedings of the International Conference on the Learning Sciences Association for the Advancement of Computing in Education.* Chicago: Northwestern University.

Richardson, J. (2000). *Researching student learning: Approaches to studying in campus-based and distance education.* Buckingham, UK: Open University Press.

Richardson, W. (2006). *Blogs, wikis, podcasts and other powerful Web tools for classrooms.* Thousand Oaks, CA: Corwin Press.

Rourke, L., & Anderson, T. (2002). Using peer teams to lead online discussions. *Journal of Interactive Media in Education, 1.* Retrieved August 15, 2007, from http://www-jime.open.ac.uk/2002/1/rourke-anderson-02-1.pdf

Rumble, G. (1999). Cost analysis of distance learning. *Performance Improvement Quarterly, 12*(2), 122–137.

Seely Brown, J., & Hagel, J. (2005, April). IT platforms for business innovation. *Milestone Group.* Retrieved August 15, 2007, from http://www.milestone-group.com/news/05_04/seely-hagel.htm

Shank, G. (1993). Abductive multiloguing: The semiotic dynamics of navigating the Net. *The Arachnet Electronic Journal on Virtual Culture, 1*(1). Retrieved August 15, 2007, from http://infomotions.com/serials/aejvc/aejvc-v1n01-shank-abductive.txt

Short, J., Williams, E., & Christie, B. (1976). *The social psychology of telecommunications.* Toronto: John Wiley and Sons.

Siemens, G. (2005). A learning theory for the digital age. *Instructional Technology and Distance Education, 2*(1), 3–10.

Sims, R. (1999). Interactivity on stage: Strategies for learner-designer communication. *Australian Journal of Educational Technology, 15*(3), 257–272.

Smith, C., Feld, S., & Franz, C. (1992). Methodological considerations: Steps in research employing content analysis systems. In C. Smith (Ed.), *Motivation and personality: Handbook of thematic content analysis* (pp. 515–535). New York: Cambridge University Press.

Smolensky, M., Carmondy, M., & Halcomb, C. (1990). The influence of task type, group structure and extraversion on uninhibited Speech in computer-mediated communication. *Computer in Human Behavior, 6*(3), 261–272.

Spivack, N. (2007). Minding the planet: The meaning and future of the Semantic Web. *Lifeboat Foundation Special Report.* Retrieved August 15, 2007, from http://lifeboat.com/ex/minding.the.planet

TOPICA. (n.d.). *TOPICA email discussion list webpage.* Retrieved August 15, 2007, from http://lists.topica.com/dir/?cid=4

Visser, J. (2000). Faculty work in developing and teaching web-based distance courses: A case study of time and effort. *American Journal of Distance Education, 14*(3), 21–32.

Vygotsky, L. (1978). *Mind in society: The development of higher psychological processes.* Cambridge, MA: Harvard University Press.

Wagner, E. D. (1994). In support of a functional definition of interaction. *The American Journal of Distance Education, 8*(2), 6–26.

Wenger, E., R. McDermott, R. & and W. Snyder, W. (2002). *Cultivating communities of practice: A guide to managing knowledge.* Cambridge, MA: Harvard Business School Press.

Wilson, B. (1997). Thoughts on theory in educational technology. *Educational Technology, 37*(1), 22–26.

Yu, J., Brown, D., & Billett, E. (2007). Design of virtual tutoring agents for a virtual biology experiment. *European Journal of Open and Distance Learning.* Retrieved August 24, 2007, from http://www.eurodl.org/materials/contrib/2007/Yu_Brown_Billett.htm

ABOUT THE AUTHOR

Terry Anderson (terrya@athabascau.ca) is a professor and Canada Research Chair in Distance Education at Athabasca University – Canada's Open University. He has published widely in the area of distance education and educational technology and has co-authored three books: Anderson and Kanuka (2002) *eResearch: Methods, Issues and Strategies*; Garrison and Anderson (2002), *Online Learning in the 21st Century: A Framework for Research and Practice*, and Haughey and Anderson, *Networked Learning: Pedagogy of the Internet.* Terry graduated with a PhD from the University of Calgary in Educational Psychology, has a MSc from the University of Oregon in Computer Education, and a BA and BEd from the University of Alberta. He teaches educational technology courses in the Centre for Distance Education at Athabasca. He is the founding director of the *Canadian Institute for Distance Education Research* (see http://cider.athabascau.ca) and currently serves as the editor of the *International Review of Research in Open and Distance Learning* (see www.irrodl.org).

CHAPTER 3

Situating Prior Learning Assessment and Recognition (PLAR) in an Online Learning Environment

Dianne Conrad
Athabasca University

INTRODUCTION

Open and distance educational institutions share a commitment to principles of access and flexibility which, in turn, reflect a set of foundational beliefs that shape learning activity. Housed within this broad mandate is an explicit recognition of the presence and value of mature learners' prior learning. This chapter describes and situates *prior learning assessment and recognition* (PLAR) as a knowledge-building process within an online post-secondary learning culture. In doing so, it briefly reviews the history and context of PLAR; discusses the pedagogy of portfolio construction; outlines PLAR's operational functionality; and considers the potential of the e-portfolio as a learning tool. Athabasca University's use of PLAR in an open and distance university setting will serve as context.

THE ROLE OF PRIOR LEARNING ASSESSMENT AND RECOGNITION IN ADULT EDUCATION AND OPEN AND DISTANCE LEARNING (ODL) ENVIRONMENTS

By definition and through practice, distance education has become synonymous with innovative models of program delivery that offer more generous open and flexible learning opportunities to wider and more diverse audiences than did traditional classrooms. The commonly accepted ways in which open and distance learning (ODL) institutions are perceived to serve diverse student populations centre around issues of scheduling and geography, typically allowing easier access to post-secondary education for those who have not previously enjoyed that option. And while the complex relationship between the concepts of diversity, access, and facilitating adults' learning through the recognition of their prior learning raises philosophical questions around social and power relationships, the presence of PLAR within post-secondary systems nonetheless provides viable alternative learning opportunities to many distance learners.

PLAR is practiced globally as a means of honouring and building on mature learners' past experiential learning. Grounded in ancient philosophies, the recognition of prior learning is defined by UNESCO as "the formal acknowledgement of skills, knowledge, and competencies that are gained through work experience, informal training, and life experience" (Vlăsceanu, Grünberg, & Pârlea, 2004, p. 55). More recent history on PLAR can be found in the works of Pestalozzi (1907), Dewey (1938), and Kolb (1984).

Dewey presented a sound pedagogical rationale for recognizing adults' experiential learning – "the beginning of instruction shall be made with the experience learners already have...this experience and the capacities that have been developed during its course provide the starting point for all further learning" (1938, p. 74) – while advocating a progressive philosophy whose real-world learning echoed through the work of many adult educators. In North America, Moses Coady (1971) and Myles Horton (1990) were among those whose parallel views were instrumental in bringing educational opportunities to the oppressed and poverty-stricken. Farther abroad, Paulo Freire's work with farm workers in South America rested on the foundational premise of their experiential learning (1970). More recently, in exploring transformational learning across the span of adults' lives, Welton (1995) cites Mezirow's understanding of the role of educators in helping learners mine their past for reflexive learning, thereby declaring the value of experiential learning as an active-learning occasion by involving the teaching role in the re-creation of learners' pasts.

ODL AND THE COMMITMENT TO PLAR AT ATHABASCA UNIVERSITY

As do other ODL institutions, Athabasca University outlines its commitment to reducing barriers to university education in its mandate and vision statements. Following on this, Athabasca University adopts as a key pillar in its foundation the process of recognizing learners' prior experiential learning. To implement a coherent and integrated prior learning recognition policy, AU maintains a central office where personnel champion, direct, and manage the PLAR process. The existence of such an internal and integrated structure makes Athabasca University somewhat unique among Canadian universities; the size of its operation places it at the forefront of university prior learning practice in Canada.

AU implements PLAR using both challenge-for-credit and portfolio assessment methods, thereby reflecting the field's general understanding of the twin practices for PLAR implementation, challenge, and equivalency (Ontario Ministry of Education, 2001). Under the challenge-for-credit policy, learners may choose to target a specific course for which they feel they already possess the required knowledge or skills. Working with the course professor, they then engage in a contractual relationship to meet the challenge conditions that have been pre-established for the course. While this processes honours their right to bring forward their prior knowledge, learners applying to have their prior knowledge recognized in this fashion are obliged to tailor their learning histories to fit into pre-determined knowledge clusters that look like Athabasca University courses. While this is just one model of PLAR – and an acceptable one – it is not a model that gives learners the opportunity to build new knowledge on the foundation of their prior knowledge. Rather, it is the process of preparing a portfolio that permits learners to demonstrate their prior knowledge through the careful selection, reflection, connection, and projection of learning artefacts. In so doing, learners can most fully exercise the scope and latitude of their prior knowledge while learners' cognitive engagement with their learning histories gives rise to new knowledge – of self, of self situated within the trajectory of growth, and of self situated within the profession.

It is important to note that the portfolio approach is necessarily guided by sets of university-provided criteria and outcomes. That said, portfolio criteria and outcomes serve as guidelines and structuring devices rather than as hard-and-fast targets. They provide signposts around which learners can rally and organize their own learning, rather than stipulating for them what they must know to be successful in their petition.

KNOWLEDGE-BUILDING THROUGH PLAR PORTFOLIOS

In many post-secondary PLAR systems, the portfolio is the vehicle through which learners' prior learning can be assessed for credit toward a university credential. More broadly, portfolios serve as repositories of achievement and methods of celebrating growth for lifelong learners. Outside of learning venues, portfolios are used as performance assessment tools for those seeking advancement in the workplace; they also serve as showcase vehicles for those seeking recognition of their accomplishments.

PLAR Paradigms and Politics

Universally, portfolios are being touted more widely than ever as an essential part of citizenship, personal performance, or learning. To this end, the European Union promotes the development of a personal portfolio for each of its citizens by 2010 (European Commission, 2005). Similarly, many post-secondary institutions now include a portfolio as an essential component for graduation from the institution. Such a portfolio would capture a graduate's entire learning history from the institution, featuring papers, assignments, reflections, triumphs, and struggles, as well as indications of present and future career aspirations. Barrett and Carney (2005) describe the many functions of portfolios in terms of low-stakes and high-stakes assessment. High-stakes assessments reap considerable rewards: learning portfolios that are submitted for university credit are prime examples of high-stakes assessment.

PLAR-by-portfolio generates controversy within the university culture, in part as a result of its existence as a high-stakes assessment tool that offers learners opportunities to sidestep course-taking or fast-track through university credentials, even though, in ODL institutions, meeting learners' needs in this way generally contributes to university mandates. More than that, however, portfolio assessment generates even deeper controversy around issues of power and voice (Harris, 1999; Michelson, 1996). Several questions arise: Who controls knowledge? How can those who step forward with non-university learning be expected to conform to the language of the university so that they can attain fair recognition of their knowledge? Peters (2005) is among many who contest the ability of academic faculty to fairly assess portfolio learning.

Promoting PLAR to its critics depends, at a meaningful pedagogical level, on being able to demonstrate a system that is rigorous, sound, and capable of initiating self-reflection and critical thinking. To do this, it is necessary to return to PLAR's first principles on two levels, the first of which is recognizing the value of mature learners' prior learning. PLAR literature is indebted to Dewey (1938) and Kolb (1984) for their work on experiential learning and its value to individuals and their societies. Of no less importance, however, is the belief in a constructivist-based approach to learning. In this view, the portfolio process allows learners to begin at a point of their own choosing and to select and reflect upon learning that is important to them. Their learning challenge is to integrate that knowledge into the knowledge asked of them by the institution. Following this view, portfolio development would be analogized as a journey, complete with all the meandering, false starts, corners, surprises, and difficulties that any journey holds.

PLAR Practice and Process

Using the metaphor of portfolio-as-journey, learners move along a route of portfolio preparation comprised of a number of cognitive stages. Somewhat glibly labelled reflect, select, connect, and project, each of these steps requires intense and laborious thought; each step may spark the "aha" moment that occasions learning. The process is described below.

Reflect

Among adult learners – and PLAR participants by definition are usually adult learners – learning is a voluntary action that centres around what is already known. From a starting point of personal meaning and relevance, adult learners enter into a relationship with their environment to construct new meaning (Angelo, 1993; Mackeracher, 2004). This process is one of thoughtful reflection, resulting in what Crites (1971) terms a movement from the mundane to the sacred – learning to understand experience beyond its isolated, secular level. Helping learners to settle at this level of interpreting their experiences is a process intended to elevate their stories beyond the confines of their own immediacy to more generic levels of knowledge. For example, a single mother who wrote about her demanding personal schedule, that included shuttling her sons back and forth to hockey practice and assuming multiple parental roles, used those experiences to highlight her organizational skills and the resultant value that her inter-collegial skills brought to her workplace. As she worked through the process of reflecting on the lessons emanating from her household tasks, she drew new meaning from those tasks and learned that she had actually been honing new skills.

Select

When preparing PLAR portfolios, applicants must mine their rich and varied learning experiences selectively for the events that can most effectively anchor the learning narrative that they are creating. Their selections constitute a type of scaffolding upon which they build the stories of their learning. In putting together this framework, they map both their histories and their futures in a form of strategizing, which is similar to the cognitive processes that would formulate the answer to an essay question asking, say, for a detailed explanation of the events leading up to the fall of the Berlin Wall. In learning portfolios, however, the value and nature of the knowledge incidents are related to self; selecting them and denoting them as valuable labels them as integral pieces in the exercise of building self-knowledge.

Connect

The act of connection occurs both subsequently to, and concomitantly with, the act of selection. As in the example of the Berlin Wall used above, once the "knowledge items" have been identified, they must be linked or arranged into an order that serves the purpose at hand. Mackeracher (2004) cites the "basic learning cycle" that incorporates the work of Kolb (1984) and other theorists into five basic phases of learning. In brief, the five phases include a) participation in experiences and activities; b) making sense of experience by giving it meaning or value, using pattern recognition and other cognitive processes; c) applying meanings and values to problem-solving and decision-making processes to make choices; d) implementing action plans; and e) receiving feedback both from others and from self-observation. The integral theme of connecting experience to meaning recurs in situated cognition theory (Brown, Collins, & Duguid, 1989) and also in transformation theory (Mezirow, 1995). Using the same processes that Mezirow outlines for engendering transformational learning by critically reflecting on and modifying current assumptions and understandings, the PLAR process also asks learners to engage in knowledge-building activity.

Project

The last step for PLAR applicants in demonstrating learning is to determine an appropriate presentation method – to project the evidence of their learning in a format deemed acceptable by the receiving institution. In conforming to a structured set of expectations, learners meet another set of learning outcomes by fulfilling process (or generic) outcomes that might be labelled thus: using and constructing documents accurately; communicating appropriately in text; understanding one's learning style; and adapting it to tasks at hand. The foundational importance of this type of learned skill is reflected in the compilation of national-level outcomes for all learners (Government of Canada, 2006).

The projection of PLAR applicants' learning, according to template-type guidelines, results in the production of a substantial portfolio document. The portfolio format itself is designed to triangulate learners' demonstration of knowledge, and in constructing such a document, learners are further encouraged to apply their organizing and prioritizing cognitive skills. The entire document should contain most of the following parts: table of contents, resume, narrative autobiography or personal narrative, chronological learning history, educational and career goals, demonstration of learning through learning statements, and documentation of learning. The documentation of learning often forms the bulkiest part of the portfolio as learners include many types of documents, including letters of attestation written by externals to validate their learning claims, and copies of credentials, awards, certificates, and other artefacts.

The heart of the knowledge construction exercise in this text-based portfolio method rests in the process of writing learning statements. Learning statements form the body of the demonstrated evidence of the learning that PLAR applicants claim to have acquired. The documentation described previously must support these claims. Based on Bloom's Taxonomy (1956), which stratifies cognitive achievement into six hierarchical categories – knowledge, comprehension, application, analysis, synthesis, and evaluation – learners compose statements that appropriately reflect the learning outcomes they feel they have achieved. The process of writing learning statements presents a vigorous cognitive challenge to most learners and most PLAR applicants struggle with this task. At the end of it, however, with the clarity that arises from successfully resolving a task, their reactions reflect both satisfaction with, and wonder at, the nature and extent of the learning that they realize has occurred.

OPERATIONALIZING PLAR
IN AN ONLINE ENVIRONMENT

Recognizing learners' prior learning may appear to provide solutions to many traditional situational, attitudinal, and institutional barriers to learning; however, the relationship between the concepts of diversity, access, and the issue of facilitating adults' learning through the recognition of their prior learning is both complex and dichotomous. An uneasy type of teeter-totter balance exists between the fact of open and distance access and PLAR processes, exacerbated by the presence of philosophical and social power relationships (Conrad, 2007). As a result, the use of PLAR processes confronts, and opens the door to, a network of resulting tensions.

Online learning environments are also viewed as opening the door to educational opportunities where none existed before, and, in many cases, this is exactly what happens. Technology, however, brings with it its own set of encumbrances and difficulties, and its successful implementation requires careful networks of student support (Davis, Little & Stewart, 2008; Moisey & Hughes, 2008; Johnson, Trabelsi, & Fabbro, 2008). Superimposing the online learning environment on top of portfolio learning opportunities requires not only sensitivity and awareness, therefore, but an acutely informed understanding of online learners and the challenges that confront them. A discussion of these areas of challenge follows.

Adult Learners, Andragogy, ODL

Not all online learners are adults, nor are all online learners mature.[1] That said, online theory supports the view that online learning holds the most potential for mature learners following a constructivist approach (Kanuka & Anderson, 1998). Experiential learning certainly favours maturity (Dewey, 1938; Kolb, 1984). Given the confluence of these two educational streams at the junction described in this chapter, it stands to reason that success in this domain requires a good understanding of what it means to be a mature learner in a distance learning environment, as regards issues of motivation, learning styles, community, and social, cognitive, and instructional presence. The pervasive problematic and underlying irony in the implementation of PLAR is that often it is not well understood in its role as a learning activity – a role that would bring into play all of the literature suggested above – and is instead relegated by both supporters and detractors to the purview of registrars, credit transfer, and credit counting. Adequate educational foundations for PLAR's operation, therefore, are often missing.

Assessment Methodology

There are many ways to assess prior learning. They include performance displays, interviews, examinations, projects, and portfolio assessments, as well as combinations of these various methods. The fact of a distance institution limits the choice, effectively ruling out interviews or performance displays, for example; Athabasca University chooses to use only the portfolio method of assessment. While not unusual in this situation, the use of only one method of assessment increases the importance of the structure and integrity of the PLAR process, specifically as it involves and relates to learners' and assessors' text-based abilities. The need for learners to be able to display their learning largely in a written format[2] demands a high level of communication structure, as discussed below.

Communication

In many other venues, PLAR is conducted in informal or semi-formal face-to-face venues where applicants are able to engage in discussion with mentoring or coaching staff. Because of the nature of the task – helping applicants grapple with understanding the extent of, and the value of, their past learning – an iterative format is best, as it allows a level of deep understanding to evolve through reflection (Schön, 1987). ODL institutions that are not privy to face-to-face access must rely on a well-developed structure and responsive systems of communications in order to accomplish the interaction necessary for the successful management of a PLAR process. Facilitating such complex communication requires excellent and continual application of written and verbal skills, and the manufacture and maintenance of high-quality resources (see the section on Resources, below).

In another communication twist occasioned by a distributed environment, internal communications among staff and faculty must also operate at a highly efficient level. At Athabasca University, for example, where PLAR is integrated across all programs, a complex many-to-many system of interactions arises from each portfolio assessment. The potential of lost or misunderstood communications is high.

Resources

It is well understood by online educators that not all learners want to forsake paper-based resources. The current generation of online learners,

at least, prefer to access their online resources in moderation.[3] In keeping
with principles of access that attempt to provide maximum opportunity
to its clientele, Athabasca University's PLAR system provides both paper-
based and online resources for potential applicants. A large web site
forms the online resource (http://priorlearning.athabascau.ca/index.
php). A virtual portfolio located on the web site permits almost-hands-on
access to the real thing. High-quality PLAR resources form one of the
bases for the strong platform of support required by distance learners.

Support

The need for generous provision of student support is well documented
in ODL literature (for example, see Moisey & Hughes, 2008). Support
for distance learners takes many forms, most obviously advising, counselling, coaching, mentoring, and supporting with technology and the web
site. Within the pedagogy of online learning, the need for community
support, also well documented, manifests itself in the form of learning
communities, communities of practice, virtual learning environments,
and applications of social software. PLAR learners require an equal
amount of support for successful completion. While numerous material
resources provide one level and type of support, an essential and more
sophisticated level of support relies on human interaction, achieved
through telephone and email contact. Ideally, collegial peer support
involving those who are concomitantly engaged in preparing PLAR portfolios would provide a high level of effective interaction. Given the positioning of PLAR as a learning activity within the institution, PLAR learner
support mechanisms should look no different than any other type of
course-oriented learner support.

INTRODUCING THE E-PORTFOLIO

What is the future of the e-portfolio in an ODL environment, therefore,
given the conditions for successful management of a portfolio system,
as described in this chapter? At Athabasca University, as in most post
secondary institutions' high-stakes assessment portfolio use, materials
must be assembled for the exact purpose of attaining credit at the institution. The learning portfolio described in this chapter

> contains work that a learner has collected, reflected, selected,
> and presented to show growth and change over time. A critical

component of an educational portfolio is the learner's reflection on the individual pieces of work (often called 'artefacts') as well as an overall reflection on the story that the portfolio tells. (Barrett, 2005, p. 4)

From this rigorous structure that is defined by educational require-ments comes a very targeted and precise document, the production of which encourages reflective learning activity in its participants and demands evidence of that learning. Does the electronic portfolio format permit learners to engage in the same type of thoughtful process? Tosh, Light, Fleming, and Haywood (2005) outline that, as with paper-based portfolios, the

e-portfolio is – or should be – part of a student-owned, student-centred approach to learning that makes it possible for students to actively engage in their learning rather than just be the recipi-ents of information. This is consistent with constructivist theory, which argues students actively construct their own knowledge rather than simply receive it from instructors, authors, or other sources. (Jonassen, cited in Tosh et al., p. 90)

Ideally, advocates of learning portfolios, whether paper-based or elec-tronic, will strive to support the concept of learners' portfolios-as-learning while adhering to the rigours and accountability of high stakes assess-ment for the purpose of credit allocation. In fact, in fields that value computer, technology, multimedia, or design skills, learners' use of e-portfolios could provide not only a more engaging demonstration of skills, but also a more technically correct demonstration of skills. However, Tosh and colleagues' contention that e-portfolios offer opportunity for learner control and promote deep learning should be true of any good portfolio process and should be no less true of the traditional paper-based portfolio. The introduction of another layer of technology brought about by e-portfolio use, however, raises several concerns for learners and educators in online environments.

Focus

If, as Barrett (2000, para. 3) suggests, "the e-portfolio draws on two bodies of literature, multimedia development (decide, design, develop, evaluate) and portfolio development (collection, selection, reflection, projection)," will the e-portfolio's necessary emphasis on software design potentially lessen learners' attention to content? Is there the potential of e-portfolios favouring form over content?

Assessment Equity

On the other side of the equation, will the e-portfolio's emphasis on software design potentially lessen the assessors' attention to content? Will assessors searching for an individual's learning story feel less attuned to the applicant who submits an electronic portfolio?

In a similar vein, e-portfolio technology has the potential to alienate assessors. Universities such as Athabasca University use assessors who tend to be academic faculty; they have the time and the inclination to contribute to the PLAR process because they are older faculty members, secure in their positions. Cumbersome as paper-based portfolios often are, some faculty prefer them due to the increased computer usage that e-portfolios require.

Diversity

Issues of diversity reshape themselves when technology is added to the portfolio mix. As outlined in the discussion above, a number of types of diversity already exist within the portfolio process; it is naïve to consider that access to PLAR offers a level playing field. Similarly, relying on technology or introducing a technological platform to the production of a portfolio privileges some learners above others. That said, critics argue that a paper platform also disadvantages some learners while privileging others.

Pedagogy

Tosh and colleagues' (2005) assumption, based on the adult education premise that learners engage more successfully when they have control (Ramsden, 2003), skirts the deeper cognitive issues of how learners connect to, or feel ownership of, their learning. Do today's learners feel more connection to electronic portfolios? Research maintains that as the number of learners who can be labelled "digitally native" increases over time, e-resources and e-materials will rise in popularity among learners (Eshet & Geri, 2007). Currently, however, as manifested in similar discussions of the merits of print-based journals versus those of e-journals, each option has supporters and detractors.

CONCLUSION

Nowhere does the practice of prior learning assessment and recognition make more sense than in the adult learning environment. That said, theory also supports the integration of PLAR processes into the online teaching and learning environment, and current practice confirms that ODL institutions, such as Athabasca University, are leaders in the implementation of PLAR at the university level.

As demonstrated through literature and practice, however, consensus remains to be found around issues of prior learning. The practice of recognizing prior learning will hopefully inform post-secondary educators' perceptions of learning while it continues to offer learners fertile ground for cognitive and personal growth.

NOTES

1. The issue of maturity is hotly debated among adult educators, as is the complementary issue of defining the term adult. Generally, a psycho-social definition that outlines individuals' acceptance of social roles in terms of their society's expectations is what is used to define adulthood. In a learning context, maturity is understood to entail responsibility and some degree of control and self-direction. While institutions and agencies are often required to attach an age to adult learner status, it is understood pedagogically that age alone constitutes arbitrary and somewhat artificial boundaries.

2. Although portfolios are classified as text-based, in reality, material may be presented in other ways. A portfolio, for example, will often contain graphics or pictures, and may contain CDs or audio recordings of some sort. A portfolio may be submitted on a CD, although it will still comprise mostly text. Some of the issues that surround the introduction of web-based e-portfolios are discussed later in this chapter.

3. Internal studies conducted by Athabasca University's Institutional Studies unit have produced statistics to support external research, which shows that learners still prefer paper-based resources, or that they are willing to spread their resource menu among various modalities. Other external research shows that learners' level of comfort with online resources is dependent on their status as digital natives;

in the future, this figure is expected to rise accordingly (Eshet & Geri, 2007).

REFERENCES

Angelo, T. A. (1993, April). A 'teacher's dozen': Fourteen general, research-based principles for improving higher learner in our class-rooms. *AAHE Bulletin,* 3–13.

Barrett, H. (2000). Electronic portfolios = multimedia development + portfolio development: The electronic development process. *electron-icportfolios.org web site.* Retrieved August 14, 2007, from http://electronic portfolios.org/portfolios/EPDevProcess.html

Barrett, H. (2005). Conflicting paradigms and competing purposes in electronic portfolio development. *TaskStream web site.* Retrieved August 13, 2007, from http://www.taskstream.com/reflect/whitepaper.pdf

Barrett, H., & Carney, J. (2005). Conflicting paradigms and competing purposes in electronic portfolio development. Retrieved April 16, 2007, at http://www.taskstream .com/ reflect/whitepaper.pdf

Bloom, B. S. (1956). *Taxonomy of educational objectives, Handbook I: The cognitive domain.* New York, NY: David McKay.

Brown, J. S., Collins, A., & Duguid, A. (1989). Situated cognition and the culture of learning. *Educational Researcher, 18*(1), 32–42.

Coady, M. M. (1971). The man from Margaree: Writings and speeches of M. M. Coady. Toronto: McClelland & Stewart.

Conrad, D. (2007). Recognizing prior learning: Exploring the diversity of learners' experiential learning through PLAR. In T. Evans, D. Murphy & M. Haughey (Eds.), *World Handbook of Distance Education.* Oxford: Elsevier.

Crites, S. (1971). The narrative quality of experience. *American Academy of Religion Journal, 39*(3), 291–311.

Davis, A., Little, P. & Stewart, B. (2008). In T. Anderson (Ed.), *Theory and practice of online learning,* 2nd ed. (pp.121–142). Edmonton, AB: AU Press.

Dewey, J. (1938). *Experience and education.* New York, NY: Macmillan.

Eshet, Y., & Geri, N. (2007). Print versus digital: Critical reading of information. New Learning 2.0? *Proceedings of EDEN Conference,* Naples.

European Commission. (2005). Implementing the 'Education and Training 2010' work programme. Brussels.

Freire, P. (1970). *Pedagogy of the oppressed.* New York: Herder & Herder.

Government of Canada. (2006). Essential skills. *Human Resources and Skills Development Canada.* Retrieved August 14, 2007, from http://srv108.services.gc.ca/english/general/home_e.shtml

Harris, J. (1999). Ways of seeing the recognition of prior learning (RPL): What contribution can such practices make to social inclusion? *Studies in the Education of Adults, 31*(2), 124–138.

Horton, M. (1990). *We make the road by walking: Conversations on education and social change.* Philadelphia: Temple University Press.

Johnson, K., Trabelsi, H., & Fabbro, E. (2008). Library support for e-learners: E-resources, e-services and the human factors. In T. Anderson (Ed.), *Theory and practice of online learning,* 2nd ed. (pp. 397–418). Athabasca, AB: AU Press.

Jonassen, D. (1991). Evaluating constructivist learning. *Educational Technology, 36*(9), 28–33.

Kanuka, H., & Anderson, T. (1998). Online social interchange, discord, and knowledge construction. *Journal of Distance Education, 13*(1). Retrieved August 14, 2007, from http://cade.athabascau.ca/vol13.1/kanuka.html

Kolb, D. A. (1984). *Experiential learning: Experience as the source of learning and development.* Englewood Cliffs, NJ: Prentice-Hall.

Mackeracher, D. (2004). *Making sense of adult learning* (2nd ed.). Toronto, ON: University of Toronto Press.

Mezirow, J. (1995). Transformation theory of adult learning. In M. Welton (Ed.) *In defense of the lifeworld: Critical perspectives on adult learning* (pp. 39–70). Albany, NY: State University of New York Press.

Michelson, E. (1996). Usual suspects: Experience, reflection, and the (en)gendering of knowledge. *International Journal of Lifelong Education, 15*(6), 438–54.

Moisey, S., & Hughes, J. (2008). Supporting the online learner. In T. Anderson (Ed.), *Theory and practice of online learning,* 2nd ed. (pp. 419–439). Edmonton, AB: AU Press.

Ontario Ministry of Education. (2001). Policy/program memorandum No. 129. Retrieved August 14, 2007, from http://www.edu.gov.on.ca/extra/eng/ppm/129.html

Pestalozzi, J. H. (1907). *How Gertrude teaches her children: An attempt to help mothers to teach their own children,* 4th ed. Lucy E. Holland & Frances C. Turner, Trans. London: Swan, Sonnenshein & Co.

Peters, H. (2005). Contested discourses: Assessing the outcomes of learning from experience for the award of credit in higher education. *Assessment & Evaluation in Higher Education, 30*(3), 273–285.

Ramsden, P. (2003). *Learning to teach in higher education* (2nd ed.). London: RoutledgeFalmer.

Schön, D. (1987). *Educating the reflective practitioner.* San Francisco: Jossey-Bass.

Tosh, D., Light, T. P, Fleming, K., & Haywood, J. (2005). Engagement with electronic portfolios: Challenges from the student perspective. *Canadian Journal of Learning and Technology, 31*(3), 89–110.

Vlăsceanu, L., Grünberg, L., & Pârlea, D. (2004). Quality assurance and accreditation: A glossary of basic terms and definitions. *Papers on Higher Education.* Bucharest:

UNESCO-CEPES. Retrieved August 13, 2007, from http://www.cepes. ro/ publications/Default.htm

ABOUT THE AUTHOR

Dianne Conrad (diannec@athabascau.ca) is a practicing adult educator with over 25 years of experience. Dr. Conrad is currently the director of the Centre for Learning Accreditation at Athabasca University in Alberta, Canada. She is actively engaged in e-learning research that focuses on the development of community among online learners and the positioning of e-learning as a societal phenomenon.

CHAPTER 4

UNDERSTANDING E-LEARNING TECHNOLOGIES-IN-PRACTICE THROUGH PHILOSOPHIES-IN-PRACTICE

HEATHER KANUKA
University of Alberta

Theory without practice leads to an empty idealism, and action without philosophical reflection leads to mindless activism.
– Elias & Merriam, 1980, p. 4

INTRODUCTION:
WHY IS UNDERSTANDING OUR PHILOSOPHIES IMPORTANT?

Existing and emerging e-learning technologies are having intense, immediate, and disruptive transformations on education systems (Archer, Garrison & Anderson, 1999); nowhere is the impact felt more than on the practitioners who teach. More specifically, education has moved into a third decade of profound change in how courses and programs are designed and delivered. During this time, many new possibilities have become apparent, but also many new challenges.

With the rise of e-learning technologies in all sectors of education, there has been one most frequently asked and investigated question: Has e-learning delivered on its promises? Leaders in the field of education have argued that e-learning technologies can effectively respond to accelerating global competition (Daniel, 2000), increase the quality of learning experiences (Garrison, 2002), remove situational barriers

(Bates, 2005), and be more cost effective (Twigg, 2003). In an effort to provide evidence for the promises forwarded by e-learning advocates, interventions and explorations into the use of e-learning technologies have been conducted. Based on these investigations, commonly cited advantages of e-learning technologies include an ability to provide just-in-time learning; increased access; removal of time, place and situational barriers; cost effectiveness; greater accountability; increased interaction; provision of future employment skills for students; and effective support for lifelong learning.

As e-learning has become more pervasive, however, expressions of uncertainty, concern, and scepticism have also emerged. The growing lists of concerns include commercialization of teaching; lack of face-time between students and teachers; techno-centric models prioritized over face-to-face culture; devaluation of oral discourse/discussion practices; centralization of decision-making and service provision; concerns that complex and deep learning cannot be satisfactorily achieved without real-time classroom experience; increased technological and pedagogical uniformity; surveillance options that violate privacy policies; recontextualization of established cultural practices, such as education as a cultural discourse; and concern about the growing digital divide and downloading of costs to students.

When this kind of schism between opinions occurs, it can be useful to step back, reflect, and consider the nature of the disagreement. If we reflect on our own as well as others' opinions about both technology and education through a philosophical lens, it is possible to become aware that these kinds of differences can be reduced to perspectives on *philosophies-in-practice*. Draper (1993) asserts that an examination of our opinion, or philosophy-in-practice, is more than an academic exercise. Our philosophy determines how we perceive and deal with our preferred teaching methods – which includes how (or if) we choose and use e-learning technologies.

WHY IS KNOWING OUR PHILOSOPHIES-IN-PRACTICE IMPORTANT?

At present, education at all levels is to a great extent minimally regulated in terms of what will be taught, how it is taught and, in particular, what role e-learning technologies play. Individual teachers, schools, colleges, and/or faculties often determine the content and scope of what they will teach, then choose methods or strategies, instructional materials, and the e-learning technologies they believe will best help the learners to gain new knowledge, skills, and/or attitudes. As such, educators have the freedom as well as the responsibility to set learner expectations and to determine the purpose and outcomes of the learning activities (Zinn, 1990) – which includes a decision on the use of e-learning technology. These decisions are embedded in our philosophical views about both education and technology; underlying these views is our interpretation of the world and our actions within it. As such, knowing our philosophical views is important.

And yet, many educators' philosophies are often unrecognized and rarely expressed, though they may be understood implicitly (Elias & Merriam, 1980). More importantly, educational practices concerned with using and choosing e-learning technologies could be conducted more effectively if basic philosophical differences were understood. Differences over the benefits of e-learning technologies are linked to differences over the ends our educational purposes are to achieve (Kanuka & Kelland, forthcoming). For example, the debate over whether or not we need to prepare our learners for a pervasively networked world revolves around what types of persons we expect our education systems to produce.

When considering the interrelationship of philosophy and the choices we make about e-learning technologies, it is important to be aware that philosophy inspires our activities and gives direction to our practices. Specifically, when we are aware of the philosophies of teaching and technology, we can then articulate our own personal philosophy. Knowing our personal philosophy helps us to understand why we act and think the way we do about using e-learning technologies, as well as why others think and act the way they do about e-learning technologies. Moreover, knowing our own and others' philosophies provides us with the ability to understand the consequences of our technological choices, as well as the effect that our philosophical orientation has on our learners. Further, it can facilitate effective communication with others when we can explain not only what we are doing, as well as why (Draper, 1993; Darkenwald & Merriam, 1982; Zinn, 1990).

The following sections of this chapter describe the philosophical orientations of teaching and technology, and discuss how our views of e-learning technologies are grounded in our philosophy-in-practice. Our beliefs about teaching and technology guide our practice and, as such, understanding our beliefs can result in informed practices where we can articulate not only what we are doing, but why.

WHAT IS A PHILOSOPHY OF TEACHING AND TECHNOLOGY?

A philosophy of teaching and technology can be defined as a conceptual framework that embodies certain values from which we view the many aspects of education (Zinn, 1990), including the field of e-learning. A philosophy of e-learning technology is necessary because too often educators are concerned with what to do with e-learning technologies without examining sufficiently why they should do it (Draper, 1993; Elias & Merriam, 1980).

Embedded in our opinions on e-learning technologies are views on the (non) neutrality of technology. The debate over technological neutrality revolves around whether or not technologies are neutral and whether or not biases can arise only from the ways in which technologies are used by teachers and students – or whether biases can occur through the technologies themselves. An analogy to contextualize and bring relevance to views on the neutrality of technologies can be gained from the catch phrase, "People kill people, not guns." A comparable catchphrase in the field of e-learning might be, "Educators reshape education, not technologies." Many educational technologists agree with Jonassen (1996), who asserts that "carpenters use their tools to build things; the tools do not control the carpenter. Similarly, computers should be used as tools for helping learners build knowledge; they should not control the learner" (p. 4). While Jonassen's argument sounds solid in its rationale, media theorist Marshall McLuhan (1964) suggests otherwise. Specifically, even though the neutrality of a tool speaks to our common sense with respect to the ways in which tools are used, McLuhan and Fiore (1962) maintain that media can profoundly transform society and the human psyche. McLuhan also made famous the aphorism, "The medium is the message," giving pause to the assumption of the non-neutrality of technology.

Building on the assumption of the non-neutrality of technologies, Chandler (1996) postulates that media shapes our experiences, and it does so in part through its selectivity. In particular, Chandler asserts that when we interact with media, we act and are acted upon, use and are used. In this respect, we can use the work by Brent (2001) to illustrate the changes caused by technologies when we look at this through the lens of a gestalt perspective, where certain elements of the learning process are brought to the foreground while others are moved to the background. Consistent with McLuhan's and Brent's views, Postman (1993) maintains that, "embedded in every tool is an ideological bias, a predisposition to construct the world as one thing rather than another, to value one thing over another, to amplify one sense or skill or attitude more loudly than another" (p. 13). Postman and McLuhan hold definitive views about the non-neutrality of technology. Others, such as Ihde (1979) and Dahlberg (2004), adopt moderate views of technological determinism, or a "nonreductionist" orientation. Ihde, for example, suggests that the use of instruments both amplifies and reduces human experiences.

Similar to mainstream philosophies of education (e.g., Zinn, 1990; see also Elias & Meriam, 1980), when we use the purposes of technology as the basis for organizing the philosophical literature, it becomes apparent that there are different and opposing perspectives. Educators who choose and use e-learning technologies should be knowledgeable about the philosophies of teaching, as well as the multidimensionality of technological determination, and be reflexive about the limits of their activities in *both* areas.

OVERVIEW OF PHILOSOPHICAL ORIENTATIONS

Knowledge of philosophical orientations provides us with insights into the nature of the use of e-learning technologies. A philosophy of teaching and technology is essential for answering e-learning questions, and their relationship to other activities within the education sector. Of course, these kinds of technologically-related concerns have recurred throughout the decades; indeed, some have even persisted over the centuries. The common thread of persistent technological debates in the field of education is that they have tended to have varying implicit assumptions about the basic nature of an education. It is apropos for those of us concerned with education to at least attempt to address the principal concerns and issues that are currently being put forward; such efforts can help legitimize and give direction to the growing field of e-learning.

The following sections in this chapter outline the differing philosophical orientations for teaching and technology. As you read the philosophies presented, you may want to ask yourself which philosophy you find yourself most in agreement with, especially regarding their aims and values.

PHILOSOPHIES OF TECHNOLOGY

In regard to e-learning technology, there is a tendency to orientate ourselves to one of three orientations (Dahlberg, 2004). The first position is referred to as *uses determinism.* This view pertains to the instrumental the uses of technological artefacts and, correspondingly, the uses effects on technological artefacts and society. The second position is referred to as *technological determinism.* This view focuses on the forms and effects that technological artefacts have on uses and society. The third position is referred to as *social determinism.* This view asserts that social contexts and cultures affect forms and uses of technological artefacts. Following is a broader discussion of each orientation.

Uses Determinism

In its simplest sense, this position emphasizes technological uses and focuses on the ways in which we use technologies within learning and teaching transactions. In this approach, technologies are perceived as neutral tools and are simply devices that extend our capacities. As users, we determine the effects of technological artefacts. Scholars commonly associated with this orientation include Fiske (1987), Harrison and Stephen (1999), Katz and Rice (2002), Sudweeks, McLaughlin and Rafaeli (1998), Garramone, Harris and Anderson (1986), Ebersole (2000), and Welchman (1997).

In educational technology, we see this view expressed by Jonassen (1996) and Clark (1994). As noted in the introduction, Jonassen asserts that "carpenters use their tools to build things; the tools do not control the carpenter. Similarly, computers should be used as tools for helping learners build knowledge; they should not control the learner" (p. 4). This view is consistent with the seminal writings of Clark (1983; 1985), who argues that our uses of instructional strategies are the active ingredient in effective learning, not the technology. In his writings, Clark claims, in part, that technologies are "mere vehicles that deliver instruction but do not influence student achievement any more than the truck that delivers our groceries causes changes in our nutrition" (1983, p. 445). Such views assert that the technological artefacts we use for educational purposes (e.g., course management systems) are neutral tools, able to serve the aims and objectives of agents (e.g., educators) employing them.

This perspective is certainly not new, emerging as a response to the pessimism of the Frankfurt School. Indeed, today the majority of e-learning technologists would likely state that this is their view of the role of e-learning technology within the learning process. This view is appealing – especially in North America – because it asserts that, as individuals, we have control and autonomy over the technology (Morley,

1989). Dahlberg (2004) observes that this should be of little surprise, given that American communications studies has been significantly influenced by the liberal pluralist *uses and gratification* model that developed in response to *effects* traditions.

While appealing in many respects, uses determinism can result in a number of contradictions and problems when educators hold this perspective in a singular fashion (Dahlberg, 2004). In particular, viewing e-learning technology as a neutral tool assumes that there is a technological fix for an educational problem. This instrumentalist line of thinking assumes that technologies exist without social or political origins, and that uses and users are the causal agents in the production of social action (Lacroix & Tremblay, 1997) – often celebrating unconstrained consumer sovereignty, and resulting in instrumentalism and/or structuralism (Golding & Murdock, 2000). The problem with instrumentalism is that there is an inclination to place emphasis upon the intentionality of agents, with an unbalanced focus on the interactions between the actors and the technologies. As a result, educators tend to narrowly focus on the role of agents and disregard the broader social structures and/or technological artefacts' effects on the learning outcomes, leading to explanations that overemphasize the power and autonomy of actors. The belief that individual actors have complete control over the effects of a technological artefact is a misguided and naïve assumption. "Such an assumption overlooks the structuring of actions by technological systems and neglects the social 'embeddedness' of these systems and their users" (Dahlberg, 2004).

Social Determinism

In this perspective, educators are concerned with the integration of technological artefacts within social systems and cultural contexts. This perspective emphasizes the way our uses of technologies are affected by the social structures and the social construction of technological artefacts. Educators holding this view are concerned about the ways that social and technological uses shape the form and content of the learning experiences. Scholars commonly associated with this orientation include Golding and Murdock (1997), Mosco (1996), Garnham (1990), Woolgar (1991a; 1991b; 1996; 2002), and Schiller (1999).

Many e-learning futurists and pundits fall within this perspective, such as Larry Ellison (chair and CEO of Oracle Corporation), Peter Drucker (author of *The Effective Executive and Management Challenges for the 21st Century*; recipient of the Presidential Medal of Freedom from

President George W. Bush; and featured on the front cover of *Forbes Magazine*), and Jaron Lanier (virtual reality pioneer). All of these suggest a looming breach of monopoly for providers of education should they not respond to accelerating globalization and increasing competition. Typically, the solution presented is a move to technologically innovative and consumer-oriented education. Peter Drucker, in an interview with *Forbes Magazine* (1997), claims that social changes will result in the physical presence of universities ceasing to exist within ten years. One might even imagine a Darwinian process emerging, with some institutions consuming their competitions in hostile takeovers.

These views rest upon the way technology is socially embedded and constituted. In particular, social choices shape the form and content of technological artefacts (Dahlberg, 2004). As with uses determinism, however, social determinism has logistical issues that are difficult to resolve. Specifically, this orientation can lead to flawed understandings of educational technology, if developed without reference to user agency or material limits (Dahlberg). The line of reasoning in this orientation – that technologies embody social choice – negates a multifaceted understanding of the place of agency in technological development. Many of the pundits and futurists cited above have an inaccurate view of the power of social context and its ability to impact education. Social contexts do not simply manipulate education systems at will. In our everyday lives, there is a dynamic mutual shaping between the social, technology, and users' environments.

Technological Determinism

Within this orientation, technologies are viewed as causal agents determining our uses and having a pivotal role in social change. Scholars most commonly associated with this orientation include Dubrovsky, Kiesler and Sethna (1991), Sproull and Kiesler (1986), Argyle (1996), Spears and Lea (1994), Marcuse (1941), Habermas (1970), Bell (1973), Lyotard (1984), Baudrillard (1983), Castells (1999), Gates (1995), Pool (1983), Toffler and Toffler (1994), Heidegger (1977), Postman (1993), and Marx (1997).

The label technological determinism has tended to have a negative connotation that educational technologists who hold this view regard technology as a distracting and potentially even harmful component of education systems. The origin of technological determinism is connected to a Marxist class analysis, which views technology as an instrument of dominance by the advantaged class over others. Within the field of education, this historical view led to a belief that technology could be a means towards the end of oppressing students – with *Technics and Civilization* (Mumford, 1934) as one of the first pieces of literature to make this analysis. By the 1960s, Mumford was joined by other critics – such as Landgon Winner (1977), Albert Borgmann (1984), and Don Ihde (1979) – responding to the changing political climate of the day. During this period, Marcuse (1964) and Foucault (1977) were also influential critics of the role of technological determinism and the formation of modern hegemonies (Feenberg, 1999).

More recently, some educators such as David Noble have been labelled as technological determinists. Noble and colleagues (Noble, 1991; Noble, Shneiderman, Herman, Agre, & Denning, 1998) have written extensively on the relationships between distance-delivered e-learning and de-professionalization of the academy. These scholars are concerned about the erosion of academic freedom, and thus they are aggressive critics arguing that the expansion of distance-delivered e-learning as a leading-edge movement to commercialize education will work to de-professionalize faculty members and erode academic freedom (e.g., Noble, 1998). Other prominent scholars who have on occasion fallen into this category include Erich Fromm (1968), Marshall McLuhan (1962), Neil Postman (1993), Hubert Dreyfus (2001), and Jean Baudrillard (1983). These scholars question modern technologies and many condemn technology for disseminating an onslaught of incoherent and fragmented trivialities to the world at the expense of engagement, reflectivity, and depth. They also argue that modern technologies and growing neo-liberalism are creating a rising capitalistic climate that includes political-economic interests such as comodification, commercialization, and corporatization of education.

The assumption underpinning these views is that technology determines our uses and impacts society – in a negative way. Although not often given the label of technological determinist, scholars who view technology as influencing our education systems in positive ways also hold the same assumption that technology determines our uses and impacts society, but in a beneficial way. In the area of e-learning, for example, Garrison and Anderson (2003) assert that educational technologies can transform the learning experiences in positive ways, resulting in increasing the quality of learning experiences.

Other positive views presented in the literature include the opinion that e-learning communication tools facilitate the development of argument formation capabilities, increased written communication skills,

complex problem-solving abilities, and opportunities for reflective delib-
eration (Abrami & Bures, 1996; Garrison, Anderson, & Archer, 2001;
Hawkes, 2001; Winkelmann, 1995). The rationale underpinning these
beliefs rests on the assumption that the technologies (e.g., asynchronous
text-based Internet tools which have a time lag when communicating)
provide the inherent potential to effectively facilitate higher levels of
learning. For example, Lapadat (2002) argues that with asynchronous
text-based Internet technology, learners have the means to compose their
ideas and thoughts into a written form of communication. This, according to Garrison and Anderson, provides learners with the ability to critically reflect on their views, which is necessary for higher-ordered learning.
In regard to educational systems, Archer, Garrison, and Anderson (1999)
have written about disruptive technologies, arguing that technologies
are a catalyst of change, resulting in the need for educators and institutions to adapt and/or transform. The assumption here is that the effects
of technical change are inevitable and unquestioned.

As these examples illustrate, both advocates and opponents of
e-learning believe that e-learning technologies determine the uses and
the agents. In less bi-polar positions, this orientation also asserts that the
effect of new media (e.g., social software) has influenced post-modern
ideas. Poster (1997), for example, puts forth the notion that the Internet
has instantiated new forms of interaction and power relations between
users, resulting in significant social impacts. Nguyen and Alexander
(1996) assert further that the Internet has produced new realities in our
everyday lives. Technological determinism is also consistent with much
of the existing technology theory, perhaps most notably, McLuhan's
(1964) "the medium is the message" slogan, as well as the idea of the
world now being a global village. These views are representative of the
cultural products of mass media and agents of socialization and political
indoctrination, and correspond with the social impact of technology
literature that emphasizes the transformations caused by technologies
acting on society.

Theorists of post-industrialism and post-modernity also view
technology as a causal agent, having a central role in social change
(Dahlberg, 2004). Lyotard (1984) and Baudrillard (1983) likewise argue
that technology is instrumental in the development of the post-modern
condition. Within the field of education, de Castell, Bryson, and Jenson
(2002) express concerns that e-learning technologies result in yet another
form of cultural colonization, resulting from curricular development
designed to mimic the cognitive styles of recognized experts.

An understanding of the impact of technology on educational systems is important for educators to know and recognize. As with the other technological orientations, however, an overemphasis on the impact of technology on the learning process can lead to problems when there is a lack of recognition of the social and user embeddedness of technology. Without question, there is a significant effect of e-learning technology on modern education, including, as Chandler (1996) notes, the numerous unanticipated consequences – which should not be underestimated. Likewise, Winner (1977) asserts that technological artefacts may embody affirmation, but may also become a betrayal. There is little doubt that education is increasingly being encompassed by e-learning technologies and that they increasingly shape the way we think and learn. Nevertheless, this impact is not as independent of human control as the techno-utopian, techno-cynic, techno-zealot, and techno-structuralism theorists indicate (Boshier & Onn, 2000). Accounts from such theorists either reify reductive consequences or claim too much for what is increasingly a shift in the growing use of e-learning technology in education.

This one-dimensional view of technology suffers similar logistical problems with the uses- and social-determinist orientations. Educators positioning themselves from a one-dimensional view of the impact of technology perceive the properties of a particular technology as having the ability to predetermine educational outcomes. Little, if any, attention is given to the effects of educational, social, and historical forces that have shaped both educational systems and educational technologies.

PHILOSOPHIES OF TEACHING

The following section highlights the philosophical orientations or frameworks that are most often used by educators in today's society. It is based on the writings of Elias and Merriam (1980), Zinn (1990), Draper (1993), and Brameld (1969). At the end of the descriptions for each teaching orientation is a description of the philosophy of technology most closely associated with it.

Liberal/Perennial

This orientation is the oldest and most enduring philosophy of education. The earliest efforts of education in the Western world were developed under the influence of this philosophy. The primary aims of educators holding this orientation are twofold: (1) to search for truth, and (2) to develop good and moral people. As such, an educated person should possess these components: rational, intellectual, and evolving wisdom; moral values; a spiritual or religious dimension; and an aesthetic sense. Its historical origins are derived from the classical Greek philosophers Socrates, Plato, and Aristotle. Some contemporary philosophers who espouse this viewpoint include Mortimer Adler (1937), Robert Hutchins (1953; 1968), Jacques Maritain (1943), and Mark Van Doren (1943).

Instructional methods used in this position lend themselves to the facilitation of rigorous intellectual training that begins with knowledge of grammar and rhetoric; extends to the national sciences, history, and literature; and ends with a study of logic and philosophy. Students are encouraged to question all assumptions – which is in keeping with the search for truth. The person who "knows the truth" will also "do the truth." The lecture method is recognized as an efficient instructional strategy when well organized and followed with dialogue. Through dialogue, students clarify the real meaning of concepts and can thus build syntheses of knowledge. Intuition and inner contemplation are also encouraged.

In this view, the teaching focus is primarily on the content of education with an emphasis on the art of investigation, criticism, and communication, through an intimate acquaintance with the Great Books (e.g., Plato, Aristotle, Aurelius, Augustine, Bacon, Descartes, Milton, Marx), philosophy, and religion. The humanities are believed to be superior to science. The teacher has a prominent role in dissemination of the content and the student is a receptacle of this information. An education system following this orientation aims to create leaders and responsible citizens. Though information and knowledge are necessary, it is only in the possession of wisdom that one truly becomes educated. The learning process moves from information to knowledge to wisdom.

Critics of the liberal orientation have argued that this form of education does not lend itself much to statements, analyses, and evaluations; has a class and elitist bias; and does not address vocational education and life-related subjects. In addition, knowledge of past civilization and culture does not itself liberate persons.

Role of Technology

Aligning most closely with technological determinism, the liberal views on demanding intellectual training would not normally involve the use of technology. For example, automated courses (quizzes, exams) with modularized units, tutorials and/or simulations, in and of themselves, cannot achieve the aim of a liberal education. As the ultimate aim and essence of education is in the development of character, a standardized curriculum typically associated with online courses and economies of scale is viewed as robbing the student of an intellectual experience. While some existing social software (e.g., synchronous audio, Internet-based tools) might be viewed somewhat more positively by educators of this orientation, the current widespread use of textual communication technologies would be in conflict with the spirit of the aims and objectives of this orientation, and with the focus on rigorous dialogic encounters.

The position that e-learning can be a flexible and convenient alternative serving the needs of the institutions' clients (students) would also be problematic for educators of the liberal orientation. Indeed, liberal educators believe that learning should not be convenient and students should not be viewed as clients or customers. Rather, students should submit themselves to the rigours of intellectual development and be stretched intellectually as far as they can go. Convenience and flexibility, in ways that meet the needs of the learners, would be at odds with this orientation. In a general sense, e-learning technology is viewed by educators closely associated with the liberal orientation as interfering with their aims and objectives.

Progressive

The aim of the progressive orientation is personal growth, maintenance, and promotion of a better society. The preferred methods of instruction include the experimental, problem-solving, and situation approaches to learning. This includes the organization of curriculum around problems and situations which relate to the experiences of the students. The focus of the learning activities is always toward movement of democratic cooperation and personal enlightenment. The chief exponent of pragmatism and progressive thought, especially as it relates to education, is John Dewey (1910; 1916; 1938) and William James (1909). Elements of progressive thought are found in the writings of all major theorists in the field of education, including Malcolm Knowles (1970), Cyril Houle (1972), Eduard Lindemen (1956), and Paul Bergevin (1967).

Education itself is viewed as both practical and pragmatic; utilitarian educators of this orientation strive to maintain the standards of competence, knowledge, wisdom, and skill. Accordingly, a good society requires these standards. Educators also see themselves as having a role in social reform and social reconstruction. Specifically, education should be aimed at improving the individual's life in society; improving individuals through education leads to a better society. Students and society cannot be separated, as the student's interests, needs, problems, and ambitions are products of their environment.

The teacher/student relationship is best characterized as a partnership. Learning is something that students do for themselves. Education involves experience, which is reflected and acted upon by the student. The result is knowledge that is inseparable from ever-changing experiences. Learning also involves liberating the learner for the potential improvement of society and culture. In particular, learning is not enough; sooner or later, students must act as a consequence of their learning. The teacher's role is to organize, stimulate, instigate, and evaluate the highly complex process of education. This can be effectively achieved by being a helper, consultant, and/or encourager. When the teacher provides a setting that is conductive to this form of learning, the teacher also becomes a learner.

The main criticism of the progressive orientation is the tendency to place too much influence on the power of education to bring about social change and to replace the fixity of ideas with the fixity of the problems. Another criticism has been that, in their view, the student should be placed at the centre of the learning process, failing to give sufficient attention to the role of the teacher and to the importance of the subject matter.

Role of Technology

Aligning most closely with uses determinism, progressives view certain educational technologies as being well suited to the learning process. For example, using the conferencing options in course management systems (e.g., *WebCT®*, *Blackboard®*, *Lotus Notes®*), learning activities can effectively be designed as an interactive partnership between and among the teacher and students. Perhaps more important is the ability of asynchronous communication technologies to give students equal opportunities to contribute. When facilitated effectively by the teacher, this can result in a democratic learning environment for all students. Further, given that the teacher's role is to organize, stimulate, instigate, and evaluate the highly complex process of education, as well as to be a helper, consultant, and/or encourager, e-learning technologies can be very effective at facilitating this kind of environment because they effectively facilitate a learner-centred environment.

Behaviourist

The ultimate goal of the behaviourist orientation is to bring about observable changes in behaviour. Methods of instruction begin with stated learning objectives, accompanied by the inclusion of rewards and punishments toward and away from the stated behavioural objectives. Examples of well-known methods include mastery learning, personalized systems of instruction, individually guided instruction, and individually prescribed instruction. The focus of the learning is on the content, with a subject-centred approach. Early behaviourists include Edward Thorndike (1932) and John Watson (1914), with the most prominent behaviourist philosophy originating from B. F. Skinner (1938). A more contemporary behaviourist is Ralph Tyler (1949), who is well known for the introduction of needs assessments in curriculum and instruction.

Behaviourists tend to view most of societies' problems arising from the behaviour of people living in them. The solution to creating a better society is to control human behaviour. Behaviourists believe that the purpose of education is to change the behaviour of people so they can work with each other to design and build a society that minimizes suffering and maximizes the chances of survival. The role of the teacher is to design an environment that elicits desired behaviour toward meeting these goals and to extinguish behaviour that is not desirable. The teacher is a contingency manager or an environmental controller. The students' role is active rather than passive, and it is essential that students act, so that their behaviour can be reinforced. As such, responsibility lies primarily with the student. According to behaviourists, students have learned something if there is a change in behaviour and if their response occurs again under similar circumstances. Learning how to learn is also an important skill, needed if one is to adapt successfully to a changing environment.

There have been many criticisms of the behaviourist orientation. Perhaps the most important criticism revolves around the stated behavioural objectives that predetermine the end product of a learning experience. This activity has been attacked for not accounting for other kinds of learning, such as incidental learning; dehumanising students and their learning; lacking in concern for the student; inhibiting creativity; and, fragmenting the curriculum into bits and pieces while overlooking the whole.

Role of Technology

Aligning most closely with technological determinism, the majority of behaviourists believe that the use of e-learning technologies, in all forms, results in effective and efficient learning. There are many positive transformations that occur through the use of technology, with the *sine quo non* being computer-based tutorials and simulations. Standardized course management systems (e.g., *WebCT®*, *Blackboard®*, *Moodle*) and the integrated use of learning objects into the learning process can also benefit educational institutions in terms of providing efficient and effective learning.

Moreover, the use of course management systems can regulate teacher activities. As such, the teaching can be controlled to student assessment and grading administration. Course management tools can track the students' activities and provide immediate feedback via the assessment tools. It is possible, then, to track exactly what the students have learned through observable changes in behaviour. Overall, behaviourists tend to view e-learning technologies as more reliable, accurate, faster, and cost-effective than humans. Social interaction can be expensive, and when the learning is content-centred, interaction is generally not an important function within the learning events. E-learning courses that focus on the content and are presented in a modularized format, with stated learning objectives and end-of-unit assessment tools to provide positive or negative feedback, are an effective and efficient way to teach students.

Humanist

The primary aim of the humanist orientation is to support individual growth and self-actualization. Key constructs emphasized in this approach are freedom and autonomy, trust, active cooperation and participation, and self-directed learning. The philosophical roots of this orientation are found in such writers as Martin Heidegger (1977), Jean-Paul Sartre (1949), and Albert Camus (1940; 1942; 1951). The Third Force psychologists who have been equally responsible for the development of this approach include Abraham Maslow (1976), Carl Rogers (1967), Malcolm Knowles (1970), and Erich Fromm (1968).

Humanists use instructional methods such as group dynamics, group relations training, group processes, sensitivity workshops, encounter groups, values clarification workshops, transactional analysis, human potential workshops, and self-directed learning to achieve their aims. Group activity is the favoured technique, but experimentation and discovery methods are also encouraged. Decisions made by the teacher about curriculum are viewed as interfering with individual students' ability to identify their own learning needs. The focus on the learning activities is always on the individual student's growth and development rather than the content, and on affective rather than cognitive aspects of education. This focus, in turn, assists in the development of responsible selfhood; fostering persons who are open to change and continuous learning; and the striving for the self-actualization of fully-functioning individuals. As such, the whole focus of education is on the individual learner rather than a body of information.

The role of the teacher is that of facilitator, helper, and partner in the learning process. The teacher does not simply provide information; he or she must create the conditions within which learning can take place. The teacher should facilitate the process of the students to be self-directed, by serving as a resource person and by encouraging students to set their own goals. The responsibility for learning therefore rests with the student. Students are free to learn what and how they want. The act of learning is a personal activity that involves intrinsic motivation, self-concept, perception, and self-evaluation. Indeed, according to humanists, self-evaluation is the only meaningful test of whether learning has taken place.

As with the other philosophical orientations, there have been numerous criticisms of the humanist orientation. For example, at times self-directed learning can be impossible or undesirable. It can also be difficult to conduct discussion groups when one considers time constraints, organizational expectations, and group size composed of many diverse learning environments. Perhaps most importantly, this orientation lacks administrative accountability in terms of what is going to be taught, what is actually taught, and what has been learned.

Role of Technology

Aligning themselves most closely with uses determinism, humanists typically would agree that e-learning technologies can, under certain circumstances, serve an important role in so far as providers of the learning activities can provide flexibility, convenience, and meet individual student needs with just-in-time learning. Specifically, uses of technology can play a critical role in providing flexible and open access to the growing needs of individual students.

For the humanists, learning is viewed as a highly personal endeavour and, as such, intrinsic motivation, self-concept, self-perception, self-evaluation, and discovery are important learning and thinking skills. Many e-learning technologies, especially social software, can provide learners with opportunities to facilitate their learning needs. Further, online classrooms make it difficult, if not impossible, for the role of the teacher to be anything but a facilitator, or a guide on the side. It should be noted that some humanists have objected to arbitrary decisions by educational institutions and/or instructors about the kinds and uses of technologies. These arbitrary decisions are viewed by most humanists as a violation of students' abilities to identify their own learning needs, which includes their choices about which technologies to use or not use. Few humanists, however, would disagree with the opinion that new group communication tools can play an important role in facilitating access for students to participate in group discussions. Group relations are an extremely important component in facilitating the learning process, and under certain circumstances, many humanists would argue that online discussions can be effective, perhaps even more effective than face-to-face discussions, due to their ability to meet the diversity of student needs.

Radical

The overarching aim of the radical perspective is to invoke change in the political, economic, and social order in society via the intersection of education and political action. Radical educators of the past include George Counts (1932), Theodore Brameld (1969), Jonathan Kozol (1972), John Holt (1967), Paul Goodman (1994), and Ivan Illich (1979). Contemporary prominent educators of this philosophic position include Paulo Freire (1973) and Jack Mezirow (1991).

Preferred instructional methods are dialogic encounters that lead to praxis. These instructional methods include problem posing and problem identification, through dialogue based on respect, communication, and solidarity. Collective dialogue, ideal speech, and critical questioning in a risk-free environment should be offered in place of traditional lecture and dissemination of information. Dialogic and problem-posing encounters will involve students engaged in questioning the basic values, structure, and practices of society.

Many radicals view traditional lecturing as offending the freedom and autonomy of the student. Indeed, these practices are viewed as a form of violence, because imposing facts and values submerges the consciousness of the student, perpetuates the evils of an oppressive society, dehumanizes, and stifles individual freedom. Education is viewed as value-laden and never neutral, because it includes the transmission and reification of attitudes and development of character. As such, the role of the teacher is to raise students' consciousness of the social and political contradictions in their culture. Radicals view their role as a catalyst to increasing the learners' objective reality or to eliciting distorted assumptions. The teacher is also a learner with equal status, but the teacher will have expert knowledge. Information, however, must be imparted in a dialogic manner with the student. In order for action to be authentic, participants must be free to create the curriculum along with the teacher. Students are viewed as unfinished and, as such, are free and autonomous learners.

Through these activities, students become enablers of radical social change. Radicals perceive education as being closely connected with our social, political, and economic understanding of cultures, and with the development of methods to bring people to an awareness of responsible social action. Learning, then, must include the development of insight into the state of the students' oppression, achieved only through critical reflection. This kind of learning can lead to action, which may significantly transform aspects of one's life.

The main criticism of the radical orientation is that the methods used to achieve perspective transformation are not doable in most educational environments. Mandatory grading in most educational systems, for example, diminishes the prospect of a risk-free environment. Another difficulty with this orientation is that knowledge is viewed as power, and power is seen as something political. Thus, when the teacher provides information, the teacher will then be exercising power and control over the student. The premise, then, that education can be neutral and non-value-laden with a knowledgeable teacher, becomes a paradox.

Role of Technology

Radicals align themselves most closely with social determinism. The biggest problem associated with the use of e-learning for radicals is not so much the technologies, per se, as the fact that most educational institutions use technologies that are owned by large corporations. Commercialized products, such as *WebCT®*, *Blackboard®*, *Lotus Notes®*, and so on, are viewed as enforcing a corporate communication paradigm onto the learning process. For example, a risk-free and trusting environment is not achievable with corporate technologies that have surveillance features. Alternatively, open-source technologies (e.g., *Moodle*) would not be problematic for most radical educators.

Analytical

The primary aim of the analytical orientation is the development of rationality, which is assisted by the fearless transmission of educationally worthwhile knowledge (e.g., truth that is morally, socially, and politically neutral). Philosophers of education in this traditional view include Israel Scheffler (1960), R. S. Peters (1967), and Thomas Green (1971).

Guided and directed by the teacher, dialogue through class discussion is considered the ideal instructional method. It is important that the dialogue include communication of information that is educationally significant. Specifically, analytical educators focus on content that is worthwhile, while emphasising the need for clarifying concepts, arguments, and policy statements. The result is to bring about deepened awareness, in meaningful touch with reality; this is accomplished through the provision of worthwhile knowledge. Education is never complete and lifelong education is a necessity for full human development.

Educators from the analytical orientation see the need for teachers to identify what the students do not know and then to determine their aims and objectives. The primary role of teachers is to make choices about the things that are educationally worthwhile. Teachers, then, are essential for introducing learners to knowledge beyond themselves; learners are subordinate to the teachers. Analyticals believe that students need to temporarily give up their freedom and subject themselves to being guided, criticized, and tested according to the standards of a discipline.

Analyticals also believe that society and education should not be linked to each other. The problem inherent in linking educational aims to social values becomes particularly acute in a multicultural or pluralistic society where there are differences of opinion as to what ends are most desirable. Based on established scientific truths, education should involve the fearless transmission of neutral knowledge, guided by the liberal studies. There is, however, a cognitive element and a need for the understanding of principles. Specifically, learning is cognitively connected with other areas of learning so that each area is understood in relation to other areas, and what is learned should be usable.

Many critics of this philosophical orientation raise the troubling question of whether any programmatic decision can be neutral or value-free. Taking a neutral position on social questions, for example, is itself a contradiction.

Role of Technology

Aligning most closely with uses determinism, analytical educators view e-learning technologies as serving the learning process well under certain circumstances. For example, lectures can be downloaded to web pages, and follow-up dialogue can be facilitated, effectively moderated, and directed by the teacher, using group communication tools.

KNOWING YOUR TEACHING AND TECHNOLOGY PHILOSOPHIES IN PRACTICE: AVOIDING MINDLESS ACTIVISM

Reflecting on and becoming aware of our philosophical orientations is important; it provides a basis for how we choose and use e-learning technologies. Education effects change, whether that change is the ability to engage in rational thought, personal growth, or to bring about political and social change (Zinn, 1990). The desired changes are based on what we believe should happen through education. This, in turn, will be reflected in how we choose and use e-learning technologies.

When we are aware of our philosophical orientation, it is then possible to make informed decisions about choosing and using e-learning technology. Without knowing our philosophical orientation, other strategies are used (Zinn, 1990). Often swept up by unbridled – but uninformed – enthusiasm by technological advocates, many decisions by educators are based on following the latest trend. Unfortunately, these strategies often lead to incongruence and inconsistency in action between and among instructors, administrators, and students, and the ensuing disagreements that revolve around the means rather than the ends of education. Moreover, when there is incongruence between beliefs and actions, the promises of what e-learning technologies can provide will never be delivered. Unless we can systematically identify what we value in education, we cannot justify the choices we make with e-learning technologies, or deliver the promises. For these reasons, it is important to take time out from our *doing* and ask *why* it is important. "Thoughtful practitioners know not only what they do, but why they are to do it. Experience combined with reflection leads to purposeful and informed action" (Darkenwalk & Merriam, 1982, p. 37).

REFERENCES

Abrami, P. C., & Bures, E. M. (1996). Computer-supported collaborative learning and distance education. *American Journal of Distance Education, 10*(2), 37–42.

Adler, M. (1937). *The revolution to education.* Chicago: University of Chicago Press.

Archer, W., Garrison, R., & Anderson, T. (1999). Adopting disruptive technologies in traditional universities: Continuing education as an incubator for innovation. *Canadian Journal of University Continuing Education, 25*(1), 13–30.

Argyle, K. (1996). Life after death. In R. Sheilds (Ed.), *Cultures of Internet: Virtual spaces, real histories, living bodies* (pp. 58–69). London: Sage.

Bates, A. W. (2005). *Technology, e-learning and distance education* (2nd ed). New York: Routledge Falmer Studies in Distance Education.

Baudrillard, J. (1983). *In the shadow of the silent majorities.* New York: Semiotext(e).

Bell, D. (1973). *The coming of post-industrial society: A venture in social forecasting.* New York: Basic Books.

Bergevin, P. (1967). *A philosophy of adult education.* New York: Seabury.

Borgman, A. (1984). *Technology and the character of contemporary life.* Chicago: University of Chicago Press.

Boshier, R., & Mun Onn, C. (2000). Discursive constructions of web learning and education. *Journal Distance of Distance Education, 15*(2). Retrieved September 27, 2007, from http://cade.athabascau.ca/vol15.2/boshieretal.html

Brameld, T. (1969). *Ends and means in education.* Westport, CT: Greenwood.

Brent, D. (2001). *Teaching as performance in the electronic classroom.* Retrieved September 27, 2007 from http://www.quasar.ualberta.ca/cpin/cpinfolder/papers/Doug_Brent.htm

Camus, A (1940). *The myth of Sisyphus.* Harmondsworth: Penguin.

Camus, A. (1942). *The stranger.* London: Vintage Books.

Camus, A. (1951). *The rebel.* Harmondsworth: Penguin.

Castells, M. (1999). *The information age: Economy, society and culture* (Vol. I, II and III). Cambridge, MA: Blackwell.

Chandler, D. (1996, February). Engagement with media: Shaping and being shaped. *Computer-Mediated Communication Magazine.* Retrieved September 27, 2007 from http://users.aber.ac.uk/dgc/determ.html

Clark, R. E. (1983). Reconsidering research on learning from media. *Review of Educational Research, 53*(4), 445–459.

Clark, R. E. (1985). Confounding in educational computing research. *Journal of Educational Computing Research, 1*(2), 445–460.

Clark, R. E. (1994). Media will never influence learning. *Educational Technology Research and Development, 42*(2), 21–30.

Counts, G. (1932). *Dare the school build a new social order.* New York: John Day.

Dahlberg, L. (2004). Internet research tracings: Towards non-reductionist methodology. *Journal of Computer Mediated Communication, 7*(1). Retrieved September 27, 2007 from http://jcmc.indiana.edu/vol7/issue1/dahlberg.html

Daniel, J. (2000, July 18). The university of the future and the future of universities. Keynote address from the *Improving University Learning and Teaching 25th International Conference.* Retrieved September 27, 2007, from http://www.open.ac.uk/johndanielspeeches/FrankfurtJuly2000.htm

Darkenwald, G., & Merriam, S. (1982). *Adult education: Foundations of practice.* Cambridge: Harper & Row.

de Castell, S., Bryson, S., & Jenson, J. (2002). Object lessons: Towards an educational theory of technology. *First Monday, 7*(1). Retrieved September 27, 2007 at http://www.firstmonday.org/issues/issue7_1/castell/

Dewey, J. (1910). *How we think.* Chicago: University of Chicago Press.

Dewey, J. (1916). *Democracy and education.* New York: Macmillan.

Dewey, J. (1938). *Experience and education.* New York: Macmillan.

Draper, J. A. (1993). Valuing what we do as practitioners. In T. Barer-Stein and J. A. Draper (Eds.), *The craft of teaching adults* (pp. 55–67). Toronto, ON: Culture Concepts.

Dreyfus, H. (2001). *On the Internet: Thinking in action.* New York: Routledge.

Drucker, P. (1997). Interview. *Forbes,* March 1997.

Dubrovsky, V., Kiesler, S., & Sethna, B. (1991). The equalization phenomena: Status effects in computer-mediated and face-to-face decision-making groups. *Human-Computer Interaction, 6*(2), 119–146.

Ebersole, S. (2000). Uses and gratifications of the web among students. *Journal of Computer-Mediated Communication, 6*(1). Retrieved September 27, 2007 from http://www.ascusc.org/jcmc/vol6/issue1/ebersole.html

Elias, J. L., & Merriam, S. (1980). *Philosophical foundations of adult education*. Malabar, FL: Robert E. Krieger.

Feenberg, A. (1999). *Questioning technology*. New York: Routledge.

Fiske, J. (1987). *Television culture*. London: Routledge.

Foucault, M. (1977). *Discipline and punish*. A. Sheridan (Trans.). New York: Pantheon.

Freire, P. (1973). *Education for critical consciousness*. New York: Seabury.

Fromm, E. (1968). *The revolution of hope, toward a humanized technology*. New York: Harper & Row.

Garnham, N. (1990). *Capitalism and communication: Global culture and the economics of information*. London: Sage.

Garramone, G. M., Harris, A. C., & Anderson, R. (1986). Uses of political computer bulletin boards. *Journal of Broadcasting & Electronic Media, 30*(3), 325–339.

Garrison, D. R. (2002). Cognitive presence for effective online learning: The role of reflective inquiry, self-directed learning and metacognition. Invited paper presented to the *Sloan Consortium Asynchronous Learning Network Invitational Workshop*, Lake George, NY, September. Retrieved December 26, 2005, from communitiesofinquiry.com/documents/SLOAN%20CP%20Chapter%202003.doc

Garrison, D. R., & Anderson, T. (2003). *E-learning in the 21st Century: A framework for research and practice*. London: Routledge Falmer.

Garrison, D. R., Anderson, T., & Archer, W. (2001). Critical thinking, cognitive presence and computer conferencing in distance education. *American Journal of Distance Education, 15*(1), 7–23.

Gates, B. (1995). *The road ahead*. New York: Viking.

Golding, P., & Murdock, G. (Eds.) (1997). *The political economy of the media* (Vol. I and II). Cheltenham, UK: Edward Elger.

Golding, P., & Murdock, G. (2000). Culture, communication, and political economy. In J. Curran & M. Gurevitch (Eds.), *Mass media and society* (3rd ed., pp. 71–92). London: Edward Arnold.

Goodman, P. (1994). *Crazy hope and finite experience: Final essays of Paul Goodman*. Taylor Stoehr (Ed.). San Francisco: Jossey-Bass.

Green, T. F. (1971). *The activities of teaching*. New York: McGraw-Hill.

Habermas, J. (1970). *Toward a rational society: Student protest, science, and politics*. Boston: Beacon.

Harrison, T. M., & Stephen, T. (1999). Researching and creating community networks. In S. Jones (Ed.), *Doing internet research: Critical issues and methods for examining the Net* (pp. 221–241). Thousand Oaks, CA: Sage.

Hawkes, M. (2001). Variables of interest in exploring the reflective outcomes of network-based communication. *Journal of Research on Computing in Education, 33*(3), 299–315.

Heidegger, M. (1977). The question concerning technology. David Krell (Trans.). New York: Harper & Row.

Holt, J. (1967). *How children learn.* New York: Pitman.

Houle, C. (1972). *The design of education.* San Francisco: Jossey-Bass.

Hutchins, R. (1953). *The conflict in education in a democratic society.* New York: Harper & Row.

Hutchins, R. (1968). *The higher learning in America.* New Haven: Yale University Press.

Ihde, D. (1979). *Technics and praxis.* London: D. Reil.

Illich, I. (1979). *Deschooling society.* New York: Harper & Row.

James, W. (1909). *The meaning of truth: A sequel to Pragmatism.* New York: Appleton.

Jonassen, D. H. (1996). *Computers in the classroom: Mindtools for critical thinking.* Englewood Cliffs, NJ: Prentice Hall.

Kanuka, H., & Kelland, J. (in press). *A deliberative inquiry with experts in e-learning: Contentions in need of further research.*

Katz, J. E., & Rice, R. E. (2002). *Social consequences of Internet use: Access, involvement, and interaction.* Cambridge, MA: MIT Press.

Knowles, M. (1970). *The modern practice of adult education.* New York: Association Press.

Kozol, J. (1972). *Free schools.* Boston: Houghton Mifflin.

Lacroix, J. G., & Tremblay, G. (1997). The 'Information Society' and cultural industries theory. *Current Sociology, 45*(4), 1–153.

Lapadat, J. C. (2002). Written interaction: A key component in online learning. *Journal of Computer Mediated Communication, 7*(4). Retrieved April 8, 2004, from http://www.ascusc.org/jcmc/vol7/issue4/lapadat.html

Lindeman, E. (1956). *The democratic man: Selected writings of Eduard Lindeman.* Boston: Beacon.

Lyotard, J.-F. (1984). *The postmodern condition: A report on knowledge.* Manchester: Manchester University Press.

Marcuse, H. (1941). Some implications of modern technology. *Studies in Philosophy and Social Science, 9,* 414–39.

Marcuse, H. (1964). *One-dimensional man.* Boston: Beacon.

Maritain, J. (1943). *Education at the crossroads.* New Haven: Yale University Press.

Marx, L. (1997). Technology: The emergence of a hazardous concept. *Social Research, 64*(3), 965–988.

Maslow, A. (1976). Education and peak experience. In C. D. Schlosser (Ed.), *The person in education: A humanistic approach*. New York: Macmillan.

McLuhan, M. (1964). *Understanding media: The extensions of man*. New York: McGraw-Hill.

McLuhan, M., & Fiore, Q. (1962). *The medium is the message*. New York: Bantam.

Mezirow, J. (1991). *Transformative dimensions of adult learning*. San Francisco: Jossey-Bass.

Morley, D. (1989). Changing paradigms in audience studies. In E. Seiter, H. Borchers, G. Kreutzner & E. M. Warth (Eds.), *Remote control: Television, audiences, and cultural power* (pp. 16–43). New York: Routledge.

Mosco, V. (1996). The political economy of communication. London: Sage.

Mumford, L. (1934). *Technics and civilization*. New York: Harcourt, Brace & Company.

Nguyen, D. T., & Alexander, J. (1996). The coming of cyberspacetime and the end of the polity. In R. Sheilds (Ed.), Cultures of Internet: Virtual spaces. *Real histories, living bodies* (pp. 99–124). London: Sage.

Noble, D. (1991). *The classroom arsenal: Military research, information technology and public education*. New York: Falmer.

Noble, D. (1998). Digital diploma mills: The automation of higher education. *First Monday, 3*(1). Retrieved September 23, 2007 from http://www.firstmonday.org /issues/issue3_1/noble/

Noble, D., Shneiderman, B., Herman, R., Agre, P., & Denning, P. J. (1998). Technology in education: The fight for the future. *Educom Review, 33*(3). Retrieved on July 26, 2005, from http://www.educause.edu/pub/er/review/reviewArticles/33322.html

Peters, R. S. (1967). What is an educational process? In R. S. Peters (Ed.), *The concept of education*. Boston: Routledge & Kegan Paul.

Pool, I. D. S. (1983). *Technologies of freedom*. Cambridge, MA: Harvard University Press.

Poster, M. (1997). Cyberdemocracy: Internet and the public sphere. In D. Porter (Ed.), *Internet culture* (pp. 201–217). New York: Routledge.

Postman, N. (1993). *Technopoly: The surrender of culture to technology*. New York: Vintage Books.

Rogers, C. R. (1967). The process of the basic encounter group. In J. F. T. Bugental (Ed.), *Challenges of humanistic psychology*. New York: McGraw-Hill.

Sartre, J. P. (1949). *Nausea.* Lloyd Alexander (Trans.). London: Purnell & Sons.

Scheffler, I. (1960). *The language of education.* Springfield, IL: Charles Thomas.

Schiller, D. (1999). *Digital capitalism: Networking the global market system.* Cambridge, MA: MIT Press.

Skinner, B. F. (1938). *The behaviour of organisms.* Cambridge, MA: B. F. Skinner Foundation.

Spears, R., & Lea, M. (1994). Panacea or panopticon? The hidden power in computer-mediated communication. *Communication Research, 21*(4), 160–176.

Sproull, L., & Kiesler, S. (1986). Reducing social context cues: Electronic mail in organizational communications. *Management Science, 32,* 1492–1512.

Sudweeks, F., McLaughlin, M., & Rafaeli, S. (Eds.) (1998). *Network and netplay: Virtual groups in the Internet.* Cambridge, MA: MIT.

Thorndike, E. (1932). *The fundamentals of learning.* New York: Teachers College, Columbia University.

Toffler, A., & Toffler, H. (1994). *Creating a new civilization: The politics of the third wave.* Atlanta: Turner Pub.

Twigg, C.A. (2003). Improving learning and reducing costs: New models for online learning. *EDUCAUSE Review, 38*(5), 29–38.

Tyler, R. (1949). *Basic principles of curriculum and instruction.* Chicago: University of Chicago Press.

Van Doren, M. (1943). *Liberal education.* Boston: Beacon.

Watson, J. B. (1914). *Behavior: An introduction to comparative psychology.* New York: Norton.

Welchman, A. (1997). Funking up the cyborgs. *Theory, Culture & Society, 14*(4), 155–162.

Winkelmann, C. L. (1995). Electronic literacy, critical pedagogy, and collaboration: A case for cyborg writing. *Computers and the Humanities, 29*(6), 431–448.

Winner, L. (1977). *Autonomous Technology: Technics-out-of-control as a theme in political thought.* Cambridge, MA: MIT Press.

Woolgar, S. (1991a). Configuring the user: The case of usability trials. In J. Law (Ed.), *A sociology of monsters: Essays on power, technology and domination* (pp. 58–97). London: Routledge.

Woolgar, S. (1991b). The turn of technology in social studies of science. *Science, Technology, & Human Values, 16*(1), 20–50.

Woolgar, S. (1996). Technologies as cultural artefacts. In W. H. Dutton (Ed.), *Information and communications technologies: Visions and realities* (pp. 87–101). Oxford: Oxford University Press.

Woolgar, S. (Ed.) (2002). *Virtual society? Technology, cyberbole, reality.* Oxford: Oxford University Press.

Zinn, L. M. (1990). Identifying your philosophical orientation. In M. Galbraith (Ed.), *Adult Learning Methods* (pp. 39–77). Malabar, FL: Krieger.

ABOUT THE AUTHOR

At time of writing, Heather Kanuka (heather.kanuka@ualberta.ca) was a Canada Research Chair and associate professor in the Centre for Distance Education at Athabasca University. Dr. Kanuka is currently academic director of the University Teaching Services unit at the University of Alberta, Edmonton, Canada. Dr. Kanuka's research interests are in faculty development, higher education, and the effects of mediated learning.

PART II

INFRASTRUCTURE AND SUPPORT FOR CONTENT DEVELOPMENT

Developing an Infrastructure for Online Learning

Alan Davis
Vancouver Community College,
British Columbia, Canada

Paul Little
Red River College, Manitoba, Canada

Brian Stewart
Athabasca University, Alberta, Canada

INTRODUCTION

Before embarking on the development of an online learning system, in part or in whole, careful stock needs to be taken of the needs of the intended learners, the curriculum to be offered, and the context for the project. This chapter considers the various factors that must be considered for the infrastructure for online learning, including planning, structural and organizational issues, the components of a system and the interfaces among them, and various related issues, such as human resources, decision-making, and training.. Once developed, any infrastructure must be able to evolve in order to accommodate changing student needs, technologies, and curricula.

In 2003, as a result of the implementation of an e-learning plan, Athabasca University (AU) declared itself to be an online institution (Athabasca University, 2002a). As for many institutions and organizations, much had changed in a very short time with respect to the adoption of information and communications technologies. With the advent of Web 2.0, another era of change is now underway. While distance education institutions and departments have been the vanguard of the development of online learning, campus-based teachers and students have increasingly been mixing and matching their classroom and online learning in all sorts of (often unanticipated) ways.

For AU, the selection of and engagement with *Moodle* as the institution's single Learning Management System (LMS) has acted as a catalyst in moving the university's course creation, production, and delivery processes online. The experiences of AU as it works its way through the transition have borne out many of the ideas and issues raised here; of note are governance and change issues. Without effective structures and processes, the selection, deployment, and ongoing performance of an online learning system will prove challenging, and perhaps unsuccessful.

Building the infrastructure for online learning has many interconnected components and many factors must be considered, so it is hard to provide a straightforward checklist or recipe to follow. Distance education has provided an understanding of how the entire system of course design, development, and delivery occurs, and how these link to related learner services and other components, all of which are vital aspects of ensuring effectiveness and quality. Elsewhere in this book, readers will find chapters that provide a wealth of information and detail the specifics of how to develop and deliver online learning. The focus here is on the planning and organization of an online learning system, and some of the associated issues that must be considered.

A concept often used by scientists, classifying systems as *ideal* versus *non-ideal* (more commonly understood as *real*) may be helpful. In this way, we can define the ideal, and then look at the deviations from the ideals that manifest themselves in the real (Lu, 2006).

The ideal online learning and teaching system is developed from scratch, with no restrictions on costs and staffing, and uninhibited by resistance to change from previous practices. A real system, however, is one where any or all of the following deviations from the ideal occur: limited resources; legacy systems that have loyal advocates; key staff who have to be retrained; unworkable policies and practices that require reinvention; inadequate governance processes; back-end administrative systems that may or may not be interfaceable; plus an evolving understanding of the pedagogical underpinnings of online learning. Furthermore, after these deviations from the ideal are initially factored in, any real system must also be able to *change* constantly, specifically because curriculum, learning technologies, and approaches evolve all the time. Using this framework, the key aspects of an ideal online learning infrastructure are described and then adjusted for real situations; some ideas are also presented on how the subsequent and inevitable change can be managed.

BASIC THINKING

Any social system is built within a context. The social context of education, in general, has evolved significantly over the centuries. The increasingly open approach to educational systems, supported by global village technologies, takes the social context of education beyond the windows and into the world. As such, for any online learning endeavour, each discipline, department, faculty, institution, or company must have its own mission, mandate, goals, and values that need to be considered when planning and designing its own ideal system. For a real system, even at the conceptual level, there will be many internal and external environmental factors, such as competing priorities, budget constraints, faculty and student preparedness, professional bodies' requirements, and so on. All these factors must be well understood and accounted for from the outset.

All teaching and learning systems should be built from two vantage points: the *needs of the intended students*, and the *intended learning outcomes* of the course or program – i.e., the knowledge, skills, and attributes that students will gain. An ideal online learning system will be based on a plan that flows from a full understanding of these two fundamentals.

For intended students, it's necessary to understand their prior learning, background with technology, expectations, financial and other resources, access to the web or other online networks, bandwidth limitations, and any other pertinent information about their preparedness and ability to participate equally and fully in the online learning experience. In reality, of course, it is rare that such a complete picture is available, and a judgement call must be made on how the system balances common solutions for maximum efficiency and yet still accommodates students' individual needs. For example, how much do we employ technologies, which we know the students are already familiar with and have access to, versus those which are new and unfamiliar and/or which are expected to become widely available? A good example of this question is the extent to which distance students have access to high-speed connectivity. Since bandwidth is expanding steadily, and depending on student demographics and other factors, a system that assumes high bandwidth might be preferred, with alternative access to certain online learning components such as CD-ROMs or DVDs for the few not yet ready.

There is also the need for clear identification of the intended learning outcomes of any course, program, or training event in order to, for instance, design a learning assessment system, determine the degree of prior learning that may be accepted, measure the quality of the offering, or use as a basic determinant of an online learning system. In applied and professional fields, describing the intent of the educational experience in terms of the knowledge, skills, and attributes expected of the successful completers is typically routine, and a curriculum and associated teaching and learning system can be devised and cross-referenced with those ends clearly in mind (Red River College, 2004).

In academic fields – the real world in this context – such outcomes are not so well, nor very often, explicitly stated. All programs claim to develop critical thinking skills, for instance, without much definition of what these are, what taxonomy is used to determine the extent of students' achievement, or how exactly the content and program design link to them. If the outcomes include the ability to work in groups, to undertake independent research from a wide range of resources, or to critically analyze case studies, these will drive the design and functionality of the online learning system needed to deliver that curriculum. Having comprehensive and clearly stated intended learning outcomes, as well as a curriculum and associated teaching approaches designed accordingly, makes the task of building the ideal online learning system so much easier. In addition, at least some understanding of and linking with good principles of teaching and learning should be in place (Chickering & Ehrmann, 1996).

Closely related to these two fundamental educational design perspectives – student needs and the learning outcomes – are the size, scope, and scalability needed for the online learning system. Whether the program is to be delivered to a well-defined and selected cohort of students once a year, or made available to all comers at all times (as driven by mandate or a business plan predicated on growth) will have a strong impact on how the system is designed.

The real situation, of course, is much less rational. Online learning initiatives often spring from the well-intentioned experimentation of an individual or small group of educators and/or technologists, oftentimes with no clear idea of what the benefit to the learning experience will be (or not be). Sometimes, the addition of a new functionality, piece of content, or tool does not add value and is ignored by students; in other cases, a simple enhancement can reap great educational and other rewards for all concerned, sometimes in ways which were unanticipated. The degree to which an organization (department, faculty, company, or institution) wants to foster and allow more random experimentation versus keeping tight control over a single online learning system will be driven by that organization's mission, mandate, core values, technological capabilities, systems architecture, and financial resources. There are interesting case studies of how institutions have adopted various strategies – intentionally or unintentionally – along this centralization/decentralization spectrum (see the *International Review of Open and Distance Learning*, 2001, 1(2)). This is a very important decision, however, since it will determine how the online learning system should be designed, developed, resourced, and governed.

Even where the student market is well understood and learning outcomes clearly defined or prescribed, the implementation of online learning often involves a good deal of trial and error. With the best information and intentions, the results and experience rarely meet expectations, and thus the ability to adapt and refine the online learning system is crucial.

OVERALL STRUCTURE AND ORGANIZATION

The ideal case is based upon a good understanding of an institution's or company's core business and values, the nature of the intended student market, and the needs of the curriculum. This understanding is expressed through the learning outcomes of the program to be developed and delivered. On this basis, an overall online learning framework can be developed. This framework shows the organization of the various components of the proposed system, after which a relatively complete business plan for the endeavour can be developed. Figure 1 describes one such framework for a post-secondary institution, on which the discussion of the various components is based.

Ideally, the learning outcomes (1) are translated into course content and resources plus appropriate strategies for the teaching and learning process that will enable students to achieve those intended outcomes. Once these basic parameters have been determined, the

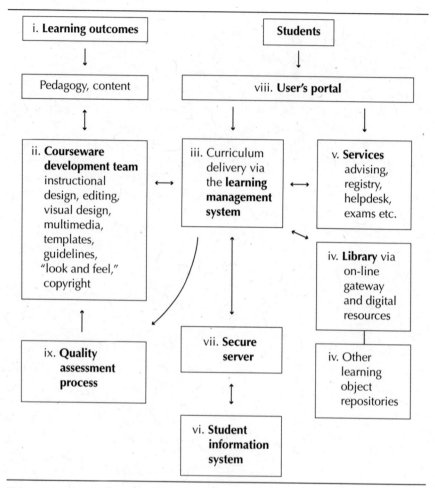

FIGURE 1. An online learning system framework

development team (2) shares the responsibility of translating the theory and intentions into practice in the form of courseware (stored on a Content Management System) and online learning functions, which are delivered by (3), the Learning Management System (LMS), which is interfaced with the library and other digital resources (4), related services (5), and the student information system (6) via a secure server (7) that can authenticate the student login.

This is but one view of an ideal system; there are increasing perceptions that LMSs in themselves may be less significant in the system.

Indeed, the context of learning is so varied or open that the confines of an LMS may be too restrictive. For our purposes here, it is enough to recognize that learning and the connection to learning resources or experiences need to be managed, and that this process can be facilitated through some sort of LMS.

The students will connect to the LMS and related services via a user-friendly portal system (8) so that, with a single login, they can also have access to their courses. Finally, to ensure ongoing improvement, an independent evaluation process for the effectiveness of the system (based on achievement of the learning outcomes and students' feedback), and an independent quality assessment process will be in place (9), which also feeds back into the development cycle.

Using this rough framework, aspects of the online learning infrastructure will be discussed, but to conclude this section on overall organization, the general relationships, particularly among the units responsible for information technology support, should be discussed. In 1990, Paul (1990) raised a number of important issues regarding the incorporation of technology into learning systems, many of which we still grapple with. Two in particular are pertinent here and are intertwined.

The first issue is the relationship between academic and administrative computing, whether they should be connected or not, and in either case, how these two information technology functions can interface with each other. These questions are a significant aspect of the centralization/decentralization issue. While the normal structure is often to have them separated and reporting through different executive officers, the online learning staff and systems need a lot of support and maintenance from the central administrative computing unit, as do key service areas such as student registration, the library, and other learning resources. The second and tightly related issue is that of centralized control versus decentralized freedom. Normally, the administrative computing units prefer a more centralized system, in order to improve integration, avoid duplication, ensure security, and minimize the divergent approaches and the subsequent complexity of support. Those involved in the design and delivery of educational programming prefer a more decentralized approach, with more freedom to innovate, and to choose platforms and applications that suit their specific needs and preferences. Of even greater possible political consequence is their deep desire for academic values and needs to have priority over those of the central administrative unit.

The separation of academic and administrative computing at an organizational level makes the implicit assumption that they can be separated on the technological level also. Such is unlikely to be the case as system interdependencies are a critical requirement of the ability to offer a seamless service to the student and, indeed, to the teacher. The growing complexity of learning systems requires a jointly developed vision for the technological architecture that provides flexibility and sustainability for both groups. Separating the activities into a bifurcated stream of development will ultimately compromise the ability of the organization to provide students with a responsive, flexible, and dynamic learning system.

In an ideal case, it should not matter how such units are organized or linked, since the overall goals and values of the institution or company surely will govern people's behaviour and attitudes, and everyone will accommodate each other's needs, responsibilities, and functions. In the real world of online learning, conflicting priorities and approaches quickly arise, and very tangible structures, clear roles and responsibilities, and processes and policies have to be established to help balance the relative needs for control/centralization and freedom/decentralization.

An additional organizational issue, more relevant to traditional institutions, is the question of discipline ownership. With much online learning emerging from the continuing/distance education departments and from the growth of online programming in other academic faculties, there is sometimes organizational conflict in who "owns" the discipline.

THE COMPONENTS OF AN ONLINE LEARNING SYSTEM

The following represent the typical components and functionality of a comprehensive online learning system.

Development of Courseware

Even at the initial stages of thinking about the development of an online learning program, it is wise to involve all those who are likely to be involved at any stage. This can be done by the sponsors of the program preparing a preliminary proposal, laying out the objectives of the program, determining the intended student market, and proposing an online learning approach. This gives various service units a chance to comment on matters that will affect them, and for fellow educators to comment on the proposed content and pedagogy. The proposal should also identify the composition of the development and delivery teams that will be established to undertake the project. The nature of these teams can vary widely. The small team could be just one person, the content expert who is also an experienced educator and well trained to use a comprehensive web-learning platform and related technologies which are already fully supported by the institution or company. This person would just need routine support from areas such as copyright, library, and other departments.

Alternatively, a very complex team involves content experts, educators, instructional designers, editors, visual designers, multimedia designers, programmers, systems staff, and so on, in the design of a course that needs new online learning functions, connects uniquely to the other systems, and involves the creation of new multimedia digital learning objects. In either case, the preliminary proposal must have sufficient information for all concerned to understand what their likely role and responsibilities would be, and what direct and indirect costs would be involved.

For those familiar with formal project management processes and techniques, the identification and discussion around the proposal with the project team will seem redundant, but in academe, it is surprising how little attention is paid to this much needed process. Much of it is just common sense, common courtesy, and good planning. Depending on the size and scope of the task, some basic understanding and application of the principles of project management is also required to develop online learning courseware. The roles of team members can vary widely, but, as a guideline, the following types of positions and the roles they play in the team are described further in Chapters 10 (Development of Online Courses) and 18 (Developing Team Skills and Accomplishing Team Projects Online) in this volume.

Learning Management System

Another key decision to be made at the development phase is the choice of Learning Management System (LMS), which leads quickly to a discussion of using commercial, proprietary software versus developing an in-house system, which may or may not also be based on freely available, imported, open-source software. For the former, there are a host of very good and comprehensive packages, some which come as an add-on to the student information system, while others can be interfaced accordingly. Training events, conferences, and meetings allow staff to be oriented and updated on the software's development and functionality.

Assessing which of the purchased options is the best fit for a particular online learning system's needs can be an onerous task. All choices must be carefully considered and aided by some independent evaluation sources (Course Management Systems, 2007).

For the in-house system, there are many free, open-source solutions also available, which emulate the functionality of the proprietary systems and can be adapted in any manner needed. This approach may require more initial development and different skill sets among staff, to ensure the robustness of the system, provide a higher level of technical support on an ongoing basis, prepare documentation and training, and interface with other systems as necessary. Having an active community supporting and contributing to an open-source application provides considerable benefit, through access to a knowledge base and a continuing stream of developments.

In the ideal case, this choice of LMS is based on the needs of the course, without worrying about costs, the availability of qualified staff, or any limitations to using existing systems. The real case, however, is often more complicated: one is either constrained to a single solution based on previous institutional or company decisions (which some would think of as ideal), or one's choice is limited (as it should be) by practicalities, such as the costs of adopting yet another proprietary LMS or the human resources needed and other implications of building or adapting an open-source LMS. Each new solution adds considerable pressure on back-end systems, especially services such as the technical helpdesk and training, and can have a negative impact on both the students' and teacher's experience having to adapt to each LMS. Lastly, there is a lock-in factor: the costs of changing systems is very high, mainly due to the organizational relearning required to switch, and although much effort is being made to develop standards for online learning that will better enable interoperability and reusability of online content, the promise has not yet been met (Friesen, 2004).

The selection of the open-source *Moodle* LMS at Athabasca was achieved through the involvement of a broad section of experts in the community. An essential first task was the development of an evaluative criteria under the following headings:
- Mandate
- Systems Administration
- Cost
- Instructional Design
- Teaching and Learning Tools

These criteria provided guidelines to the evaluators to try out the applications under consideration and helped to establish a degree of objectivity to the process. A final report, produced for the entire Athabasca University community, outlined the reasons for the selection of *Moodle* (Stewart, 2007). The process proved effective in gaining acceptance of the selection within the institution, which has proven essential to its subsequent deployment.

Content Management System

The potential afforded by the LMS to have a more contextualized and dynamic learning environment sets in motion the need for a responsive, flexible, and potentially real-time content development system. Thus, upon deployment of an LMS, the provision of course materials or courseware using efficient and effective workflows will require the adoption of a Content Management System (CMS). There is no single description of a CMS or its functionality and there are many varieties available. In the main, these divide into two essential although not exclusive types: web content management systems and document management systems. The essential capabilities required for courseware are a system that can manage web content and provide a secure, accessible, and collaborative environment for the creation and storage of content in XML format. The importance of XML is that it allows content to be rendered through different media, such as print, web, and mobile devices.

As with LMSs, there are a considerable number of both open-source and proprietary choices available (MIT, 2006). The selection and adoption of a CMS should follow closely in both time and methodology the choice of the LMS, although the expert groups may be different. A CMS will provide the functionality for the creation, collaboration, production, and publishing of learning materials. As the delivery will be through the LMS it needs to be integrated into a seamless environment from the user's perspective, requiring that both systems be technologically compatible.

Library and Digital Resources

Linking the course or program LMS to the necessary online resources is now a key element of any online system. Institutional and public libraries have been leaders in the development of systems and protocols to acquire and share resources. Many now have electronic gateways to their own holdings; those housed elsewhere; digital databases of journals, magazines and government publications (including much in the way of full-text materials); and specially developed supplementary databases of materials selected for a particular course. In addition, learning objects will increasingly be accessible through in-house and external digital repositories. A key contribution to the development of online delivery is the librarian's understanding of knowledge management and intellectual property issues. These components are discussed in much more detail in Chapter 16, but the key point in developing the infrastructure for online learning is that the availability of such online resources should be ensured or at least anticipated, so that the courseware is developed accordingly, the LMS is appropriately configured, and any access for the student is enabled.

Learner Services

Most attention in online learning must be paid to the courseware and delivery platform. Those who have worked in various forms of distributed learning for many years know only too well the vital importance of the non-academic learner support needed to ensure student success and satisfaction. Depending on the enterprise involved, this support would include technical help, educational advising, various forms of counselling, services for learners with special needs, and so on (see Chapter 17). In an ideal online learning system, these aspects would be given equal priority and developed in concert with the curriculum. In a real situation, such services likely already exist, but are designed for traditional educational environments, and so their conversion and enhancement for online learning is needed, with the ability to adapt and change as new options and learner expectations change.

Interface with the Student Information System

Ideally, the LMS is linked to the Student Information System (SIS) in such a manner that the right student is automatically placed in the right course at the right time with all the right student information easily available to the right instructor and to anyone else who needs it. This interface avoids the need to input student names into the LMS, with all the associated errors and wasted time. Instructors should be able to manipulate the student data as needed for the course (e.g., submitting and editing final marks), and to contact the students as a group, in subgroups, and individually.

All these capabilities require integration between the LMS, CMS, portal, and the SIS, allied to strong identity and access management that will authenticate students to enter their individual learning space. An integrated SIS/LMS system may seem attractive if one is building an online learning system from scratch. However, in many real situations, there are one or more LMSs, each of which needs to be interfaced as needed to the SIS, and any or all of these may be proprietary, imported, or home-built systems.

The User's Portal

As for most sophisticated online enterprises (travel, banking, shopping, and so on), the nature of the portal provided to the learner (and indeed to staff in various ways) is important. At minimum, the portal should allow the learner, with one secure login, to access everything that is of interest to them: the LMS (and from there to other essential links), their grades, other applicable documentation on their student file, and related learner services and accounts. The portal environment should also be open for students to exhibit their preferences through the customization of the interface and the information and user communities they choose to access or give accesses to.

The growth in portal sophistication represents a major improvement in student services that is only achievable through online delivery. The ability to personalize a student's experience is not economically or practically conceivable in the off-line world. Further, the involvement of students in the creation of their own personal spaces provides a level of control and convenience that, by itself, adds significantly to the student's understanding of their learning environment.

Initial forays into this portal-enabled space include social networking, e-portfolios, and course support applications. On the horizon are automated support capabilities, such as e-advising and e-counselling, that would review the information provided through the institution's SIS to provide students with advice as to choice of programs, course schedules, and related communities of practice. The network ability of portals enables an interconnected and real-time analysis of Internet-available information to be used in the provision of such services. Although such services will not provide a complete picture or replace the higher-level counselling or advising functions, they can provide real-time assistance to students that will improve both their learning experience and learning outcomes.

Quality Assessment

Most institutions and organizations have a unit dedicated to providing thorough and independent evaluation of any enterprise, as part of the routine process of quality assurance and improvement. Ideally, the development of an e-learning system should include a plan for the independent evaluation of all aspects of the system, but especially the degree to which it enables or enhances the achievement of the stated learning outcomes (especially in the opinion of its users). Furthermore, such an evaluation would also provide information about the system's return on investment, especially the unanticipated or unseen costs of implementation from back-end systems, staff attitudes, infrastructure, and so on.

In the real situation, where there may be a variety of systems in place, the tendency will be for each group to undertake its own research, which can often be biased (intentionally or not) and difficult to compare with others, unless a strict and common framework is in place. Even if only one system exists, larger corporate pressures may ensure that a project is "doomed to succeed." This is an aspect of online learning where a strong and centralized approach is preferred. The type, scope and framework for evaluation must be independent and structured if the results are to lead to real improvement in systems and good decisions on whether to scrap the systems or build on them with new resources.

RELATED ISSUES

Many institutions and organizations who have shifted significant areas of their core business to an online environment may have noticed the predicted and unanticipated effects on all aspects of their enterprise. For online learning, some of these impacts are straightforward and can be factored in early on, with systematic updates.

- Back-end hardware (servers, switches, etc.) and connectivity will need to be estimated up front, then routinely adjusted as the number of users grows and the system evolves, as well as standards and expectations for up-time (usually 24 hours, seven days a week). With the expectations that video will be increasingly used routinely in online learning, this back-end element will be under ever-increasing demands.
- Polices related to access to servers, security, and the use of the online learning system need to be in place, to balance the need for stability and security with the need to innovate (Athabasca University, 2003).
- Technical help and helpdesk support needs to be in place, possibly linked to a training, orientation, and documentation function,

which can provide support to students and staff on the online learning system. Since this function can be spread among the core information service and the teaching units, clear mandates and lines of responsibility must be in place to avoid duplication of effort or gaps in support.

- A host of human resource issues need to be addressed. Some are tied to collective agreement and employment contract terms and conditions, especially those related to service standards and expectations (which go beyond the normal working day) and the automatic flexibility that online learning provides not only to the student, but also to the staff in terms of the place and times that they work. By way of examples, online activities such as chatting, discussion within forums, blogging, pod-casting, and wiki editing, will likely be new to many faculty and need to be integrated into accepted practice. Such integration may require new policies on attendance and standards for being in touch with the central office for administrative matters.

- Another human resource issue is the constantly shifting nature of the work that staff undertake. Many individuals working in online learning have had no official (or dated) training, but have learned and adapted successfully to new approaches and new technologies. There are many stories of staff who entered organizations at a junior level and worked their way into key roles in online learning, often quite unexpectedly, as organizational needs and their abilities evolved. Traditional approaches to hiring, appointment, promotions, position classification, access to training and professional development have to be adapted in order to maximize the opportunity to invest in and reward staff in such in such a dynamic environment, and/or to avoid exploiting staff who may be working well above the level for which they are paid. The long-term sustainability of the online learning system will depend, to a large extent, on how this new human resource environment is addressed, if only to retain valuable staff. The online learning system itself should inspire new types of flexible training for staff, with inter-institutional and intrainstitutional support groups and learning communities, information links, and so forth.

- Lastly, the process for decision-making and resource allocation related to online learning in an institution or organization must be carefully considered. If new committees are to be established to provide recommendations on direction and investments, care must be taken to balance the discussion between those who know and understand a lot (but may proselytize one approach in favour of another), central technical staff, decentralized technical staff who directly support the online system (and who often want more freedom), the central administration (who likely do not know as much, but are accountable for the success and effectiveness of the system), and the users (teachers and learners). The role of independent and thorough evaluation becomes very important in this process.

Organizational Change

Any educational endeavour, if it is of any credibility, is dynamic in nature, responding to new knowledge, understanding, and approaches to the disciplines, to new employment market needs, to changing student demographics, and so on. In a traditional campus or classroom environment, the expectation is on the teachers and/or curriculum developers to ensure this currency, and the same is true in online systems. In the online system, however, change is more complicated, because any change in content or approach can have wide impact on a number of aspects of the system. Online learning technologies themselves evolve just as quickly as the curriculum, as do students' expectations, their level of connectivity, and so on (sometimes in unexpected ways). In short, the organization's capacity and capability of effectively managing change is of vital importance.

Assuming that the organization as whole respects and encourages change in such systems, there still remains the matter of how it is to be managed within the context of online learning. The first issue is balance: specifically, between every time a new idea or product comes into view (including those good for students) versus sticking with an established system (typically for administrative ease and staff convenience). In short, such changes often take place long after they have been superseded by better, proven systems.

The degree of centralization or decentralization of a system (or systems) also drives the change process. To what extent will some units be free to explore and try new systems, and to what extent will those lagging behind be forced to update their approaches? Such questions, since they relate to core aspects of an organization's business and culture, can only be answered within that context. Thus, following the dimensions of an online system infrastructure would appear to be the key to handling change well.

Leadership

As for any organizational issue, effective change starts with leadership. Having the right attitude towards change, its importance and value, is essential. Change should be embraced, and not seen to be just another headache to be dealt with. Kotter (1996) gives a concise explanation of why change is inevitable and crucial in modern business, and provides specific ideas on how change can be led. Organizations have different mandates, cultures, leadership styles, and competitive positions. Universities, for example, have consensual cultures, and therefore leaders of change in such environments require the ability to understand the needs of the broad group of stakeholders before implementing change initiatives.

Scouting Reports

Some staff, as part of their work, must look around for emerging trends and ideas in online learning systems, and provide a place for others to feed information they come across. These scouting reports need to be compiled and shared. In addition, staff members who support online learning applications, particularly in cases where open-source software is used, need to incorporate themselves into the communities that plan and develop applications. By so doing, they may influence and contribute to the applications' development roadmaps, while providing a knowledge base for the organization's community. This function is well supported by regular reports such as the annual Horizon Report (2007).

Governance

A governance body is needed that deals not only with current issues related to online systems, but also provides a forum for discussion of emerging trends, organizes meetings and events to share and demonstrate new ideas, and revisits the vision for the online learning system regularly (e.g., every year or two). This vision should be detailed enough to allow affected managers to adjust their plans and budgets accordingly, within the context of the organization's regular cycle. The terms of reference and reporting relationship of this body should be commensurate with the importance of online learning to the organization.

Membership in such a body can be difficult to determine. The first impulse is typically to include those most intimately involved in online systems – technical experts and educational technology champions – simply because their opinions are valuable. A more important criterion for membership for such an expert, however, is an individual's willingness to consider a wide variety of alternatives, and to not stubbornly defend their own particular preferred approach. In addition, users of the online systems, neophyte teachers, students, and user support staff, provide an important balance to discussions which otherwise can degenerate into purely technical banter. Finally, this body should be chaired by the highest possible level of relevant management.

The governance body also plays an important role in the allocation of resources to specific initiatives. Such decision-making ability and authority is essential to effective governance; a broad strategic perspective should be channelled through the governance body to prioritize and allocate limited resources to projects with the most potential to achieve the institution's objectives. Without effective governance, initiatives are not likely to be funded on the basis of best fit or strategic importance, but instead on more local or individual concerns.

At the same time, governance must not stifle innovation. Governance, therefore, should have three levels of decision-making: enterprise, departmental, and individual, each level with defined criteria for acceptance, and each level armed with a clear understanding of how the technology will be used. Having clear guidelines will help engender innovation while ensuring its effective usage within the larger community.

Communication

The requirement to continuously communicate at all levels of the organization cannot be overstated. From concept to commissioning, all stakeholders must be aware of what is going on. The adoption of transparent processes with effective governance provides the basis for developing trusting relationships among the greater community, and serves to lessen the inevitable apprehension that change typically engenders.

Through the governance body, there needs to a process whereby developments and ideas in online education are regularly broadcast internally though newsletters and in multiple forums, and, where appropriate, externally via journals and conferences. Simplicity of language is important, as is the opportunity to receive input and explain any apparent inconsistencies in approach.

Pilot Projects and Evaluation

An important dimension of change is the use of pilot projects for new developments, plus effective evaluation of their impact before proceeding to wider adoption. The governance body could provide the approval for such pilots, and have pool of resources to allocate accordingly. Unfortunately, pilots often become the first phases of deployment, and actions taken eventually result in the organization scrambling to retroactively provision and support what has essentially become an operational system. Having clear expectations of the pilot communicated to the project owners in advance of the project will help to ensure that such misunderstandings are avoided from the outset. Evaluation of any pilot system should be at arm's length, and the results should be shared widely throughout the community. In this way, the organization can receive the fullest benefit and intelligence from its pilots, and the process of innovation can be seen by all involved to be open and effective.

Change Management

As implied, new ideas and approaches must be fostered, not only by words, but also by financial and in-kind resources. Moreover, these resources must be coordinated via an open and widely representative governance body. The goal here is to balance the organization's need for control over implementing innovations (which can deviate rapidly if separate units are left to their own devices) versus the organization's need to constantly explore new innovations and foster the culture of change needed to support such innovation. For the human resources involved, the same balance of recognition and rewards for individuals' contributions to implementation and innovation must be found.

A defined process must also be employed to provide a framework for any proposed changes. As mentioned above, project management provides transferable practices which can be used for this purpose, particularly as the changes are typically complex, ranging from developing a new module in-house to deploying an existing, turnkey module. The process must also allow broad input into both the approval process and the precise specifications of the desired change.

Change is a concomitant outcome of all technological developments. Indeed, even relatively minor amendments to existing work practices can have disruptive effects. As the impact is in the mind of the changed and not the changer, effective change management requires a high level of sensitivity and understanding, to help assist the group to adapt to the new environment. It should always be kept in mind, however, that any technological innovation is only as effective as the weakest user's ability to use it. An adequate technology that is well accepted will be more effective than a good technology that is not. All change initiatives therefore need to have the usability of the system as their main goal and focus on organizational change; in other words, in the people, not the functionality of a particular piece of technological wizardry.

CONCLUSION

In order to develop an infrastructure that supports excellence in online leaning, the issues to be addressed are almost all the same as for any post-secondary educational enterprise: a clear understanding of the goals of the curriculum and the characteristics of the intended students' needs, coupled with a healthy working environment with committed staff, where implementation can proceed and where constant change is understood to be the norm. Within these general areas, there are, of course, a host of technical, procedural, and policy decisions to be made. Nonetheless, online learning is now mature enough that such decisions need not be made haphazardly: there are many successful examples of online learning systems to learn from and plenty of research and information available, including this online text. As opposed to those who were the vanguard of this exciting educational development, new contributors can now focus their efforts on getting the basic principles and goals in order before proceeding to implementation. Ultimately, as with any educational system, online learning is fundamentally a human endeavour, with technology available to support the agreed-upon principles and goals, not vice-versa.

REFERENCES

Athabasca University. (2002a). *Athabasca University Education Plan web page*. Retrieved December 1, 2002, from http://intra.athabascau.ca/reports/edplan_0ct4_02.doc

Athabasca University. (2002b). *Athabasca University Student Academic Services web site*. Retrieved December 1, 2002, from http://intra.athabascau.ca/reports/ student_satisf_acad_services_2002.doc

Athabasca University. (2003). *Athabasca University Sever Policy web page*. Retrieved May 19, 2007, from http://www.athabascau.ca/policy/computingservices/serverpolicy.htm

Chickering, A., & Ehrmann, S. C. (1996, October). *Implementing the seven principles: Technology as lever*. Retrieved May 19, 2007, from http://www.tltgroup.org/programs/seven.html

Course Management Systems. (2007). *Course management systems on www. edutools.info web site.* Retrieved May 19, 2007, from http://www.edutools. info/course/index.jsp

Friesen, N. (2004). Editorial: A gentle introduction to technical e-learning standards.
Canadian Journal of Learning and Technology, 30(3). Retrieved March 6, 2007, from http://www.cjlt.ca/content/vol30.3/normeditorial.html

Horizon Report. (2007). *NMC.org 'Horizon Report' web page.* Retrieved May 19, 2007, from http://www.nmc.org/horizon/

International Review of Open and Distance Learning. (2001). *International Review of Research in Open and Distance Learning, 1*(2). Retrieved May 19, 2007, from http://www.irrodl.org/index.php/irrodl/issue/view/10

Kotter, J. P. (1996). *Leading change.* Boston, MA: Harvard Business School Press.

Lu, M. (2006). *SparkNotes on ideal gases.* Retrieved May 19, 2007, from http://www.sparknotes.com/chemistry/gases/ideal

MIT. (2006). *Peer review of course/learning management systems.* Cambridge, MA: MIT. Retrieved May 19, 2007, from http://www.wcet.info/services/publications/MIT07-19-06.pdf

Paul, R. H. (1990). *Open learning and open management: Leadership and integrity in distance education.* New York: Nichols Publishing.

Red River College. (2004). *Red River College, learning outcomes web page.* Retrieved May 19, 2007, from https://me.rrc.mb.ca/LearningOutcome Support/

Stewart, B., Briton, D., Gismondi, M., Heller, B., Kennepohl, D., McGreal, R., & Nelson, C. (2007). Choosing Moodle: An evaluation of learning management systems at Athabasca University. *Journal of Distance Education Technologies, 5*(3), 1–7.

ABOUT THE AUTHORS

Alan Davis is vice-president of Education at Vancouver Community College. Since 1989, Dr. Davis has held senior positions at the BC Open University, Athabasca University, and Niagara College. His original discipline was chemistry, and he received his doctorate from Simon Fraser University in 1980. He has special interests in learning assessment and accreditation, the management of online learning, and higher education consortia.

Paul Little is dean of the School of Learning Innovation, Red River College, Winnipeg, Canada.

Brian Stewart is the chief information officer at Athabasca University – Canada's Open University.

TECHNOLOGIES OF ONLINE LEARNING (E-LEARNING)

RORY MCGREAL
Athabasca University

MICHAEL ELLIOTT
Mosaic Technologies

INTRODUCTION

This chapter includes an examination of some of the most exciting technologies and features used in online instruction today, and those we may use tomorrow. Education is one of the fastest-growing economic and social sectors in the world, and the use of new technologies is an integral and driving component of that growth. Multimedia applications have long been popular on the Web, and these combined with streaming audio and video podcasts, such as the myriad music sites or video sites like YouTube, are opening up different opportunities for educators. Audio chat using Skype has become common, and web conferencing is used for teaching and for creating podcasts. Other useful applications in this chapter include instant messaging and peer-to-peer file sharing. The possibilities of using the new hand-held third-generation mobile technologies are also explored along with blogs, RSS, wikis, learning objects, digital games, and virtual worlds.

Many of these applications are seamlessly combined in the latest social networking sites such as Facebook, MySpace, and Bebo. These sites allow students, in classes or as informal learners, to create a community online. Although the sites are public, individuals or groups can choose to close off their space, limiting it to "friends" or to their classmates.

MULTIMEDIA ON THE INTERNET

Multimedia incorporates text, graphics, and audio media (often with real video or animations) and combines them, using a computer. Almost every personal computer built today is capable of delivering multimedia presentations for entertainment, advertising, or education. *Edutainment* is a word for applications that incorporate multimedia entertainment with educational objectives.

Multimedia on the Internet is still not an everyday reality in the same sense as multimedia on CD-ROM or DVD, which may be commonplace in the home or classroom. Internet connection speeds limit the quality and quantity of what can be transmitted. Even with wired/wireless and high-speed advances, the transmission of large sound, animation, and video files can be time-consuming and often frustrating.

With the introduction of *streaming multimedia* in the past five or six years, however, large multimedia files can now be delivered even over modem connections. Streaming multimedia is an Internet data transfer method that facilitates the transfer of audio and video files from computer to computer in a "stream." Streamed media packets can be played as soon as the data starts arriving at the receiving computer – users do not have to wait until the full file has been downloaded. Streaming audio has been more successful than video, which has generally been limited to small picture sizes or low resolution (grainy) video projections, but as the bandwidth increases, higher quality, full-screen video becomes possible.

The key to this breakthrough is the format in which the files are distributed, or served, over the Internet. Large audio or video files are converted into a format that can be sent as a continuous stream of small pieces to a user's computer. At the user's end of the connection, special software interprets the stream of data and begins to play the sample. While the first part of the sample is being played, the next is being downloaded. The second sample begins seamlessly, the first is deleted, and the third is downloaded. Using this format, hours of audio and video content can be received over a slow modem connection.

Recommended Links

The following links provide some good examples of educational multimedia on the Web:

- Athabasca University Astronomy 230: Northern Lights/Northern Skies: http://astro.whytespace.ca/
- Math Open Reference – Plane Geometry: http://www.mathopenref.com/index.html
- Kbears (Knowledge Bears): http://www.kbears.com/
- National Museum of American History: http://americanhistory.si.edu/kids/athome.cfm
- University of Washington, EDGE streaming video web site: http://www.engr.washington.edu/edge/streaming.html
- Free-ed.net: http://www.free-ed.net/free-ed/
- Malloy, T. Understanding ANOVA Visually: http://www.psych.utah.edu/stat/introstats/anovaflash.html

STREAMING AUDIO

Audio was the first type of multimedia to be delivered over the Internet in a streaming format; concerts and live radio broadcasts were among the first examples of streamed audio to appear. A wide range of streaming audio formats is in use on the Web today, but while each is different in name, the basic technology remains the same.

When a sound file is prepared for streaming, it is compressed to reduce the overall size of the file. For example, a news broadcast consisting of a single recorded voice would normally be a smaller file than an orchestral sample. In some cases, compression also means that the quality of the file is affected.

Different programs are available for receiving streaming audio, each with its own proprietary sound or media format. Quality varies from format to format, but all are compatible with modem connections. Recently, these programs have become more generic, which is good news for the end user, who no longer faces the hassle of installing three different programs in order to listen to three different sound formats. Instead, the newer, more powerful media players can decode, decompress, and play a variety of proprietary sound samples.

Many of the Internet's most widely-publicized firsts have happened as a result of streaming media events. The longest continuous Internet broadcast in history was in the form of a "jam session" held during the Canadian East Coast Music Awards in Moncton, New Brunswick, in 1997; that record was bettered during the following year's ceremony (East Coast Music Association, n.d.). Producing a live, continuous stream of music (and in subsequent years, video) for over 80 hours was truly an impressive feat. Another, more widely known first was Paul McCartney's 1999 return to The Cavern, the bar in Liverpool where the Beatles first played (Fab Four, n.d.). This live broadcast over the Internet was the most listened-to sound production in Internet history.

Educational Uses

Streaming audio is currently used as a supplement to classroom-based and online course delivery, usually in the form of prerecorded lectures, interviews with guests, student projects, samples of student classroom interaction, or sound bytes of content relevant to the course of study. For music or English composition courses, it can be used by teachers or students to record samples of their work and make them available to the teacher and other students. Streaming on demand is becoming a key feature in web-based education. For example, listen to Gustav Holst's musical interpretation of *The Planets* included in the list of recommended links given below.

Recommended Links

- Trussler, B., Gustav Holst: The Planets Suite: http://www.aquarianage. org/lore/holst.html
- Internet.com News Channel: http://www.Internet.com/sections/ news.html
- East Coast Music Association, Your Music: http://www.ecma.ca
- Streaming Media World: http://www.streamingmediaworld.com

STREAMING VIDEO

First came radio, and then television. And on the Web, first came streaming audio, and then streaming video. When a video sample is presented in electronic format, there are many more "layers" of data to be converted and compressed than with audio alone. As a result, when this multimedia format is delivered over the Internet in a streaming delivery system, more technical and educational issues must be taken into consideration.

Size is the first issue. Video files are much larger than audio files, and video combined with audio is larger still. Video samples also demand more processing power on the part of the receiving computer. It is relatively simple to record sound – music, voice, or both – even on a home computer. Recording video and saving it in an electronic format, however, is more demanding on hardware and requires additional software. Because of the size and other issues, video has taken longer to become an industry standard, and it is harder to find educational applications for streaming on the Web.

Receiving streaming video feeds on a home computer is not difficult. Newer versions of Windows®, Apple OS®, and Linux come with pre-installed streamers for audio and video. Generally, these streamers are sufficient for most educational applications. As is the case with streaming audio, different formats require different applications; however, most multimedia applications now available for the home market have been designed to receive both audio and video streams. Superbowl XXXV (Clancy, n.d.), held in January 2001, saw the recreational and commercial use of streaming multimedia go to new heights. Long known for its glamorous halftime shows and extremely expensive commercials, this event was different from those of past years because of the means by which the commercials were broadcast. For those unable or unwilling to sit through hours of football to see a few commercials, several online video streaming sites encoded and broadcast the commercials within minutes of their traditional broadcast. By noon of the next day, hundreds of thousands of people had a chance to see what they had missed the night before. This application illustrates how events or sequences can be decomposed to extract only the relevant components. This technique is now driving the creation of modular, chunk-sized content objects, often referred to as *learning objects,* or more precisely, as *knowledge objects.*

Educational Uses

The stiff, unemotional "talking head" of a professor or tutor in the corner of an e-learning web page is the image that most quickly comes to mind when one considers video clip use in an online educational situation. In such a presentation, a professor or tutor delivers a prepared lecture or shows an example of a hands-on activity; however, almost any video sample with educational value can be converted to a streaming format, and many will serve as excellent additional resources on an educational web page, for classroom courses, or for online courses delivered synchronously. When implemented wisely, video can alleviate the page-turning boredom of many online courses. The LearnAlberta.ca project, included in the list of recommended links below, is an example of an educational video streaming project with a variety of video-based curricula for Alberta teachers and students. This project was established to define and deploy a prototype K–12 application.

Recommended Links

- YouTube: http://www.youtube.com/
- University of Washington, EDGE, Streaming Video Site: http://www.engr.washington.edu/edge/streaming.html
- CyberTech Media Group, Streaming Video over an Intranet: http://www.cybertechmedia.com/intranet.html
- MP3, Top 40 Charts: http://www.mp3charts.com

AUDIO CHAT AND VOICE-OVER INTERNET PROTOCOL

Text chat has long been a popular feature of the Internet. Within the past decade, audio chat has also emerged and become quite popular (Romero, 2000). Point-to-point audio connections can be made between almost any two computers on the Internet, and some Internet service providers (ISPs) and online services are now offering free Internet-based long-distance service that connects individuals calling through a personal computer to the public telephone system.

Although the robustness of Internet phone calls, or Voice-over Internet Protocol (VoIP), is currently somewhat inferior to that of dial-up long-distance telephone, consumers are increasingly attracted to Internet telephony. Most of the time, the quality is very high, and the price is free when calling computer to computer, or extremely cheap when calling telephones. The success of *Skype* and other *VoIP* services is due to the relative simplicity of making a call, requiring only an Internet hookup, headphones or speakers, and a microphone. After signing up with an Internet telephony provider, users can make local or long-distance calls to people with any type of phone. However, since voice transmissions are carried over the Internet in small packets, in the same manner as data transmissions, conversations can be subject to delays. Without a high-speed Internet connection, the quality of an Internet call can deteriorate affecting the robustness of the call, but companies are working to improve it.

Educational Uses

Classroom-based, email pen pal programs have been used for a long time as a way of making intercultural connections between schools. Internet telephony will add an opportunity for students to speak to others in their age group, almost anywhere in the world. It will therefore facilitate more fluid and natural communication between different cultural groups, and will be especially useful for foreign language exposure and practice.

Teacher or tutor and student communication can be greatly enhanced by opportunities to speak with one another, to discuss an assignment or a difficult concept without the expense of long-distance tolls. An electronic blackboard can be used along with VoIP for synchronous teaching. This practice is known as audio-graphic teleconferencing. Microsoft's NetMeeting is can be used in this manner.

Recommended Links

- Skype: http://www.skype.com/
- ICUII.com. ICUII Video Chat (I See You Too, audio and video phone): http://www.icuii.com
- PC-Telephone.com: http://www.pc-telephone.com
- Microsoft Corp., NetMeeting: http://www.microsoft.com/windows/netmeeting

WEB CONFERENCING

Web conferencing is a form of graphic teleconferencing, used in combination with VoIP as a single tool in general web applications that support real-time collaboration. The "whiteboarding" feature emulates writing or drawing on a blackboard. With a whiteboard, both teachers and learners can create, manipulate, review, and update graphical information online in real time while participating in a lecture or discussion. Using a mouse, an electronic stylus with a tablet, or even a large electronic classroom-sized whiteboard, users can annotate by writing, cutting and pasting, or clicking, dragging, and dropping. In web conferencing, content can be saved and used in future presentations. Imported graphics can be used as underlays that the user can trace over, using an "onionskin," "placed" on top of the image; for example, routes can be drawn and redrawn on maps. The providers listed in the Recommended Links section below sell or rent virtual classrooms, with size (i.e., number of simultaneous logons permitted) determined by the license and the bandwidth available at the central site. These products are now incorporating small video images, "web safaris" in which the teacher leads the class to visit various sites, and application sharing which allows any of the distributed users to control a single application.

Educational Uses

These audio and graphics-enhanced web conferencing applications allow for the emulation of classroom lessons. Students in different locations can participate actively and collaboratively with the teacher and with other students in the creation and adaptation of graphical information. This application is particularly appropriate for brainstorming sessions.

Recommended Links

- Saba Centra Software, Inc. Saba Centra.com: http://www.saba. com/products/centra/
- Elluminate, Inc., Elluminate.com: http://www.elluminate.com
- Luidia Inc., eBeam: http://www.e-beam.com
- WBD Whiteboard (open source): http://www-mice.cs.ucl.ac.uk/ multimedia/software/wbd/

INSTANT MESSAGING

ICQ (I seek you), a commercial product distributed freely over the Net, can be described as an Internet paging device. It has some similarities to other modes of text-based communication, such as email or Internet Relay Chat (IRC). ICQ allows short messages to be sent electronically from computer to computer. As with email, the messages are stored on a central server until the recipient collects them; however, ICQ is more dynamic, in that it shows all of the group members when the recipient logs on. Thus, the exchanges are often very rapid and work much like synchronous text exchanges. Attachments and web addresses (URLs) can also be sent. Unlike email, however, ICQ also allows group chat sessions to be opened and voice chats to be established. In addition, and unlike most email systems, ICQ is highly transportable: a user could have ICQ on a computer at work, at home, and on a laptop, and receive "pages" only on the active computer.

ICQ is one of a growing number of instant messenger services that are available online. Users can also choose from MSN Messenger (MSN.com), AIM, and a bevy of similar applications. ICQ has been popular for some time, especially with technically proficient Internet users. More recently, because of the capacity of central servers, immediate and delayed message delivery, and increased functionality, instant messaging has become a popular choice for millions of users.

Educational Uses

Instant messaging has not yet been used as an efficient content-delivery teaching tool. Its strength lies in its ability to facilitate immediate contact with other students and teachers, or with a tutor who is supervising chat sessions.

Recommended Links

- ICQ, Inc., ICQ: http://www.icq.com
- MSN.com, MSN Messenger: http://messenger.microsoft.com
- AIM Instant Messenger: http://www.aim.com/
- Instant Messaging Planet: http://www.instantmessagingplanet. com
- International Engineering Consortium, Instant messaging (tutorial): http://www.iec.org/online/tutorials/instant_msg

HAND-HELD AND WIRELESS TECHNOLOGIES

Imagine the power of the Internet in the palm of your hand, using a Portable Digital Assistant (PDA), a third generation (3G) mobile phone, or even an iPhone®. Wireless technologies, cellular modems, and hand-held devices are moving from elite gadgetry into the mainstream. How will this cord-free revolution change how we work and learn? Hand-held devices are very powerful small computers. They are now used not only for voice communications, but also for listening to music, downloading email, sending Short Message Service (SMS) messages, and surfing the Web. Some are now using mobile devices to pay bills or pay for soft drinks at dispensing machines. Many people are choosing mobile devices over desktop computers. These include ultra-notebook computers, e-books, web pads, and tablet computers.

Mobile computing has arrived. Already, wireless devices are being chosen over desktop and even laptop computers, not only as the preferred

Internet access tool, but also for common computing applications such as word processing and spreadsheets. These devices are disguised as telephones, tablets, e-books, and web pads, and now include a web browser, an instant messenger, and an email feature, along with other functions.

So your next computer probably will not be just a computer. It will also be a phone and an organizer, and will include other serious and gaming applications. You will use it to check your bank balance, buy groceries, and bet on the lottery. Cordless devices, pocket PCs, and PDAs are the wallets, cheque books, calculators, and Rolodexes of the 21st century. The size of a calculator (or even smaller), these devices are capable of basic computing tasks such as handwriting-recognition text processing and contact management. More complex and higher-end hand-helds have multimedia capabilities, wired or wireless Internet access, and the ability to send and receive data and text alike. With the advent of infrared networking, these hand-held computer devices can offer students and teachers a previously unknown degree of flexibility.

Athabasca University is preparing for the mobile and wireless world with its digital reading room, that has made course-related library materials accessible to a wide variety of mobile devices. And the AU English Second Language project has put a full basic English grammar course on the Web, accessible to mobile devices.

Educational Benefits and Uses

As affordable access to high bandwidth increases, and the cost of wireless devices that can incorporate all the features of a PC decreases, the educational possibilities are unlimited. It might mean the end of paper-based teaching and learning, lost homework, missing tests, and costly textbooks. In the Philippines, for example, people living in rural environments, even in communities without electricity, are using their cellular phones for text-based digital messaging. Newer applications for small devices are opening up the possibility of using wireless to deliver graphics and video to users, no matter where they are. Learning becomes universally accessible.

Recommended Links

- PDA Verticals Corp., pdaED.com: http://www.pdaed.com
- Palm Inc., Palm Products: http://www.palmone.com/us/products/
- Tucows, Mobile/PDA (PDA and handheld device software): http://tucows.com/PDA

- Athabasca University Digital Reading Room: http://library. athabascau.ca/drr/
- Athabasca University ESL Grammar: http://eslau.ca

PEER-TO-PEER FILE SHARING

Perhaps the most publicized Internet event in the past couple of years has been the controversy surrounding peer-to-peer, or file-sharing, applications. Peer-to-peer applications allow users, regardless of location or connection speed, to share practically any kind of file with a limitless population of other Internet users. In contrast to the currently predominant client-to-server model, where users retrieve information from a centralized server, the peer-to-peer model allows members of its "community" to transfer files directly between users, without having to access or be constrained by a centralized server.

Of all the peer-to-peer (P2P) applications, Napster became the most well known, because of its popularity and its ultimate demise in the courtrooms. Napster became prominent because of its focus on facilitating the distribution and sharing of files, and especially of copyright-protected media (mainly music files) encoded in the MP3 format. While P2P software and services have been considered mainly a means of downloading music files, the technology and goals behind the peer-to-peer concept allow for much more wide-ranging uses.

Andy Oram, editor of *Peer-To-Peer: Harnessing The Power of Disruptive Technologies,* notes that communities on the Internet have been limited by the flat interactive qualities of email and network newsgroups, and that users have great difficulty commenting on each other's postings, structuring information, and so forth. As such, he recommends the use of peer-to-peer applications with structured metadata for enhancing the activities of almost any group of people who share an interest (Oram, 2001).

Educational Uses

It is easy to make connections between learning objects, intelligent educational systems, and the peer-to-peer model. Research and other materials can easily be offered online and "harvested" by a well-designed P2P program, offering students or teachers a wealth of knowledge that might not otherwise be available.

Recommended Links

- Napster (the infamous P2P application): http://www.napster.ca/
- Audiogalaxy: About the satellite (the next generation of P2P): http://www.audiogalaxy.com/satellite/about.php
- Kazaa Media Desktop (P2P continues): http://www.kazaa.com/us/index.htm

BLOGS (WEB LOGS)

Blogs are becoming very popular. They are generally personal journals or newsletters that are more or less frequently updated by the owner. Most blogs are available to the general public. Blogging software exists so that people who are not technically sophisticated can maintain one without difficulty. Blogs range from the deeply philosophical to the mundane, from the generic to those dedicated to very specific issues, such as sports, politics, or travel. Many blogs serve as mini-portals, containing links of interest to the blog owner, or to the community which they serve; these are sometimes called *linklogs*. Visitors to a blog site can normally add comments and ideas. Blogs can serve as effective communications tools for people who wish to maintain connections. Although primarily text-based, some blogs can support different types of media, including audio and video. One of the most popular is the *vlog* or *video blog*. Other blogs define themselves by the type of device, such as specialty blogs for PDAs or other mobile devices.

Educational Uses

Blogs have many uses in education, including their importance for knowledge sharing in any specific subject area, either with other students, the instructor, or external professionals. Blogging can also provide key networking opportunities between students and with outside professionals in the field. Blogs can also be used by teachers for assigning coursework, and serve as a place for students to submit their work. Course announcements and annotated links to readings, along with advice on how to approach their studies, can also be delivered using blogs. Blogs are used successfully in creative or reflective writing courses, and in courses that require journals or e-portfolios. And they also provide students with experience in real-world digital knowledge management, working with groups, and information sharing.

Recommended Links
- Edublogs: http://edublogs.org/
- Blogdigger.com: http://www.blogdigger.com/
- Technorati.com: http://technorati.com/
- University of Houston. Blogs in Education: http://awd.cl.uh.edu/
  blog/

RSS AND ATOM FEEDS

Rich Site Summary or Really Simple Syndication (RSS) is a subset or protocol of the XML programming language that supports the distribution of content over the World Wide Web. RSS *aggregators* are computer programs which subscribe to a feed through a hyperlink that checks relevant sites for new content. RSS is heavily used for delivering news items, comments, descriptions, or images to subscribers, and enables the personalization of news items, by allowing a user's computer to fetch information that is of interest, using their PC, notebook, PDA, or mobile phone. This information can be tracked and personalized, using RSS. It facilitates access to the vast store of information that is increasing daily on the Web. Rather than having to go and search specific web sites or blogs, RSS sends the information directly to the user's web site as it becomes available. Atom is a proposed standard that attempts to overcome the problem of incompatible RRS formats with poor interoperability.

Educational Uses

Sharing of information with other teachers is probably one of the main uses of RSS for educators. As content is updated, relevant teaching content can be aggregated in a timely fashion. From one site, information will be available to view from a wide variety of relevant sources, including podcasts and videocasts. More recently, RSS feeds have been used to support social networks of students with peer-produced content. Another area for RSS sharing is in open-source productivity applications and educational games.

Recommended Links

- RSS – A quick start guide for educators by Will Richardson: http://
  weblogg-ed.com/wp-content/uploads/2006/05/RSSFAQ4.pdf
- RSS Ideas in Education: http://www.teachinghacks.com/wiki/
  index.php?title=RSS_Ideas_in_Education

- RSS, The next killer app for education by Mary Harsch: http://technologysource.org/article/rss/
- Feedster: http://www.feedster.com/
- Syndic8: http://www.syndic8.com/

WIKIS

A wiki is a web site or, more accurately, a collection of web sites where users can insert and edit content collectively. Users can also insert relevant hyperlinks, using a simple markup language. A wiki exists on an easy-to-use database and is normally maintained by the user community. Many wikis are open to the public, although some are closed and require users to log in. *Wikipedia* is the best-known wiki.

Educational Uses

Wikis can be used effectively by instructors for posting course information or lecture notes and inviting participation from students. These notes can be distributed in the form of simple text, PowerPoint slides, or audio and video components. Students can participate by adding their own notes and comments, along with relevant links that they may have found, creating a discussion environment for a particular topic. Students or groups of students can be invited to create their own wiki, either with personal information or project information related to the topics being studied. Wikis can also be used as e-portfolios of students' work, for evaluation by the instructor. Brainstorming activities can be especially powerful using a wiki, and FAQ pages are also possible.

Recommended Links

- Wikipedia: http://www.wikipedia.org
- Curriki: http://www.curriki.org
- Wikiversity: http://en.wikiversity.org/wiki/Wikiversity_Reports
- Wiki Pattern's Blog on Wiki use in Education: http://www.ikiw.org/
- Wikiineducation.com's A Wiki book: http://www.wikiineducation.com/display/ikiw/Home

VIRTUAL WORLDS

Virtual worlds are sometimes referred to as 3D Internet or *metaverses*. Perhaps the most well-known example is *Second Life*, which is used by millions of people. A virtual world is a simulated environment that exists on a server and is accessed by users via the Internet. Users interact with *avatars*, which are simulated characters that may or may not resemble the actual user. Normally, virtual worlds are inhabited by many users simultaneously. Real-time communication is possible in these worlds, using VoIP or live video. Virtual worlds are used for massive multiplayer gaming, particularly role-playing games.

Educational Uses

Virtual worlds can be exploited by educators who are interested in flexible environments that are limited only by the imagination. Learning can be promoted in these worlds using traditional methods, such as lectures and other classroom-based types of activities, or through computer-based simulations, new media applications, electronic gaming, and other forms of experiential learning. Learners can practice skills and try out new ideas in a safe environment, and thus learn from their mistakes without adverse consequences. Students and instructors from anywhere in the world can participate together in these simulated worlds.

Recommended Links

- Virtual World Comparison Page: http://oz.slinked.net/compare.php
- Second Life: http://secondlife.com/
- ActiveWorlds: http://www.activeworlds.com/
- Open Source Metaverse Project: http://metaverse.sourceforge.net/

DIGITAL GAMES

Computer games are very popular. The most popular types include shoot-em-ups, racing, and sports games that normally include two or more simultaneous players. Games which are used extensively in education include puzzlers, crosswords, sudoku, and types of chess. Role-playing games require users to adopt a character who must reach an end goal, typically by overcoming obstacles and traversing several levels. Strategy games are used for military training as well as for entertainment.

Educational Uses

Educational games are becoming very popular. For the most part, educational games today are used to reinforce learning that has been introduced in traditional ways. Games reinforce learning by their ability to offer immediate feedback and recurring gratification. In addition, they can be used to support students who learn differently. They prolong the interest of learners, keeping them on task while reinforcing the concepts taught. Above all, games motivate learners by making learning enjoyable.

Recommended Links

- Learning Light: e-Learning Centre, Games-based Learning: http://www.e-learningcentre.co.uk/eclipse/Resources/games.htm
- Prensky, M. *Twitchspeed*: http://www.twitchspeed.com/site/news.html
- Carlton College's Game-based Learning: http://serc.carleton.edu/introgeo/games/index.html

LEARNING OBJECTS

Knowledge objects are discrete items that can be integrated into lessons as, for example, a text, graphic, audio, video, or interactive file. *Learning objects* are more highly developed, consisting of discrete lessons, learning units, or courses. For example, a video clip from a speech is a simple knowledge object, but it becomes a learning object when a lesson is added to it. Many different learning objects can be created from one such component; for example, lessons in politics, history, ethics, media studies, and many other subjects could be created from a single video clip. They could subsequently be made available in online databases, using international standards for efficient access by learners. Imagine having seamless access to a vast store of learning objects in the form of animations, videos, simulations, educational games, and multimedia texts, in the same way that Napster users had access to music files.

Educational Uses

The principal benefit of knowledge and learning objects comes from their reusability. As discrete units, they can be incorporated into a wide range of courses or learning scenarios. Their standards-based structure makes them available for use in many different learning management systems and other applications. They also appear to be pedagogically effective:

> NETg compared typical expositive courses with a blend of case-based learning and self-study learning objects. They found that the students who used the objects-based course enjoyed a 41% drop in the time required to complete the task that was taught. (Clark & Rossett, 2002)

Recommended Links

- MERLOT, Welcome to MERLOT!: http://www.merlot.org/merlot/index.htm
- CAREO: http://www.careo.org
- Connexions: http://www.connexions.com
- Longmire, W., A primer on learning objects: http://www.learning circuits.org/2000/mar2000/Longmire.htm
- McGreal & Roberts, 2001. *A primer on metadata for learning objects*: http://auspace.athabascau.ca:8080/dspace/handle/2149/231

CONCLUSION

Does the Web offer us the potential to expand our classrooms and study halls beyond the school grounds, beyond provincial and national boundaries? Can our educational systems evolve into entirely new institutes that support learning by taking full advantage of the emerging technologies? Certainly, distance education and traditional correspondence courses will never be the same because of the World Wide Web. All levels of education stand to benefit from what the Internet has to offer. For educators, web participation could range from simply putting class notes and lecture materials online for absent students, to integrating dynamic online quizzing systems, to preparing classes for upcoming tests and examinations, all the way to enabling learners to participate in highly interactive, true-to-life simulations and games.

With the evolution of more user-friendly applications and interactive content encapsulated in learning objects, one need not be a coding expert to take advantage of the learning opportunities that are becoming available on the Web. Many instructors and learners are already bridging the divide by using hybrid access and delivery models, complete with an Internet component. As the cost of hardware, software, and telecommunications declines, even developing countries can look forward to a future where access to the wealth of the world's knowledge is commonplace. The future has arrived.

REFERENCES

ActiveWorlds. (n.d.). *ActiveWorlds: Home of the 3D Chat, virtual reality build-ing platform web page.* Retrieved September 1, 2007, from http://www. activeworlds.com/

AIM Instant Messenger. (n.d.). *AIM 6.5.* Retrieved March 7, 2008, from http://www.aim.com

AOL Canada. (2002). *AOL Instant Messenger.* Retrieved August 15, 2007, from http://www.aol.ca/aim/index_eng.adp

Athabasca University. (n.d.). *Astronomy 230: Northern Lights/Northern Skies web site.* Retrieved September 1, 2007, from http://astro. whytespace.ca/

Athabasca University. (n.d.). Athabasca University ESL Grammar. *Athabasca University Mobile ESL web site.* Retrieved September 1, 2007, from http://eslau.ca

Athabasca University. (n.d.). *Digital Reading Room.* Retrieved September 1, 2007, from http://library.athabascau.ca/drr/

Audiogalaxy. (2003). About the satellite. Retrieved August 15, 2007, from http://www.audiogalaxy.com/satellite/about.php

Blogdigger. (n.d.). *Blogdigger.com home page.* Retrieved September 27, 2007, from http://www.blogdigger.com/

CAREO. (2002). *Campus Alberta Repository of Educational Objects (CAREO) home page.* Retrieved August 15, 2007, from http://www.careo.org

Carlton College. (n.d.). Game-based learning. In *Starting point: Teaching entry level Geoscience.* Retrieved September 27, 2007, from http://serc. carleton.edu/ introgeo/games/index.html

Clancy, K. J. (n.d.). Super Bowl XXXV: Advertising's night of nights? In *Copernicus Marketing Communications.* Retrieved September 1, 2007, from http://www.copernicusmarketing.com/about/superbowl.shtml

Clark, R., & Rossett, A. (2002, September 10). Learning solutions – learn-ing objects: Behind the buzz. *Chief Learning Officer online.* Retrieved

August 15, 2007, from http://www.clomedia.com/content/templates/clo_feature.asp?articleid=24&zoneid=30

Connexions. (n.d.). *Connexions telecommunications web site.* Retrieved September 1, 2007, http://www.connexions.com

Curriki. (n.d.). *Curriki home page.* Retrieved September 1, 2007, from http://www.curriki.org

CyberTech Media Group. (n.d.). *Streaming video over an Intranet.* Retrieved August 15, 2007, from http://www.cybertechmedia.com/intranet.html

East Coast Music Association. (n.d.). *Your music.* Retrieved September 1, 2007, from http://www.ecma.ca

Edublogs. (n.d.). *Edublogs home page.* Retrieved September 27, 2007, from http://edublogs.org/

Elluminate, Inc. (2007). *Elluminate V.8, web site.* Retrieved August 15, 2007, from http://www.elluminate.com

Fab Four. (n.d.). *Paul McCartney rocks the Cavern Club.* Retrieved September 1, 2007, from http://www.fabfour.addr.com/paulcavern.htm

Feedster. (n.d.). *Feedster 2.0 beta version home page.* Retrieved September 27, 2007, from http://www.feedster.com/

Free-ed.net. (n.d.). *Free-Ed.Net: Free education on the Internet web site.* Retrieved September 26, 2007, from http://www.free-ed.net/free-ed/

Harsch, M.(2003) RSS: The next killer app for education. *The Technology Source.* Retrieved March 7, 2008, from http://technologysource.org/article/rss/

ICQ. (n.d.). *ICQ hompage.* Retrieved September 1, 2007, from http://www.icq.com

ICUII.com. (n.d.). *ICUII 8.0 Video Chat.* Retrieved August 15, 2007, from http://www.icuii.com

Instant Messaging Planet. (n.d.). *Instant Messaging Planet home page.* Retrieved September 27, 2007, from http://www.instantmessaging-planet.com/

International Engineering Consortium. (2003). *Instant messaging (Tutorial).* Retrieved September 27, 2007, from http://www.iec.org/online/tutorials/instant_msg

Internet.com. (n.d.). *Internet.com news channel.* Retrieved September 26, 2007, from http://www.Internet.com/sections/news.html

Kazaa V3.2.5. (n.d.). *Kazaa P2P Desktop.* Retrieved September 1, 2007, from http://www.kazaa.com/us/index.htm

kbears.com. (n.d.). *Knowledge Bears home page*. Retrieved September 27, 2007, from http://www.kbears.com/

Learning Light. (n.d.). Games-based learning. In *Learning light e-learning centre*. Retrieved September 1, 2007, from http://www.e-learningcentre. co.uk/ eclipse/Resources/games.htm

Luidia. (1997). *eBeam*. Retrieved August 15, 2007, from http://www. e-beam.com

Longmire, W. (2000, March). A primer on learning objects. *Learning Circuits: ASTD's online magazine all about e-learning*. Retrieved September 1, 2007, from http://www.learningcircuits.org/2000/mar2000/ Longmire.htm

Malloy, T. (2000). Understanding ANOVA visually. *University of Utah Faculty of Psychology*. Retrieved September 1, 2007, from http://www. psych.utah.edu/stat/introstats/anovaflash.html

Math Open Reference. (n.d.). *Plane geometry*. Retrieved March 7, 2008, from http://ww.mathopenref.com/index.html

McGreal, R., & Roberts, T. (2001). *A primer on metadata for learning objects: Fostering an interoperable environment*. Retrieved April 29, 2004, from http://auspace.athabascau.ca:8080/dspace/handle/2149/231

MERLOT. (n.d.). Welcome to MERLOT! *Multimedia Educational Resource for Learning and Online Teaching (MERLOT) home page*. Retrieved September 1, 2007, from http://www.merlot.org/merlot/index.htm

Microsoft Corporation. (n.d.). *NetMeeting*. Retrieved September 1, 2007, from http://support.microsoft.com/ph/2457

MP3.com Inc. (n.d.). *Top 40 charts*. Retrieved September 1, 2007, from http://www.mp3charts.com

MSN.com. (n.d.). *MSN Messenger.* Retrieved September 1, 2007, from http://webmessenger.msn.com/

Napster, LLC. (n.d.). *Napster.* Retrieved September 1, 2007, from http:// www.napster.ca/

National Museum of American History. (n.d.). Kids: Things to do at home. *National Museum of American History web page*. Retrieved September 27, 2007, from http://americanhistory.si.edu/kids/athome. cfm

NeoPlanet, Inc. *(n.d.). NeoPlanet Browser.* Retrieved September 1, 2007, from http://www.neoplanet.com/site/products/browser.html

Open Source Metaverse Project. (n.d.). *Metaverse open source software project homepage*. Retrieved September 27, 2007, from http://metaverse.source- forge.net/

Oram, A. (Ed.). (2001). *Peer-to-peer: Harnessing the power of disruptive technologies.* Sebastopol, CA: O'Reilly and Associates.

Palm Inc. (n.d.). *Palm products.* Retrieved September 1, 2007, from http://www.palm.com/us/products/

PC-Telephone.com. (n.d.). *PC Telephone web site.* Retrieved September 1, 2007, from http://www.pc-telephone.com

PDA Verticals Corp. (n.d.). *pdaED.com.* Retrieved September 1, 2007, from http://www.pdaed.com/vertical/home.xml

Prensky, M. (n.d.) *Twitchspeed: Reaching younger workers who think differently.* Retrieved March 7, 2008 from http://www.marcprensky.com/writing/Prensky%20-%20Twitch%20Speed.html

Richardson, R. (2005). *RSS – A quick start guide for educators.* Retrieved September 27, 2007, from http://weblogg-ed.com/wp-content/uploads/2006/05/RSSFAQ4.pdf

Romero, S. (2000, July 6). IP: Millions phoning online: Price is right even if quality isn't. *New York Times,* C1. Retrieved September 1, 2007, from http://query.nytimes.com/gst/abstract.html?res=F30F13FD355D0C758CDDAE0894D8404482

RSS Ideas in Education. (n.d.). *Teaching Hack.com's wiki entry.* Retrieved September 1, 2007, from http://www.teachinghacks.com/wiki/index.php?title=RSS_Ideas_in_Education

Richardson, W. (2006). A quick start guide for educators. Retrieved March 7, 2008 from http://weblogg-ed.com/wp-content/uploads/2006/05/RSSFAQ4.pdf

Saba Centra Software. (n.d.). *Saba Centra.com.* Retrieved August 15, 2007, from http://www.saba.com/products/centra/

SecondLife. (n.d.). *SecondLife home page.* Retrieved September 1, 2007, from http://secondlife.com/

Skype. (n.d.). *Skype.com web site.* Retrieved September 1, 2007, from http://www.skype.com/

Streaming Media World. (n.d.). *Streaming Media World.com web site.* Retrieved September 1, 2007, from http://www.streamingmediaworld.com

Syndic8.com. (n.d.). RSS 2.0. *Syndic8.com home page.* Retrieved September 1, 2007, from http://www.syndic8.com/

Technorati.com. (n.d.). *Technorati.com web site.* Retrieved September 27, 2007, from http://technorati.com/

Trussler, B. (1995). Gustav Holst: The Planets Suite. *AquarianAge web site.* Retrieved September 1, 2007, from http://www.aquarianage.org/lore/holst.html

Tucows. (n.d.). *Mobile/PDA.* Retrieved September 1, 2007, from http://tucows.com/PDA

University of Houston. (n.d.). *Blogs in education.* Retrieved September 27, 2007, from http://awd.cl.uh.edu/blog/

University of Washington. (n.d.). *Education at a Distance for Growth and Excellence (EDGE) Streaming Video.* Retrieved September 1, 2007, from http://www.engr.washington.edu/edge/streaming.html

Virtual World Comparison Page. (2004). *Oz World's Virtual World Comparison web page.* Retrieved September 27, 2007, from http://oz.slinked.net/compare.php

WBD Whiteboard. (n.d.). *Department of Computer Science, University College London.* Retrieved August 15, 2007, from http://www-mice.cs.ucl.ac.uk/multimedia/ software/wbd/

WikiinEducation.com. (n.d.). Using wikis in education: A wiki book. *Wikineducation.com web site.* Retrieved September 27, 2007, from http://www.wikiineducation.com/display/ikiw/Home

Wiki Patterns. (n.d.). *Wiki Pattern's blog on wiki use in education.* Retrieved September 27, 2007, from http://www.ikiw.org/

Wikipedia. (n.d.). *Wikipedia homepage.* Retrieved September 1, 2007, from http://www.wikipedia.org

Wikiversity. (n.d.). *Wikiversity home page.* Retrieved September 27, 2007 from http://en.wikiversity.org/wiki/Wikiversity_Reports

YouTube. (n.d.). *YouTube web site.* Retrieved September 1, 2007, from http://www.youtube.com/

ABOUT THE AUTHOR

Rory McGreal is Associate Vice President, Research, at Athabasca University – Canada's Open University. Previously, he was the executive director of TeleEducation New Brunswick, a province-wide bilingual (French/English) distributed distance learning network. Before that, he was responsible for the expansion of *Contact North* (a distance education network in Northern Ontario) into the high schools of the region. His present interest in mobile learning research grows from his investigations into learning objects and standardization for interoperability among different applications and devices. He is leading efforts at AU to build a learning object repository that will facilitate data output to a wide variety of mobile devices.

In the past, he has worked in Canada as a teacher and teacher representative, and abroad in the Seychelles, the Middle East, and Europe in various capacities, as a teacher, union president, ESL technological training co-ordinator, instructional designer, language and computer laboratory co-ordinator, and educational advisor. He was the recipient of the US Wedemeyer Award for excellence as a distance education practitioner.

CHAPTER 7

CHARACTERISTICS OF INTERACTIVE ONLINE LEARNING MEDIA

PATRICK J. FAHY
Athabasca University

INTRODUCTION

This chapter describes technologies used to overcome distance in online learning. Online learning media are tools for cooperation, collaboration, and communication. These devices allow for provision of individual amounts of teaching presence, structure, learning and technology support, orientation to new roles and processes, and interaction (dialogue) with the tutor and others. Multimedia principles applicable to online pedagogy are described, as are the specific characteristics of individual media-based tools. Developments such as new intranets, inexpensive and more robust hardware, and open-source and social-collaborative tools are discussed. The chapter concludes that distance educators should monitor technological trends in society, as such trends tend to translate rapidly from the culture to the (virtual) classroom.

Online technologies for learning and teaching have continued to evolve and become more varied, though more in developed than developing countries (UC College Prep, 2006). In 2006, the Internet was estimated to have achieved a penetration of 65–75% in economically developed countries, while the rate in developing countries was only 10–20% ("Fun Facts," 2007). However, the consensus was emerging that media in widely varying socio-cultural and economic contexts could give "global reach to individual voices...killing once and for all the idea that togetherness requires physical proximity" ("Wireless Nonstop," 2005).

The impact of media has become dominant in teaching and learning. In 2005, the largest university in the United States was the University of Phoenix, a for-profit institution featuring distance and distributed learning; one of the largest law schools in the U.S. was Concord Law School, all of whose courses are online; and the University of Monterey grew rapidly, using teleconferencing to offer courses throughout Mexico and Latin America. Going online has not, however, proven to be a guarantee of growth and success for educational institutions. For example, Columbia University, Wharton University of Pennsylvania, Temple University, and New York University (NYU) all experienced expensive failures in online programming during this same period ("Higher Education Inc.," 2005).

In North America, the personal computer (PC) has been the technology of choice for education and training. Early in the new millennium, it was estimated that two-thirds of Canadians over the age of 15 had used a computer in the previous 12 months; 60% of Canadians (90% of students) had a computer at home; and 50% of Canadians (70% of students) had Internet access from their homes (Statistics Canada, 2001). The computer has become so important in developed countries that Negroponte (an architect and computer scientist best known as the founder and Chairman Emeritus of the Massachusetts Institute of Technology's Media Lab) was able to gain support from countries such as Brazil, Argentina, Libya, Thailand, Nigeria, and China for his *$100 Laptop or One Laptop Per Child* plan, an initiative that was initially regarded as "wildly ambitious" and a "pipe dream" (Surowiecki, 2006). Today, that verdict has begun to appear both technologically and pedagogically accurate ("Today's Startup Lesson," 2007; "Of Internet Cafés," 2008), but by whatever criteria are applied, it is clear that the computer had demonstrated impressive adaptive capabilities worldwide.

At the same time, a better understanding of some of the limitations of computer-based technology has developed. Oliver and McLoughlin (1998) argue that computers alone cannot transform the learning experience, and Vrasidas and McIsaac (1999) warn that "intrusive technologies" could actually create barriers to interaction in the online learning climate. Rovai and Barnum (2003) summarize the debate over "media and learning" with the observation that course design and pedagogy are always more important than media, and Walther, Gay, and Hancock (2005) remind technophiles that previous research should not be ignored in their enthusiasm for new tools.

Experience with new media, as technologies and as innovations, might now allow a more balanced assessment of impacts and shortcomings. Advantages, such as greater flexibility for learners, reduced spending on construction, greater computer and technical literacy of graduates, alleviation of overcrowding on campus, the capability to reuse course materials, more capability for transfer and collaborative credit, improved graduation rates, and more attention to the requirements of special-needs students are counterbalanced by disadvantages, such as concerns about quality, issues related to fair treatment of distance faculty, continuing (but declining) scepticism of some employers about graduates of distance programs, and reduced opportunities for spontaneous interaction between faculty and students (Newby, Stepich, Lehman, & Russell, 2000; Grandzol & Grandzol, 2006). A balanced view of technology considers all potential impacts and outcomes.

This chapter attempts to provide a balanced assessment of common distance teaching and learning media. It is based on the assumption that no medium, however technologically elegant, is *de facto* appropriate for all student audiences or learning contexts. The task of practitioners and the purpose of this chapter are to understand and better appreciate the implications of the various affordances and limitations of technologies, and to monitor their readiness for use in online teaching and learning, as they change and develop.

MEDIA IN DISTANCE LEARNING

The following is a discussion of media's perceived relation to learning, the impact of media on learners' perceptions of isolation (transactional distance vs. community), and the role of teaching presence in meeting individual learning needs. Santoro, Borges, and Santos (2004) describe the key uses of media as coordination, cooperation, and co-construction. This view reflects the importance of both group goals ("common and shared") and individual priorities. While these authors do not use the term "learning communities," they do nicely describe the process by which learning communities are constructed.

Interactive media support communities, based on *what* people do together, not *where* or *when* (Rovai & Barnum, 2003). Community becomes a *process*, not merely a *place* (Cannell, 1999), in which "structured and systematic" social interaction, using media, is essential to significant learning (Fulford & Zhang, 1993; Ragan, 1999; Dilworth & Willis, 2003; Garrison & Cleveland-Innes, 2005; Conrad, 2005).

In addition to helping communities to develop and evolve, media allow individualized learning, reducing *transactional distance* (Moore, 1991). Online learners experience transactional distance differently (if at all – learning styles and preferences affect perceptions of isolation), requiring varying forms and amounts of interaction, including instructor support (Fahy & Ally, 2005). A major implication is that all interaction is not equally useful; interaction should be adjusted to individual needs and preferences (Walther, 1996; Chen & Willits, 1998).

Responding to individual online learning preferences requires skilled uses of media. In most traditional learning, the learner is largely passive (Garrison & Cleveland-Innes, 2005); online learning designs, on the other hand, usually expect the learner to exercise more autonomy and control (Vrasidas & McIsaac, 1999). Research showing that field-dependent students experience less success and satisfaction with online learning because it is less compatible with their preferred communication style confirms the importance of these learner characteristics (Maushak, Chen, Martin, Shaw, & Unfred, 2000). Another difference concerns structure in the learning environment, usually plentiful in face-to-face situations, and potentially essential where sound study skills or habits may be lacking (Loomis, 2000). The finding that undergraduates tend to benefit less than graduate students from distance methods suggests the importance of maturity, and of a "watchful and helpful" instructor stance (Davies, 1981; Bernard et al., 2004).

To summarize: individual participant's success with online communication depends on effective use of the technical resources available, along with the guidance and leadership provided by a skilled instructor-moderator (Garrison & Cleveland-Innes, 2005), and tempered by the learner's own capabilities and preferences for collaborative, cooperative, active, and self-directed learning (Oliver & McLoughlin, 1998). Combined, these factors enable online learners to engage in both collaborative and autonomous adult learning experiences (Knowles, 1980).

It should be emphasized here, however, that individuals do differ and not all students are capable of, nor do they necessarily desire, the same kinds or amounts of autonomy or self-direction in their learning experiences (Grow, 1991). They also differ in important skills. Biesenbach-Lucas (2004) points out that online learners must not only understand ideas and concepts, they must be able to explain them articulately to others, using text. Successful online learners need an environment where they can both acquire and exercise their skills to achieve personal learning goals, and receive compensating media-based assistance and support as required.

The formal learning process should not be a lonely one. Dialogue, as pointed out by Moore (1991), affects perceived isolation and can reduce the need for structure. Mere interaction, however, does not in itself constitute critical discourse (Garrison & Cleveland-Innes, 2005), and talking together does not assure collaboration or "social thinking" among group members (Oliver & McLoughlin, 1998). A key role of instructor-moderators is to provide individually required amounts of structure and dialogue online, through their *teaching presence* (Anderson, Rourke, Garrison, & Archer, 2001).

Teaching presence is the leadership and facilitation necessary for individuals to achieve "meaningful understanding" through interaction and collaboration (Garrison, Anderson, & Archer, 2001). Teaching presence recognizes that students may not spontaneously use discussion effectively, and that collaboration, especially among those still learning its forms, is facilitated by appropriate amounts of structure (Biesenbach-Lucas, 2004). In the terms of Garrison et al. (2001), teaching presence includes design and organization, discourse facilitation, and direct instruction. The inclusion of design as a specific element of the role shows the importance attached by these observers to the systematic provision of structure. It also supports purposeful interaction (discourse) in learning, whether the environment is online or not (Chickering & Gamson, 1987; Beaudoin, 1990; Chickering & Ehrmann, 1996; McCabe, 1997; French, Hale, Johnson, & Farr, 1999).

In summary, two findings in the research on distance education compared with face-to-face instruction, reported by Bernard et al. (2004), are particularly important here, and applicable to the rest of this chapter. First, media research confirms that what the *learner* does with media is more important than what the *teacher* does; second, in terms of student learning outcomes, the *teaching experience* of the instructor does not matter as much as the *instructor's experience with technology*. This finding underscores the importance to online learners of appropriate media and design, supported by media-competent instructors (Mandell & Herman, 1996; Ragan, 1999; Conrad, 2005).

MEDIA, MODES, AND LEARNING

The following section presents principles that affect the impact of multimedia in learning, distinguishes between media and modes of presentation, and then applies these principles to a discussion of specific tools used in online learning.

Multimedia Principles

The impact of multimedia in teaching, whether online or face-to-face, is dependent upon certain principles. Mayer (2001, p. 184) has suggested seven *multimedia principles*, each with implications for online design and instruction:

1. *Multimedia principle:* Students learn better from words with graphics or pictures than from words alone.
2. *Spatial contiguity principle:* Students learn better when corresponding words and pictures are presented closer to each other on the page or screen.
3. *Temporal contiguity principle:* Students learn better when corresponding words and pictures are presented simultaneously rather than successively.
4. *Coherence principle:* Students learn better when extraneous words, pictures, and sounds are excluded rather than included.
5. *Modality principle:* Students learn better from animation and audible narration than from animation and on-screen text.
6. *Redundancy principle:* People have a limited capacity to process visual and auditory material that is presented simultaneously; therefore, students learn better from animation and narration than from a combination of animation, generation, and on-screen text.
7. *Individual differences principle:* Design effects are stronger for low-knowledge learners than for high-knowledge learners, and for high-spatial-ability learners than for low-spatial-ability learners (Note: *Spatial ability* is the mental capacity to generate, maintain, and manipulate visual images.).

These seven principles and variants independently arrived at by others are referred to in the following discussion.

Media and Modes of Learning

Technologies, as *channels* through which *modes* (symbols acting as stimuli) pass, differ in the responses they evoke. For example, text is a mode of presentation. Print-on-paper is one possible *medium* (channel) for text, but there are others: a computer monitor, overhead projection, a television screen, film (moving or still), the screen of a PDA or smart-phone, and so on. Wherever text is used, it retains its characteristic affordances and limitations (highly portable and compact, but demanding of literacy, for example). Despite their differences, useful online teaching and learning media have in common their ability to bring students into timely contact with their tutors, the content, and their peers (Moore, 1989), by reducing transactional distance (Chen & Willits, 1998).

Although similar in producing these outcomes, the differences in how various technologies accomplish their effects have important implications for online teaching practice. The following is a discussion of some salient differences among media and modes of interaction in distance learning and teaching. (The generic term *tools* can be used to avoid unnecessary distinctions between media and modes of teaching and learning.)

Characteristics of Specific Tools

The following discussion of online tools includes print and text, video and graphics, audio, mobile devices such as PDAs and smartphones, and the Internet. The intention is to summarize some of the technical and pedagogical characteristics of each, in the context of their potential usefulness as tools for online teaching and learning. In the next section, promising developments affecting these tools are presented.

Print and Text

There is still no medium more ubiquitous than print, and no mode of presentation more familiar than text in its many forms. Print was part of the first teaching machine – the book – and books were the first mass-produced commodity (McLuhan, 1964). Print was the dominant medium initially in distance education (Scriven, 1993), and distance students have traditionally spent much of their time in solitary study of text-based materials (Bates, 1995). The strengths and weaknesses of text and print include the following:

Strengths:
- Cost: Print is one of the lowest cost one-way technologies (Bates, 1995).

- Flexibility and robustness (Koumi, 1994).
- Portability and ease of production: Especially with desktop publishing, printing has become enormously simpler and its quality much higher (Bates, 1988). Costs may be further reduced with in-house production.
- Stability: Text-only print and online materials can be reorganized and resequenced with relative ease by cut-and-paste operations, using word processors and editors (Kozma, 1991).
- Convenience, familiarity, and economy: Instruction and feedback are facilitated, as are, for the appropriately skilled, higher-order thinking and concept formation (Pittman, 1987).

Weaknesses:

- Print is static, sometimes failing to produce adequate involvement from low-functioning readers; attention, perception, and recall, and active learner participation, may also be reduced.
- Print is relatively non-interactive or non-responsive, and may lead to passive, rote learning.
- Revisions to print materials are more costly and slower than revisions to online databases.
- Print may be seen by some as the "slightly seedy poor relation" of other instructional media (Pittman, 1987).

Text's lack of appeal is somewhat ameliorated by multimedia-based alternatives to reading, and improvements in voice reproduction technologies that make reading less critical for users, including for the visually impaired (Hadenius, 2004; "Speak to Me, " 2006). With these developments, non-print multimedia-based technologies and utilities that translate text to voice are cost-effectively available in situations where high levels of literacy cannot be assumed, where learners prefer or find auditory content more convenient, or where the costs of reading inaccuracies or inefficiencies are high.

Technical developments may affect the economies and appeal of text and print. Downloadable books, such as the *Sony Reader,* HP's *ebook,* the *E Ink initiative,* and the Philips *Readius,* make books more available (though not necessarily inexpensive: Amazon's *Kindle* came to market in 2007 at $400 [Epstein, 2008]). Some books that are not meant to be read from cover to cover (i.e., directories, encyclopaedias, cookbooks, technical references) are increasingly available in easily searchable digital forms (Makris, 2005; "Readius," 2005; Greene, 2006; "Not Bound By Anything," 2007; "White OLEDs Brighten," 2007; "Displays To Keep An Eye On," 2007).

A worrying finding in relation to technology and literacy is the suggestion that extensive technology use early in life may inhibit reading later: a national survey of children in Britain in 1997 found that 23% said they did not like reading, a proportion that by 2003 had risen to 35% ("Catching Up," 2006). This trend obviously must be monitored and its relation, if any, assessed as to the timing of technology introduction.

Given the above, the trend to make online reading materials even more accessible may seem somewhat ironic. *Google*'s book digitizing project, intended to place all non-copyright books on the Web, continues (Roush, 2005), and e-textbooks have been piloted in Canada at Mount Royal College in Calgary and the University of British Columbia in Vancouver (Schmidt, 2007).

Graphics and Video

Earlier research showed that graphics can increase the motivation of users to attend, prompt their perception and aid recall, and assist in the development of higher-order thinking and concept formation (Saettler, 1990; Szabo, 1998). Furthermore, still (non-animated) graphics combine high information content (illustrating abstract or unfamiliar concepts) with relatively low production and distribution costs. Online compression formats, such as JPEG, permit ready distribution of high quality graphics. This factor is particularly relevant when delivery is to PDAs, smart-phones, or other mobile devices with limited bandwidth, display, storage, or memory.

The advantages of various forms of video content in actual practice continue to be debated. In some studies, animation has been shown to result in "more efficient learning" (Szabo, 1998, p. 30). There is, however, also some indication that when compared with "highly imaginative examples and illustrations," the advantages of animated simulations are less obvious (Rieber & Boyce, in Szabo, 1998, p. 30).

General graphics principles include the following (Dwyer, in Szabo, 1998, p. 20):

- Visuals that emphasize the critical details relevant to learning are most effective. Unnecessary visuals may be distracting, especially to learners with limited attention spans or discrimination skills. (See Mayer's [2001] multimedia principles, above.)
- The addition of detail and realism to displays may not increase learning; unnecessary detail can add to learning time without increasing achievement, and increase transfer times. Depending

on the relevance of detail to the learning task, simple line drawings may be superior to photographs or more realistic drawings.

- Winn (in Szabo, 1998) cautions that diagrams, charts, and graphs should not be assumed to be self-explanatory; graphics should include clearly written supporting captions.

Colour is routinely expected in online instructional materials, but designers and user should be aware that, with the exception of instruction that directly employs colour for teaching (e.g., identifying colour-coded elements), there is little evidence that colour enhances learning, and it may even distract some users (Dwyer, in Szabo, 1998, pp. 38–39). Some other generalizations about colour follow:

- Colour may increase the speed at which lists can be searched.
- Too many colours may reduce the legibility of a presentation.
- The most highly recommended colours are vivid versions of green, cyan, white, and yellow.
- Colours may be displayed differently by various receiving technologies.
- End-users should be able to control colour in displays, given the prevalence of colour-blindness (found to some degree in 8% of men and 0.5% of women); the best colour display combinations are blue, black, or red on white; or white, yellow, or green on black (Rockley, 1997).

Based on his review of the data, Szabo (1998) concludes that "the disparity between effectiveness and perceived effectiveness is nowhere as great as it is in the realm of colour" (p. 27).

For online uses of still graphics, the following characteristics of the computer as a delivery medium should be noted by developers (Rockley, 1997):

- A PC screen is about one-third of a piece of paper in display area (hand-held devices may be much smaller), and most display devices are less sharp than the best laser printers or photographic reproductions. What works on paper may not work, without translation or redesign, online. (Also, designers should not assume that users have superior equipment; design should be for displays of mid-range quality.)
- Screen positioning is critical: important information should go to the top-left; the lower-left is the least noticed area of the page/screen.

- Single-colour backgrounds, with a high contrast ratio between the background and the text, are easiest for readers; white or off-white is best for the background (see above).
- Textured backgrounds display differently on various systems, and should be used with care, if at all.
- Sans serif fonts, with mixed upper and lower case, are best for legibility and reading ease.
- The size of the font depends on the purpose. For extended reading, smaller (12–14 point) fonts are suitable; for presenting information that will be skimmed or scanned, larger fonts may be more appropriate.
- Font changes (size and type) can be effective for emphasis, as can capitals, underlining, and especially bolding. The use of colour alone for emphasis should be avoided.

All of the above techniques should be used sparingly, to preserve their impact (Rockley, 1997).

Videoconferencing

According to Roberts (1998), videoconference sessions have the following pedagogic characteristics. They

- add a sense of direct involvement and physical presence among geographically dispersed learners.
- provide quality learning opportunities (as good as or better than those offered by other methods and technologies).
- provide live, interactive learning opportunities to distant sites, including delivery of global expertise to remote learners.
- eliminate or reduce travel time.

The following strengths of videoconferencing for learning and teaching can be exploited with appropriate instructional strategies. Teleconferencing

- fosters social presence and cohesion among users, and may improve motivation.
- permits the sharing of visual resources, including demonstrations.
- makes collaborative learning more attractive and feasible.
- may help in the teaching of abstract, time-protracted, hazardous, or unfamiliar concepts.

Design is important in videoconference-based learning. According to Roberts (1998, p. 96), critical issues in video-based training include

1. proper training of instructors
2. user self-consciousness
3. integration of other media into video-based presentations
4. optimum length of sessions and size of groups
5. session variety
6. technical design and support
7. professional quality visual elements

Cost and accessibility remain issues with online video of all kinds (Bates, 1995). Costs vary enormously in video implementations (Simpson, Pugh, & Parchman, 1993). The Halo videoconferencing system, launched in late 2005 and highly regarded ("Halo: Video Conferencing Done Right," 2006), was priced at its inception at $550,000 to install, and $18,000 per month to run. Its customers, including DreamWorks, HP, PepsiCo and other multinationals, could afford the high costs ("Halo Effect," 2005), but potential educational users likely could not. If one-way video and two-way audio are used, costs drop dramatically, as does the bandwidth needed. The least expensive variant (when amortized over large numbers of users) is one-way video with one-way audio (a broadcast), but there are significant pedagogical implications.

Audio: iPods®, MP3 players, and VoIP

The *iPod®*, Apple's downloadable audio device, has become the standard for portable music (sales reached 100 million units and 2.5 billion songs in 2007 ("Apple Said," 2007). Pontin (2007) regards the iPod® (along with the Palm® and the Blackberry®) as not only highly functional but "beautiful designs" for technology (p. 10). The fact that Apple has made *iTunes®* software compatible with the Microsoft operating system, a previously unthinkable concept, suggests that this protocol and the iPod® will remain this medium's standard ("You've Heard This Song Before," 2006). In comparison, early versions of *Zune*, Microsoft's iPod® competitor, were not capable of receiving podcasts or video downloads (Ulanoff & Costa, 2007).

In Canada, experiments in learning with iPods® have been conducted at the University of Guelph, the University of Saskatchewan, and Carleton University (Hounsell, 2006). Video iPods® provide full lecture downloads (sound and pictures), or live streaming. Some observers question whether these technologies will be commercially successful beyond the early adopters who made them popular initially (Miller,

2006a); others (in one case, a Google vice-president) predict continued evolution and expansion for educational purposes ("Pocket Power," 2007). Standards defining best practices for the design of mobile-learning (m-learning) materials have appeared (Rabin & McCathie-Nevile, 2006), largely driven by security threats (Rubenking, 2007).

With MP3 software, users can download or *rip* (copy), mix, encode, convert, clean, and organize audio files, and then *burn* (copy) them to CDs, DVDs, or flash-based devices like iPods® ("Make Your Own Music," 2004). The MP3 compression algorithm employs "psychoacoustic theories" to achieve smaller file sizes (Murphy, 2005). The software also permits editing and copying of JPEG video files.

Podcasts permit iPods® and MP3 players (or other portable or mobile digital media players) to download lectures or other presentations. Interest in these media appears age-dependent: 50% of 18- to 28-year-olds have engaged in podcasts, compared with only 20% of 29-year-olds and up ("Podcasting Hits the Mainstream," 2005).

Voice-over Internet protocol (VoIP), like the other broadband-dependent technologies in this group, was regarded as a highly promising new technology immediately after it appeared (Pescovitz, 2003). Subsequent rulings in the United States by the Federal Communications Commission (FCC), reducing regulations and oversight of VoIP, made this a "new standard for voice communications" (Miller, 2004, p. 7). Versions of VoIP (*Vonage, Skype*) that allow users to plug traditional telephones into computers to make free long-distance phone calls globally have great social (and educational) potential ("The War of the Wires," 2005). For teaching, synchronous voice-based tools such as *Elluminate* (see http://www.elluminate.com/), *iLinc* (see http://www.ilinc.com/), Dimdim (see http://www.dimdim.com/), and *Paltalk* (see http://www.paltalk.com/) provide a virtual space for learning interactions, including excellent audio, whiteboard (with *PowerPoint* display capability), web-touring and desktop control, textbox chat, small-format videocam, and various teacher tools (i.e., hand-raising, microphone control, individual note exchange, quiz utility, graphing capability for math, and tools for students to provide feedback to the presenter. (Dimdim is open source.)

Audio in teaching raises technical – storage and bandwidth – as well as pedagogical challenges. Online audio can be particularly useful in teaching for several reasons (recall Mayer's [2001] multimedia principles):

• An audio summary of previous material can aid recall, help retention, and promote concept formation and higher-order thinking.

- Although audio in many formats may be asynchronous (DVDs, *iPods®*, blogs), and therefore one-way and non-interactive (like a lecture or a radio broadcast), these access-delivery formats offer significant learner control (Morgan, 2007).
- DVDs persist because they are relatively easy and cheap to produce and ship, but downloadable audio (and video) are more accessible to the end-user, and increasingly preferred by users.
- The mode of presentation most often found in this medium, the human voice, is a familiar and powerful teaching tool.
- Audio may be more motivating than print alone, and together with print may form a powerful alternative and aid to reading alone (Newby et al., 2000).

An important issue in selecting a mix of other technologies for use with synchronous audio is the relative pedagogic importance of *relationship building* vs. *information exchange*. Picard (1999) sees synchronous audio's key contribution as its ability to promote relationship-building. The need for other technologies, according to Picard, is dependent upon the degree to which there is also a need to exchange information (for which, she warns, audio may not be particularly effective).

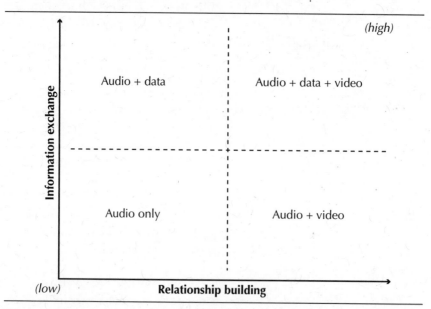

FIGURE 1. Association of synchronous audio, data exchange, and video presence, with information exchange and relationship-building objectives (Picard, 1999)

In Picard's (1999) analysis, when the needs for relationship building and information exchange are both low, audio alone may suffice. When both needs are high, however, audio, video, and data (including text) should all be present. Relationship building can be enhanced by combining audio-conferencing and video with data, especially text. (Text has formidable relationship-building capabilities, as anyone who has ever had a pen pal knows, but literacy is required, and the absence of non-verbal cues, especially body language, can be inhibiting, as noted earlier.) Video increases the likelihood that interaction will promote relationships, while audio alone is less capable of promoting this outcome. Data exchange alone seems to do little to promote relationships among those with access to no other form of interaction.

As technological evolutions permit more audio-based delivery, both synchronous (interactive such as VoIP or wireless) and one-way (streaming) audio research findings become applicable (Szabo, 1998):

- Learning gains from one-way audio alone are, at best, weak (a form of Mayer's [2001] *multimedia principle*).
- Learners possessing higher verbal skills usually do not benefit from audio added to text (Mayer's *individual differences principle*).
- There are little or no apparent immediate recall effects between text-only and text-plus audio, except that, on occasion, audio may lengthen the time required to complete instruction (Mayer's *modality* and *redundancy principles*).
- The quality and utility of digitized speech depend upon the amount of compression, the sampling rate, the bandwidth available, and the quality of the device.
- Users may relatively quickly become accustomed to synthetic speech; however, more cognitive effort is needed, and increased demands on short-term memory may reduce retention. (Synthesized speech may be more useful in reading back a learner's work, for example from a word processor, than in presenting unfamiliar learning content.)
- For general audiences, the possible benefits of audio must be weighed against the increased costs. Exceptions include uses such as language training, music instruction, and as an aid to the visually impaired.
- Where possible, the learner should be able to decide whether or not to use available audio (another form of Mayer's individual differences principle).

PDAs

The probable future direction, at least in the short term, of video for online teaching can be seen in *personal digital assistants* (PDAs), smart phones, and other handheld devices. PDAs are small, wireless, highly mobile Internet receivers which, despite their size, can deliver movie-length video. On PDAs, a feature film requires a megabyte of memory for each minute, permitting a 128 Mb memory card to store two hours of video (Rupley, 2003). The emergence of very small, high-capacity (2GB) *microdrives* boosted the popularity of PDAs for a time (Rupley, 2005), but the emergence of highly capable *smart phones* has led some observers to comment that PDAs might become a "dying breed" (DeFeo, 2004; "The Device That Ate Everything?" 2005).

High bandwidth is essential for mobile video. Ultrabroadband, wireless video cellphones support voice- and email, web access, MP3 audio, picture-taking capability, video clips, and, of course, telephony. With robust support, high broadband speeds and an accepted mobile wireless standard ("Mobile Net," 2007), and assuming the threat of phone viruses can be controlled (Hutson, 2005; "Airborne Outbreak," 2005; "Why Wait for WiMax?" 2005), a major delivery vehicle for distance education and training may evolve from this technology (Copeland, Malik, & Needleman, 2003). Paulsen (2003) and Rekkedal (2005) report the use of devices such as pocket PCs/PDAs with portable keyboards and mobile phones at Norway's NKI, as part of accessibility projects (although Rekkedal added that the team was still "uncertain" as of his report whether such technologies comprised a mobile learning "future solution").

The Internet

As noted at the outset of this chapter, *online learning* almost always denotes learning on the Internet, which offers both advantages and challenges to educators and trainers. The advantages arise from the Internet's enor-mous capacity to link participants with information and with each other (Haughey & Anderson, 1998). Problems with navigation, structure, inter-activity, complexity, security, stability, and time wasted by undisciplined or confused users does affect its usefulness, however.

The Internet is potentially a powerful linking and communication vehicle, surpassing one hundred million web sites in 2007 ("Watching the Web Grow Up," 2007). Heinich, Molenda, Russell, and Smaldino (1996) suggest that the Internet's power lies in its capacity for providing rapidly growing numbers of connections to potentially engrossing, multi-sensory experiences, while remaining adaptable to individual needs. The fact that the Net can be modified by teachers themselves, can be tailored to individual students' needs, and can support meaningful collaboration and interaction also makes it a potentially powerful learning tool.

At the same time, there are weaknesses. The Web's inherent lack of structure may result in some users getting unintentionally "lost in cyberspace" or making poor use of their time (surfing or exploring interesting but irrelevant minutiae). Also, especially in "Web 1.0" (Borland, 2007), Internet materials may lack interactivity, providing merely a one-way presentation of information. The reliability of information on the Internet may also be suspect. Finally, successful use of the Internet currently demands proficient literacy and computer skills.

The Internet offers a means for gaining the attention of learners, and of presenting opportunities for focusing perceptions and prompting recall. Learner participation can also be supported, especially with computer-mediated communications (CMC) and the use of collaborative learning projects. Providing instruction and assuring appropriate organization, sequencing, and higher-order outcomes are less easily accomplished with the Internet, for reasons discussed below.

Web 2.0 and the emerging Web 3.0 are intended to address some of these problems. Web 2.0 is characterized by tagging, social networks, and user generation of content, using tools such as Wikis, blogs, and podcasts. Web 2.0 is called the "writing web," because it allows individual users to create and circulate their own materials (Borland, 2007). The present web (Web 1.0) was originally planned to be two-way, but as it grew exponentially in the late 1990s, publishing tools failed to keep up with web browsers in ease of use; now, with the rise of blogs and wikis, the balance is being redressed ("Watching the Web Grow Up," 2007).

Growth and acceptance of Web 3.0, called the "Semantic Web," is predicated on three areas of development: 1) the spread of Internet access to millions of new users via mobile devices; 2) growing interest in this technology's potential socially; and 3) the practice of consistently labelling information so that it makes sense to machines as well as people ("Watching the Web Grow Up," 2007). The Semantic Web incorporates widespread mobile broadband access to full web services, including technologies that allow computers to organize and draw conclusions from online data. In Web 3.0, online content is encoded so that computers are capable of locating and extracting the information. In this version of the Web, machines will be able to read web pages much as humans do, and software agents will "troll the Net and find what they're looking for" in an Internet that will resemble "one big database" (Metz, 2007, p. 76).

Many authorities believe the above cannot happen within the existing Internet, due to the fact that the present Web has become increasingly "fragile" (Talbot, 2005), and because of the immense challenge of accurately ascribing standardized forms of metadata to the millions of items already on the Internet.

PROMISING DEVELOPMENTS

Developments such as new versions of the Internet, more equable Internet access globally, social software, and the open-source movement constitute promising new developments in media evolution.

New Internets

New versions of the Internet are being developed to address the weaknesses of the old. Because of problems described above, both Canada and the U.S. have projects to create a new high-speed Internet to serve the research and academic communities worldwide. As well, the National Science Foundation (NSF) in the U.S. is studying the feasibility of developing "clean-slate" Internet architectures that will be secure, accommodate new technologies, and be easier to manage (characteristics the current Internet manifestly lacks). Talbot (2005) reports that among these are the university-based programs PLANETLAB (Princeton), EMULAB (University of Utah), DETER (USC, Information Sciences Institute), and WINLAB (Rutgers). Two National Science Foundation initiatives are the Global Environment for Networking Innovations (GENI), and Future Internet Design (FIND). GENI is a redesign project for Internet protocols and applications, and FIND is intended to generate a new vision of the future Internet ("Reinventing the Internet," 2006). Shibboleth, an open-standard authentication system under development at Brown University, is an element of the Internet2 project, and a sign that the new Internets will better address present security and management concerns (Talbot, 2006a).

All of the above initiatives are prompted by various assumptions, some of which are applicable to virtual and distance education:
- Present world-wide Internet growth, already very high, will continue.

- World-wide Internet-based research, and academic, government, and corporate cooperation and collaboration, will continue and increase.
- The Internet has proven it is a powerful tool for productive collaboration and communication.
- Governments have a responsibility, in the national interest, to fund and maintain such a network (NGI, 2001).
- Ease of use, power/speed, cost, and accessible content determine the growth of wireless Internet developments (Machrone, 2001).
- Designers will assure that new Internets will not be more failure-prone as they become more complex, employing more leading-edge technologies (Talbot, 2005; "The Next Internet," 2005).

Reality-based Internet Access for the Developing World

In much of the developing world, or where necessary infrastructure elements (such as reliable power) cannot be assumed, sophisticated computer-based communications and access systems are not feasible. In such instances, technologies must recognize both socioeconomic and technological issues. Alternate-powered technologies are more suitable, in the form of wind-up medical devices ("Power From The People," 2008), communications tools ("Human-Powered Health Care," 2004), radios (Freeplay Foundation, 2006), and computers that derive their power from springs (Miller, 2006b), or even from the energy of the typist's keystrokes (Pontin, 2005). The ability of developing societies to skip over stages of infrastructure growth (adopting wireless, for example, without first becoming fully "wired") is a major reason that emerging nations move more quickly than developed ones to adopt new technologies ("Of Internet Cafés," 2008).

Other technologies, such as the cellphone, may also turn out to be more useful than computers in some societies. There were 2.8 billion active cellular telephones (cellphones) worldwide in 2007 ("A World of Connections," 2007), and purchases of cellphones that also function as PDAs vastly increased in the preceding two-year period (Roush, 2005). At that time, some 80% of the world's population lived within range of a cellphone network, but only 25% owned a cellphone ("Less is More," 2005). These facts make cellphones a potentially important global wireless communications technology, a "genuine productivity tool" (Kamen, 2003) capable, in the minds of some, of spurring economic growth and timely learning ("Cellphones vs. PDAs," 2004). Some believe the economic impact of cellphones could powerfully affect social development in third-world countries, improving gross domestic product (GDP) and reducing poverty ("Calling an End to Poverty," 2005). The potential of this technology can be seen in the Bangladesh Grameen Phone project ("Power to the People," 2006; "Yogurt or Cucumber?" 2008); the TradeNet initiative in Africa, which exploits the fact that over 60% of the population now have cellular coverage – expected to rise to 85% by 2010 ("Buy, Cell, Hold," 2007; "A Cash Call," 2007); and the benefits that downloading books from satellites to Linux-based PDAs, avoiding print altogether, has had on the availability of quality training resources in rural areas of developing countries (Talbot, 2006b; "Calling For a Rethink," 2006).

Social Software

Social software refers to software that supports group interaction (Shirky, in Owen, Grant, Sayers, & Facer, 2006). Lefever (cited in Anderson, 2005) is less general, and suggests the educational potential of these tools: "Where normal software links people to the inner workings of a computer or network, social software links people to the inner workings of each others' thoughts, feelings and opinions" (p. 4).

Boyd (in Owen, et al., 2006) refines the definition further, specifying three types of interaction support provided by social software:

- Support for *conversational interaction between individuals or groups*, from real-time instant messaging to asynchronous collaborative teamwork, including blogs.
- Support for *social feedback*, in which a group rates the contributions of others, producing a *digital reputation* for participants.
- Support for *social networks* to explicitly create and manage participants' personal relationships, and to help them develop new ones.

Owen and colleagues (2006) have observed that social software also causes changes to community function: the group benefits from others acting in more social, community-oriented ways – the social whole becomes greater than the sum of its parts. This concept reflects the belief that important knowledge and significant learning opportunities may be missing from mainstream institutions and traditional learning environments, and that the design of most learning management systems and related software fosters isolation and competition rather than community. Social software emphasizes the importance of interpersonal interaction in groups that are dedicated to learning and teaching. There is the expectation that learning structures, including tools and environments, will reflect and facilitate social equality, collaboration, cooperation, and mutual support.

In education and training situations, social software encourages *collaborative, community-oriented learning,* based on *voluntary affiliation and participation.* Members join these learning groups motivated by intrinsic interests, rather than the pursuit of credentials, credits, or other extrinsic motivations. Instead of being assigned membership in classes or programs, participants seek out others who possess the knowledge that matches their needs or interests, join voluntarily, and, using social software systems, contribute to group success by learning and, when appropriate, teaching (Wikipedia, n.d.a). Groups are based upon trust and are democratically governed. Conrad (2005) found that such groups, drawing on the group's resources, were more able to identify – and survive – poor teaching.

Any medium that promotes collaboration, group formation, and support could qualify as social software. Anderson (2005) suggests that social software is defined by the activities it supports, such as "meeting, building community, providing mentoring and personal learning assistance, working collaboratively on projects or problems, reducing communication errors, and supporting complex group functions" (p. 4), and by its other affordances, such as "combinations of blogging, portfolio management, discussion and file sharing, group file management, and search and linking capacity" (p. 8).

Presently, examples of social software include instant messaging, Internet relay chat (IRC), Internet forums, blogs (weblogs), wikis, social network services, peer-to-peer social networks, massively multiplayer online games, virtual presence sites, even social shopping applications (Wikipedia, n.d.a). (Note: Wikis are "an effective tool for *collaborative authoring,*" and "a type of *web site* that allows the visitors themselves to easily add, remove, and otherwise *edit* and change some available content, sometimes without the need for registration" [Wikipedia, n.d.b])

Social software, though popular, has its critics. Dvorak (2006) calls virtual immersion experiences "a complete waste of time," since "there's no hint of reality and its consequences in these worlds" (p. 138). *Second Life* itself has been called "lawless" (Talbot, 2008). Recognizing these criticisms, New York University planned a "Facebook in the Flesh" session for incoming freshmen in 2007, believing that undergraduates immersed in online interaction might need help relating to classmates face-to-face (Shulman, 2007).

Further, some research shows that social networks do not benefit from Metcalfe's Law, which, in relation to traditional networks, holds that the value of a network is proportional to the square of the number of users. Social networks, on the other hand, appear to lose value as membership increases; one Silicon Valley forecaster comments, "the value of the social network is defined not only by who's on it, but by who's excluded" ("Social graph-iti," 2007, p. 83). By this perspective, exclusivity, not accessibility, is an online social network value (Costa, 2007), because "people want to hobnob with the chosen few, not to be spammed by random friend-requests" (p. 83).

Finally, there is also evidence that participation in some of these more self-revelatory virtual environments may be short-lived for many who try them. Dalton (2007) reports that, while 175,000 new blogs were started daily in early 2007, half of those blogs were abandoned within three months, leaving 200 million inactive blogs on the Internet. While some observers disagree (citing the trend to commercialization and corporate uses of blogs as an indication of their vitality), Dalton predicted that the number of authentically active blogs would level off after 2007, at about 30 million.

Open Source

Open source began as a reaction to the power that proprietary software makers were seen to wield (sometimes symbolized by Microsoft's alleged monopolistic practices). Open-source supporters advocate the use of software that is open to modification, and is free (or nearly so), as a way of supporting experimentation and competition, features they regard as lacking in both the organizations and the software packages of the big software producers. While open source may have begun as a reaction, it has become a credible movement, representing a growing and diverse community of seasoned information technology professionals who, because so many are involved and check each other's work, produce software of consistently high relative quality (Constantine, 2007; Goldman, 2007).

The appeal of open source is broad: the movement is supported by companies such as Sun Microsystems, AOL, American Express, Novell, and Bank of America, as well as the UK's Ministry of Defense and the French tax authority. Corporate users of Linux, the open-source operating system, include Orbitz, Schwab, L.L Bean, and the New York Stock Exchange; Linux is supported by IBM, Hewlett-Packard, Dell, Intel, Oracle, and Google, (Null, 2003; Miller, 2003; Ferguson, 2005; "Business,"

2005). In late 2006, Linux was selected to become the operating system of the world's fastest computer (Rupley, 2006). It was predicted that, by 2008, 6% of operating systems shipped by commercial vendors would be Linux-based (Roush, 2004). Linux server software was growing at 40% annually in 2005, while the rate for similar Windows products was less than 20% and Unix usage was declining (Ferguson, 2005). The suggestion that Linux servers were considerably more resistant to malware attacks than Windows servers helped to pique interest (Vaughan-Nichols, 2005).

The desire to address the problem of too-centralized software development may ironically contain another serious issue, however:

> Because there are so many individual voices involved in an open-source project, no one can agree on the right way to do things. And, because no one can agree, every possible option is built into the software, thereby frustrating the central goal of the design, which is, after all, to understand what to leave *out*. (Gladwell, 2005, 132)

There may also be questions of intellectual property rights in open-source products, since no one author is completely responsible for them ("Open, But Not As Usual," 2006). Obviously, if not addressed, these criticisms could constitute serious obstacles to the eventual success of the open-source movement. There are also strong opposing arguments for the standards, support, and sheer endurance of commercial software, such as Windows (Miller, 2005).

CONCLUSION

Online learning continues to mature in relation to media and technologies, and to an appropriate pedagogy for their use. There are many outstanding and, in some cases, vexing issues: costs, though declining, still limit widespread access, especially in the developing world, and for those whose purchases (including seemingly constant upgrades) are not subsidized; further training remains a need for many (teachers, trainers, and learners) to assure mature use of online media and systems (Garfinkel, 2003; Bernard, et al., 2004); administrators and policy-makers often misread or oversell the likely impacts of going online (Nikiforuk, 1997; Dvorak, 2002), resulting in confusion, disappointment, and, in the worst cases, recriminations and disillusionment; systems and inter-faces generally remain too complex (Fahy, 2005); and the relation of learning outcomes to technology use, for specific populations and in particular circumstances, remains unclear, at least partially because it is under-theorized, (Garrison, 2000; Walther, et al., 2005), but also because so much research on technology use in distance learning is weak (Rovai & Barnum, 2003).

At the same time, there are promising signs, especially in post-secondary education and training ("Higher Education Inc.," 2005; Rhey, 2007). Access to the Internet is improving, especially for some previously disenfranchised groups (U.S. Department of Commerce, 2004; OECD, 2007; Miller, 2006b; "Fun Facts," 2007). For example, women as a group have for some time exceeded men in numbers of Internet users (Pastore, 2001). Some consensus about good practice is emerging, including models of clearly successful uses of technology to meet persistent user (including learner) needs ("Inculcating Culture," 2006). And much needed in-service training is increasingly available to users and potential users (Biesenbach-Lucas, 2004).

Will these useful trends continue? Change has been a constant in the online learning world, so that as technical capabilities come out of the lab, they are quickly packaged and made available to users by entrepreneurs. Education could keep pace and avoid the costs and uncer-tainties of invention by following the technological lead of the corporate sector, and of society in general, and learning from their experiences.

Whether online learning follows this path or not, it has a good chance to grow, because online access to training using various media is an established social and economic reality globally ("The Best is Yet To Come," 2005). Whether one deplores or applauds this fact, it is still true that as a society, we increasingly go online for a widening array of purposes, including learning. The implications for every educator – espe-cially distance educators and trainers – are becoming more obvious.

REFERENCES

A cash call. (2007, February 17). *The Economist, 382*(8516), 71–73.

Airborne outbreak. (2005). *Technology Review, 108*(4), 22.

A world of connections. (2007, April 28). Special Report on Telecoms. *The Economist, 383*(8526), 3–4.

Anderson, T. (2005). Distance learning – Social software's killer app? Paper presented at the *Open and Distance Learning Association of Australia (ODLAA) Conference.* November, 9–11, 2005, Adelaide, South Australia. Retrieved May 10, 2007, from www.unisa.edu.au/odlaaconference/ PPDF2s/13%20odlaa%20-%20Anderson.pdf

Anderson, T., Rourke, L., Garrison, D. R. & Archer, W. (2001). Assessing teaching presence in a computer conferencing context. *Journal of Asynchronous Learning Networks, 5*(2), 1–17.

Apple said. (2007, April 14). *The Economist, 383*(8524), 7.

Bates, A. W. (1988). Technology for distance education: A 10-year prospective. *Open Learning, 3*(3), 3–12.

Bates, A. W. (1995). *Technology, open learning and distance education.* New York: Routledge.

Beaudoin, M. (1990). The instructor's changing role in distance education. *The American Journal of Distance Education, 4*(2), 21–29.

Bernard, R., Abrami, P., Lou, Y., Borokhovski, E., Wade, A., Wozney, L., Wallet, P. A., Fiset, M., & Huang, B. (2004). How does distance education compare to classroom instruction? A meta-analysis of the empirical literature. *Review of Educational Research, 74*(3), 379–439.

Biesenbach-Lucas, S. (2004). Asynchronous web discussions in teacher training courses: Promoting collaborative learning – or not? *Association for the Advancement of Computing In Education, 12(2).* Retrieved August 29, 2007, from http://www.aace.org/pubs/aacej/temp/03lucas155-170.pdf

Borland, J. (2007). A smarter web. *Technology Review, 110*(2), 64–71.

Business. (2005). *The Economist, 377*(8447), 9.

Buy, cell, hold. (2007, January 27). *The Economist, 382*(8513), 48.

Calling an end to poverty. (2005, July 9). *The Economist, 376*(8434), 51–52.

Calling for a rethink. (2006). *The Economist, 378*(8462), 57–58.

Cannell, L. (1999). Review of [distance education] literature. Winnipeg: Distance Education Association of Theological Schools. Unpublished paper.

Catching up. (2006, December 23). *The Economist, 381*(8509), 86–87.

Cell phones vs. PDAs. (2004). *Business 2.0, 5*(1), 32.

Chen, Y. & Willits, F. (1998). A path analysis of the concepts in Moore's theory of transactional distance in a videoconferencing environment. *Journal of Distance Education, 13*(2), 51–65.

Chickering, A. & Ehrmann, S. (1996). Implementing the seven principles: Technology as lever. *American Association for Higher Education Bulletin,*

49(2), 3–6. Retrieved August 29, 2007, from http://www.tltgroup.org/ programs/seven.html

Chickering, A. & Gamson, Z. (1987, March). Seven principles for good practice in undergraduate education. *AAHE Bulletin, 39,* 3–7.

Conrad, D. (2005). Building and maintaining community in cohort-based online learning. *Journal of Distance Education, 20,*(1), 1–20.

Constantine, L. (2007, January/February). The open-source solution. *Technology Review, 110*(1), 26.

Copeland, M., Malik, O. & Needleman, R. (2003). The next big thing. *Business 2.0, 4*(6), 62–64.

Costa, D. (2007, November 6). My Space is not your space. *PC Magazine, 26*(21/22), 62.

Dalton, A. (2007, March 6). All typed out? *PC Magazine, 26*(5), 17–18.

Davies, R. (1981). *The rebel angels.* Toronto: Penguin.

DeFeo, J. M. (2004). Sony halts the Clie. *PC Magazine, 23*(13), 17.

Dilworth, R. L., & Willis, V. J. (2003). *Action learning: Images and pathways.* Malabar, FL: Kreiger.

Displays to keep an eye on. (2007, March 10). *The Economist, 382*(8519), Monitor 4–Monitor 6.

Dvorak, J. C. (2002). The nine assassins of broadband. *PC Magazine, 21*(2), 55.

Dvorak, J. C. (2006, December 26). Unreal life? Get a life. *PC Magazine, 25*(23), 138.

Epstein, J. (2008, March/April). What's wrong with the Kindle? *Technology Review, 111*(2), 12–13.

Fahy, P. J. (2005). Two methods for assessing critical thinking in computer-mediated communications (CMC) transcripts. *International Journal of Instructional Technology and Distance Learning, 2*(3) (March). Retrieved June 1, 2005, from http://www.itdl.org/Journal/Mar_05/ article02.htm.

Fahy, P. J., & Ally, M. (2005). Student learning style and asynchronous computer-mediated conferencing. *American Journal of Distance Education, 19*(1), 5–22.

Ferguson, C. (2005). How Linux could overthrow Microsoft. *Technology Review.com.* Retrieved May 17, 2005, from http://www.technologyreview. com/ articles/05/06/issue/feature_linux.asp?p=1

Freeplay Foundation. (2006). What is Lifeline radio? Retrieved August 29, 2007, from http://www.freeplayfoundation.org/

French, D., Hale, C., Johnson, C. & Farr, G. (Eds.) (1999). *Internet-based learning.* London: Kogan Page.

Fulford, C. P., & Zhang, S. (1993). Perception of interaction: The critical predictor in distance education. *The American Journal of Distance Education, 7*(3), 8–21.

Fun Facts: Worldwide Internet usage. (2007, March 6). *PC Magazine, 26*(5), 21.

Garfinkel, S. (2003). Class struggle. *Technology Review, 106*(3), 33.

Garrison, D. R. (2000). Theoretical challenges for distance education in the twenty-first century: A shift from structural to transactional issues. *International Review of Research in Open and Distance Learning, 1*(1). Retrieved August 29, 2007, from http://www.irrodl.org/index. php/irrodl/article/view/2/333

Garrison, D. R., Anderson, T., & Archer, W. (2001). Critical thinking, cognitive presence, and computer conferencing in distance education. *The American Journal of Distance Education, 15*(1), 7–23.

Garrison, D. R. & Cleveland-Innes, M. (2005). Facilitating cognitive presence in online learning: Interaction is not enough. *The American Journal of Distance Education, 19*(3), 133–148.

Gladwell, M. (2005, September 5). The bakeoff. *The New Yorker,* 124–133.

Goldman, R. (2007). Open source and you. *Technology Review, 110*(2), 34.

Grandzol, J. R., & Grandzol, C. J. (2006). Best practices for online business education. *International Review of Research in Open and Distance Learning, 7*(1). Retrieved August 29, 2007, from http://www.irrodl. org/index.php/irrodl/article/view/246/ 475

Greene, K. (2006, March/April). Stretchable silicon. *Technology Review, 109*(1), 70.

Grow, G. (1991). Teaching learners to be self-directed. *Adult Education Quarterly, 41*(3), 125–149.

Hadenius, P. (2004). No. 6,529,871 – A voice of approval. *Technology Review, 107*(4), 68.

Halo effect. (2005, December 17). *The Economist, 377*(8457), 63.

Halo: Video conferencing done right. (2006, March 7). *PC Magazine, 25*(4), 22.

Haughey, M., & Anderson, T. (1998). *Networked learning: The pedagogy of the Internet.* Montreal: Chenelière/McGraw-Hill.

Heinich, R., Molenda, M., Russell, J. D., & Smaldino, S. E. (1996). *Instructional media and technologies for learning* (5th ed.). Englewood Cliffs, NJ: Prentice Hall.

Higher Education Inc. (2005). *The Economist, 376*(8443), 19–20.

Hounsell, K. (2006, February). Lectures just a download away. *University Affairs*, p. 5.

Human-powered health care. (2004). *The Economist, 373*(8404),14–50.

Hutson, S. (2005). Wireless devices catch bad code through the air and then infect supposedly secure computer systems. *Technology Review.com*. Retrieved April 19, 2005, from http://www.technologyreview.com/ articles/05/05/ issue/feature_emerging.asp?p=9

Inculcating culture. (2006, January 21). *The Economist, 378*(8461), 11–12.

Kamen, D. (2003). Technology where it's needed. *Business 2.0, 4*(6), 124.

Knowles, M. (1980). *The modern practice of adult education: From pedagogy to andragogy* (2nd edition). New York: Association Press.

Koumi, J. (1994). Media comparisons and deployment: A practitioner's view. *British Journal of Educational Technology, 25*(1), 41–57.

Kozma, R. (1991). Learning with media. *Review of Educational Research, 61*(2), 179–211.

Less is more. (2005, July 9). *The Economist, 376*(8434), 11.

Loomis, K. D. (2000). Learning styles and asynchronous learning: Comparing the LASSI model to class performance. *Journal of Asynchronous Learning Networks, 4*(1), 23–32.

Machrone, B. (2001). The price of wireless shopping. *PC Magazine, 20*(6), 77.

Make your own music. (2004). *PC Magazine, 23*(11), 28.

Makris, S. (2005, June 18). Creative new designs make computing fun. *The Edmonton Journal*, F-1.

Mandell, A., & Herman, L. (1996). From teachers to mentors: Acknowledging openings in the faculty role. In R. Mills & A. Tait (Eds.), *Supporting the learner in open and distance learning* (pp. 3–18). London: Pitman Publishing.

Maushak, N., Chen, H. H., Martin, L., Shaw, B., & Unfred, D. (2000). Distance education: Looking beyond the no significant difference. Annual proceedings of *Selected Research and Development Papers, National Convention of the Association for Educational Communications and Technology*, Denver, October. ERIC Document: ED 455 779.

Mayer, R. E. (2001). *Multimedia learning*. New York: Cambridge University Press.

McCabe, M. (1997). *Online classrooms: Case studies of computer conferencing in higher education*. Unpublished PhD dissertation. Columbia University Teachers' College.

McLuhan, M. (1964). *Understanding media: The extensions of man.* Toronto: McGraw-Hill.

Metz, C. (2007, April 10). Web 3.0. *PC Magazine, 26*(7/8), 74–79.

Miller, M. J. (2003). IBM takes on the world. *PC Magazine, 22*(16), 8.

Miller, M. J. (2004). Consumer electronics leads the way. *PC Magazine, 23*(4), 5.

Miller, M. J. (2005). Windows at 20: Competition is a good thing. *PC Magazine, 24*(19/20), 7–8.

Miller, M. J. (2006a, February 7). The phone as a platform. *PC Magazine, 25*(2), 7–8.

Miller, M. J. (2006b, June 27). Will digital access make the world a better place? *PC Magazine, 25*(11), 61.

Mobile net. (2007, January). *PC Magazine, 26*(1/2), 16.

Moore, M. G. (1989). Three types of interaction. *American Journal of Distance Education, 3*(2), 1–6. Retrieved August 29, 2007, from http://www.ajde.com/ Contents/vol3_2.htm#editorial

Moore, M. G. (1991). Editorial: Distance education theory. *The American Journal of Distance Education, 5*(3), 1-6.

Morgan, R. (2007, March 20). Believe the hype. *PC Magazine, 26*(6), 87.

Murphy, D. (2005). Audio format glossary. *PC Magazine, 24*(12), 122.

Newby, T., Stepich, D., Lehman, J., & Russell, J. (2000). *Instructional technology for teaching and learning* (2nd ed.). Upper Saddle River, NJ: Merrill.

NGI. (2001). Next Generation Internet (NGI) Initiative. Retrieved August 29, 2007, from http://ecommerce.hostip.info/pages/794/Next-Generation-Internet-Initiative-NGI.html

Nikiforuk, A. (1997, Oct. 4). The digerati are bluffing. *The Globe and Mail,* D15.

Not bound by anything. (2007, March 24). *The Economist, 382*(8521), 93–94.

Null, C. (2003). At Orbitz, Linux flies first-class. *Business 2.0, 4*(6), 53.

OECD. (2007). *Key ICT indicators.* Retrieved August 29, 2007, from http://www.oecd.org/document/23/0,3343,en_2825_495656_33987543_1_1_1_1,00.html

Of Internet cafés and power cuts. (2008, February 9). *The Economist, 386*(8566), 75–77.

Oliver, R. & McLoughlin, C. (1998). Interactivity in telelearning environments. *Open Praxis: The Bulletin of the International Council for Open and Distance Education, 1,* 9–13.

Open, but not as usual. (2006, March 18). *The Economist, 378*(8469), 73–75.

Owen, M., Grant, L., Sayers, S., & Facer, K. (2006). *Social software and learning: An open education report from Futurelab*. Retrieved August 29, 2007, from http://www.futurelab.org.uk/resources/documents/ opening_education/Social_Software_report.pdf

Pastore, M. (2001). Women maintain lead in Internet use. *Cyberatlas.com*. Retrieved July 18, 2002, from http://cyberatlas.Internet.com/big_ picture/demographics/ article/05901_78679100.html

Paulsen, M. F. (2003). *Online education and Learning Management Systems: Global e-learning in a Scandinavian perspective*. Oslo: NKI Forlaget.

Pescovitz, D. (2003). The best new technologies of 2003. *Business 2.0, 4*(10), 109–115.

Picard, J. (1999, June 10). *Creating virtual work teams using IP videoconferencing*. Presentation at the Distance Education Technology '99 Workshop, Edmonton, Alberta.

Pittman, V. V. (1987). The persistence of print: Correspondence study and the new media. *The American Journal of Distance Education, 1*(1), 31–36.

Pocket power. (2007, January). *PC Magazine, 26*(1/2), 16.

Podcasting hits the mainstream. (2005). *PC Magazine, 24*(9), 23.

Pontin, J. (2005). Mediating poverty. *Technology Review, 108*(8), 14.

Pontin, J. (2007). On beautiful machines. *Technology Review, 110*(3), 10.

Power from the people. (2008, February 9). *The Economist, 386*(8566), 87.

Power to the people. (2006, March 11). Technology Quarterly. *The Economist, 378*(8468), 37–38.

Rabin, J., & McCathie-Nevile, C. (2006.) *Mobile web best practices 1.0: Basic guidelines*. Retrieved August 29, 2007, from http://www.w3.org/TR/ mobile-bp/

Ragan, L. C. (1999). Good teaching is good teaching: An emerging set of guiding principles and practices for the design and development of distance education. *CAUSE/EFFECT Journal, 22*(1).

Readius: The ultimate e-reader? (2005). *PC Magazine, 24*(19/20), 24.

Reinventing the Internet. (2006, March 11). Technology Quarterly. *The Economist, 378*(8468), 32–33.

Rekkedal, T. (2005). Online flexible distance education or Internet based e-learning – The evolutionary development of the NKI Internet college. Presentation, *eLearning Project (Exemplo – Elex) Conference*, Rome,

December 15-16. Retrieved August 29, 2007, from http://www.nki. no/eeileo/research/nki/tor1.htm

Rhey, E. (2007, January). Top 10 wired colleges. *PC Magazine, 26*(1/2), 112–123.

Roberts, J. (1998). *Compressed video learning: Creating active learners.* Toronto: Chenelière/McGraw-Hill.

Rockley, A. (1997). *Intranet publishing.* Stouffville, ON: The Rockley Group.

Roush, W. (2004, April). An alternative to Windows. *Technology Review. com.* Retrieved October 1, 2007, from http://www.technologyreview. com/articles/04/09/ roush0904.asp?trk=nl

Roush, W. (2005, May). The infinite library. *Technology Review.com.* Retrieved October 1, 2007, from http://www.technologyreview.com/ articles/05/05/issue/ feature_library.asp?trk=nl

Rovai, A. P. & Barnum, K. T. (2003). Online course effectiveness: An analysis of student interactions and perceptions of learning. *Journal of Distance Education, 18*(1), 57–73.

Rubenking, R. (2007, May 8). Invasion of the data snatchers. *PC Magazine, 26*(10), 42.

Rupley, S. (2003). Tiny film festival. *PC Magazine, 22*(9), 23.

Rupley, S. R. (2005). A 60GB microdrive? Never say never. *PC Magazine, 24*(9), 24.

Rupley, S. (2006). Meep! Meep! Roadrunner will be the fastest PC ever. *PC Magazine, 25*(19/20), 23.

Saettler, P. (1990). *The evolution of American educational technology.* Englewood, CO: Libraries Unlimited, Inc.

Santoro, F. M., Borges, M. R. S., & Santos, N. (2004). Evaluation of collaborative learning processes. *Advanced technologies for learning, 1*(3), 164–173.

Schmidt, S. (2007, January 24). E-books far from a bestseller with students. *The Edmonton Journal,* A-5.

Scriven, B. (1993). Trends and issues in the use of communication technologies in distance education. In G. Davies & B. Samways (Eds.), *Teleteaching* (pp. 71–78). North Holland: Elsevier Science.

Shulman, M. (2007, September 17). Social studies. *The New Yorker,* 37.

Simpson, H., Pugh, H. L., & Parchman, S. (1993). Empirical comparison of alternative instructional TV technologies. *Distance Education, 14*(1), 147–164.

Social graph-iti. (2007, October 20). *The Economist, 385*(8551), 83–84.

Speak to me. (2006). *PC Magazine, 25*(14), 19.

Statistics Canada. (2001, March). *Overview: Access to and use of information communication technoplogy.* Catalogue No. 56-505-XIE. Retrieved August 27, 2007, from http://www.statcan.ca/english/freepub/56-505-XIE/0000156-505-XIE.pdf

Surowiecki, J. (2006). Philanthropy's new prototype. *Technology Review, 109*(5), 48–56.

Szabo, M. (1998). *Survey of educational technology research.* The Educational Technology Professional Development Project (ETPDP) Series. Edmonton, AB: Grant MacEwan Community College and Northern Alberta Institute of Technology.

Talbot, D. (2005, November 29). Next-generation networks. *Technology Review.* Retrieved August 29, 2007, from http://www.technologyreview.com/InfoTech-Search/wtr_15937,308,p1.html

Talbot, D. (2006a, March/April). Universal authentication. *Technology Review, 109*(1), 65–66.

Talbot, D. (2006b, May/June). Beaming books. *Technology Review, 109*(2), 21–22.

Talbot, D. (2008, Jan.–Feb.). The fleecing of the avatars. *Technology Review, 111*(1), 58–62.

The best is yet to come. (2005). *The Economist, 376*(8443), 20–22.

The device that ate everything. (2005). Rational Consumer. *The Economist, 376*(8441), 16.

The next Internet. (2005). *PC Magazine, 24*(18), 20.

The war of the wires. (2005). *The Economist, 376*(8437), 53–54.

Today's startup lesson: Fewer orders = higher price. (2007, 30 October). *The Globe and Mail,* B 13.

UC College Prep. (2006). The state of online learning in California: A look at current K-12 policies and practices. Santa Cruz: University of California, UC College Prep Online.

Ulanoff, L., & Costa, D. (2007, January). iPod enemy #1. *PC Magazine, 26*(1/2), 42.

U.S. Department of Commerce. (2004). Economics and Statistics Administration. (2004). *A nation online: Entering the broadband age.* National Telecommunications and Information Administration. Retrieved August 29, 2007, from http://www.ntia .doc.gov/reports/anol/NationOnlineBroadband04.htm#_Toc78020933

Vaughan-Nichols, S. J. (2005). Linux lasts longer. *PC Magazine, 24*(9), 64.

Vrasidas, C., & McIsaac, M. S. (1999). Factors influencing interaction in an online course. *American Journal of Distance Education, 13*(3), 22–36.

Walther, J. B. (1996). Computer-mediated communication: Impersonal, interpersonal and hyperpersonal interaction. *Communication Research, 20*(1), 3–43.

Walther, J. B., Gay, G., & Hancock, J. T. (2005). How do communication and technology researchers study the Internet? *Journal of Communication, 55*(3), 632–657.

Watching the Web grow up. (2007). *The Economist, 381*(8519), 31–32.

White OLEDs brighten. (2007). *Technology Review, 110*(1), 18.

Why wait for WiMax? (2005). *The Economist, 376*(8440), 51.

Wikipedia (n.d.a). *Social software.* Retrieved August 29, 2007, from http://en.wikipedia.org/wiki/Social_software

Wikipedia (n.d.b). *Wiki.* Retrieved August 29, 2007, from http://en.wikipedia.org/wiki/Wiki

Wireless non-stop. (2005). *Technology Review, 108*(8), 18.

Yogurt or cucumber? (2008, February 23). *The Economist, 386*(8568), 103.

You've heard this song before. (2006). *The Economist, 381*(8503), 75.

ABOUT THE AUTHOR

Patrick J. Fahy, Ph.D. (patf@athabascau.ca), is a professor in the Centre for Distance Education (CDE), Athabasca University. His career has included high school and adult teaching, and research from basic literacy to graduate levels, private sector management and training, and private consulting. Currently, in addition to developing and teaching educational technology courses in the Master of Distance Education (MDE) program, Pat coordinates the MDE's Advanced Graduate Diploma in Distance Education Technology program and the CDE's annual Distance Education Technology Symposium, and he is designing and will teach the first doctoral course. Pat is Past-President of the Alberta Distance Education and Training Association (ADETA), the Alberta Association for Adult Literacy (AAAL), and the Movement for Canadian Literacy (MCL). His current research interests include measures of efficiency in online and technology-based training, interaction analysis in online conferencing, and ethics in online research.

"IN-YOUR-POCKET" AND "ON-THE-FLY:" MEETING THE NEEDS OF TODAY'S NEW GENERATION OF ONLINE LEARNERS WITH MOBILE LEARNING TECHNOLOGY

MAUREEN HUTCHISON, TONY TIN,
& YANG CAO
Athabasca University

INTRODUCTION

Mobile devices are ubiquitous in today's business and social environments, and they are shaping the way that individuals learn, communicate, and share information. A given technology for those approaching and just entering adulthood, mobile devices have also become central to the business demographic, who have a need or expectation to be always connected, mobile, and online. Today's online learners require flexibility, and mobile devices are a solution to remove the barrier of a fixed time, place, and mode of learning. Tailoring online education to meet the needs of those who wish to learn "anywhere, anytime," however, will be an ongoing challenge.

The emergence of the "Net Generation" into the halls and cyberspace of higher education has challenged educators to better understand the makeup of a new generation of learners within our highly connected, technological society. As Canada's leading distance education and e-learning institution, Athabasca University (AU) is exploring tools, techniques, and the learning preferences of this tech-savvy demographic who are now just crossing our threshold. This chapter outlines what mobile learning is, its benefits and challenges, and discusses several of the issues faced. We also provide examples of how Athabasca University has applied mobile learning and mobile technology to support online teaching and learning, and offer our "lessons learned" in practice.

WHAT IS MOBILE LEARNING?

Although mobile learning is considered to be a relatively new concept, it has experienced significant growth with the onset of the new millennium. Mobile technologies, such as mobile phones, personal digital assistants (PDAs, such as *Palm®, iPAQ®*); smartphones (integrated telephony, computing, and communication devices, such as *BlackBerry®, Treo™, iPhone™*); and portable media players (such as MP3 players, *iPod®*) have become embedded in our social and business milieu, transforming the way we work, live, and, indeed, learn. According to a recent Statistics Canada *Innovation Analysis Bulletin* (McDonald, 2006), over 16.6 million Canadian individuals subscribed to mobile communications services by the end of 2005, and from 1997 to 2004, Canadian households increased their total communications expenditures on wireless services by 253% and on Internet access by 600%.

Mobile learning (m-learning) is the delivery of electronic learning materials with built-in learning strategies on portable computing devices, to allow access from anywhere and at any time (Ally, 2004). In the continuum of educational technology, m-learning is emerging to build on the advances of e-learning, or the use of Internet and learning management systems (Georgiev, Georgieva, & Smrikarov, 2004). Milrad (2003) concurs and describes the differences between m- and e-learning: e-learning is "learning supported by digital 'electronic' tools and media," whereas mobile learning is "e-learning using mobile devices and wireless transmission" (p. 151).

Everywhere today, people are connected: they are checking email on their PDAs; they are text-messaging, listening to music, or playing games on their cellphones or *iPods®*; and they are surfing the Internet via a wireless connection for sports scores, stock prices, and even for dinner and flight reservations. The rise of mobile devices is allowing a broad range of consumers – from those owning a basic cellphone to those on the periphery with cutting-edge smartphones – to connect in ways that foster learning and the exchange of ideas within a more universal social "mind," beyond the restrictions of age, gender, national identity, and socio-economic status.

MOBILE LEARNING AND THE NET GENERATION

Mobile learning allows individuals to connect with just the right content, using just the right technology, at just the right time. In today's egoistic society, learning, too, can be on demand and attuned to the specific interests of the individual.

The *Net Generation* (also known by the monikers Net Gen, Generation Y, Millennials, the Google Generation, iGeneration, Me Generation) describes a demographic born between 1980 and 1994 who are very tech-savvy, accustomed to multi-tasking, and expect to control what, when, and how they learn (Tapscott, 1998). This demographic poses a new challenge for educators, who must consciously be aware of being made technically obsolete by the younger generation. According to Richard Sweeney (cited in Carlson, 2005), a university librarian at the New Jersey Institute of Technology, "higher education was built for us [baby boomers and previous generations] under an industrial-age model" (p. A34); the Net Generation is far from this design. This new generation of learners is smart but impatient, creative, expecting results immediately, customizing the things they choose, very focused on themselves, and reliant on an "arsenal of electronic devices – the more portable the better" (Carlson, 2005, p. A34). They are more apt to learn and work in teams, are very achievement-oriented, are comfortable in image-rich environments, crave interactivity, and prefer to learn by doing rather than reflecting (Oblinger & Oblinger, 2005).

The e-book *Educating the Net Generation* (Oblinger & Oblinger, 2005) is a compilation of articles that explores this theme and discusses how higher education must better understand the Net Generation to remain relevant for today's and tomorrow's learners. One key to understanding the Net Generation, however, is recognizing that this demographic is not specifically about technology; rather, it is about the activities or experiences that technology enables (Roberts, 2005). Technology is merely a tool that may or may not support the various learning activities that are available, as part of one's individualized approach to learning, for selection from a cafeteria-style array of learning services.

Today's learners have what Oblinger and Oblinger (2005) describe as "multiple media literacy" (p. 2.14). As such, educators today must not only prepare students for future careers, but also prepare students for the "real world," where state-of-the-art technologies will be encountered on a regular basis. Alvin Toffler's book *The Third Wave* (1980) illustrates society's transition from a brute force economy (the Agricultural and Industrial Revolutions) to a brain force economy (the Information Revolution). Toffler's subsequent book, written a decade later and titled *Powershift: Knowledge, Wealth, and Violence at the Edge of the 21st Century* (1990), explores power, based on individualism, innovation, and information. In today's economy, workers are increasingly dependent on knowledge and technology. Levy (2005) further builds on Toffler's ideas with his concept of "the fourth revolution," a movement to develop the full potential of knowledge workers, in order to gain maximum return from human capital. Emphasis is placed on the knowledge container, the "knower" whereby the learner is in full control and learning is no longer linear. These learners have the freedom and power to select what they wish to learn – central characteristics of the Net Generation. A key issue to consider for educators of this new demographic, therefore, is how to measure quality, given the new demographics' preference for learner-centred, cafeteria-style educational choices to meet their learning needs. If the learner is in control and can choose what he or she wishes from a selection of educational materials, can quality be achieved? How will we credential and certify learning competence?

If one assumes that the learner is in full control, what influence does this have on preferences for mobile learning? Given our knowledge of the Net Generation, Wagner and Wilson (2005) argue that mobile learning – while enabling equal opportunity access, ubiquitous connectivity, multi-generational uses and users, services for the mobile worker, and services for the mobile learner – will benefit most those who can leverage their digital communication skills in a world that has been levelled by mobile technologies.

MOBILE LEARNING IN DISTANCE EDUCATION TODAY

Muirhead (2005), in his paper, "A Canadian Perspective on the Uncertain Future of Distance Education," sees distance education to be at a "critical juncture in its historical development," and views distance educators as no longer leaders in an environment of "technology-enhanced, hybrid, flexible learning environments" (p. 239). The educational marketplace is increasingly literate and competent with information and communication technologies, a phenomenon that forces distance educators to adapt to a rapidly changing technological social and learning environment. Muirhead believes that "distance education must focus on how to reconceptualize itself and reconcile the increasing role of computer technology in everyday educational activities, with the growing adoption of distance-like educators" (p. 253). According to Clyde (2004), "the challenge is to identify the forms of education for which m-learning is particularly appropriate, the potential students who most need it and the best strategies for delivering mobile education" (p. 46).

In 1996, the University of Hagen and FernUniversität, Germany's Open University, developed a virtual university system, the first e-learning platform and university in Germany offering services via the Internet. Within the past five years, the University of Hagen has evolved this virtual university model to the *pocket university*, where m-learning is being investigated for teaching and learning (Bomsdorf, Feldmann, & Schlageter, 2003). As with Athabasca University, the University of Hagen's typical students are employed, study part-time, prefer to attend virtual events asynchronously, and need access to information and materials while travelling. For these students, efficient learning is key to educational success, and the flexibility to learn at a time and place which they choose is critical.

Researchers cited in this chapter are focusing on the tools, techniques, style, structure, user interface, and the multitude of formats available for mobile learning and mobile devices. As such, educators are discovering various advantages and disadvantages of mobile devices for education. While some benefits of mobile devices include portability, collaboration and sharing, anytime-anywhere flexibility, "just-in-time" learning, and advantages for learners with learning difficulties and disabilities, there are also disadvantages in using mobile devices for learning (Riva & Villani, 2005).

Central disadvantages of using mobile devices are the small display screen (Rekkedal & Dye, 2007), reduced storage capacity, and reliance on a battery-powered device. Waycott and Kukulska-Hulme's (2003) research found that using PDAs for reading and note taking was not ideal. For older learners, diminishing eyesight makes viewing small screens a challenge. In addition, the lack of a common platform among the various manufacturers and equipment available (e.g., smartphones, cellphones, PDAs), complicates the development of content. There are also security issues inherent in using a wireless device and connecting to an "outside" environment. Also, as more users access a wireless network, bandwidth can be compromised, affecting the immediacy expected by today's learners. Some educators opine that mobile devices are not the be-all, end-all solution to addressing the needs of today's learners, and that performance improvement and optimized environmental conditions for learning should be the focus – rather than the technology itself (Rushby, 2005). Nonetheless, these emerging technologies appear to complement many of the characteristics of today's learners and of other media used for delivery of distance education programming.

Next-generation learning environments are being designed to be highly interactive, meaningful, and learner-centred. Kirkley and Kirkley (2005) believe these elements are important, as educators consider how to use technological affordances to provide a learning environment that reflects the same cognitive authenticity as the domain area or environment being trained. In *Going Nomadic: Mobile Learning in Higher Education,* Alexander (2004) describes the emergence of *learning swarms,* wherein the socializing powers of mobility and wirelessness are influencing the way we look at traditional education methods and the traditional, physically sedentary campus. Alexander (2003) argues that "m-learning shifts the educational center of gravity towards students, raising fundamental and practical questions about learning for every instructor and campus" (p. 3). Knowing the intended learning audience allows for more options to engage them in the learning process. Chris Dede (2005) of Harvard University's Graduate School of Education argues that campuses which make strategic investments in "physical plant, technical infrastructure, and professional development will gain a considerable competitive advantage in both recruiting top students and teaching them effectively" (p. 15).

MOBILE LEARNING AND EDUCATIONAL OPPORTUNITIES

What does mobile learning mean to providers of higher education today? Removing barriers to enable learning anytime, anywhere for learners worldwide and increasing the equality of educational opportunities can be provided by using mobile devices, as several of the researchers and educators cited earlier in the chapter have noted. Dede suggests that new methods of teaching and research must be explored to better serve students. Various university mandate statements affirm several of the themes relating to mobile learning discussed earlier, such as accessibility, flexibility, meeting the needs of the learner *and* the workplace, and a commitment to research, learning technologies, and individualized distance education methods (Athabasca University, 1999, 2002, 2005; University of Waterloo, 2002; Royal Roads University, 2004).

Although technology has regularly transformed the preparation and delivery of distance education materials (from print to television to online, to mention just a few technologies), institutional mandates give impetus to further work in the field of learning technologies and methods, and to the newest evolution of e-learning. The methods and outputs of print-based educational publishing have been replaced largely with a new digital paradigm. Faculty and subject matter experts now interact with increasingly specialized team members skilled in multimedia and digital communication. Gone is distance higher education's reliance on paper-based manuscripts, hard-copy texts, broadcast technologies, and traditional course packs. Institutions once at the vanguard of the distance education movement must now compete with newcomers to the e-learning environment, as well as with the traditional bricks-and-mortar institutions, in the new arena of online, individualized, and collaborative learning.

MOBILE LEARNING AT ATHABASCA UNIVERSITY

In what ways has Athabasca University addressed the needs of the new generation of learners with mobile learning and associated technologies? How is Athabasca University different from other educational providers, and how can the university capitalize on its rich history of distance education, individualized approaches to learning, and the removal of barriers to learning? In October 2006, Athabasca University illustrated its commitment to mobile learning by hosting *mLearn 2006,* the fifth world conference on mobile learning, in Banff, Alberta (see: http://www.mlearn2006.org/). Topics of discussion included building and implementing m-learning strategies in educational institutions, corporations, and government; m-learning theory and pedagogy; cost-effective management of m-learning processes, digital rights management, and m-learning management systems (mLMSs); emerging hardware and software for m-learning; creating interactive and collaborative m-learning environments; intelligent agents, learning objects, and metadata for m-learning; mass personalization and socialization; m-learning in developing countries; and the evaluation, implementation, instructional design, student support, and quality of m-learning. Various case studies, papers, poster sessions, workshops, and speeches were presented by conference attendees from around the globe. Several Athabasca University projects have since applied e-learning and m-learning pedagogy to support learners, and are discussed below.

THE DIGITAL READING ROOM

The Digital Reading Room (DRR) at Athabasca University enables students to access library materials that have been selected by faculty for a particular course. The DRR is an interactive online reading room, offering digital files for course readings and supplementary materials. It can accommodate a range of formats, including online journal articles, electronic books, audio or video clips, web sites, and learning objects. In 2007, the DRR housed more than 20,780 resources, serving 235 courses (Tin, 2007). The resources available have been specially selected by faculty, are organized by course and by lesson for the convenience of students, and are accessible using *persistent links* (PURLs). The library's Web Access Management (WAM) function manages access to licensed resources, including password protection of copyrighted intellectual property (Magusin, Johnson, & Tin, 2003). The Athabasca University DRR can be accessed at http://library.athabascau.ca/drr/

The Mobile Deployment

Mobile access has been used to articulate the resources that are also suitable for m-learning, currently available in the Athabasca University DRR. This work has resulted in the implementation of a comprehensive mobile library web site that contains relevant digital reading files, application tools and software, and learning resources. These materials include
- mobile device-ready learning objects, including MP3 versions of journal articles, video clips, and e-books
- existing AU library electronic resources, organized for m-learning
- an m-library web site
- a comprehensive list of m-learning application tools
- A best-practice document for m-learning instructional design.

Figure 2 illustrates how the desktop version of the DRR has been adapted for mobile display.

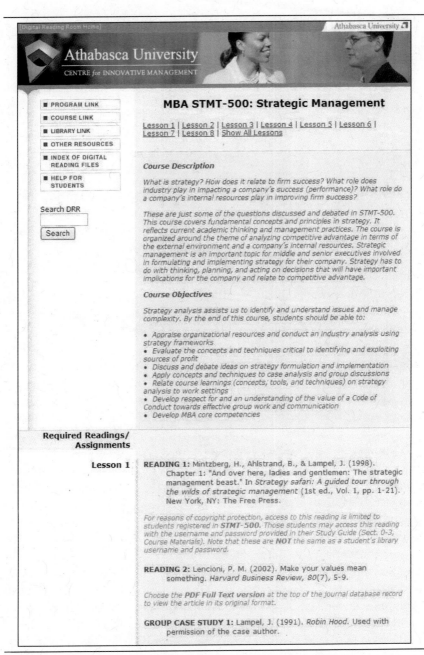

FIGURE 1. Athabasca University DRR interface for MBA program (desktop display)

FIGURE 2. DRR desktop display (left) and mobile display (right)

Mobile ESL Project

E-learning, or using computers to study, is a well-established pedagogy in Canada. Athabasca University has taken e-learning one step further by using mobile phones to deliver interactive course materials. The AU Mobile English as a Second Language (ESL) Project provides English grammar lessons and interactive exercises to anyone with a mobile device (cellphone, PDA, or smartphone) and access to the Internet. Students can brush up on their English language skills while waiting for a bus, over their lunch break, or whenever they have time to review grammar. The AU Mobile Learning Project was sponsored by the Canadian Council on Learning, Alberta Science and Research Authority, Canada Foundation for Innovation, Athabasca University, Canadian Virtual University, and the National Adult Literacy Database.

The digital ESL content is based on Penguin's bestselling introductory English grammar lessons and exercises, which was released by the author as open-source material (O'Driscoll, 1988; 1990). Students have access to the basic tools of English grammar in an interactive modular format, accessible on mobile and fixed computing devices. The course content consists of 86 lessons and related exercises that teach the basics of the English language, ranging from the difference between *is* and *are* to verb tenses, countable nouns, and other aspects of basic grammar. These digital lessons have been adapted into reusable multimedia learning objects that are accessible to anyone on the Internet, either as stand-alone lessons, groups of lessons in units, or as full-course modules. The content materials are in a digitized format with interactive elements added to enhance flow and learner motivation. Specifically, the content has been rendered interactive by using a variety of multiple-choice, short-answer, jumbled-sentence, matching/ordering and fill-in-the-blank exercises on the World Wide Web. The content is specifically formatted for output on small mobile devices. Figure 3 illustrates the mobile ESL content on a basic cellphone. This familiar learning context lends a sense of security to teachers and learners when using the mobile devices for learning. It adheres to the principle of introducing new technologies in a familiar context, as one would introduce new pedagogical approaches in traditional contexts. The course site has been developed to also auto-detect for desktop display; PDF and Microsoft® Word documents are provided for download or printout, should the learner prefer to use these document formats.

FIGURE 3. Mobile ESL display on a basic cellphone

Adult learners from three institutions – the Edmonton Mennonite Centre for Newcomers, the Chinese Evangelical Baptist Church, and Global Community College – assisted Athabasca University by pilot testing this project. The pilot testing indicated the following interesting results (Woodburn and Tin, 2007):

a) *Test Scores*: A slight improvement was shown after the students accessed and studied the grammar units on the mobile phone. The improvement was still noted the week following the pilot testing.

b) *Accessibility*: Almost all participants (90%) either "agree" or "strongly agree" that the mobile technology provided flexibility for them to learn anytime and anywhere.

c) *Quality of Learning*: Most participants (69%) thought that learning with mobile technology increased the quality of their learning experience.

d) *Taking More Mobile Lessons*: Most of the students (60%) chose either "5- Strongly Agree" or 4- Agree" when asked if they would like to take more lessons using mobile technology.

e) *Recommend to Friends*: Most (60%) agreed that this technology could be useful to others.

Mobile ESL learners have reported three main benefits from this project. First, students are provided with immediate feedback. As students work through the exercises one by one, they receive instant feedback on how they scored (after clicking *Submit*, they are told which questions they answered correctly or incorrectly); if they have answered incorrectly, they can try again and learn from their initial mistake. Second, this project allows for cross-referencing to other sites and resources. Mobile devices with constant wireless online access enable users to surf the World Wide Web and view related web sites on grammar that may assist them in their language learning. Last, this project increases motivation and opportunity for learning. Having the content online and right at students' fingertips, "one click away," means they can learn wherever they are, despite the constraints of busy work and personal schedules which take them from place to place. Moreover, as students achieve success and progress through the exercises, they may be motivated to learn more of the English language. The Athabasca University mobile ESL project can be accessed at http://eslau.ca

Athabasca University AirPac

The Athabasca University AirPac project is another example of mobile learning technology. AirPac is a software module of Innovative Interfaces

Inc. (III), an automated library system specially designed for compatibility with wireless mobile devices. AirPac runs on the library's server and sends out JavaServer Pages (JSP), formatted for mobile devices requesting information. AirPac allows mobile users with wireless Internet access to search and browse the library catalogue, check due dates, request materials, and view their patron records in real time. Library staff and patrons, including people with disabilities, can now access the online public catalogue via wireless LANs, WiFi, 802.11b, and Bluetooth. Digital information is reformatted "on-the-fly" for different browsers and screen resolutions. AirPac also recognizes that information needs to be formatted in Wireless Access Protocol (WAP). If the user submits a search from a wireless PDA (such as a mobile phone or handheld computer), AirPac formats a response for that type of device. For example, a mobile phone will receive a minimal display to accommodate the smaller screen area, while AirPAC will send a larger display to a PDA with more screen area available. Athabasca University's AirPac can be accessed at http://aupac. lib.athabascau.ca/airpac/.

The DRR and MP3 Technology

Moving Picture Experts Group Audio Layer III – more commonly known as MP3 – is a format that compresses digital audio file size, yet retains nearly the original quality of the audio. The DRR takes advantage of this new technology by offering MP3 audio-reading files for curriculum use. In particular, the DRR features the use of *MP3Producer*, a CD-ripping and MP3-encoding program (see http://www.softsia.com/MP3Producer-download-8ts0.htm). Using *MP3Producer*, a series of CD audio tracks were converted to MP3 files for use in French language lessons at Athabasca University. The resulting encoded files are more compact, suitable for playback on an *iPod®* or on a media player program on a mobile device.

In another Athabasca University example, pre-coded MP3 files were obtained with copyright permission and streamed for use in the Global Strategic Management (EGSM-646) course of Athabasca University's online MBA program. These Harvard University clips complement the study of several specific Harvard cases in the course. Students commented favourably on the learning value they provided; the video clips also provided the instructor with another medium for teaching course concepts. The MP3 files were converted into Realplayer's Real Media (rm) streaming format. They are available in both high-speed and low-speed versions, to accommodate bandwidth restrictions and thus remove another barrier for learning (see http://library.athabascau.ca/

drr/mba _template.php?course=mba&id=585). This type of technology is ideal for busy, time-pressed executive or adult learners engaged in graduate studies such as the MBA, undergraduate studies, or specific work-related training, while juggling family and business commitments, including travel. Although typically older than members of the Net Generation, Athabasca University students embrace many of the characteristics of this younger demographic, especially given their multiple-media exposure through the technologies and practices of business, the expectation of "digital connectedness" at all times, and the need to be highly efficient at multitasking. Today's office, like today's learning environment, increasingly knows no boundaries.

The Mobile DRR also features the use of text-to-speech (TTS) technology to convert machine-readable text into MP3 audio files. Using a software program called *River Past Talkative* (*RPT*; see http://www. riverpast.com/), a curriculum guide for a Master of Arts in Integrated Studies course, was converted from text into an audio-WAV file, providing a choice of natural human voices (see http://library.athabascau.ca/ drr/view.php?course=mais&id=496&sub=0).

Once created, these audio files can be saved as MP3 files and listened to on a mobile device or portable MP3 player. The interface contains simple and readily accessible controls for different voices, including *AT&T® Natural Voices*™ (see http://www.naturalvoices.att.com). This program is also used to convert books and articles into MP3 audio books and audio articles for use in the mobile DRR. For an example, see http:// library.athabascau.ca/drr/view.php?course=demo&id=418. To further enhance the audio books and articles with full-text display and content reading aloud, a software program called *MP3 Stream Creator* is used (see http://www.guangmingsoft .net/msc/).

IRRODL and MP3 Technology

The *International Review of Research in Open and Distance Learning* (www. irrodl.org) is a renowned, refereed, open-access e-journal that aims to disseminate research, theory, and best practices in open and distance learning worldwide. IRRODL is housed at Athabasca University's Open University Press web site. It is available free of charge to anyone with access to the Internet. IRRODL has pioneered the use of MP3 technologies for e-journal development (Killoh, Smith & Wasti, 2007). Individuals with *iPods®*, mobile phones, and other mobile devices are able to access IRRODL's content anytime, anywhere. The inclusion of MP3 audio technology increases access for those with disabilities. IRRODL has featured more than 40 MP3 audio articles for download and *iPod®*-casting. IRRODL uses NeoSpeech's *VoiceText®* technology to convert the written text into MP3 audio files. The MP3 version of IRRODL is available at http://www.irrodl .org/index.php/irrodl/index.

Podcasting

Podcasting is a term that describes the combination of a Rich Site Summary (RSS) feed and multimedia materials. It has become popular as multimedia-capable devices such as the Apple *iPod®* and other hand-held "smart" devices have become ubiquitous. Most podcasts are in MP3 audio format. The *iPod®* is not wireless-enabled, so it functions simply as an audio player. Using the DRR, Athabasca University researchers added multimedia clips of different formats and created a podcast RSS channel. Athabasca University has aimed at testing and exploring three different groups of multimedia clips: audio, video, and enhanced audio with pictures, and chaptering capabilities and their applications.

Podcasting works like a radio, but with better audio quality and no need to tune in at a specific show time. With a combination of *iTunes®* on the desktop and the mobile *iPod®*, students can retrieve materials when they connect the device at their desk, or listen to the materials on the road. *iPod®* is far superior to analog devices such as cassette tapes. Educational developers can add chapters in the clip, allowing learners to jump to the appropriate section. For some MPEG 4 audio files, pictures can also be encapsulated for each chapter. *iPod®* allows students to listen to audio lectures, anytime and anywhere. The subscription model streamlines the process for students to locate and retrieve newly available learning materials. As such, podcasting opens up a new and better way to deliver audio clips.

EFFECTIVENESS AND FUTURE OF MOBILE LEARNING

Is m-learning effective? Avellis and Scaramuzzi (2004) remind us that, although there is great potential for m-learning, there are relatively few successful implementations from which best practices can be studied. The "distinction between software and supporting learning is blurred because of the way the application runs, which affects its educational effectiveness, and the educational purpose, which underlies the design of the software... therefore, both aspects must be carefully considered" (p. 16). Further, Avellis and Scaramuzzi state that it is "difficult to develop a pre-defined set of standards against which the educational value of the software can be defined, because it is not possible to define a unique and general instructional approach" (p. 16). One group of researchers has developed a set of "quality function deployment" tools to identify and classify four types of learning, using mobile devices and learning environments: context, presentation, management, and communication (Baber, Sharples, Vavoula, & Glew, 2004). These aspects are reflective of the functions considered important for mobile learning, such as the ability to "adapt functionality for learner characteristics and learning context; discover, access, evaluate, store, retrieve learning objects; monitor, utilise, evaluate learning outcomes; assist in the recovery of breakdowns and errors during and due to learning; support the learner's mobility" (p. 23).

Although mobile technology is still in its infancy, it holds unbounded promise and potential as a key medium for learning and training in the future. The challenge for higher educators and learning professionals, therefore, is to harness the burgeoning growth of this technology and transform it into educational formats that speak to today's new generation of online learners.

REFERENCES

Alexander, B. (2003, April 7). Teaching in the wireless cloud. *TheFeature, 3*. Retrieved May 1, 2003, from http://www.thefeature.com/

Alexander, B. (2004). Going nomadic: Mobile learning in higher education. *EDUCAUSE Review 39(5)*. Retrieved August 25, 2007, from http://www.educause.edu/pub/ er/erm04/erm0451.asp?bhcp=1

Ally, M. (2004). Using learning theories to design instruction for mobile learning devices. Paper published in the *Mobile Learning 2004 International Conference Proceedings*. Rome, July 2004.

Athabasca University (1999). *Athabasca University mandate statement.* Retrieved August 26, 2007, from http://www.athabascau.ca/aboutAU/mission.php

Athabasca University (2002). *Athabasca University mission statement.* Retrieved August 26, 2007, from http://www.athabascau.ca/aboutAU/mission.php

Athabasca University (2005). *Athabasca University strategic university plan: 2006-2011*. Retrieved August 26, 2007, from http://www.athabascau.ca/sup/ SUP_highlights_09_08.pdf

Avellis, G., & Scaramuzzi, A. (2004). Evaluating non-functional requirements in mobile learning contents and multimedia educational software. In J. Attewell & C. Savill-Smith (Eds.), *Learning with mobile devices: Research and development*. London: Learning and Skills Development Agency.

Baber, C., Sharples, M., Vavoula, G., & Glew, P. (2004). A 'learning space' model to examine the suitability of different technologies for mobile learning. In J. Attewell & C. Savill-Smith (Eds.), *Learning with mobile devices: Research and development*. London: Learning and Skills Development Agency.

Bomsdorf, B., Feldmann, B., & Schlageter, G. (2003). Pocket university: Mobile learning in distance education. *Learning Technology Newsletter, 5*(2), 19–21.

Carlson, S. (2005). The net generation goes to college. *The Chronicle of Higher Education, 52*(7), A34.

Clyde, L. A. (2004). M-learning. *Teacher Librarian, 32*(1), 45–47.

Dede, C. (2005). Planning for neomillenial learning styles: Implications for investments in technology and faculty. In D. Oblinger & J. Oblinger (Eds.), *Educating the Net Generation* (p. 15.19). Washington, DC: EDUCAUSE.

Georgiev, T., Georgieva, E., & Smrikarov, A. (2004). M-Learning: A new stage of E-Learning. *International Conference on Computer Systems and Technologies*. Rousse Bulgaria, June. 28–31. Retrieved August 26, 2007, from http://ecet.ecs.ru.acad.bg/cst04/Docs/sIV/428.pdf

Killoh, K., Smith, P., & Wasti, S. (2007, July). OJS-MP3 article usage: A pilot study. Presented at the *PKP Scholarly Publishing Conference 2007, at Simon Fraser University*, July 13–16. Retrieved August 24, 2007, from http://pkp.sfu.ca/ocs/pkp2007/index.php/pkp/1/paper/view/39

Kirkley, S. E., & Kirkley, J. R. (2005). Creating next generation blended learning environments using mixed reality, video games and simulations. *TechTrends, 49*(3), 42–53.

Levy, J. (2005). The fourth revolution. *T+D, American Society for Training and Development*, 64–65.

Magusin, E., Johnson, K., & Tin, T. (2003). Library services: Designing the digital reading room to support online learning. In Proceedings of the *19th Annual Conference on Distance Teaching and Learning*. Madison, WI: University of Wisconsin, Madison.

McDonald, C. (2006). Are cell phones replacing traditional home phones? *Innovation Analysis Bulletin, 8*(2), 12–13.

Milrad, M. (2003). Mobile learning: Challenges, perspectives, and reality. In N. Kyiri (Ed.), *Mobile learning essays on philosophy, psychology and education*. (pp. 151–164). Vienna: Passagen Verlag.

Muirhead, B. (2005). A Canadian perspective on the uncertain future of distance education. *Distance Education, 26*(2), 239–254.

Oblinger, D., & Oblinger, J. (2005). (Eds.) *Educating the Net Generation.* Washington, DC: EDUCAUSE.

Oblinger, D., & Oblinger, J. (2005). Is it age or IT: First steps towards understanding the Net Generation. In D. Oblinger & J. Oblinger (Eds.), *Educating the Net Generation.* Washington, DC: EDUCAUSE.

O'Driscoll, J. (1988). *Basic English grammar.* London: Penguin Books.

O'Driscoll, J. (1990). *English grammar exercises.* London: Penguin Books.

Rekkedal, T., & Dye, A. (2007). Mobile Distance Learning with PDAs: Development and testing of pedagogical and system solutions supporting mobile distance learners. *International Review of Research in Open and Distance Learning, 8*(2). Retrieved August 25, 2007, from http://www.irrodl.org/index.php/irrodl/article/view/349/871

Riva, G., & Villani, D. (2005). CyberEurope. *CyberPsychology & Behavior, 8*(5), 510–511.

Roberts, G. R. (2005). Technology and learning expectations of the Net Generation. In D. Oblinger & J. Oblinger (Eds.), *Educating the Net Generation* (pp. 3.1–3.7). Washington, DC: EDUCAUSE.

Royal Roads University (2004, July 21). *RRU policy on quality.* Retrieved August 26, 2007, from http://www.royalroads.ca/NR/rdonlyres/776F046C-BEDC-4BB0-9006-22797347AA07/0/CurriculumQualityAssurancePolicy.pdf

Rushby, N. (2005). *Editorial.* In N. Rushby (Ed.), *British Journal of Educational Technology, 36*(5), 709–710.

Tapscott, D. (1998). Growing up digital: The rise of the Net Generation. New York: McGraw-Hill.

Tin, T. (2007). *DRR report Athabasca University. Internal report.* Athabasca, AB: Athabasca University.

Toffler, A. (1980). *The third wave.* New York: Bantam.

Toffler, A. (1990). *Powershift: Knowledge, wealth, and violence at the edge of the 21st century.* New York: Bantam.

University of Waterloo. (2002). *2002 strategic directions.* Retrieved August 26, 2007, from http://www.adm.uwaterloo.ca/infocist/Directions2002/Strategies2002.html

Wagner, E. D., & Wilson, P. (2005). Disconnected: Why learning professionals need to care about mobile learning. *T+D, American Society for Training and Development, 43,* 40–43.

Waycott, J., & Kukulska-Hulme, A. (2003). Students' experiences with PDAs for reading course materials. *Personal and Ubiquitous Computing,* 7(1), 30–43.

Woodburn, T., & Tin, T. (2007). *Athabasca University Mobile ESL Research Project.* Unpublished. Athabasca, AB: Athabasca University.

ABOUT THE AUTHORS

Maureen Hutchison (maureenh@athabascau.ca) is the manager of Learning Services at Athabasca University's Centre for Innovative Management. Her work bridges the operational and academic elements of course development, production, and deployment for the centre's business courses and programs. Her career with CIM began as a course production coordinator, working closely with CIM faculty in the development, editing, instructional design, and production of online MBA courses.

Maureen holds a B.A. (with distinction) in English literature from the University of Western Ontario and a Management Development certificate (with distinction) from the University of Alberta.

Tony Tin (tonyt@athabascau.ca) is the electronic resources librarian at Athabasca University Library. Tony holds a BA and MA in History from McGill University and a BEd and MLS from the University of Alberta. He maintains the Athabasca University Library's web site and online resources, and is the Digital Reading Room project leader. Tony is the co-coordinator of the Athabasca University Mobile library and Mobile ESL learning project. He was also the recipient of the Athabasca University's Sue and Derrick Rowlandson Memorial Award For Service Excellence.

Yang Cao (yangc@athabascau.ca) is the digital objects & repository network developer in Library Services at Athabasca University. Yang received her BEng from Northeastern University and her MSc in Computer Science from the University of Saskatchewan. Her research interests are in the areas of e-learning, mobile learning, and the application of advanced technology in online distance education. Yang develops and maintains Athabasca University Library's web site and other online applications, including Digital Reading Room (DRR), Digital Theses and Project Room (DTPR), and mobile-friendly library web sites. In 2006, Yang and her team won the Athabasca University's Sue and Derrick Rowlandson Memorial Award for Service Excellence.

CHAPTER 9

SOCIAL SOFTWARE TO SUPPORT DISTANCE EDUCATION LEARNERS

TERRY ANDERSON

INTRODUCTION

This chapter discusses the challenges of developing modes of distance education that afford maximum freedom for learners, including the ability to enroll continuously and to pace one's own learning, and yet still create opportunities and advantages to working cooperatively in learning communities with other students. To resolve these often conflicting priorities, a new genre of networked-based learning tools, known as Educational Social Software (ESS), is defined, described, and its attributes discussed. These tools have applications for both on-campus and blended-learning applications, but my focus is on distance education – specifically, their use in self-paced, continuous enrolment courses. Finally, I briefly discuss the open-source social software tool, ELGG, and our plans for deploying it with both cohort-based and self-paced continuous enrolment courses at Athabasca University.

SOCIAL CHALLENGES IN DISTANCE AND ONLINE EDUCATION

The integration of information technologies, and especially of communications technologies, into distance education programming has significantly altered both the processes and the content of much of this programming. Nonetheless, distance education, especially those forms that maximize individual freedom by allowing continuous enrolment and individual pacing, is often perceived and experienced as a lonely way to learn. It is likely that the implicit requirement for self-motivation reduces accessibility to many students who have little exposure to, or sufficient experience with, programming that is not structured and orchestrated by a live (and often face-to-face) teacher. This challenge, to permit maximum student freedom while supporting opportunities for community building and mutual individual support in cost-effective ways, is perhaps the greatest challenge (and opportunity) facing the distance education community.

Many programs attempt to meet these challenges of isolation and self-direction by developing models of learning based upon cohort groups of students, interacting either through real-time audio, video or immersive conferencing, or asynchronously through text conferencing with a teacher and other students. However, this model has not been demonstrated to be cost-effective (Annand, 1999; Fielden, 2002) when compared to self-paced distance learning (Rumble, 2004). Few published accounts of such cohort-based programming support more than 30 students per teacher in a class, and a very frequent outcome is that teachers find such models of delivery require more time expenditure than equivalent classes delivered on campus (Jones & Johnson-Yale, 2005; Lazarus, 2003).

Much of the high cost of such programming is related to the time requirements placed upon instructors to interact with students. Although I have argued elsewhere (Anderson, 2003) that student-teacher interaction can be substituted by student-student and student-content interaction, it is not easy to orchestrate and support such interactions, and both traditionally minded students and teachers easily slip into cost-ineffective models of e-learning. A 2005 study of e-learning programs (Ramage, 2005) offered by 12 U.S. colleges concludes that all but two of these are cost-inefficient and again highlights the need to create cost effective e-learning by gaining economy of scale or changing the nature of the instructional processes. Before arguing for the capacity of new social software tools to alleviate these concerns, I briefly overview theoretical models that highlight social presence and interaction issues in distance education programming.

SOCIAL PRESENCE

Randy Garrison and I worked to develop a model of e-learning that we refer to as the Community of Inquiry model. Figure 1 revisits this model.

Note the pivotal role of social presence, not only in setting the educational climate but in supporting discourse and creating the educational experience. We define social presence as "the ability of learners to project themselves socially and affectively into a community of inquiry" (Rourke, Anderson, Archer, & Garrison, 1999). We spent some time

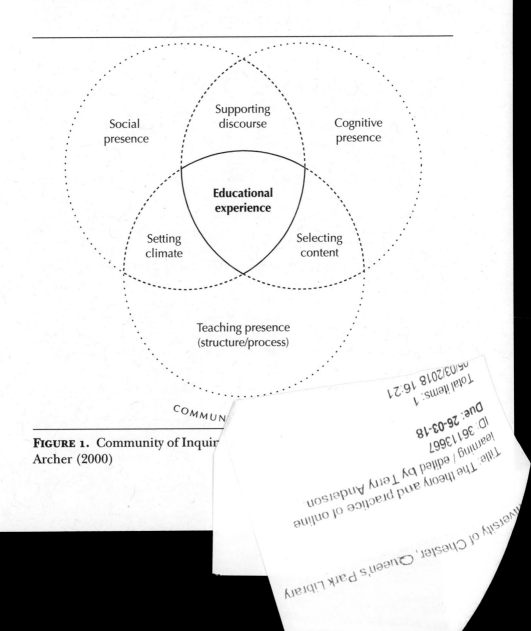

FIGURE 1. Community of Inquir[...] Archer (2000)

developing tools to measure social presence in asynchronous text-conferencing systems and validating these tools via interviews and surveys (Rourke & Anderson, 2002; Arbaugh, 2007). This work has been extended and quantified by a number of researchers (Tu, 2002; Stacey, 2002), demonstrating amongst other findings that social presence correlates with student satisfaction and higher scores on learning outcomes (Richardson & Swan, 2003).

Although the key variable, interaction, is critical in all three of the presences, it is perhaps most important in the development and support of the participants' sense of social presence. Assuming that interaction is necessary to develop social presence leaves us with the questions: which forms of interaction are most critical, and amongst which partners is the interaction most critical and most cost- and learning-effective?

LEARNER FREEDOM AND SOCIAL PRESENCE

Beyond access to content, perhaps the greatest benefit to both formal and lifelong learners afforded by the Net is the freedom to control one's learning experience in a number of dimensions. Paulsen (1993) models these forces in a "theory of cooperative freedom," in which six different dimensions of freedom are described. These include the familiar freedom of space and freedom of time that have defined much traditional distance education programming. But he also describes the freedom to pace one's learning in response to individual competencies or time availability. A fourth dimension concerns the freedom of media, that allows choice of learning medium to match a host of media access and usability constraints, as well as communication system qualities and preferences. Fifth is the freedom of access that includes removal of the barriers of prerequisites and high costs. Finally, Paulsen's sixth dimension, freedom of content, allows the learner to have control over the subject and instructional style of their learning. I have suggested to Paulsen the need for a seventh dimension, freedom of relationship, where learners are allowed to engage in the type of learning relationship with other learners that best fits their individual social needs and capacities.

Paulsen argues that individual learners are more or less concerned with each of these dimensions of freedom and are interested in learning designs and activities that meet their individual freedom preferences and constraints in each dimension. Further, these dimensions are not stable, but shift in response to individual and group preferences, constraints, and opportunities. Traditional campus-based programming developed into the form it takes today because it evolved in times of very severe personal constraints imposed in each of these dimensions. For example, the first universities offered classes centered around rare volumes of text found in medieval libraries. Later, school schedules were designed to allow students to work on their parents' farms in summer months. As these constraints are reduced by technical and social innovation, opportunity and demand are created for the development of much freer learning opportunities that are evolving to co-exist with traditional campus-bound educational programming (Friesen & Anderson, 2004). Recent interest in blended learning (Bersin, 2004; Garrison & Kanuka, 2004) shows that it is very possible to combine different formats and media of delivery. However, the challenge is to select and invent those forms of education that offer the greatest degrees of freedom and yet retain high levels of cost- and learning-effectiveness.

Social Software

The term *social software* is often attributed to the writing and promotion of Clay Shirky (2003), who defined it as "software that supports group interaction". This definition is so broad that it includes everything from email to Short Message System (SMS), so it has been qualified by a number of authors. Allen (2004) notes the evolution of software tools as the Net gains in its capacity to support human interaction, decision making, planning, and other higher-level activities across boundaries of time and space, and less adeptly, those of culture and language. Levin (2004) builds on Allen's historical description by noting how much the technology has defined the field and how that technology has radically changed and improved since the earlier generations of software that were designed to connect and support human communications. Similar to Anderson's (2004) affordances of the *semantic web*, Levin notes the ubiquity of the Net and especially the "findability" of content afforded by even current generations of brute-force searching with tools like *Google*. Second, she notes the pervasive and multiple formats of communication supported, ranging from synchronous to asynchronous; from one-to-one, to many-to-many, from text to full multimedia, from communications in a dedicated home theatre to that supported on a mobile phone while in transit. Finally, Levin notes the affordance of the Web to support new patterns of interconnection that "facilitate new social patterns: multi-scale social spaces, conversation discovery and group forming, personal and social decoration and collaborative folk art."

Coates (2002) provides functional characteristics of social software to extend human communications capabilities. Coates describes the enhanced communications capacity provided by social software over time and distance (the traditional challenges of access addressed by distance education). He goes on to note that social software adds tools to help us deal with the complexities and scale of online context, such as filtering, spam control, recommendation, and social authentication systems. Finally, he argues that social software supports the efficacy of social interaction by alleviating challenges of group functioning, such as decision making, maintaining group memory, documenting processes, and so on. Butterfield (2003) is much broader in his discussion of the qualities of social software. He characterizes social software as tools that support communication, using the five "devices" of identity, presence, relationships, conversations, and groups.

Cervini (2003) also notes the capacity of social software to perform directed searches for specific people or for those with specific interests or skills in complex social networks. She argues that, "without the ability to execute directed searches, through a social network, the transition cost of finding other users within the system is simply too high to warrant using the system" (p.2). Obviously, in educational systems characterized by high degrees of freedom, it becomes much more difficult to find fellow students and initiate and develop supportive learning interactions.

Just as social software defies precise definition, the classification and categorization of social software tools is also evolving. Stutzman (2007) makes an interesting distinction between social software tools and suites that are focused upon objects (object-centric) and upon people (ego-centric). Object-centric sites allow users to share, comment upon, and display a wide range of digital media, such as photos, music, books owned or read, citations, or music recordings. Ego-centric sites usually contain profiles, personal diary spaces (blogs), lists of friends, community discussions, and other tools that allow users to locate, work, and play with each other. Jon Dron and I (Dron & Anderson, 2007) have also been classifying the functions of social software into the tools that support groups, that support networks, and that support collectives or aggregated users.

Social software shares some of the defining features of what Tim O'Reilly first referred to as Web 2.0 tools. O'Reilly (2005) defines Web 2.0 as the network as platform, spanning all connected devices; Web 2.0 applications are those that make the most of the intrinsic advantages of that platform: delivering software as a continually-updated service that gets better the more people use it, consuming and remixing data from multiple sources, including individual users, while providing their own data and services in a form that allows remixing by others, creating network effects through an "architecture of participation," and going beyond the page metaphor of Web 1.0 to deliver rich user experiences.

Many social software tools are network-centric, and most get better as more people use them, creating network effects and building on an "architecture of participation." However, social software predates Web 2.0, and it focuses more on supporting the social relationships than the more technical and network-intensive applications referred to as Web 2.0. To summarize, many of the newer social software tools can also be described as Web 2.0 tools, but not all Web 2.0 tools are focused on meeting social needs.

One can see both common threads and divergences in the definition and classification of this relatively new genre of tools. Social software tools can be applied to many tasks and in many domains. A few social software tools have been developed with explicit educational goals; however, most are general purpose tools that can be used by individuals, groups, or networks of users, either as a component, support, or not associated at all with formal education.

Since there no single definition of social software has evolved in the literature, and none specifically related to education applications – I have coined my own (Anderson, 2006a)! I have tried to combine the sense of freedoms from Paulsen's categories to *define educational social software as networked tools that support and encourage individuals to learn together while retaining individual control over their time, space, presence, activity, identity, and relationship*. Obviously, popular educational tools such as computer conferencing and email qualify as social software under this definition. However, these and other common communication tools are primitive examples of a variety of tools, services, and support that distributed networked learners require.

In summary, a concise and precise definition of social software still seems to elude us, but it is clear that the problems social software addresses (meeting, building community, providing mentoring and personal learning assistance, working collaboratively on projects or problems, reducing communication errors, and supporting complex group functions) apply to educational use, and especially to those models that maximize individual freedom by allowing self-pacing and continuous enrolment. Educational social software (ESS) may also be used to expand, rather than constrain, the freedoms of their users. In the next section, I turn to the requirements of educational social software, with examples.

FEATURES OF EDUCATIONAL SOCIAL SOFTWARE (ESS) APPLICATIONS

In this section, I overview functions and features of social software that are can be used be used to enhance distance education processes. The details below are condensed and updated from those presented in an earlier book chapter (Anderson, 2006a).

Presence Tools

ESS tools should allow learners to make known (or conceal) their presence, both synchronously and asynchronously. An example of presence notification was provided in my early experience with computer conferencing software. The first full course I taught used the First Class system and notified learners when other members of their cohort were currently online. This notification allowed one to see and communicate (by an instant text message) with other students. Students could then agree to meet in the chat room for more sustained and perhaps larger-group, real-time interaction. When I changed educational institutions, I began teaching with WebCT, which lacked this notification of presence, and I found that the built-in chat rooms were almost never used, and certainly not in a spontaneous fashion. Hanging out in an empty chat room waiting for someone to drop by is not an engaging activity!

Presence notification can also operate to support presence in physical space, as provided by the tools for mobile social networking, or for helping to identify those in social proximity who share a common interest in an educational- or discipline-related interest. Presence indicators are also being added to text, audio, and video communication and conferencing tools to allow us to see which of our friends or colleagues are available for instant answers, feedback, and interaction. Of course, this sense of presence must be under the control of the individual learner; there are times when I welcome the presence of other "kindred souls," while there are other times when I need the freedom to protect and maintain my privacy and anonymity.

Notification

Contributing to a learning community and not receiving feedback or acknowledgment of that contribution quickly discourages and tends to extinguish further participation. Good ESS provides both pushed and pulled forms of notification. Using push tools such as RSS, instant messaging, or even email provides notification to the learner when new content or communication is entered into a learning space. Quality ESS tools also allow historical and persistent display and searching of these interventions, so that the learning space can be searchable and span across significant lengths of time.

Filtering

The assault on our systems, caused by both legitimate avalanches of potentially useful information as well as non-legitimate spam, creates the need for ESS to contain collaborative filtering systems. These systems need to be able to filter out illegitimate information, as well as filtering in items of potential interest. Filtering out is being handled with various degrees of success by many of the commercial spam filters. But filtering in relevant information is a greater challenge. Downes (2005) discusses the use and limitations of various semantic web tools such as RSS and FOAF to create and maintain critical dimensions of identity. The solutions (like most other semantic web applications) seem inviting and even plausible, but many have noted the slow emergence of relevant and effective semantic web applications.

Cooperative Learning Support

Paulsen (2003) makes a distinction between cooperative learning activities in which learners are encouraged (though not required) to cooperate in learning activities that are alluring to the individual learner, and collaborative activities where members are compelled to work together through the duration of an activity. This distinction between collaboration and cooperation, based upon the compulsion to interact, is unique and fits well with ESS programming. Cooperative activities are generally short term, bounded in temporal space (for example, a week-long project), and often not time-centric, such that learners can cooperate outside of the knowledge of where and in which order they are studying, and can cooperate with both those engaged in the class and that larger group of family, friends (virtual and face-to-face), and colleagues not formally enrolled in a program of studies. Colleagues at the Dutch Open University (Kester et al., 2007) have been supporting the emergence of "ad hoc transient communities" of self-paced learners in which cooperative activities, cooperative problem solving, and team-teaching activities are designed.

Referring

Humans and other social animals tend to flock to activities in which others are engaged. ESS tools track activities which students engage in, noting indicators of success (time spent, assessments attempted and past, formal evaluations, and so on). These referrals can be used by students to select learning activities and courses, and by teachers and administrators to evaluate, refine, and continuously improve the learning activities. Koper (2005b; 2005a) has developed interesting models of implicit referral systems in which students' activities leave trails, much like the pheromone trails left by ants to guide other members of the colony to food sources. His simulations of these models show how individual student experiences can be used to improve learning networks and provide useful referral services to new students. Dron (2007; 2004) has expanded this further and defines such *stigmergic* activities as one of ten design features of effective social software.

Student Modelling

Much of the previous functionality depends upon or is enhanced when it is possible to identify, classify, and quantify the individual profiles of learners. Such systems might capture interests, learning styles, goals and aspirations, accomplishments, and progress through a course of studies; personal characteristics such as professional interest and experience; family status; and other individual and group information (Towle & Halme, 2005). These profiles can then be used by ESS software to customize referrals, notification, filters, and so on. Considerable work is being done in this area by scholars working in the field of artificial intelligence in education (see, for example, Boticario, Santos, & Rosmalen, 2005; Shute & Towle, 2003). Such systems usually produce an XML-based learner profile that is explicitly altered by the learner. Others (McCalla, 2004) use more active techniques, where the learner profile is updated in real time by activities, assessments, and interactions between the learner and other learners, teachers, and content. These systems are all migrating to exposure in XML that can be read and interpreted by both humans and autonomous agents. Various standards bodies, including the IMS (see http://www.imsglobal.org/profiles/), are working to create standardized schemas for formally defining learner profiles in such as way that they can be read and interpreted as components of the Educational Semantic Web (Anderson & Whitelock, 2004). It is worth emphasizing that learner profiles must be under the ultimate control of the learner if critical issues of trust and privacy are to be maintained in ESS systems.

Stephen Downes (2005) argues that we need to link resources with the humans who have built, used, recommended, or otherwise commented upon them. This "explicit conjunction of personal information and resource information within the context of a single distributed search system will facilitate much more fine-grained searches than either system considered separately." This step would take learner profiles beyond their instantiation as a means to modify content, and to allow systems where learners can meet with and engage with others based on their individual experience of learning activities and outcomes.

Introducing Learners to Each Other

Some of the most successful commercial social software (for example, LinkedIN and Facebook) are based upon providing selective referrals to other persons for social or commercial motivations and effective encounters. Most of these referral systems assume that those people you regard as friends are more likely to be become friends of each other than of a random selection of individuals. Thus, mining both weak and strong connections allows us to become acquainted with, and possibly work or learn together with others, with a greater probability of developing profitable exchanges. This system can provide distance learners with the well-known capacity of campus-based education systems to serve as meeting places for diverse individuals from many groups, as well as for developing stronger links to those sharing common cultural identities. Thus, ESS tools can serve distance learners as environments in which learners are free to share their interests, connections, communities, and friends. It is also worth noting that ESS tools facilitate the development and sharing of reputation, since documented postings and interactions can be used as referencing trails to determine the past contribution of learners to other learners or, more broadly, to the learning community.

Helping Others

The study group and study buddies have long been features of successful campus-based learning systems. Developing these groups in virtual and

independent study contexts is challenging. Very interesting work has
taken place at the University of Saskatchewan in the development of the
I-Help system (Greer et al., 2001). For each student, the I-Help system
configures an autonomous agent that knows its owner's skills, preferences, and fiscal capacity (in real or play money) to provide and request
help from other students. When students require help, they release their
agent into the learning space to negotiate with the agent of another,
more skilled learner. These negotiations may lead to a request for help
by email or telephone, the subsequent exchange of funds, and evaluation by both the helper and the helped. Of course, this help can also be
used for activities that violate academic standards and morals, such as
cheating and plagiarism. In my own institution, providing our independent students with the capability to meet each other has raised some
faculty concerns about the increased possibility and efficacy of such
activities; it threatens our on-demand, continuous exam system that
seems to be based upon an assumption that students are not in contact
with each other. Since these concerns also affect campus-based systems,
technical and social fixes have been developed to at least partially constrain these opportunities. More importantly, ESS will force us to develop
competency-type examinations that build upon and exploit social
learning, rather than attempting to eliminate it.

Documenting and Sharing of Constructed Objects

Much formal learning is based on students learning and relearning a
very slowly evolving body of knowledge. Educational strategies designed
for such contexts are not highly productive in contexts when useful
information and knowledge is under continuous revision. More currently, educational authors (Grabinger & Dunlap, 2002; Collis, B., &
Moonen, 2001) have argued that students should be actively creating
rather than consuming knowledge. Our own experiences of assigning
students the tasks of creating learning portals and learning objects for
each other have been very positive (Anderson & Wark, 2004). But often,
the co-creation of content has assumed that students are actively working
and designing learning content in synchronous fashion. ESS tools will
need to support students working continuously to update content that
was initiated months or even years before by other students. Wikis and
collaborative blogs are first-generation tools to support this type of interaction. However, more sophisticated tools are needed, capable of including multimedia, tracking both contributor and learner use, controlling
access to creation tools, and assessing learning outcomes.

From the generic potential functionality of ESS, this chapter now moves to specific descriptions of ESS tools, focusing on those that are open source and available. In particular, I give an overview of our initial design-based study, using the ELGG system developed by David Tosh and his colleagues at the University of Edinburgh.

CURRENT EDUCATIONAL SOCIAL SOFTWARE (ESS) TOOLS

Many of the social software tools developed for business, social, and entertainment activities can be used for educational application. However, many are proprietary offerings providing a service, but not distributing the software itself. Such solutions may be useful for individual student exploration and small class work, but they do not allow the freedom to design and create value-added instances of ESS that are customized for particular groups of learners, nor do they provide the type of security and control demanded by many formal education institutions.

Generally, ESS tools that have been developed to date offer combinations of blogging, portfolio management, discussion and file sharing, group file management, and search and linking capacity. Due to ideological issues, low budgets and our desire to have control, we limited our search for a development platform for our use to open-source products. In our search, we found a number of generic database/content management tools (notably Plone http://plone.org and Drupal http://drupal.org/) that could be developed as ESS applications. However, the programming and customization work would be considerable. Fortunately, we discovered two OS tools that were already focused on ESS use. BarnRaiser offers an interesting program known as the Aroundme platform (http://www.barnraiser.org/index.php?wp=software). The current version (1.5) offers the usual blogging, polls, group tasks, and a very interesting tool to measure the "social capital" of contributors. The second tool, ELGG (version 0.90, http://elgg.org), offers many of the same tools, and was chosen for our installation due to the strength of its ad hoc folksonomie-style linkages, its provision for individual control of personal information and postings, its support for e-portfolios, and its Canadian connection (David Tosh, one of the principal developers, is a Canadian with whom we have developed a long-distance friendship and is friend of a number of our friends – how social!).

An instance of ELGG was installed at Athabasca (with minimal problems) and rechristened me2u.athabascau.ca (Figure 2).

FIGURE 2. Me2U.athabascau.ca

We were interested in testing an ESS application within formal education programs, and have chosen to create a resource that is exclusive to students registered at our institution. Downes (2005) and others argue that such "silos" are inherently restrictive, but they do offer a safer, more controlled environment for educational testing. Naturally, these environments should support RSS and other notification tools such that learners are not expected to spend a great deal of time waiting for action on their institutional ESS installation. ELGG has what we believe to be the most versatile privacy control system in current ESSs. Figure 3 illustrates how the display of every field of information in a learner's profile, plus all the items in their e-portfolio and their blog postings, can be restricted to only the author, their friends, particular communities, logged-on members (registered Athabasca University students), or the general public (including search-engine spiders).

There has also been considerable debate about the role of ESS in relationship to the more firmly established learning management systems, such as *Blackboard* or *Moodle*. I have compared the affordances of both systems elsewhere (Anderson, 2006b) and concluded that "personal learning systems" do not offer the types of document control and learner management currently built into LMS systems. It is also interesting to note the inclusion of blogs, profiles, wikis, e-portfolios, and other

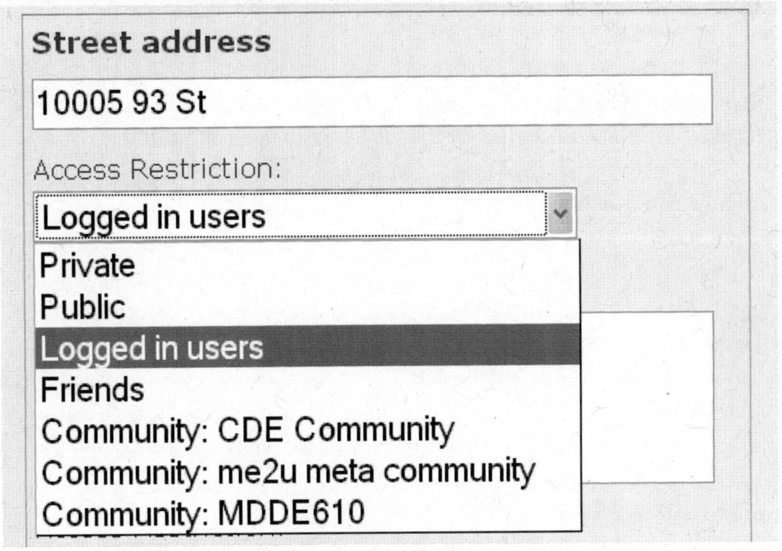

Street address

10005 93 St

Access Restriction:

Logged in users

Private
Public
Logged in users
Friends
Community: CDE Community
Community: me2u meta community
Community: MDDE610

FIGURE 3. Selecting Access provisions in ELGG

social tools in the ever-growing, monolithic LMS systems. Debate about the advantages of personal versus institutional systems is beyond the scope of this chapter, but current developments portray an interesting future as Web 2.0 tools increase the capacity for working together (mash-ups). This development will allow for very fine-tuned customization of learning contexts, not just by teachers and administrators, but by students, as they gain control over their own learning environments.

Design-based Research Development of Me2U

The final section of this paper describes our research design used to assess this intervention. Bannan-Ritland (2003) describes four stages of design-based research and maps these to more traditional forms of education research and publication. The first stage is informed exploration. Our earlier 2004 survey of student experience with interactive interventions and consultations with global distance educators (Anderson, Annand, & Wark, 2005) has set the stage and detailed the need for social software solutions. Our primary focus is on students enrolled in unpaced and continuous enrollment courses. We hope to design an informal place for the development of social presence and tools to allow students to engage in voluntary, for-credit learning activities that contain cooperative learning components. Through engagement in these learning activities, as well as through profiling services allowing them to connect online or in person with other students, we hope to allow them to form relationships with other learners in loosely structured learning communities. We also continue to track innovations in social software and to develop conceptual models for their effective adoption in formal learning educational contexts.

In the second stage of development, we have installed the ELGG tools and are developing support documentation and systems to facilitate its use in pilot applications. We plan to work with our colleague (Morten Paulsen) at the Norwegian Knowledge Institute in Norway to develop an optional student profile system that encourages learners to develop and share their individual learning plans. Finally, development in this phase includes adoption and development of new learning designs that create compelling, but optional learning activities to support the learning community while retaining student freedoms.

In the third phase, our educational social software interventions are piloted in one or more local contexts. We are working with designers, program and course managers, and faculty in a selected number of academic departments at Athabasca University. Our approach will move towards a grounded theory model, in which we will use a variety of data sources (interviews, observations, final exam scores, completion rate data, student perceptions of learning, cost accounting, machine-log analysis, and transcript analysis) to develop and test a grounded theory of educational social software use in learner-paced e-learning.

The fourth phase of a design-based research project focuses on understanding the innovation's effect in multiple contexts. Working with national and international partners, we will provide the tools and techniques developed and tested in Phases 2 & 3 to a wider variety of contexts. The evaluation tools that have proved most useful in pilot testing and development in Phase 3 will be refined and used to gather data across these diverse sites. And the theory that has emerged in Phase 3 will be validated, tested, and refined in this phase. We will use the community and repository tools developed at the Canadian Institute for Distance Education Research (http://cider.athabascau.ca) to build and support a community of researchers and practitioners in their own implementations of ESS theories and tools developed in the earlier phases of this research.

CONCLUSION

This overview of ESS tools is perhaps yet another instance of "it will be perfect when..." ESS tool development and application is in its very early stages, and doubtless there are many blind alleys as well as very productive avenues yet to explore. I remain convinced that using the tools and affordances of the emerging educational semantic web will result in very significant improvements (both in cost- and learning-effectiveness) to our current practice and theory of distance education. Social software needs a "killer app" and distance education needs new cost- and learning-effective tools, to develop and enhance the creation and maintenance of social presence. These are indeed exciting times!

NOTES

This chapter is a revised and updated version of a paper presented in 2005 at the 17th Biennial Conference of the Open and Distance Learning Association of Australia, held in Adelaide Australia.

REFERENCES

Allen, C. (2004). Tracing the evolution of social software. *Life with alacrity*. Retrieved Dec 14, 2007, from http://www.lifewithalacrity.com/2004/10/tracing_the_evo.html

Anderson, T. (2003). Getting the mix right: An updated and theoretical rational for interaction. *International Review of Research in Open and Distance Learning, 4*(2). Retrieved Dec. 14, 2007, from http://www.irrodl.org/index.php/irrodl/ article/view/149/708

Anderson, T. (2004). The educational semantic web: A vision for the next phase of educational computing. *Educational Technology, 44*(5), 5–9.

Anderson, T. (2006a). Higher education evolution: Individual freedom afforded by educational social software. In M. Beaudoin (Ed.), *Perspectives on the future of higher education in the digital age*. New York: Nova Science Publishers.

Anderson, T. (2006b). PLEs versus LMS: Are PLEs ready for Prime time? *Virtual Canuck*. Retrieved Dec., 2007, from http://terrya.edublogs.org/ 2006/01/09/ples-versus-lms-are-ples-ready-for-prime-time/

Anderson, T., Annand, D., & Wark, N. (2005). The search for learning community in learner-paced distance education programming or "having your cake and eating it, too!" *Australian Journal of Educational Technology, 21*(2), 222–241. Retrieved Dec. 12, 2007, from http://www. ascilite.org.au/ajet/ajet21/res/anderson.html

Anderson, T., & Wark, N. (2004). Why do teachers get to learn the most? A case study of a course based on student creation of learning objects. *e-Journal of Instructional Science and Technology, 7*(2). Retrieved Dec.11, 2007, from http://www.usq.edu.au/electpub/e-jist/docs/Vol7_no2/ FullPapers/WhyDoTeachers.htm

Anderson, T., & Whitelock, D. (2004). The educational semantic web: Visioning and practicing the future of education. *Journal of Interactive Media in Education, 1*. Retrieved Dec. 16, 2007, from http://www-jime. open.ac.uk/2004/1

Annand, D. (1999). The problem of computer conferencing for distance-based universities. *Open Learning, 14*(3), 47–52.

Arbaugh, B. (2007) An empirical verification of the community of inquiry framework. *Journal of Asynchronous Learning Networks, 11*(1). Retrieved Dec. 14 2007, from http://www.aln.org/publications/jaln/v11n1/pdf/ v11n1_9arbaugh.pdf

Bannan-Ritland, B. (2003). The role of design in research: The integrative learning design framework. *Educational Researcher, 32*(1), 21–24. Retrieved Dec. 14, 2007, from http://www.aera.net/uploadedFiles/ Journals_and_Publications/Journals/Educational_ Researcher/3201/3201_Ritland.pdf

Bersin, J. (2004). Blended learning: Finding what works. *Chief Learning Offficer, 1*. Retrieved Dec., 2007, from http://www.clomedia.com/ content/templates/clo _feature.asp?articleid=357&zoneid=30

Boticario J.G., Santos, O.C., & Rosmalen, P. (2005). Technological and management issues in providing adaptive education in distance learning universities. EADTU. Retrieved Dec. 19, 2007 from http://www. ia.uned.es/~jgb/publica/ TechMngIssuesALMS-jgbosmpvr.pdf

Butterfield, S. (2003). Sylloge. Retrieved Feb. 12, 2008, from http://www. sylloge .com/personal/2003_03_01_s.html

Cervini, A. (2003). Network connections: An analysis of social software that turns online introductions into offline interactions. Unpublished

Master's thesis. New York University. Retrieved Mar. 21, 2008, from http://www.frimfram.com/thesis/ print.html

Coates, T. (2002). My working definition of social software... *plasticbag. org blog*. Retrieved January, 16, 2006, from http://www.plasticbag.org/ archives/2003/05/my_working_definition_of_social_software/

Collis, B., & Moonen, J. (2001). *Flexible learning in a digital world*. London: Kogan Page.

Downes, S. (2005). Semantic networks and social networks. *The Learning Organization, 12*(5), 411–417. Retrieved Dec.,10, 2007, from http:// www.downes .ca/cgi-bin/page.cgi?post=31624

Dron, J. (2004). Termites in the schoolhouse: Stigmergy and transactional distance in an e-learning environment. In *AACE* (Ed.). Retrieved Dec. 14 2007, from http://www.cmis.brighton.ac.uk/staff/jd29/papers/ dronedmedia2004.doc

Dron, J. (2007). *Control and constraint in e-learning: Choosing when to choose*. Hershey, PA: Information Science Pub.

Dron, J., & Anderson, T. (2007). Collectives, networks and groups in social software for e-Learning. Paper presented at the *Proceedings of World Conference on E-Learning in Corporate, Government, Healthcare, and Higher Education* Quebec. Retrieved Feb. 16, 2008, from www.editlib. org/index.cfm/files/paper_26726.pdf?fuseaction=Reader. DownloadFullText&paper_id=26726 -.

Fielden, J. (2002). Costing e-learning: Is it worth trying or should we ignore the figures? London: The Observatory on Borderless Higher Education. Retrieved Sept. 16, 2005, from http://www.obhe.ac.uk/ products/reports/pdf/August2002.pdf

Friesen, N., & Anderson, T. (2004). Interaction for lifelong learning. *British Journal of Educational Technology, 35*(6), 679–688.

Garrison, D. R., Anderson, T., & Archer, W. (2000). Critical inquiry in text-based environments?: Computer conferencing in higher education. *The Internet and Higher Education, 2*(2-3), 87–105. Retrieved Dec. 14, 2007, from http://communitiesofinquiry.com/documents/CTinText EnvFinal.pdf

Garrison, D. R., & Kanuka, H. (2004). Blended learning: Uncovering its transformative potential in higher education. *Internet and Higher Education, 7*(2), 95–105.

Grabinger, S., & Dunlap, J. (2002). Applying the REAL model to web-based instruction: An overview. In P. Barker & S. Rebelsky (Eds.), *Proceedings of 2002 World Conference on Educational Multimedia, Hypermedia and Telecommunications* (pp. 447–452). Chesapeake, VA: AACE. http://www.editlib.org/index.cfm?fuseaction=Reader.ViewAbstract& paper_id=10128

Greer, J., McCalla, G., Vassileva, J., Deters, R., Bull, S., & Kettel, L. (2001). Lessons learned in deploying a multi-agent learning support system: The I-Help experience. *Proceedings of Artificial Intelligence in Education, 2001.* Retrieved Dec. 4, 2007, from http://julita.usask.ca/Texte/Aied01-camera.pdf

Jones, S., & Johnson-Yale, C. (2005). Professors online: The Internet's impact on college faculty. *First Monday, 10*(9). Retrieved Sept. 13, 2007, from http://firstmonday.org/issues/issue10_9/jones/

Kester, L., Sloep, P., Van Rosmalen, P., Brouns, F., Kone, M., & Koper, R. (2007). Facilitating community building in learning networks through peer tutoring in ad hoc transient communities. *International Journal of Web Based Communities, 3*(2), 198–205. Retrieved Dec. 16, 2007, from http://dspace.ou.nl/bitstream/1820/ 609/4/Facilitating +Community+Building+-+titlepage.pd

Koper, R. (2005a). Designing learning networks for lifelong learners. In R. Koper & C. Tattersall (Eds.), *Learning Design* (pp. 239–252). Berlin: Springer.

Koper, R. (2005b). Increasing learner retention in a simulated learning network using indirect social interaction. *Journal of Artificial Societies and Social Simulation, 8*(2). Retrieved Jan.8, 2006, from http://jasss.soc.surrey.ac.uk/8/2/5.html

Lazarus, B. (2003). Teaching courses online: How much time does it take. *Journal of Asynchronous Learning, 7*(3). Retrieved Dec. 1, 2003, from http://www.aln.org/publications/jaln/v7n3/v7n3_lazarus.asp

Levin, A. (2004). Social software: What's new. *Many 2 Many*. Retrieved Dec., 2007, from http://www.alevin.com/weblog/archives/001492. html

McCalla, G. (2004). The ecological approach to the design of e-learning environments: Purpose-based capture and use of information about learners. *Journal of Interactive Media in* Education, *10*. Retrieved Dec. 12, 2007, from http://www-jime.open.ac.uk/2004/7/

O'Reilly, T. (2005) What is Web 2.0: Design patterns and business models for the next generation of software. Retrieved Feb, 2008, from http://www.oreilly.com /pub/a/oreilly/tim/news/2005/09/30/what-is-web-20.html

Paulsen, M. (1993). The hexagon of cooperative freedom: A distance education theory attuned to computer conferencing. *DEOS, 3*(2).

Retrieved Dec. 16, 2007, from http://www.nettskolen.com/forskning/ 21/hexagon.html

Ramage, T. (2005). A system-level comparison of cost-efficiency and return on investment related to online course delivery. *E-Jist, 8*(1). Retrieved Dec. 14, 2007, from http://www.usq.edu.au/electpub/ e-jist/docs/vol8_no1/fullpapers/ Thomas_Ramage.pdf

Richardson, J. C., & Swan, K. (2003). Examining social presence in online courses in relation to students' perceived learning and satisfaction. *Journal of Asynchronous Learning Networks, 7*(1). Retrieved Dec. 14, 2007, from http://www.sloan-c.org/publications/jaln/v7n1/pdf/v7n1_ richardson.pdf

Rourke, L., & Anderson, T. (2002). Exploring social presence in computer conferencing. *Journal of Interactive Learning Research, 13*(3), 259–275. Retrieved Dec.14, 2007, from http://communitiesofinquiry. com/documents/ Rourke_Exploring_Social_Communication.pdf

Rourke, L., Anderson, T., Archer, W., & Garrison, D. R. (1999). Assessing social presence in asynchronous, text-based computer conferences. *Journal of Distance Education, 14*(3), 51–70.

Rumble, G. (2004). *Papers and debates on the economics and cost of distance and online learning.* Oldenburg: University of Oldenburg.

Shirky, C. (2003). A group is its own worst enemy. *Clay Shirky's writings about the Internet.* Retrieved Dec. 14, 2007, from http://www.shirky. com/writings/ group_enemy.html

Shute, V., & Towle, B. (2003). Adaptive e-learning. *Educational Psychologist, 38*(2), 105–114. Retrieved Dec. 2, 2007, from http://www.leaonline. com/doi/abs/ 10.1207/S15326985EP3802_5

Stacey, E. (2002). Social presence online: Networking learners at a distance, education and information technologies. *Education and Information Technologies, 7*(4), 287–294. Retrieved Dec. 16, 2007, from http:// www.springerlink.com/content/ m3370313r055xh73/

Stutzman, F. (2007). Thoughts about information, social networks, identity and technology. *Unit Structures.* Retrieved Dec.3, 2007, from http:// chimprawk.blogspot.com/2007/11/social-network-transitions.html

Towle, B., & Halme, M. (2005). Designing adaptive learning environments with learning design. In R. Koper & C. Tattersall (Eds.), *Learning Design* (pp. 215–226). Berlin: Springer.

Tu, C.H. (2002). The measurement of social presence in an online learning environment. *International Journal on E-Learning, 1*(2), 34–45.

PART III

DESIGN AND DEVELOPMENT OF ONLINE COURSES

THE DEVELOPMENT OF ONLINE COURSES

Dean Caplan
Canadian Pacific Railway

Rodger Graham
Athabasca University

INTRODUCTION

In an ideal world, instructional media developers – those who will actually create the planned instructional materials with which the student will interact – are included in the course development process from the beginning, to consult with and advise course team members on development-related topics as they arise. Then, on receiving a detailed design document from the subject matter expert or instructor, developers will set to work, assured that

- the instructional designs of the learning materials are stable because they have been based firmly on sound, proven learning theories
- these instructional designs will meet the institution's identified and articulated internal and external standards for quality, usability, and interoperability
- appropriate media have been selected to meet these standards

- the technologies selected for course delivery are not superfluous – rather, the course design will exploit the unique characteristics of the selected media to engage and support both learners and teachers (such characteristics may include accessibility of content, multimedia, hyperlinking, multiple or global perspectives, ease of revision, and accommodation of many forms of interaction)
- the designs are practical and can be developed in a cost-effective and timely way.

Of course, most of us do not have the luxury of working in an ideal world. There is a good chance that a very thick file has just landed on your desk(top), and you are not sure where to start! The first part of this chapter discusses the infrastructures that must be in place to support the development of course materials. The second part considers the key roles on a course production team, a few instructional development models, and some technical issues in the process of developing an online course.

WHAT MUST BE IN PLACE BEFORE DEVELOPMENT CAN OCCUR

Computer-mediated distance education is becoming ubiquitous, and is now being demanded more and more by students. Despite what some might believe, however, Internet-based instruction is by no means the magic bullet that automatically guarantees a rich learning environment. Although research continues to confirm that there is no significant difference among student outcomes based on mode of course delivery (Russell, 1999), we must keep in mind that web-based distance education technology and pedagogy is still very much in its infancy. Hence, those of us working in Internet-based instruction are blazing new trails to develop the essential elements and processes that will lead to high quality, active, online learning environments.

It is generally agreed that the World Wide Web is a compelling, resource-rich, multimedia environment with great potential to serve large numbers of widely dispersed students at relatively low cost. Although many educational institutions have undertaken strategic planning for the systematic implementation of web-based distance education, not all have succeeded. The fundamental requirement to gain support for web-based instruction from faculty, administrators, and students is an institutional model that is distinct from the traditional instructional-planning model and supports the design, development, and implementation of high-quality instruction on the Internet. Each of these stakeholder groups

– faculty, administrators, and students – must be assured that web-based instruction is a viable means of delivering courses and programs, and of accommodating student needs. To create those assurances, the web-based instructional model that is to be implemented must deal with some fundamental issues that may have never been addressed before.

Definition of an Online Course

What does it mean for a course to be considered *online?* Since the web-based delivery option is new to many institutions, there is no standard or accepted definition of what constitutes an online course. An examination of Internet-based courses currently offered reveals two basic categories, with a large middle ground: courses that are primarily text-based (the text being delivered either online or by mailed hard copy), with computer-mediated enhancements; and courses that are designed specifically for the distributed Internet setting, and that merge several smaller educational components into a single course of study.

In the early days of online learning, from the mid 1990s to the early 2000s, the majority of distance-education courses found on the Web were of the former type, involving text that had merely been converted to electronic form and placed on a web site for students to read, or, more likely, to print and then read. The advantages of this method of delivery included circumventing postal delays and getting the materials to the student almost immediately; facilitating easy searching and manipulation of the text by the student; cutting the costs of publishing and shipping; and increasing the ease of development (often using a course template), updating, and revision. In addition, the communication capacity of the Internet allows for a variety of forms of student-student, student-content, and student-teacher interactions, which could be used to augment the students' independent interaction with the printed course contents.

The loudest criticisms of this type of course are that it does not make any use of the multi-modal, computer-mediated instructional means that are available, and that the printing costs are off-loaded onto the student. Also, these text-based online courses are often supplemented by electronic interactive tools, such as discussion forums and chats, which are typically implemented as "extras" or afterthoughts to the course, and thus their pedagogical value is often artificial and suspect.

As the nature of Internet users evolves, so do their demands and expectations from e-learning. Since the beginning of the twenty-first century, there has been a marked shift in online course development toward the second type of course mentioned above, which attempts to take advantage of the strengths of the Internet as a teaching and learning environment: its open, distributed, dynamic, globally accessible, filtered, interactive, and archival nature (McGreal & Elliot, 2008). In the first generation of this type of online course, where all course materials and activities are Internet-based, text can still play a part in instruction, although it generally appears in short, concise "chunks." The instruction is also distributed among other multimedia components, commonly known as *learning objects*; ideally, learning objects are designed to be shareable, reusable, and repurposed so that they can work in multiple contexts (McGreal & Elliott).

The first-generation, learning-object-based online course is often delivered through a learning management system (LMS), a software application suite that organizes and standardizes learning content, dividing the course into modules and lessons, supported with quizzes, tests and discussions (Downes, 2005). Today, most LMSs afford developers the use of text; email; asynchronous discussion boards; synchronous utilities such as voice over Internet protocol (VoIP); instant-messaging chat features; desktop and application sharing; on-demand video clips and demonstrative animations; interactive activities, simulations, and games; self-grading exercises, quizzes, and examinations; and secure assignment "drop boxes" where students and instructors exchange assignments and feedback one-on-one.

Some well-known examples of Learning Management Systems are *Blackboard®, Moodle,* and *Desire2Learn®.* The eduSource Canada Network of Learning Object Repositories brings together several online collections of learning objects, which can be searched and contributed to by developers free of charge.

> While debate and research continues about the value of the first generation online courses, the ground is shifting beneath our feet. As we approach the halfway mark of the new millennium's first decade, the nature of the Internet, and just as importantly, the people using the Internet, have begun to change. These changes are sweeping across entire industries as a whole, and are not unique to education; indeed, in many ways education has lagged behind some of these trends and is just beginning to feel their wake. One trend that has captured the attention of numerous pundits is the changing nature of Internet users themselves. Sometimes called 'digital natives' and sometimes called 'n-gen,'

these new users approach work, learning and play in new ways.
(Tapscott,1997, in Downes, 2005)

In learning, these trends are manifest in what is sometimes called *learner-centred* or *student-centred* design. This is more than just adapting for different learning styles or allowing users to change the font size and background colour; it is the placing of the control of learning itself into the hands of the learner (Marzano, 1992).

What is emerging from the learner-centred approach to online learning is "E-learning 2.0," the next generation of online learning that is characterized primarily by a shared domain of interest where members interact and learn together, and develop a shared repertoire of resources (Wenger, 1998). In other words, the shift in learning is moving from the didactic teacher-to-learner model to a networked, community-based model of learner-to-learner. This evolution, of course, has significant implications for instructional design and development, the scope of which is not the intent of this chapter. As instructional developers, however, we are being called upon to become familiar with a new set of tools that will facilitate those engaged in e-learning 2.0.

The type of online learning you are planning to develop might fall into one of the two categories above, or it might fit somewhere in between, and it might contain any combination of learning objects. Regardless of how you define your online instructional materials, your course should contain certain administrative documents to help instructors organize, prepare, and orient students, especially if they are new to online learning. These documents could include

- a personalized letter of welcome for each new student
- general information about online learning, technology requirements, and the resources available to students for technical help, and for obtaining the proper software and Internet services required for the course
- information on how to access the course on the Web, and how to navigate it successfully
- student log-in and password information for course web site
- rules, procedures, and help for use of the interactive tools
- a course syllabus (preferably on public pages so that prospective students can browse in advance of registration); course overview; course schedule; list of required text and materials (if applicable); clearly defined pre-requisite academic and computer skills; course expectations; instructions on activities, assignments, and deadlines;

faculty and tutor contact information and office hours; and student support information

- administrative regulations, including guidelines on plagiarism, privacy, academic appeal procedures, library facilities, and access to counselling and advisory services

Faculty Buy-in

While the World Wide Web has been with us for well over a decade now, only in the past few years has it begun to be accepted as a workable vehicle for the delivery of instruction. Consequently, many faculty members working in post-secondary educational institutions were not hired with the expectation that they would use educational technologies in their teaching. This new mode of learning is also redefining teaching. Access to new cohorts of students and new media makes it possible, sometimes necessary, to teach in new and innovative ways.

Some faculty take to these new methods immediately, while others are unsure if they have, or even want, the technical abilities to develop an online course. Do not underestimate the importance of the degree to which faculty feel they are receiving encouragement and support in all areas of online development. Administrators can initiate certain policies designed to encourage and support faculty acceptance of online teaching. Faculty should be reassured that they are not about to lose their jobs to technology, but that they can expand the ways they do their jobs by employing technology. Finally, it is crucial to adequately reward all who undertake the considerable personal effort and risk to develop courses and teach online, especially within the merit award and promotion processes associated with performance reviews.

Focus on Sound Pedagogy

Any instructional strategy can be supported by a number of contrasting technologies – old and new – just as any given technology might support different instructional strategies. For any given instructional strategy, however, some technologies are better than others: "Better to turn a screw with a screwdriver than a hammer – a dime may also do the trick, but a screwdriver is usually better" (Chickering & Ehrmann, 1996, para. 4).

Faculty concerns about using new teaching methods and media often centre on pedagogy. Unfortunately, many examples of poor pedagogical application in web-based instruction can be found, often in the form of the text-based online courses described above. The prevalence of such examples is largely due to the novelty of online instruction, or the fact that critical mass has yet to be achieved in design or practice, to prove the value of online learning. One way to address concerns about inferior pedagogy online is to dictate that the same educational standards must apply to the development of instruction for the Internet as to any other delivery medium, such as the classroom.

The American Association of Higher Education's *Seven Principles for Good Practice in Undergraduate Education* is one such set of standards (Chickering & Gamson, 1987). Originally written for classroom instruction, it was later revised to include online educational practice, and is now widely accepted by post-secondary institutions. Good practice in undergraduate education

1. encourages contacts between students and faculty
2. develops reciprocity and cooperation among students
3. uses active learning techniques
4. gives prompt feedback
5. emphasizes time on task
6. communicates high expectations
7. respects diverse talents and ways of learning (p. 3)

Arthur Chickering and Steve Erhmann have recently updated these practice guidelines to illustrate how communications technologies, and especially the Internet, can be used to support these seven "good practices" (see http://www.tltgroup.org/programs/seven.html).

Another set of standards is presented in the Western Interstate Commission for Higher Education's (WICHE) *Balancing Quality and Access: Principles of Good Practice for Electronically Offered Academic Degree and Certificate Programs.* (n.d.). Some of these principles are paraphrased as follows:

- Programs provide for timely and appropriate interaction between students and faculty, and among students.
- The institution's faculty assumes responsibility for and exercises oversight over distance education, ensuring both the rigour of programs and the quality of instruction.
- The institution provides appropriate faculty support services specifically related to distance education.
- The institution provides appropriate training for faculty who teach in distance education programs.
- The institution ensures that students have access to and can effectively use appropriate library resources.
- The institution provides adequate access to the range of student services appropriate to support the programs, including admissions,

financial aid, academic advising, delivery of course materials, and placement and counselling.

Your institution may have its own set of standards. The point, however, is that all instructional endeavours, regardless of their medium of delivery, should be measured equally against an explicitly stated set of criteria.

NEW TEACHING PARADIGM

The unique possibilities inherent in web-based instruction originate not from the Web itself, but from the instructionally innovative ways in which it may be used. It is helpful to consider the Web not simply as a new medium for distance education delivery, but also as a partnership offering a new teaching paradigm and new technology, creating the potential for fundamental changes in how we undertake teaching and learning. Instructors and other members of the online course development team should strive to create learning environments that exploit the features inherent in computers and the Web, to promote active learning that resides in the control of the student, and that can effectively lead to the development of high-order and critical thinking skills. In addition to the AAHE's seven principles cited above, Fox and Helford (1999) list several more suggestions specific to effective teaching online. They are paraphrased below:

- Develop tolerance for ambiguity (recognize that there may be no "right" answer to a given question, and emphasize cognitive flexibility).
- Use scaffolding principles (create material that is slightly too difficult for the student, to encourage cognitive "stretch").
- Use problems that require students to understand and manipulate course content.
- Create opportunities for high levels of interaction, both student-student and instructor-student.
- Integrate formative assessment throughout the course.

TEACHER EDUCATION IS CRITICAL

One of the WICHE principles of good practice recommends appropriate training for faculty who use technology to teach by distance education.

Many of the skills that faculty had honed in face-to-face settings no longer apply online; indeed, some teachers must unlearn certain teaching methods as much as they need to learn new ones. For the sake of both teacher and learner, faculty should undergo some training before beginning to teach online.

One way for faculty to become familiar with the skills and resources needed to be successful online teachers is to become online learners themselves. Many institutions advocate that their online teaching faculty initially enrol in an online course that teaches them how to develop online instruction. This strategy often proves valuable, as teachers experience the same challenges that their students typically will face: problems with inadequate computer abilities, learning about the variety of interactive tools, and underestimating the amount of time needed to complete the online readings and homework. To be successful in the online course, faculty must not only develop new pedagogical skills; like their students, they must also gain new administrative and technical skills. The lists below summarize the most crucial of these new skills.

Pedagogical Proficiencies

- Think of the online environment as just a different kind of classroom for interacting with students.
- Look at other online courses, take some yourself, and ask colleagues if you can access theirs.
- Be prepared to invest the time and effort necessary to deliver a course online. Exploit technology to respond to students' questions and requests for assistance, as well as to provide timely feedback on assignments and grades.
- Always remember to weigh how important something is against how much time it will take to transmit and receive it. And remember to ask yourself whether or not users can see and hear exactly what you intended to communicate.
- Be creative in planning how to use technology to teach more effectively. To inform your planning, invest time and effort in gaining a basic understanding of how the technology works (see *Technical Skills* below).

Administrative Skills

- Teaching online often requires more anticipatory effort than the teaching effort which is typical of a face-to-face classroom setting. Lay out your ground rules right away. Unless you explicitly tell students otherwise, they will want to interact with you at the moment they need you. Create a course syllabus. This syllabus should include the class rules, and you must make sure that your students read it, so that they are aware of the rules. Then stick to those rules.

- Find out where your help is, and know when use it. As mentioned in the WICHE principles paraphrased above, your institution should have people whose job it is to support you (e.g., computing help-desk staff or media development departments). Find out who those people are before you need them, and do not wait to call on them, when you first discover you need them.

Technical Skills

- Determine whether you possess basic PC skills (at minimum, a familiarity with file structure, with opening, copying, saving, and moving files, with creating and managing backup files, with keyboard and mouse functions, with screen and windows features, and with web browser functions.
- Determine whether you need to learn new software applications for teaching online, and if so, whether you are willing to learn them, and to use support systems outside of your institution.
- Determine whether your institution supplies regular training in new software applications.
- Make certain that you are very comfortable with using email. It may be the most common means of communication with students.
- Make certain that you understand basic Internet functionality, bandwidth, and connections speed issues. Your computer and computing environment is probably not like the ones that your students are using (i.e., some students will be dealing with low bandwidth situations). At work, you are likely to be using a local area network (LAN), but when you log on using a modem and an older computer, you will get a better sense of what your some of your students will see and experience.
- Make certain that you have a basic understanding of how web browsers on different types of machines affect the appearance and functionality of your material.

TIME AND RESOURCE MANAGEMENT

During the semester in which the course is implemented, the instructor's time is frequently taken up with responding to student emails, marking assignments, and dealing with other interactive components of the class, such as discussion forums and chats. Due to the inherent nature of web courses, student interaction will likely be sporadic, and will at times produce a surge of email messages for the instructor to respond to. For example, an instructor should expect to receive many email messages at the beginning of the course (students will initially have many questions about online learning), if technical problems make course material inaccessible or students experience difficulty in submitting their assignments. To deal with the influx of email messages, instructors can

- solicit help from a technical assistant (graduate student, teaching assistant) to respond to course emails,
- create a frequently asked questions (FAQ) page, where students can find the information typically needed throughout the course,
- create a protocol in which students must ask questions over the course forum (bulletin board), prior to emailing the instructor,

or

- refer students to a help-desk contact to handle the inevitable technological obstacles that are inherent in accessing a web-based course.

In short, it is important that you get your course online, but it is equally important that you plan and design your course completely before it is opened to students. Indeed, positive first impressions in this new medium are vital for the success of teachers and learners. And remember, trying to develop course materials while teaching the course can be overwhelming. Many instructors typically underestimate the time and assets required to develop, maintain, and offer an online course. Efficient planning and time management are fundamental to its success. Faculty are therefore strongly advised to become familiar with their institution's web development unit, technical training unit, information technology unit, and other support units, and to build a strong working relationship with those support units.

REWARDING FACULTY

A final strategic building block in the success of online course offerings is the institutional development of a process that encourages and inspires faculty to be creative in a web-based environment. Faculty can often be suspicious about technology-based instruction, and many will be hesitant to experiment with it. Establishing the supportive systems described above will go a long way toward gaining faculty "buy-in." It is often more meaningful, however, for faculty members to know that they will receive recognition for their willingness to engage in innovative online education activities, and that their efforts will reward them with tenure, promotion, salary merit increases, and other tangible benefits.

ONLINE COURSE DEVELOPMENT

Online course development is a complex endeavour, and it is not reasonable to believe that a high calibre online course of instruction can be created by just one or two people. Quality courseware production requires a highly organized, concerted effort from many players.

Centralizing the Online Development Unit

Centralizing web development roles into one departmental unit has proved beneficial to ensure that courses are of high quality and meet institutional guidelines. Members of this department may be described as *para-academics*, a role comparable to that of paramedic in medicine. Para-academics are the "first on the scene" of course development; they liaise with the course author or subject matter expert (SME) throughout the authoring process to prevent or remove any instructional barriers that might arise. They also look after the interests of the institution (e.g., obtaining copyright permissions for images used in the course) and undertake other routine tasks that must be dealt with before a course can be published. Roles in this group include project manager, copy editor, information technology expert, HTML and XML coder, media developer, instructional designer, graphic designer, administrative assistant and, sometimes, copyright officer.

Reusable Learning Objects

There has been some development in recent years toward creating repositories of reusable learning objects, where educators can submit, use, or exchange learning objects. Some examples of successful repositories are Merlot (see http://www.merlot.org), EDNA (see http://www.edna.edu.au/edna/go), and SMETE (see http://www.smete.org/smete/). When these and other repositories first appeared, the vision was to build a large infrastructure of networked repositories, to provide the education community with reusable, interoperable, searchable learning objects, and to some extent they have achieved this goal. However, there are still issues around interoperability that limit the usefulness of these objects. It remains difficult to build an object specific enough to meet the requirements at hand, yet generic enough to be adapted to other unknown requirements.

Web 2.0

Web 2.0 is not an update to the Web, but a phrase that refers to a different way we use the Web, based more on social networking and virtual communities running on hosted services. This new use includes blogs, wikis, podcasts, RSS feeds, multi-user domains, and so forth. The potential benefits of Web 2.0 for education are especially apparent when considering the opportunities for social networking now available. From simple discussions to more complex social software, it becomes easier and more effective for learners to engage with one another as well as with the content.

The Course Development Team

The core of an online course development team might comprise as few as five key roles: SME or author, graphic designer, web developer, programmer, and instructional designer. In larger commercial organizations, it is not uncommon for development teams to be much larger, as the expertise in each of these five roles is typically further subdivided and specialists are employed. In non-profit education circles, however, where budgets are tight, it is more likely that a few people will fulfill hyphenated roles, such as *web developer-programmer*, for example.

There are both advantages and disadvantages to these hyphenates. Although one person who performs multiple roles can often exercise more creative control, their workload can, in essence, double. Hyphenates can also see their capabilities and their output become "watered down" as they end up working in areas in which they may not have expertise. The reality is that, in online educational development today, those who already possess strong skills in at least one of the areas described above are considered even more valuable if they also possess the ability and desire to learn new skills in other areas.

It is worth noting that, as the popularity of the Internet continues to increase, software applications and other development tools that combine and automate several development tasks into a single package are being introduced. Macromedia's *Flash®* application is one such example: it allows its users to create script-based interactions without actually writing any programming code, and to automatically export the results in a web-based format, without having any in-depth knowledge of web development. Although the team roles are described and discussed linearly here, each member works with other team members, often in different combinations and at different stages within the development process.

Subject Matter Expert

Subject Matter Experts (SMEs) ensure that the content of the online course is an appropriate alternative to the lecture content normally given in a traditional course. In addition, the SME must write the exercises, activities, and examinations needed to reinforce the new learning. It is also essential that SMEs commit to working as an integral part of the team throughout the development process, ensuring that the online course content is easy to access and interesting for students. Other tasks that SMEs perform include

- identifying or creating textbooks, readings, and resources
- ensuring a pedagogical match among the course objectives, content, exercises, examinations, and assignments
- identifying materials that require copyright clearance, and providing the instructional designer with the necessary information
- providing other team members with a legible copy of any written material

Instructional Designer

While there are hundreds of instructional design models, certain generic processes emerge from their common features (Seels & Glasgow, 1998). These processes are described as follows.

- Analysis – the process of defining what is to be learned
- Design – the process of specifying how learning will occur
- Development – the process of authoring and producing the materials
- Implementation – the process of installing the instruction in the real world

- Evaluation – the process of determining the impact of instruction (Seels & Glasgow, p. 7)

In practical terms, the instructional designer

- helps to make the SME aware of appropriate pedagogical strategies and options
- helps to determine, create, and adapt instructional resources
- provides advice on how best to present information
- writes statements of learning outcomes
- sequences learning outcomes
- sequences activities
- evaluates instruction
- arranges technical production and services
- usually acts as project manager
- acts as editor
- acts as web developer

Web Developer

One of the challenges that web course designers face is to create an atmosphere of confidence in the process during the early stages of development. Web developers should show faculty examples of online materials which illustrate various kinds of content and interactive options that are available to them. They should then describe to faculty how their courses can be produced using a consistent organizational template that provides students with knowledge of the learning objectives, an outline of the content, assignments, evaluation information, resources, links, a list of requirements, and FAQs.

Other roles of the web developer include

- helping the SME or instructor to use tools to create the course web pages, and to maintain the course when complete
- helping the instructor or tutor to use the tools needed, such as email and chat utilities, to make the course interactive
- working with the graphic designer to conceptualize the screens, backgrounds, buttons, window frames, and text elements in the program
- creating interactivity, and determining the look and feel of the interface
- creating design storyboards

In a small production group, the web developer may also act as the graphic designer, photographer, and director, and as the editor of video, audio, and animations. In a larger group, the web developer would typically consult with other team members for the additional aspects of the program; for example, collaborating with the sound designer on the music, or working with the programmer on functionality issues.

Graphic (Visual) Designer

Visual design for Athabasca University courses, whether print-based or electronic, is driven by the needs of students and academics, and by the content of the course itself. Distance education can be enhanced by including technical drawings, illustrations, graphics, and photography to interpret course content. Visual design for electronic courses, or optional electronic enhancements of print-based courses, includes the development and creation of generic or customized templates, navigational icons, icons or images to aid recognition of location within a non-linear presentation of materials, and visuals or graphics to enhance textual content (Athabasca University, 2007).

The World Wide Web has turned the Internet into a compelling visual medium; however, in production terms, good visual design and development can often consume the largest amount of time in a project. As the Web allows educational media to rely more and more on visuals, clear visual design is essential. The visuals that students, especially those new to online learning, encounter in an online course often set the tone for their entire learning experience.

As content is being developed, the graphic designer works with the web developer and the author to create a unique course look, while at the same time integrating the course's functionality into the common institutional template. The use of these common elements provides familiarity for online students and makes it possible for them to take several courses while learning how to learn online only once. The graphic designer ensures continuity for the faculty by designing consistent graphical elements when courses are updated or revised.

For graphic designers, *Adobe Photoshop*® has been the must-have software tool for years. For those developing specifically for online delivery, *Photoshop* has recently incorporated the features of an adjunct application, *ImageReady*®, which formats bitmap images for the Web. Other applications that are becoming more important in the visual designers tool box create vector-based images (as opposed to bitmaps); examples include *Adobe Illustrator*® and *Macromedia Freehand*®.

Programmer and Multimedia Author

The programmer is responsible for program functionality. The programmer uses specialized software tools to enable the interactivity that is suggested and desired in online courses. In the most productive teams, programming is treated as a highly specialized and separate discipline.

Many software applications are available to programmers, who each seem to have a favourite working tool. Programmers should endeavour to provide development team members with a basic understanding of the two classes of programming tools and their capabilities: code-based programming languages and graphical-user-interfaced (GUI) authoring programs. Code-based languages require that programmers use a proprietary computer language to create applications, which can then be delivered over the Internet. For example, these languages enable the processing of information which users supply on web-based forms. GUI authoring programs enable similar processes, but they also offer some automated generation of computer code.

This chapter is not meant to be a comparison of these tools – hundreds of articles cover that – but currently, there does seem to be a clear line between the followers of code-based programming techniques and those who prefer GUI applications. One clear advantage of code-based programming is that these tools are often open source; that is, they are created from freely available, stable code that encourages collaborative development. Commercial GUI software often requires less technical expertise to use than code programming, but such software can be expensive, and the companies who publish these proprietary software programs update them often, rendering earlier versions obsolete and constantly forcing developers who rely on them to purchase new versions.

Below is a partial list of the types of applications that programmers typically work with in a web-based course. Open-source code-based programming languages include
- Hypertext markup language (HTML)
- Java
- Javascript
- Perl
- Extensible markup language (XML)
- PHP
- MySQL

Proprietary GUI web-development software packages include
- Macromedia *Dreamweaver®, Flash®, Director®, Authorware®*
- Microsoft *.NET®, Visual Basic®*
- Adobe *GoLive®, Photoshop®, Illustrator®*

CONCLUSION

Developing effective instructional materials depends on a great deal of planning, collaboration, and concerted efforts from many people skilled at using the right tools. These requirements are even more crucial in online multimedia and course development, which is highly dependent on ever-changing computer technologies. Pedagogical standards must not be compromised, regardless of the instructional medium employed. Employing the principles and guidelines offered in this chapter will help all stakeholders involved in online instructional development to ensure that their efforts are rewarded, ultimately, with satisfied learners.

REFERENCES

Athabasca University. (2007). *Visual design.* Athabasca, AB: Athabasca University. Retrieved October 10, 2007, from http://emd.athabascau.ca/service_design.htm

Chickering, A., & Ehrmann, S. (1996). Implementing the seven principles: Technology as lever. *American Association for Higher Education Bulletin, 49*(2), 3–6. Retrieved October 10, 2007, from http://www.tltgroup.org/programs/seven.html

Chickering, A., & Gamson, Z. (1987). Seven principles for good practice in undergraduate education. *American Association for Higher Education Bulletin, 39*(7), 3–7. Retrieved October 10, 2007, from http://www.umflint.edu/resources/centers/tclt/resources/evaluating_teaching/pdf-bin/Development%20and%20Adaptations%20of%20the%20Seven%20Principles%20for%20Good%20Practice%20in%20Undergraduate%20Education.pdf

Downes, S. (2005). Are the basics of instructional design changing? In *Stephen's web.*
Retrieved April 17, 2007, from http://www.downes.ca/cgi-bin/page.cgi?post=6

Fox, M., & Helford, P. (1999). Northern Arizona University: Advancing the boundaries of higher education in Arizona using the World Wide Web. *Interactive Learning Environments, 7*(2–3), 155–174.

Marzano, R. (1992). *A different kind of classroom: Teaching with dimensions of learning.* Alexandria, VA: Association for Supervision and Curriculum Development. Retrieved October 10, 2007, from http://pdonline.ascd.org/pd_online/ dol02/1992marzano_chapter1.html

McGreal, R., & Elliott, M. (2008). Technologies of online learning: E-learning. In T. Anderson (Ed.), *Theory and Practice of Online Learning* (2nd. ed.). Edmonton, AB: AU Press.

Russell, T. (1999). *The no significant difference phenomenon.* Raleigh, NC: North Carolina State University.

Seels, B., & Glasgow, Z. (1998). *Making instructional design decisions* (2nd. ed.). Upper Saddle River, NJ: Merrill.

WICHE. (n.d.). *Balancing quality and access: Principles of good practice for electronically offered academic degree and certificate programs.* Boulder, CO: Western Interstate Commission for Higher Education. Retrieved October 10, 2007, from http://www.wiche.edu/Telecom/projects/balancing/principles.htm

Wenger, E. (1998). *Communities of practice: Learning, meaning, and identity.* Cambridge, UK: Cambridge University Press.

ABOUT THE AUTHORS

Dean Caplan was employed as an instructional media analyst at Athabasca University until 2002 and is currently an instructional designer at Canadian Pacific in Calgary, Alberta. Dean's professional interests include the design, development, usability, and usage of multimedia in computer-mediated communications. He earned a B.Mus.Ed and an MEd from the University of Saskatchewan.

Rodger Graham (rodgerg@athabascau.ca) joined Athabasca University as an instructional media analyst in 2003. Since 2007 Rodger, has been Acting Manager, of Course Design in the Educational Media Development department. He received a BA and a BEd from the University of Alberta, and an MEd from the University of Saskatchewan.

CHAPTER 11

VALUE ADDED – THE EDITOR IN DESIGN AND DEVELOPMENT OF ONLINE COURSES

JAN THIESSEN & VINCENT AMBROCK
Athabasca University

INTRODUCTION

The editor has traditionally played a key role in the design and development of instructional and educational materials. As the Web and the technology and processes for delivering instructional materials on it have evolved, so too has the editor's role in course design and delivery. The dynamic nature of the Web and the explosive growth of user-driven collaborative applications such as blogs, wikis, and social software – the Web 2.0 – have expanded the scope of most editors' roles even further. The typical web editor in education has a broad and changing range of responsibilities, from editing and verifying course content to evaluating the efficacy of online instructional tools, from unsnarling copyright issues to testing and applying new multimedia applications. One aspect of the editor's role, however, has remained unchanged in the course development process – the editor adds value to the course development value chain by improving course material quality, enhancing students' learning experiences, and ensuring that course-quality standards are set and maintained for the delivering institution.

Our model for defining and studying the online editor's role in the course development process is the School of Business at Athabasca University (AU). The School of Business has taken a leadership role in delivering online distance education courses at AU, by adding online features for existing print-based courses, converting print courses to online formats, or designing and developing new courses for exclusive web delivery. The multimedia instructional design editor (MIDE) is a key member of the School's online course design, development, and production team. The job title, MIDE (and the particular configuration of skills and duties associated with it), is unique to the School of Business, combining, as it suggests, the tasks of integrating multimedia instructional components into online course materials, applying instructional design principles, and editing course materials. Although the MIDE is unique to Athabasca University's School of Business, many of the duties and responsibilities of the job are typical of other online course development projects.

The School of Business has developed the MIDE role to achieve a number of course development objectives. To ensure that standards of product and pedagogical quality are achieved (an institutional objective), the MIDE is responsible for editing course materials before they are delivered to students. In addition, the MIDE applies instructional design principles and strategies to online courses and course materials. Many School of Business courses were instructionally designed for print-based delivery, so converting them for online delivery has raised a host of instructional design issues. Other School of Business print-based courses make use of some online features; the MIDE assesses the pedagogical value of multimedia components and online interactivity tools, and develops or incorporates them in each course.

The MIDE's role adds value to the School of Business' online course development process in three ways: first, by linking other participants in the value chain, and so increasing the effectiveness and efficiency of the entire process; second, by increasing the ability of value chain participants to produce effective online learning experiences; and third, by providing a measure of quality control to ensure that online courses are consistent, technologically innovative, and pedagogically sound.

DISTANCE EDUCATION AND THE ONLINE
INSTRUCTIONAL ENVIRONMENT

School of Business courses are delivered at a distance. Course materials for distance education, whether online or print, "take a learner-centred approach, rather than the traditional content-centred approach of text-books" (Swales, 2000, p. 1). This learner-centred feature enables students "to become involved and motivated by the materials and to take ownership of the skills and knowledge that they acquire" (p. 1). It also means that distance education course materials are a key to motivating, engaging, directing, and supporting students, which makes the course editor an important contributor. The hybrid role of the MIDE is particularly well suited to a distance delivery model, especially when courses are delivered online.

In online delivery, the *learning environment* becomes a particular and important consideration. Kuboni (1999) notes that the term learning environment has emerged "as one of the key metaphors associated with teaching and learning through the new telecommunications and computer-networked technologies" (p. 1). As a context in which learning takes place, the online learning environment has several features: it encourages a reduction in the emphasis on the didactic role of the teacher, while emphasizing collaboration; it enables the development of process skills and knowledge building, rather than information and knowledge acquisition; and it supports collaborative group activities (Kuboni).

Like other departments at AU, the School of Business has faced a number of challenges in developing an online learning environment that delivers all of these envisioned features. Building the tools that support online collaboration and self-directed learning requires resources and time, so logistical issues, such as resource acquisition and allocation, have a significant impact on course development, and on design considerations such as increasing the longevity, currency, and applicability of learning tools and materials. In addition, technology constraints and demands must both be considered in designing the learning environment; most students expect self-directed, web-accessible course materials and resources, online access to AU services (such as the registrar and the library), and the ability to communicate with other students, administrative staff, and faculty. Lastly, Athabasca University has built its reputation and student base on providing certain continuous-intake course delivery models (i.e., self-paced, individualized study; paced group seminars), and adapting these models to fit their new online environment requires some ingenuity. In response to all of these considerations, the

School of Business has built a learning environment in *Lotus Notes®* that is web-accessible and supports a range of collaborative applications and tools. The Notes platform provides an interface for accessing individualized study, self-paced courses and paced, grouped courses, as well as other AU web-based services and administrative and technical support.

If the online instructional and learning environment presents opportunities and challenges not found in conventional face-to-face or traditional distance delivery, so too do the multimedia tools used within it. Nunes and Gaible (2002) contend that multimedia is "the most effective and egalitarian of computer-based resources available." Multimedia, and the online learning environment that delivers and supports it, provides for "artful interaction between learners and content." As with conventional distance delivery practice, it is possible to offer "learning in different locations...for students working at different rates and levels, [as well as] repetition when repetition is warranted" (p. 95). Nunes and Gaible state that multimedia is especially well suited to "dynamic fields" and that "web-based multimedia content ware is itself dynamic" (p. 95). That multimedia and the online environment are dynamic seems an obvious conclusion when we imagine the myriad ways in which learners can interact with content in text, visual, audio, animated, and other forms, through graphic and other interfaces. This conclusion is reinforced by the online environment's possibilities for learner interaction with teachers and other learners, at any time, and from any place.

The Concise Oxford Dictionary defines the word "dynamic" as the opposite of static; it is the reverse of "stationary; not acting or changing; passive" (Thompson, 1995, p. 1,361). As dynamic entities, multimedia and the online environment offer opportunities for various kinds of interaction and active learning, and for "the chance to work with current and even cutting-edge knowledge" (Nunes & Gaible, 2002, p. 95). Rather than confine the design, development, and delivery of learning content to technical and production experts, it may be possible to "engage all stakeholders in the education system...in the development of multimedia learning resources" (p. 95).

The dynamic nature of the online environment, however, also presents unique challenges for course developers and editors. Web content, links, and interactive elements are always changing and require constant vigilance to maintain their currency. Moreover, taking full advantage of the many multimedia and graphic enhancements available in this dynamic environment comes at a price. A simple-looking but effectively designed multimedia tool often requires many resources, a significant amount of time to produce and test, and increases the workload and knowledge level required of instructional, technical, and production staff to implement and maintain it.

The online environment has the *potential* for fast and easy interaction among diverse and distributed users, a fact that raises a number of issues about how this interaction is accomplished, when it is appropriate, and how it is managed. Similarly, although a myriad of learning experiences and opportunities are available through the online environment, questions of how much diversity to offer, what instructional purposes each tool serves, and how to manage the tools selected, also become important. The MIDE addresses these issues from a learner's (student's) perspective in both the multimedia and instructional design components of the job. More recently, as learners and instructors have become more skilled in using web-based collaborative (social) software and user-driven applications, and as online information sharing and communication has moved closer to the connectivity promised by Web 2.0, new questions have arisen about the pedagogical value and methods of providing learners and instructors with more choices and control over their learning environment and interactions, while adhering to instructional standards and goals. When determining the effectiveness of online learning and interactive tools and technology, the MIDE must consider all these perspectives.

These varied demands present great challenges for the MIDE, who must apply precise editorial and instructional design standards across the various course components. Increasing the number of people engaged in the development process and the number of times learning content is subject to revision or change makes it difficult to achieve and maintain control over these standards. Furthermore, the MIDE requires an ever-growing range of skills, as well as flexibility in defining the scope of their duties, to check and evaluate the diverse components that make up an online course, and faces a constant challenge in balancing the learning needs of students against technological and course production constraints and requirements.

COURSE DEVELOPMENT IN AN ONLINE ENVIRONMENT – THE ROLE OF THE MIDE

As a School of Business course moves from concept through production to online delivery, the MIDE guides the production process and plays an integral role in each stage of course development.

Multimedia Development

In their capacity as editors, School of Business MIDEs develop an intimate knowledge of the content of each course. They are one of the final links in the content chain, reviewing all online course components when they are ready to be integrated into the web-based delivery template. The MIDEs occupy a unique position in the design and development process, far enough along that they see a course in its entirety and can clearly identify good locations for using particular multimedia and interactive components, but early enough to develop and integrate those components and to explore new ideas for enhancing educational materials.

As a means of making course production more efficient, and in keeping with a general trend toward collecting and reusing effective multimedia tools, the MIDEs play an important role in identifying online components and tools that have widespread applicability for use in several courses. The School of Business is still exploring ways to store these components and simplify their use across an array of course materials; the trend at Athabasca University, and in online learning in general, toward storing and reusing multimedia applications, learning objects, and databases presents many choices and opportunities for research. The MIDE is a vital link in this research, working as a liaison between School of Business academics, production teams, and other departments throughout the university that are developing data and learning object storage strategies (e.g., the library and the Educational Media Development department).

Instructional Design

All new or significantly revised online courses are submitted to School of Business instructional staff for a preliminary assessment of their design, content, and learning objectives. At this point, the MIDE performs a cursory instructional design (ID) assessment of the proposed course. At this stage, too, a School of Business instructional designer also reviews the proposal and offers ideas to the course author for improving the course's instructional efficacy. However, as courses and their constituent elements often undergo significant transformation between proposal and delivery, the bulk of the MIDE's ID evaluation necessarily happens after the course has been written or revised, when it is submitted for editing and production. Although this strategy can shorten the amount of time available for evaluating and testing new ideas for ID and multimedia tools in a course, it is, overall, a good use of limited resources. New courses are reviewed by the School of Business instructional designer, but existing courses (often high enrolment courses) that are being revised or converted for online delivery might or might not have had the benefit of ID at some point in their development (the School has only one instructional designer, but many new courses that require ID). In many cases, the content of a course has been revised regularly, but issues related to its instructional efficacy have not been systematically addressed in the revisions. This is where the ID role of the MIDE and its late application in the production process is especially useful in assessing and dealing with instructional quality issues, without returning a course to the beginning stages of development.

As part of their instructional design role, MIDEs also check and evaluate course design and layout for instructional efficacy, providing input to authors and production staff. The MIDE ensures that all resources are relevant, linked, and coordinated. It is essential that course components intended to present and deliver information are clearly differentiated from learning activities, which are designed for application or practice. The purpose of the learning activities must be clearly presented, and it must be obvious to learners what action the learning activities require, as well as how and where to obtain feedback. The MIDE also determines if the learning resources work, if they work as intended, and if the instructions for their use are clear. This function is particularly crucial with multimedia components.

While working with existing courses in the instructional design role, the MIDE reviews course components at a number of levels (Swales, 2000). At a course level, the MIDE determines if the course components support and conform to course objectives. At the unit level, it is essential that unit objectives support, build toward, and align with the larger course objectives. Each learning objective in each unit or lesson is assessed to ensure that it is clear, unambiguous, measurable, and related to the content in the lesson or unit. The MIDE determines whether or not the lesson and review activities, as well as technical elements such as multimedia components and interactivity tools, contribute to students' ability to meet the learning objectives of the course, and to see for themselves that they have done so. In online courses, as with traditional distance delivery, this "seeing" must take place in the absence of same-time and face-to-face interaction with a teacher.

Editing

The MIDE's primary role in course development is as an editor. In the online course development and production process, the MIDE provides feedback at the same point as editors in more traditional course development models. The MIDE reviews all course materials and components, revising and, in consultation with course authors, clarifying content, ensuring that the text is grammatically correct, concise, and online-ready. As do all editors, the MIDE ensures that the tone of the course materials is appropriate for the audience, and helps learning to happen; the MIDE also checks that coauthored materials communicate either a consistent voice or a clearly defined set of individual voices, as desired by the authors and as is suitable for the content. Editors ensure that course materials and do not contain bias or plagiarism and that all necessary copyright clearances have been obtained. Finally, web-ready content is copy edited to ensure that all i's are dotted and t's crossed, and that the rules of grammar and punctuation have been correctly and consistently applied.

As editors, more so than in their other roles, the MIDEs serve as proxies for the learners who will work through all components of the online course. They ensure that the information about assignments, including instructions to students, assignment questions, guidelines for assignment marking, and examination guidelines, is correct, consistent, and readily available. Well-edited course materials anticipate and address learner concerns and needs for information, preventing work at the "back end" of the course delivery process (instructor and technical support assistance calls), and building student confidence in and satisfaction with School of Business online course materials.

ADDING VALUE – THE MIDE IN THE DESIGN
AND DEVELOPMENT PROCESS

The MIDE, then, contributes to many aspects and levels of course design and development, and at each level affects the online-learning value chain. The effects of this contribution, however, are difficult to measure empirically. The MIDE works in the design and development component of the online learning value chain, between upstream logistics (described in earlier chapters as infrastructure for online learning, technology choice, and attributes of various media) and downstream logistics (to be discussed in subsequent chapters, and including learner supports such as tutoring, call centres, and electronic library and other digital resources). As such, the MIDE's contribution to the online delivery process is perhaps best measured through their interactions with the other participants in the value chain.

In each role – instructional design, multimedia development, and editing – the MIDE is concerned with facilitating communication between the author and the learner, and between the author and the technical staff who create the multimedia tools and instructional technology used in course delivery. The MIDE explores new resources and opens lines of communication between the many participants in the design and development value chain, and looks for solutions to instructional issues that will satisfy technical staff, academic experts, students, and upstream and downstream support resources. The MIDE searches for and evaluates ways to enhance the overall instructional efficacy of each course, and constantly works to bring the various elements of the online-delivery value chain together as efficiently and effectively as possible.

But just as the MIDE brings together elements and participants in the value chain, they also add value to the course development process by enhancing the ability of other participants to produce effective online learning experiences. Rowntree (1990) refers to this role in course development as the *transformer*, "a skilled communicator who can liaise with any subject specialists whose writing is obscure, winkling out their key ideas and re-expressing them in ways learners will be able to understand" (p. 21). The MIDE helps authors to refine and distill the material they want learners to grasp, and looks for the best tools and techniques for presenting this material concisely and effectively. MIDEs review and evaluate each element in the content and design of a course, so they have an opportunity to share their expertise and knowledge with the course development team and to facilitate communication and knowledge sharing among authors, production and support staff, and technical personnel. This knowledge sharing benefits everyone in the process, and enhances the ability of all value chain participants to make an effective contribution to course development.

The MIDE's most important contribution to the course design and development value chain is quality control. This function has become more critical, and more challenging to define and maintain, as more courses have incorporated multimedia components and moved into the online learning environment, and as learners and course creators have gained knowledge and demanded more control over their learning environment and interactions. The MIDE plays a balancing act between ensuring that rigorous institutional, instructional, and aesthetic standards are applied to learning materials, and providing learners and instructors with some degree of flexibility and control over their learning environment. McGovern (2002) points out that "trillions of words are published on millions of web sites [and] much of this publishing is of appalling quality" (para. 2).

On the surface, online publishing, which has eliminated the highly technical tasks of typesetting, printing, and distribution, appears deceptively simple. In particular, revising online material seems to be quick, simple, and straightforward. And in many ways, it is: open the source document, use a simple text editor, save the changes to the server, and every course can contain what Nunes and Gaible (2002) refer to as "cutting-edge knowledge" (p. 95). If consistent presentation and appearance were the only issues to address, this capacity for multiple participants to revise courses "on-the-fly" would be a serious enough concern for the MIDE. However, "technology is founded on the promise of automation" (McGovern, para. 4), and "you simply can't automate the creation of quality content" (para. 8). Putting poor content into the online learning environment can have especially serious consequences, both for students and for the delivering institution.

As editors do in any course development project, the MIDEs ensure that all course materials are complete and functional, and that they meet the instructional, aesthetic, and editorial standards established by Athabasca University and other educational and publishing institutions. With the course learning goals in mind, the MIDE critically evaluates course materials from the learner's perspective, and considers the learner's needs and likely responses to the information presented in the course. The MIDE ensures that all the pieces of a course work toward the same goal, and that the pieces fit together in a unified whole to provide effective instruction for students. By ensuring that the course materials delivered to students are of consistently high quality, the MIDE contributes to students' confidence in School of Business courses, removes material-based obstacles to their learning, and enhances Athabasca University's reputation as a credible, learning-centred distance education institution.

REFERENCES

Kuboni, O. (1999). Designing learning environments to facilitate reflection in professional practice: Some initial thoughts. Paper presented at *TEL-isphere '99, The Caribbean and technology-enhanced learning [conference]*, St. Michael, Barbados, November 24–27, 1999. Retrieved July 16, 2007, from http://www.col.org/colweb/webdav/site/myjahiasite/shared/docs/kuboni.pdf

McGovern, G. (2002, October 14). Words make your web site a success. *New Thinking*. Retrieved July 16, 2007, from http://www.gerrymcgovern.com/nt/ 2002/nt_2002_10_14_words.htm

Nunes, C. A. A., & Gaible, E. (2002). Development of multimedia materials. In W. D. Haddad & A. Draxler (Eds.), *Technologies for education: Potentials, parameters, and prospects* (pp. 95–117). Paris and Washington, DC: UNESCO and Academy for Educational Development.

Rowntree, D. (1990). *Teaching through self-instruction: How to develop open learning materials*. London: Kogan Page.

Swales, C. (2000). *Knowledge series: Editing distance education materials*. Vancouver, BC: Commonwealth of Learning.

Thompson, D. (Ed.). (1995). *The concise Oxford dictionary* (9th ed.). Oxford: Clarendon Press.

ABOUT THE AUTHORS

Jan Thiessen is a multimedia instructional design editor (MIDE) in Athabasca University's School of Business. She received a BEd (English) from the University of Alberta, and MA in Distance Education from Athabasca University. Her research on faculty attitudes towards interaction in distance education helps inform her work with course authors and teams, developing quality distance learning materials and experiences.

Vincent Ambrock also works as a multimedia instructional design editor (MIDE) in the Athabasca University School of Business. He holds a BA (Honours) in English Literature from the University of Alberta, and has worked extensively as an editor and writer on an array of electronic and print-based publishing projects.

CHAPTER 12

Making Relevant Financial Decisions about Technology in Education

David Annand
Athabasca University

INTRODUCTION

This chapter shows how *relevant costs* can be used by managers in educational institutions like universities, or related sub-units like computer services, to make more informed financial decisions about the use of technology. *Fixed* and *variable* cost behaviours are described, as well as the nature of *cost-volume-profit analysis* and how it is used to predict net revenue for a given level of services or production. *Time value of money* (present value) concepts and the effect of time horizons on planning and investment decisions are introduced. Finally, the means to cost services through *time-driven, activity-based costing* is described.

DIRECT AND INDIRECT COSTS

Cost objects are items for which a separate measurement of costs is desired. They are usually measured in a currency like dollars. In an online learning environment, cost objects can be courses, registration services, projects, students, departments, or academic programs.

Direct costs can be associated with a cost object in a cost-effective manner. They are generally material in amount, linked to a specific area or responsibility, or related to a particular cost object by *contractual* requirements. Let's assume that the cost object is an academic program at an institution. Direct costs would include the salary for the program coordinator, salaries of contracted faculty who teach only in the program, and the cost of a learning software system used exclusively to deliver the program of study. A rule of thumb to determine a direct cost is to consider whether the cost would disappear if the cost object was eliminated. In the example above, the salaries of the program coordinator and faculty, and the software system costs would cease if the program was discontinued, so they are direct costs.

Indirect costs do not bear a discernible relationship to a particular cost object, or cannot be determined in a cost-effective manner. So, if the cost of an online program is the cost object, insurance for the entire institution would be an indirect cost of operating this program. It is required for the institution to function, but would not be affected if a particular online program was discontinued. The means to allocate these indirect costs to cost objects is discussed later in this chapter.

Classifying costs as direct or indirect is often determined by the particular cost object. For example, building maintenance costs might be relatively immaterial when calculating the costs of several online courses, and thus be an indirect cost. The same maintenance costs would be important direct costs if the cost object was a particular campus building.

FIXED AND VARIABLE COSTS

Variable costs change as the activity level of a cost object changes. For example, if an institution provides all textbooks for online students, these costs vary in direct proportion to the number of students registered in a program. *Fixed costs* remain unchanged over a given period of time – for example, salaries for tenured faculty members would be fixed costs if the objective was to forecast the costs of operating Faculty of Medicine programs. All costs tend to be variable over time or a wide range of activity. For instance, faculty salaries may be fixed for a particular year, but will vary as long-term registration levels fluctuate. They may be fixed if a 2% increase in registrations levels is forecast in the next year, but not for a 20% increase. Thus, determining the *relevant range* is necessary when categorizing costs as fixed or variable.

The distinction between fixed and variable cost behaviours is important. Unit costs can misinform if they contain elements of fixed costs. For example, if you are a bookstore manager and have a choice between a) buying textbooks from a supplier for $600 per year for a class of students (with 15 students presently registered); or b) buying texts for $30 per student; what choice would you make? At 15 students, the per unit cost under the first option is $40 per student ($600/15). This comparison suggests that paying the variable rate of $30 per student under the second option would be preferable. However, if registrations turn out to be for 20 students, the average cost per student under the fixed level is the same as under the variable (per student) option ($600/20 = $30). If registration levels exceed 20 students, then the flat purchase price of $600 should be chosen, all other factors remaining constant.

Though this is a simple example, the point is that making financial decisions based on per unit costs which include a fixed cost component can produce incorrect decisions. This error often occurs when calculating relative costs of online versus traditional classroom delivery, because each of these modes has a fundamentally different cost structure. Most forms of online course delivery have a significantly greater fixed-cost component than classroom instruction; there may be a need to invest in computers, communication equipment, and production staff, for instance. Because of the different behaviours of fixed and variable costs over a certain level of activities, when comparing costs among alternative modes of delivery, it is necessary to identify both the fixed and variable components. Using *cost-volume-profit* analysis more accurately predicts total costs over a range of activity levels, once costs have been classified into variable- and fixed-cost categories.

COST-VOLUME-PROFIT RELATIONSHIPS

Multiple revenue and cost drivers (causal factors) can be used to predict total revenues and costs over a range of activity. It is often useful, however, to focus on only one such causal factor and study how variations in this factor affect revenues and costs. CVP analysis does this by first calculating the *total contribution margin* (total revenue less total variable costs), then the *net revenue* (total contribution margin less fixed costs). In other words,

	Measure:	*Calculated as:*
	Total Revenue	Units of output times selling price per unit
Less	Total Variable Costs	Units of output times variable cost per unit
Equals	Total Contribution Margin	
Less	Total Fixed Costs	
Equals	Net Revenue	

CVP analysis assumes that
1. total costs can be divided into fixed and variable components;
2. the behaviour of total revenues and total costs is linear in relation to units of output, within the range of output under consideration (for example, no per unit cost savings result from purchasing large volumes of instructional material);
3. selling price and variable costs of one unit of output are known;
4. time value of money is ignored. This assumption will be relaxed later.

Using CVP analysis, the *break-even point* can be determined. This is the point where Total Contribution Margin equals Total Fixed Costs and net revenue is therefore zero. The formula is:

$$\text{Break-even in units} = \frac{\text{Total Fixed Costs}}{\text{Per-unit Contribution Margin}}$$

For instance, a university pays $3,000 to an instructor per online course. Tuition fees are $300 per course. Variable costs for Course A are $100 per student, which represents the cost of the textbook. Fifteen students must be registered for the course to break even, calculated as $3,000/($300–100) = 15 students. An income statement prepared in *contribution margin* format would show the following:

	PER STUDENT	TOTAL
Revenue	$300	$4,500
Variable costs	100	1,500
Contribution margin	$200	3,000
Fixed costs		3,000
Net revenue		$ -0-

TABLE 1. Course A Net Revenue

Now suppose that Course B is offered and the instructor is paid $2,400. Tuition is $280 and the textbook costs $180. Twenty-six students are enrolled. The net revenue at this registration level is:

	PER STUDENT	TOTAL
Revenue	$280	$7,280
Variable costs	180	4,680
Contribution margin	$100	2,600
Fixed costs		2,600
Net revenue		$ -0-

TABLE 2. Course B Net Revenue

Each course is operating at its break-even point, as net revenue is zero in each case. Using the break-even formula, the minimum number of students necessary in each course to cover fixed costs – the break-even point – can also be calculated as follows:

Course A: $3,000/($300–$100) = 15 students
Course B: $2,600/($280–$180) = 26 students
Total in A and B   = 41 students

CVP analysis can inform other financial decisions. For instance, if a student is indifferent between choosing Course A or B, which course should be recommended if the institutions wants to maximize net revenue? The answer is Course A, as the contribution margin per student is $200 ($300–100), versus $100 for Course B ($280–180). That is, for every additional student registered in Course A, an extra $200 is contributed to net revenue, as opposed to only $100 for Course B. This assumes, however, that fixed costs will not increase if one more student enrols in either course. At some point, another instructor will need to be hired for Course A. Just prior to that point, students should be directed to Course B, until another instructor needs to be hired for that course.

SEGMENT MARGIN ANALYSIS

Let's assume that Course B is not needed for program requirements. If only 25 students are enrolled, should Course B be offered at all? The operating loss at this level is $100, because there is one student less than the break-even point of 26 students and the contribution margin per student is $100. This question brings up another important point with respect to cost and revenue analysis. In the example above, fixed costs are all assumed to be direct costs. In other words, if either or both Courses A and B were cancelled, the associated fixed costs ($3,000 and $2,400 respectively) would disappear. Fixed costs, however, can also be indirect costs. Some or all of these fixed costs may remain whether or not Course A or B is cancelled. The process of expanding the contribution margin analysis by analyzing the fixed cost components as direct or indirect costs is called *segment margin* analysis.

Using the same example, let's assume that the fixed costs of Courses A and B – $3,000 and $2,600 respectively – are composed of the following:

	Course A	Course B
Course-specific costs	$2,000	$1,600
Central administration salaries, allocated equally between Courses A & B	1,000	1,000
Total	$3,000	$2,600

Disclosing direct and indirect costs separately, a segment margin analysis of both courses would show the following:

	COURSE A		COURSE B		COMBINED TOTAL
	PER STUDENT	TOTAL	PER STUDENT	TOTAL	
Revenue	$300	$6,000	$280	$7,000	$13,000
Variable costs	100	2,000	180	4,500	6,500
Contribution margin	$200	4,000	$100	2,500	6,500
Direct fixed costs		2,000		1,600	3,600
Segment margin		$2,000		$900	2,900
Indirect fixed costs					2,000
Net revenue					$900

TABLE 3. Segment Margin Analysis – Courses A and B

Based on this analysis, Courses A and B both have positive segment margins ($2,000 and $900 respectively). At the given registrations levels, both courses help to cover central administration salaries. Course B should not be cancelled. If it was, overall net revenue for the institution would decrease by the amount of Course B's segment margin – $900 – to zero. Using segment margin analysis, the recalculated break-even points are as follows:

Course A: $2,000/($300–100) = 10 students
Course B: $1,600/($280–180) = 26 students
Total in A and B = 36 students

Segment margin analysis illustrates the danger of making decisions based on arbitrary allocations of costs. It is important to remember that direct fixed costs only include costs that can be controlled by the organizational unit or activity under consideration, and that would disappear if the unit or activity was discontinued. In the above example, central administration salaries were allocated to Courses A and B as if these were direct fixed costs. When these indirect fixed costs are appropriately segregated, the registration levels at which direct fixed costs are covered are significantly lower, and more accurate financial decisions result.

RELEVANT COSTS

In the context of making financial decisions about online education, the avoidance of arbitrarily allocating costs is one component of determining *relevant costs*. Relevant costs fall into three categories. First, they must be costs that *differ* between alternatives. In the above example, allocated indirect fixed costs of administrative support staff were irrelevant to the decision because these costs remained whether or not Courses A or B were offered.

Second, relevant costs are *future* costs. Past costs (those that have already been incurred) are referred to as *sunk costs*. They are irrelevant to future decisions because they cannot change the course of future events once they have been incurred. For example, a community college decides to implement an institution-wide document management system. Costs over the three-year implementation period are estimated at $1,000,000. Savings over the life of the system are estimated at $1,200,000. As a result of the estimated $200,000 overall savings, the project is approved. Two years into the project, however, incurred development costs amount to $2,000,000. Additional costs are virtually certain to amount to another $800,000. In other words, the project will cost $2,800,000, not the once-estimated $1,000,000. Estimated savings remain at $1,200,000. At this point, the Board of Governors decides to cancel the project based on the following analysis:

Estimated total savings	$1,200,000
Estimated total costs	2,800,000
Net cost of project	$(1,600,000)

This decision, however, is incorrect. At the end of Year 2, the project should still go ahead to minimize loss, based on this analysis:

Estimated future savings	$1,200,000
Estimated future costs	800,000
Net incremental benefit	$400,000

In other words, the $2,000,000 project costs to date are sunk costs and irrelevant to the decision at the end of Year 2. If they are considered and the project is cancelled at the end of Year 2, the college will lose $2,000,000. If the project is completed, the college will only lose $1,600,000. Granted, the project should not have been started in the first place, but this conclusion is based on hindsight. To minimize loss at the current point of decision, the college should ignore the sunk costs and continue with the project to completion.

Third, relevant costs are only those that involve *cash outlays*. An important example of this concept relates to amortization of capital assets. *Amortization* is a process that allocates the cost of acquiring something with future benefit over more than one year (for example, a computer) over its estimated useful life. Suppose the nursing faculty in a university develops a series of online courses for its Bachelor of Nursing program. Based on projected revenue exceeding costs over the five-year estimated life of the project, the nursing faculty is given a capital grant of $100,000 by the university to purchase the computers to launch this initiative. The computers are expected to have a useful life of five years and be worthless at the end of this period.

Amortization cost of $20,000 ($100,000/5 yrs.) is netted against the revenue generated by this online program. A programmer is hired by the faculty to develop the learning platform. Courses in the program are taught by faculty, who are paid additional money to teach them. These are all direct costs of the program.

At the end of Year 3, the following financial report is prepared by the administrative staff in the Faculty of Nursing:

	YEAR 1	YEAR 2	YEAR 3
Revenue			
Capital grant	$100,000	$ -0-	$ -0-
Registration revenue	5,000	100,000	120,000
Total revenue	105,000	100,000	120,000
Costs			
Faculty salaries	20,000	30,000	40,000
Programmer salary	60,000	60,000	60,000
Amortization	20,000	20,000	20,000
Total costs	100,000	110,000	120,000
Net revenue (loss)	$5,000	$(10,000)	$(10,000)

TABLE 4. Three Year Net Revenues for Online Program Faculty of Nursing

At the end of Year 3, the dean considers whether to cancel the program. Losses of about $10,000 per year are expected to continue since registrations in the online program are not expected to grow after reaching Year-3 levels.

Despite the appearance that the program will continue to lose money into the future, the online program should be continued. The reasons for this may not be readily apparent, but the financial analysis needs to be revamped to exclude the amortization costs, as these do not involve cash outlays. Also, the purchase of the computers needs to be recorded in its entirety in Year 1, as this is when the related cash outflow occurs. After this point, the cash outlay is a sunk cost. Restated on these bases, the financial results would be as follows:

	YEAR 1	YEAR 2	YEAR 3
Revenue			
Capital grant	$100,000	$ -0-	$ -0-
Registration revenue	5,000	100,000	120,000
Total revenue	105,000	100,000	120,000
Costs			
Faculty salaries	20,000	30,000	40,000
Programmer salary	60,000	60,000	60,000
Computers	100,000	-0-	-0-
Total costs	180,000	90,000	100,000
Net revenue (loss)	$(75,000)	$10,000	$20,000

TABLE 5. Revised Three Year Net Revenues for Online Program Faculty of Nursing

The restated results indicate that the program should be continued. Not considering cash flows and recording amortization in Years 1–3 obscures the fact that a net cash inflow is being generated by the project in Years 2–3. The program will contribute net revenue of $20,000 in Years 4 and 5 if the same results as Year 3 are achieved. If the program is dropped at the end of Year 3, no net revenue will be generated in Years 4–5.

Overall, however, the university will not recoup its initial investment over the five-year period. The final results are projected to show an overall $5,000 net cash outflow, as follows (table 6).

If these results had been known at the start of the project, it might not have proceeded. After the initial decision to proceed has been made,

	YEAR 1	YEAR 2	YEAR 3	YEAR 4	YEAR 5	TOTAL
Revenue						
Capital grant	$100,000	$ -0-	$ -0-	$ -0-	$ -0-	$100,000
Registration revenue	5,000	100,000	120,000	120,000	120,000	465,000
Total revenue	105,000	100,000	120,000	120,000	120,000	565,000
Costs						
Faculty salaries	20,000	30,000	40,000	40,000	40,000	170,000
Programmer salary	60,000	60,000	60,000	60,000	60,000	300,000
Computers	100,000	-0-	-0-	-0-	-0-	100,000
Total costs	180,000	90,000	100,000	100,000	100,000	570,000
Net revenue (loss)	$(75,000)	$10,000	$20,000	$20,000	$20,000	$(5,000)

TABLE 6. Five Year Net Revenues for Online Program Faculty of Nursing

however, the program should continue because a positive cash flow is generated in Years 2–5. A significant re-investment will be needed to replace the computers at the end of Year 5, so the decision whether to continue the program should be made at that point.

EXAMPLES OF VARIOUS DECISIONS USING RELEVANT COSTS

Relevant costing concepts can be used to inform a variety of financial decisions in a university context – for example, whether to accept one-time orders for services at a price that is less than usual. Let's assume you are the dean of your university's Faculty of Extension. An important part of your faculty's mandate is to contract with outside institutions and businesses to develop, market, and deliver online courses for their employees. Your unit is required to generate net revenue for the university. The Faculty's online learning system staff and related technological infrastructure can feasibly produce and support about 50 courses per year, about 20 more than at present. Average production costs are $20,000 per course, based on 30 courses per year and calculated as follows:

	Per-course Cost	
Production staff time	$4,000	(all variable on a per course basis)
Instructors	4,000	(all variable on a per course basis)
Online delivery system	10,000	($300,000/30 = $10,000 total per course; $9,000 fixed + $1,000 variable)
Marketing	2,000	($60,000/30 = $2,000 total per course; $1,500 fixed + $500 variable)
Total cost per course	$20,000	

An outside firm has asked your unit to develop, market, and deliver a suite of six courses. The firm has offered to pay $19,000 per course for these services. Let's assume that by accepting this contract, the Faculty of Extension will incur no additional fixed costs. The question is whether this offer should be accepted.

Using average costs per course, accepting the offer would produce a loss of $6,000 on the contract, calculated as follows:

Total revenue (6 × $19,000)	$114,000
Total costs (6 × $20,000)	120,000
Net loss	$(6,000)

It appears that a price of $19,000 per course is insufficient. Remember, however, that only costs that differ among alternatives and involve future cash flows are relevant. Using these two criteria, the allocated fixed costs associated with the online delivery system ($9,000) and marketing ($1,500) are irrelevant. They will not change if the outside contract is accepted. Eliminating these costs from the analysis and using the contribution margin format, the restated results would show the following incremental revenues and costs if the contract is accepted:

	Per Course	Total
Revenue	$19,000	$114,000
Variable Costs		
Production staff time	$4,000	24,000
Instructors	4,000	24,000
Online delivery system	1,000	6,000
Marketing	500	3,000
Total variable costs	9,500	57,000
Contribution margin	$9,500	$57,000

Since an additional $57,000 would be contributed to the faculty, the offer to produce the six courses should be accepted. In the original analysis, including allocated fixed costs that will not change produces the wrong decision. Relevant costing eliminates this conflating factor, because the fixed costs that do not change are identified and omitted.

Now let's use the same information as above, except that an additional fixed online delivery platform cost of $40,000 must be incurred to accommodate development and delivery of the additional six courses. Should these still be produced for $19,000 revenue per course?

The answer is that yes, they should, if other factors remain the same. Incremental net revenue will be $57,000 − 40,000 = $17,000 higher. As we can see in this example, fixed costs can be relevant if incurred as a result of the decision at hand. Again, the essential cost characteristics represent *cash flows* that can be *expected in the future* and are *different* under the various alternatives.

Having said this, non-quantitative factors always need to be weighed and subjectively assessed. In the above example, for instance, lower prices may be demanded by current on-campus customers if the potential contract with the outside firm is accepted and the terms become known. Though these subjective considerations are not within the scope of this chapter's analysis, the point is that relevant costing concepts can improve financial decision making in any environment, for profit or otherwise.

Often, cost-volume-profit decisions need to consider competing alternatives. For instance, let's assume that you are the manager of the learning technology division of your university. You enter into contracts with various Faculties to produce multimedia courses. Your division also has the opportunity to produce courses for either the Faculty of Medicine or the Faculty of Arts, and can sell all the courses that can be produced to these faculties. Detailed information about course production costs is as follows:

	Faculty of Arts	Faculty of Medicine
Revenue per course	$30,000	$80,000
Variable production costs per course	$20,000	$50,000
Contribution margin per course	$10,000	**$30,000**

In this case, the Faculty of Medicine opportunity should be pursued, since each additional course will produce an additional $30,000 of contribution margin compared to only $10,000 for each Faculty of Arts course. What happens, though, if the learning technology unit is operating at capacity? This is a *capacity* constraint. Under capacity constraints, managers should look at the highest contribution margin *per unit of the scarce resource*, not just total contribution margin.

Assume that a total of 40 person-hours are available per day in your unit. Faculty of Arts courses take 1,000 person-hours to produce and Faculty of Medicine courses take 4,000 person-hours to produce. The appropriate analysis is as follows:

	Faculty of Arts	Faculty of Medicine
Contribution margin per unit (see above)	$10,000	$30,000 (a)
Person-hours to produce	1,000	4,000 (b)
Contribution margin per person-hour	$10	$7.50 (a/b)

In this case, with other factors being equal, the Faculty of Arts courses should be produced because this activity produces the highest contribution margin per unit of scarce resource ($10 per hour). Looking at this decision another way, the learning technology unit can produce only one Faculty of Medicine multimedia course in the same time that it can produce four Faculty of Arts courses. Because each Faculty of Arts course contributes $10,000, a total of $40,000 of contribution margin can be generated in the same time it takes to produce one Faculty of Medicine course that produces only $30,000 of contribution margin. This difference may not be apparent unless the contribution margin is recast in terms of the scarce resource – in this case, of staff time.

Relevant cost concepts can also be applied to capital asset replacement decisions. *Capital assets* are tangible items like machines or buildings that have value to an organization for some time into the future, generally for longer than one year. The key to this type of analysis is to recognize that past costs, like the purchase price of capital assets in the past, are irrelevant to replacement decisions. These costs are sunk. Only future cash flows that differ among alternatives are relevant – for example, the cost of a new machine to be purchased, the amount that the old machine can be sold for, and differences in future maintenance costs or production efficiency savings.

Let's assume you have a photocopier that cost $20,000 when purchased yesterday. Today, you find out that you can buy another photocopier for $25,000, and it will save you $.03 per page in production costs compared to yesterday's purchase. Each machine has an estimated useful life of 1,000,000 pages. The expected life of both machines is five years. The maintenance contract with the vendor will remain at $50 per 10,000 pages produced, regardless of whether the newer machine is purchased. The one-day-old machine can be sold for $2,000. Should the one-day old machine be replaced?

Yesterday's cash outlay of $20,000 is irrelevant, as it is a sunk cost. Maintenance costs are irrelevant, as they do not differ between the two alternatives. Focusing on future cash flows that differ among the alternatives, the relevant cost analysis would be as follows:

	Cash Inflow (Outflow)
Purchase price of new machine	$(25,000)
Sale of one-day old machine	2,000
Production savings over estimated life of new machine (1,000,000 × $.03)	30,000
Net cost savings if new machine is purchased	$7,000

As a result, the new machine should be purchased. Net costs savings of $7,000 will be realized.

TIME VALUE OF MONEY

Recall that future, differing cash flows are the only relevant costs for a variety of decisions. Because these cash inflows and outflows may occur over several future years, however, the *time value of money* needs to be considered. This factor considers that a dollar received today is worth more than a dollar received in the future, because interest can be earned on the money in the meantime.

Let's assume you can invest $100 at 8% per year. By the end of the first year, your $100 would grow to $100 × 1.08 = $108. By the end of the second year, your investment of $108 would grow to $108 × 1.08 = $116.64 (earning interest on the accumulated interest is known as *compounding*). By the end of the third year, the investment would total $116.64 × 1.08 = $126. In general mathematical terms, the future value of your investment can be calculated as

$$F = P(1 + r)^n \text{, where } P = \text{present value}$$
$$F = \text{future value of P}$$
$$r = \text{rate of return}$$
$$n = \text{number of periods}$$

Substituting the information in the above example, the future value (F) of $100 received today (P), assuming that interest of 8% is paid and compounded at the end of each year, is

$$100(1.08)^3 = 100 \times 1.08 \times 1.08 \times 1.08 = \$\underline{\mathbf{126}}$$

P is the *present value* of some amount to be received in the future. It is simply the inverse of future value. In this case, the present value of $126 received three years from now is $100, assuming the funds can be invested in the interim at 8%. Similarly, the general mathematical equation to calculate present value is merely the inverse of the future value equation:

$$P = F/(1 + r)^n$$

As an example, if you could receive $100 two years from now, what amount of money would you be indifferent to receiving today, assuming that you could invest the money in the meantime at 10%? Substituting into the equation, you would get $P = \$100/(1.10)^2 = \$82.60$. In other words, if you received $82.60 today, you could invest this at 10% per year and have $100 at the end of two years ($82.60 × 1.10 × 1.10 = $100). You should therefore be indifferent between receiving $82.60 now, or $100 two years from now.

Mathematical tables have been developed to make present value calculations easier. (Refer to Appendix A.) The present value of $1, compounded annually at 10% for a period of two years, is .826 (see bolded cell in Appendix A). Applying this factor to the amount to be received in the future ($100) would produce a present value of $100 × .826 = $82.60, as above.

A somewhat similar process is available to determine the present value of a *series* of equal payments received at the end of each year, for a number of years into the future. For instance, if you received $100 per year at the end of each year for three years, and could invest this at 8% per year, how much money would you have at the end of three years? To calculate this, determine what the future value of each $100 amount received would be at the end of Year 3 and total these. At the end of

Year 3, the total of each year's revenue would grow to $324.64, calculated as follows:

Yr. 1: $100 × 1.08 × 1.08   = $116.64
Yr. 2: $100 × 1.08   = 108.00
Yr. 3:   = 100.00
Total future value $324.64

There is also a general mathematical formula to determine this:

$F = P[(1 + r)^n - 1]/r$, where P = amount of *each* revenue payment
F = future value of *all* revenue payments
r = rate of return
n = number of periods

Substituting the information from the example above,

$$F = \frac{100[(1.08)^3 - 1]}{.08} = \$324.64$$

However, this formula does not tell us how much we would require if we wanted to receive just *one lump sum today*, invest this amount for three years at 8% per year, and have $324.64 at the end of the third year. Similar to the present value of a one-time payment to be received at a future date, the present value of a *future revenue stream* received at the end of each year can be determined by a mathematical formula. This formula is:

$P = F[(1 + r)^n - 1]/r$, where P = present value of *all* future revenue streams
F = future value of *each* revenue amount
r = rate of return
n = number of periods

In the example at hand, this formula can determine the lump-sum amount one would be indifferent to receiving today rather than receiving

$100 at the end of each of three years, assuming the money could be invested at 8% in the meantime:

$$\frac{P = 100[(1 + .08)^3 - 1]}{.08} = \$257.70$$

Proof: $257.70 × 1.08 × 1.08 × 1.08 = **$324.64**

Note that the $324.64 amount is the same as the future value calculated above, assuming a revenue stream of $100 received at the end of each of three years. As shown in Appendix B, a mathematical table can also be used to determine this amount. Referring to the bolded cell in Appendix B, the present value of a future revenue stream received at the end of each of three years and invested at 8% compounded each year is **2.577**. $100 × 2.577 = $257.70, the same present value amount calculated above.

TIME VALUE OF MONEY AND RELEVANT COSTS

The essential relevant cost concepts – *future cash flows* that *differ* among alternatives – combined with the concept of the time value of money are the essential components of discounted cash flow (DCF) analysis. This technique enables decision makers to translate future cash flows that are projected to occur at different times back to the same point in time by using present value techniques, and thus to more accurately assess investment alternatives.

Capital budgeting is the process of planning purchases of assets that will be used for more than one year. Using the same relevant costing concepts discussed previously, future cash inflows and outflows that differ among alternatives are evaluated. Based on when these relevant cash flows are projected to occur, they are translated back to present values, using the techniques discussed above.

Let's assume you are the dean of the Faculty of Business. You are trying to determine whether to replace equipment in a multimedia classroom. The new equipment will cost $240,000. This new equipment, however, should require less maintenance time and expenditures, saving approximately $6,000 per year over the four-year estimated life of the new equipment. The old equipment was purchased five years ago for $100,000. You estimate that this equipment can be sold for $8,000, but that it will likely take one year to find a buyer. Assume that you will have to borrow money from the university's central revenue fund, at 10% annual interest, to finance this possible capital purchase.

To evaluate this decision, first calculate the relevant costs. Ignore the time value of money concepts for now. Note that the $100,000 original purchase price of the old equipment is irrelevant to this decision; it is a sunk cost. The relevant cash inflows (outflows) are as follows:

Purchase price of new equipment	$(24,000)
Maintenance savings over life of new equipment ($4 \times \$6,000$)	24,000
Sale of old equipment	8,000
Net cost savings	$8,000

Based on this analysis, the new equipment should be purchased. To account for the differing time frame in which cash inflows and outflows will occur, however, they need to be discounted back to the present, using discounted cash flow analysis as follows:

Cost of purchasing new equipment today ($\$24,000 \times 1$)	$(24,000)
Maintenance savings over life of new equipment ($\$6,000 \times 3.170$ – see app. B)	19,020
Sale of old equipment ($\$8,000 \times .909$ – see app. A)	7,272
Discounted net cost savings	$2,292

Note that the net cost savings, using discounted cash flow analysis, is still positive. This indicates that the new equipment should be purchased, all other things being equal. The positive cash flow, however, is now much lower than when cash flows are not discounted back to the present. Cash inflows related to the maintenance savings and the sale of the old equipment are worth less in present value terms because they are not realized until some time in the future.

Now assume that the university requires all its centrally-funded projects to earn a return of 20% per year. Recalculate the cash flows.

Cost of purchasing new equipment today ($24,000 × 1)	$(24,000)
Maintenance savings over life of new equipment ($6,000 × 2.589 – see app. B)	15,534
Sale of old equipment ($8,000 × .833 – see app. A)	6,664
Discounted net cost	$(1,802)

The discount applied to future cash inflows is much higher if a higher rate of return is required. This calculation reduces the present value of the future cash flows to amounts that are less than the purchase price of the new equipment today. In this case, the equipment should not be replaced, since the discounted net cost is $1,802.

ACTIVITY-BASED COSTING

Recall the earlier example about whether to produce six multimedia courses. In this analysis, the fixed online delivery system and marketing costs were irrelevant to the decision at hand because they did not differ between the alternatives. There are instances, however, where all costs need to be identified and allocated on some rational basis: to determine what price should be charged for a product or service. For instance, *time-driven, activity-based costing* (TDABC) is a means to accomplish this; it estimates the cost of all resources needed to produce a product or service.

Let's examine the case of a multimedia unit at a community college. The unit must break even on an annual basis; revenues must cover all costs incurred. The unit staff consists of a manager, a programmer, and an administrative assistant. The unit rents computers and space in a privately owned building near the campus. It is also responsible for purchasing liability insurance against unforeseen legal actions, and for paying all utilities. The estimated annual cash outlays are as follows:

Programmer salary	$60,000
Manager salary	80,000
Administrative assistant salary	40,000
Office supplies	3,000
Rent	12,000
Utilities	8,000
Liability insurance	2,000

Various academic units at the college and, at times, private firms, contract with your multimedia unit to produce online course material. You need to determine the amount you should charge for each project to ensure that your unit's costs do not exceed revenues. To accomplish this, the following steps should to be taken.

1. Identify the direct costs of producing multimedia courses, but only to the point where this exercise is worth the time and effort involved. In the example above, the programmer's time would likely be a direct cost, as this could be identified with the production of a specific online course (e.g., if time sheets are maintained).

2. Combine the remaining (indirect) costs into various "cost pools." Each cost pool should consist of indirect costs that are incurred by the same general sort of activity. For example, the manager's and administrative assistant's salaries could be grouped together with office supplies, as these relate to general day-to-day activities of the unit. Call this the Administrative cost pool. Utilities and rent could be lumped into another cost pool, as these relate to the costs of maintaining the physical premises, without regard to the level of course production activity. Call this the Building cost pool. Liability insurance (the Insurance cost pool) could be a third cost pool, assuming that legal action is equally possible for any project.

3. Identify a basis for cost allocation that has some relationship to the incurrence of costs for each indirect cost pool. For example, the manager's and administrative assistant's salaries, as well as office supplies, could be allocated on the basis of the manager's estimated hours incurred on a project. Building costs could be allocated based on the estimated number of working days that a project is active. Liability insurance could be allocated based on the number of expected projects in a year.

4. Calculate an appropriate hourly rate for each type of cost. To do this, it is important to choose a realistic allocation base, not an ideal one. For instance, although ideally staff might work 1,920 hours per year [(52 weeks-4 weeks holidays) × 8 hrs/day], their actual hours worked will be less than this, due to sickness, breaks, socializing, and training time. A more realistic estimate might be 80% of 1,920 hours, or 1,536 hours per year. On this basis, the allocation of the programmer's $60,000 salary would amount to ($60,000/1,536 hours) = $39 per hour. Using the same estimate of hours per year, the first indirect cost pool (Administration) application rate could also be calculated, as follows:

	Cost	Allocation Base	Allocation Amount	Application Rate
Manager salary	$80,000			
Admin. Assistant salary	40,000			
Office supplies	3,000			
Total	$123,000	Mgr.hours/yr	1,536 hrs.	$80/hr.

TABLE 7. Calculation of Application Rate Cost, Pool 1 – Administration

Let's assume that an estimated 40 projects will be completed in the upcoming year and that there are 250 business days per year. The second type of indirect costs (Building) can be allocated as follows:

	Cost	Allocation Base	Allocation Amount	Application Rate
Rent	$12,000			
Utilities	8,000			
Total	$20,000	Project-days/yr (40 × 250 days)	10,000	$2/day

TABLE 8. Calculation of Application Rate Cost, Pool 2 – Building

The third type of indirect costs (Liability Insurance) can be allocated across the estimated number of projects to be completed, as follows:

	Cost	Allocation Base	Allocation Amount	Application Rate
Insurance	$2,000	Projects/yr	40	$50/project

TABLE 9. Calculation of Application Rate Cost, Pool 3 – Liability Insurance

To provide an estimated cost for the project, these rates can now be combined, as applicable, with estimates of the programmer's and manager's time, the number of days the project will be active, and a fixed amount to cover liability insurance ($50 per project). Assume that Project 1 is estimated to take 280 hours of the programmer's time and 60 hours of the manager's time, and should be completed over a period of 150 days. The quoted price would be:

Programmer's time (280 hours × $39)	$10,920
Administration (60 hours × $80)	4,800
Building (150 days × $2)	300
Insurance	50
Quoted price	$16,070

Let's assume that the terms are accepted and the project proceeds. In the end, it turns out that Project 1 actually took 300 hours of programmer time to complete, over a period of 200 days. The manager's time on this project amounted to 50 hours. The net revenue on this project would be calculated as follows:

Revenue, as quoted		$16,070
Less actual costs		
Programmer	300 hrs. × $39	11,700
Administration	50 hrs. × $80	4,000
Building	200 days × $2	400
Insurance		50
Total costs		16,150
Net loss, Project 1		$(80)

TABLE 10. Calculation of Net Loss – Project 1

At this point, if the loss of $80 is deemed significant, the manager would compare the actual allocated costs to the original estimated costs to determine if inaccurate estimates were used. If warranted, rates for estimating total costs would then be adjusted. Also, if additional types of fixed costs are incurred, new cost pools and application rates can be created and the estimated cost of the new activity included in future price quotations.

At the end of a reporting period (let's assume one year for this example), total costs for all projects and for each cost pool can be calculated and compared to the actual costs incurred for the year in each category. This process will indicate further adjustments that may be needed to estimate future costs more accurately.

Assume that 35 projects were actually completed during the year, and that the financial results for the year's activities are as follows:

	PROJECT 1 (SEE ABOVE)	PROJECTS 2 THROUGH 35 (SUMMARIZED)	TOTAL COSTS ALLOCATED	TOTAL ACTUALLY INCURRED	(UNDER)- OVER- ALLOCATED	
Revenue	$16,070	$182,000	N/A	N/A	N/A	
Less costs						
Programmer	11,700	50,000	$61,700	58,000	$3,700	(a)
Administration	4,000	115,000	119,000	125,000	(6,000)	(b)
Building	400	18,000	18,400	21,000	(2,600)	(c)
Insurance	50	1,700	1,750	2,000	(250)	(d)
Total costs	16,150	184,700	$200,850	$206,000	$(5,150)	
Net revenue (loss)	$(80)	$(2,700)	N/A	N/A	N/A	

TABLE 11. Calculation of Net Revenue – All Projects

Analyzing this information indicates the following:

a. More of the programmer's time was assigned than actually incurred, resulting in a $3,700 over-application of this cost to all projects. Two possible causes should be investigated to inform future pricing decisions:

   i. The salary actually paid may be less than the original estimate. This appears to be the case, as the programmer's salary was estimated at $60,000 at the start of the year, but actually only amounted to $58,000.

   ii. In total, the actual hours billed to individual projects may add up to more than the original estimate of 1,536 hours.

b. Less of the Administration cost pool was allocated to the year's projects than actually incurred, resulting in a $6,000 under-application of this cost pool. This may have occurred for the following reasons:

   i. Salaries actually paid to the manager and administrative assistant, or actual office supplies costs may have exceeded estimates.

   ii. Fewer manager's hours may have been charged to individual projects than estimated.

c. Less of the Building cost pool wasallocated than incurred, resulting in a $2,600 under-application. Part of the cause is the fact that fewer projects werecompleted than originally estimated (35 vs. 40). There are other possible causes:

   i. Actual costs may have exceeded original estimates. This appears to be the case. Estimated building costs at the start of the year were $20,000. Actual costs totalled $21,000.

   ii. The average number of days to complete each project may have been less than the original estimate of 250 days.

d. Less of the professional liability insurance costs wereallocated than incurred. Since the actual costs incurred were the same as originally estimated ($2,000), the cause of this under-application is solely the result of fewer projects being completed than originally estimated.

All of these possible explanations should be investigated to determine if the estimated application rates for each type of cost are reasonable. If not, appropriate adjustments should be made to future estimates. Also, notice that initial estimates do not need to be extremely accurate. If they are grossly in error, the results will be obvious over time and adjustments can be made. Overall, the use of TDABC can provide more accurate information about the costs and underlying efficiency of value-creating processes.

CONCLUSION

Decision-makers in any organization need to base financial decisions on relevant costs. These include only the estimates of future cash flows that differ among alternatives. When cash flows from investment decisions will occur over a longer period of time, techniques should also be used to equate these amounts back to their present values. Finally, time-driven activity-based costing is a useful and relatively powerful method to inform pricing decisions. With increased interest in online learning and greater reliance on revenue-generating activities, all of the concepts discussed in this chapter are useful means to analyze the financial decisions that all institutions of higher learning face.

ABOUT THE AUTHOR

David Annand, Ed.D., M.B.A., C.A., is the Director of the School of Business at Athabasca University. His research interests include the educational applications of computer-based instruction and computer-mediated communications to distance learning, and the effects of online learning on the organization of distance-based universities.

APPENDIX A

Present Value of $1
$P = F / (1 + r)$

Periods	2%	4%	6%	8%	10%	12%	14%	16%	18%	20%	Periods
1	0.980	0.962	0.943	0.926	0.909	0.893	0.877	0.862	0.847	0.833	1
2	0.961	0.925	0.890	0.857	**0.826**	0.797	0.769	0.743	0.718	0.694	2
3	0.942	0.889	0.840	0.794	0.751	0.712	0.675	0.641	0.609	0.579	3
4	0.924	0.855	0.792	0.735	0.683	0.636	0.592	0.552	0.516	0.482	4
5	0.906	0.822	0.747	0.681	0.621	0.567	0.519	0.476	0.437	0.402	5
6	0.888	0.790	0.705	0.630	0.564	0.507	0.456	0.410	0.370	0.335	6
7	0.871	0.760	0.665	0.583	0.513	0.452	0.400	0.354	0.314	0.279	7
8	0.853	0.731	0.627	0.540	0.467	0.404	0.351	0.305	0.266	0.233	8
9	0.837	0.703	0.592	0.500	0.424	0.361	0.308	0.263	0.225	0.194	9
10	0.820	0.676	0.558	0.463	0.386	0.322	0.270	0.227	0.191	0.162	10

APPENDIX B

Present Value of a Future Revenue Stream of $1
$P = F[(1 + r)^n - 1] / r$

Periods	2%	4%	6%	8%	10%	12%	14%	16%	18%	20%	Periods
1	0.980	0.962	0.943	0.926	0.909	0.893	0.877	0.862	0.847	0.833	1
2	1.942	1.886	1.833	1.783	1.736	1.690	1.647	1.605	1.566	1.528	2
3	2.884	2.775	2.673	**2.577**	2.487	2.402	2.322	2.246	2.174	2.106	3
4	3.808	3.630	3.465	3.312	3.170	3.037	2.914	2.798	2.690	2.589	4
5	4.713	4.452	4.212	3.993	3.791	3.605	3.433	3.274	3.127	2.991	5
6	5.601	5.242	4.917	4.623	4.355	4.111	3.889	3.685	3.498	3.326	6
7	6.472	6.002	5.582	5.206	4.868	4.564	4.288	4.039	3.812	3.605	7
8	7.325	6.733	6.210	5.747	5.335	4.968	4.639	4.344	4.078	3.837	8
9	8.162	7.435	6.802	6.247	5.759	5.328	4.946	4.607	4.303	4.031	9
10	8.983	8.111	7.360	6.710	6.145	5.650	5.216	4.833	4.494	4.192	10

THE QUALITY DILEMMA
IN ONLINE EDUCATION REVISITED

NANCY K. PARKER
Athabasca University

INTRODUCTION

With the proliferation of online learning providers, and the challenges presented by the distance education sector to state regulators and accrediting bodies, it is not surprising that "buyer beware" is the watchword for students, institutions, and public agencies alike. In the current environment, organizations must demonstrate the quality of their services in ways that are intelligible to potential students and their employers; faculty and staff; regulators; and government agencies. The admirable attempts to define quality standards and best practices for online education, however, have done little to assuage the scepticism of representatives in the academy who are more accustomed to face-to-face delivery, directed to bounded communities. Fully addressing the roots of such scepticism is beyond the scope of this paper; however, its presence informs much of the technical discussion around quality assurance frameworks, in higher education in general, and in online delivery in particular.

Purveyors of online learning programs may be inclined to attribute a lack of broad acceptance among their colleagues to the paradigm shift that higher education has been undergoing in the past 15 years. In many cases, however, it must be admitted that the potential of electronic delivery modes has not been fully realized in the implementation of online courses. Some have suggested that these shortcomings are the result of trying to replicate the classroom environment, instead of maximizing the new configurations of knowing and community formation possible in an interactive online environment (Schank, cited in Caudron, 2001). Others have traced some of the potentials and limitations of online education to issues resident in the founding principles of distance education (Larreamendy-Joerns & Leinhart, 2006).

Finding appropriate comparators for the efficacy of any particular mode of delivery is difficult when the broader questions of quality assurance in higher education are far from settled. The spectrum ranges from detailed critiques of the regulatory burdens and dubious outcomes of quality assurance audits in Australia (Reid, 2005) and England (Harvey, 2005) on one end, to the accreditation debates spawned by the Spellings Commission in the United States on the other (Zemsky, 2007). An examination of definitional issues points to a long-standing conflict in values between business modelling and public services. It is important to acknowledge these tensions fully before turning to the more technical, but admittedly value-laden, exercise of reviewing the standards proposed by different quality assurance agencies.

After a discussion of the contexts of quality assurance activities in higher education in general, and of the competing paradigms highlighted by online learning, this chapter examines quality standards that have been proposed for the delivery of online instruction in four different jurisdictions. The full range of state licensing, voluntary accreditation, and market-driven seals of approval reveals tensions between externally driven compliance and internally driven improvements. Although the regulatory frameworks for quality assurance vary dramatically in Australia, England, Canada, and the United States, there is still enough common ground to establish some general characteristics for a scholarly approach to online teaching and learning. At a basic level, the characteristics of quality educational delivery demonstrated in these frameworks include providing clear statements of educational goals; sustaining the institutional commitment to support learners; and engaging in a collaborative process of discovery; which contributes to improving the teaching and learning environment.

Another area of commonality is the fact that, while self-review can be a key component for any of the frameworks, to a large degree they are being driven by external concerns. Changes in the sources and levels of funding, the rise of an international market, and the ever-present concern over "rogue operators" have challenged higher education institutions and their state regulators alike. These issues, in turn, have spawned an international dialogue around accreditation processes and guidelines for the transnational – or cross-border – delivery of higher education made viable through web-based technologies (UNESCO/OECD, 2005). While the articulation of standards may propose base levels of operational integrity, the rhetoric of most regulatory bodies and accrediting agencies suggests much more than minimal compliance.

On a wider level, each of the projects seeking to establish quality standards for online education appears to aim at inculcating a set of values that prizes management by measurement. A confluence of what might be considered "best practices" is mixed in with suggestions for regulatory minimums in a number of these statements of standards. In the past decade, the process of measurement has gained greater complexity, with the various iterations of e-learning benchmarking projects undertaken in New Zealand (Marshall, 2006), Australia (Bridgland & Goodacre, 2005), and England (Morrison, Mayes & Gule, 2006). A consistent area of contention, the degree to which quality assurance activities can or should be targeted to outcomes, as opposed to internal processes, is addressed in a separate section. Recognizing that the terms *quality* and *online education* are burdened with assumptions enough to create their own problematic is a necessary prelude to what follows.

DEFINITIONAL ISSUES

The greatest challenge for trying to define quality in any product or service is that quality remains a relative experience, realized in large part through an individual's level of expectation. Since quality necessarily rests in the eye of the beholder, at first glance, systems developed around the concept must necessarily be exercises in systematic subjectivity. In higher education, quality is a construct

> relative to the unique perspectives and interpretations of different stakeholder groups (students, alumni, faculty, administrators, parents, oversight boards, employers, state legislatures, local

governing bodies, accrediting associations, transfer institutions,
and the general public). (Cleary, 2001, p. 20)

It follows, therefore, that the effectiveness of any quality improvement activities will be as much a function of the ability to foster agreement
around common goals as of any substantive input or process adjustments
attempted by an institution. Fostering agreement, however, is much more
difficult when the term quality is burdened with the legacy of failed
management fads.

In many circles, quality is understood as shorthand for Total
Quality Management (TQM) or its close cousin, Continuous Quality
Improvement (CQI). Some may believe that these fads peaked and
retreated in the last century (Birnbaum, 2001). However, recent modeling (Widrick, Mergen & Grant, 2002), and examples of the pursuit, by
individual institutions, of the Malcolm Baldridge Awards (Spahn, 2000)
or ISO9000 recognition suggest that TQM still has a foothold in higher
education, in spite of the problems posed by the fact that its language
carries a corporate flavour (Banta & Associates, 2002). The Sloan
Consortium "Quality Framework" explicitly references CQI in its aims
to "establish benchmarks and standards for quality" for asynchronous
learning networks (Moore, 2005. p.1). The pressure to apply management techniques to higher education came from a perceived crisis in
confidence with post-secondary systems, and from the growth of state-
sponsored accountability systems.

For supporters, it "has long been understood in organizations
that when you want to improve something, you first must measure it"
(Widrick, Mergen, & Grant, 2002, p. 130). But measurement systems are
about much more than the technical specifications of various indicators
– they are about control. The first iteration of TQM/CGI provoked a
debate about its social as well as technical implications, and demonstrated the "disconnect between the philosophy of the management
process and the purposes of the institution[s] for which it was being
proposed" (Birnbaum, 2001, p.107). The engineering (or re-engineering)
of systems designed to guarantee that manufacturing processes would
meet technical specifications seems to imply a uniformity that may not
be possible, or even desirable, in the dynamic and heterogeneous environment of higher education. The International Standards Organization
(ISO) makes clear the central principle of the pursuit of quality: to
establish processes that will maximize service to customers. To many

within the academy, the "learner as consumer/information as commodity" world presupposed by the business model of higher education remains antithetical to independent scholarship in pursuit of the advancement of knowledge (Bok, 2003).

Traditionally, universities achieved quality in intellectual endeavours through the professionalism of academics, the principles of scholarship, and the rigours of peer review; they gained standing in society by communicating those standards to political and social elites. More recently, massification, diversity, and cuts to funding, along with a wider political movement to demonstrate efficiency and responsiveness, have spawned different conceptions of accountability (Brennan & Shah, 2000). The attempt to lift the meaning of quality education to something beyond short-term fiscal efficiencies and taxpayer benefits is a matter of trying to regain some of the ground lost in previous decades. It is also an encounter with what has been represented as a paradigm shift in higher education, highlighted by the advent of online education.

It must also be admitted at the outset that, with the shift to mobile wireless technologies, "online" education may well appear to be outmoded shorthand for computer or web-enabled activities. The term has appeal, however, since it carries the sense of a linked community of learners. It still resonates of bounded communities with the possibilities of transformative experiences, rather than the sporadic or strictly utilitarian viewing of information on screens. It has been suggested that online learning is best conceptualized as "an environment that integrates collaboration, communication, and engaging content with specific group and independent learning activities and tasks" (Sims, Dobbs, & Hand, 2002, p. 138). More particularly, the ability of students to engage in "asynchronous interactive learning activities" has been described as the "signature characteristic of this technology" (Phipps & Mertisotis, 2000, p. 6). The importance of the flexibility inherent in asynchronous activities challenges the assumption that emulating the classroom constitutes best practice in online teaching and learning environments. However, the degree to which technology has driven, or simply enabled, the paradigm shift in higher education, is debatable. Whether their adherents have overstated the changes that have taken place as a result of web-enabled learning technologies is another question worthy of consideration.

PARADIGM SHIFT

Although there had been many examples of applications of computer technology in classrooms for at least a decade before 1995, Michael Dolence and Donald Norris have been credited with issuing a wake-up call for higher education administrators. In *Transforming Higher Education*, Dolence and Norris (1995) purport to offer ways for colleges and universities to survive the transition from the Industrial Age to the Age of Information. Even though their vision for the future has not been realized on a wide scale, many of the conceptual juxtapositions they offer have gained currency in higher education. These juxtapositions include a shift from episodic access to clusters of instructional resources, to integrated perpetual learning, with a separation of teaching and certification of mastery, and a re-conceptualized role for faculty – from deliverers of content to mentors and facilitators of learning. The most pervasive of these changes is the shift from a *provider focus* to a *learner focus*, with its suggestions for mass customization through individualized learning systems.

Elaborations on this theme indicate that the capabilities of the Internet have overturned "the traditional roles of the college or university as the leading (1) research source and knowledge creator, (2) archivist and gateway to knowledge, (3) disseminator of advanced knowledge, and (4) referee and evaluator of truth" (Quinn, 2001, p. 32). If the production and dissemination of knowledge are no longer the restricted purview of higher education, the roles of post-secondary institutions in the worldwide network are increasingly vulnerable. Students and faculty alike need to be more open and to promote capacities to analyze, interrelate, and communicate about facts gleaned from network-based knowledge.

The traditional quality measures associated with accreditation or state-administered quality assurance frameworks do not match this new climate of teaching and learning. One of the most common measures, "seat time" does not translate to an online or even a blended environment. Even when adapted to an online environment, other common measures rely on inputs (averages of entering students; number of students; qualifications of instructors; systems development) or outputs (numbers completing courses; satisfaction ratings by students and alumni; revenue generated from tuition, intellectual property, or commercial partnerships), but lack in measures to address the fundamental integrity of the online learning environment.

Wallace Pond (2002) summarizes some of the old and new paradigms for accreditation and quality assurance as follows. The old paradigm measures could be characterized as teacher-institution-centred, centralized, hegemonistic, "one-size-fits-all," closed "us versus them," quantitative, prescriptive, time-as-constant with learning-as-variable, teacher-credentialed, consolidated experience, regional/national, static, single-delivery mode, process, infrastructure. In contrast, the new paradigm measures can be seen as learner-centred, local, deferential, tailored, open, collaborative, qualitative, flexible, learning-as-constant with time-as-variable, teacher-skilled, aggregated experience, international/global, dynamic, distributed-delivery model, outcomes, services (Pond, 2002). The degree to which these measures might apply is discussed the next section, but they do not address some of the other questions generated by the university's entry into online course delivery.

The first questions must ask the degree to which online learning environments have delivered, or can deliver on, their promises. The greater access afforded through web-based delivery systems has been one of the key advantages cited by observers of the technological transformation in higher education. Whether depicted as an advantage in developing greater economies of scale for delivery systems or in ameliorating social inequalities, broader access has been lauded as a key feature of the new paradigm. Electronic learning systems, however, are not always as billed. Academic leaders doubt the faculty's acceptance of the legitimacy of online education (Allen & Seaman, 2006). Potential employers also remain doubtful (Adams & DeFleur, 2006). Despite student-focused rhetoric, the administrative momentum for distance delivery can overwhelm the voices of mature students who may not be as confident with technologies, and of younger students with expressed preferences for face-to-face instructional contact (Arthur, Beecher, Elliot, & Newman, 2006). Some faculty doubt that the necessary social integration, particularly needed to improve the success of first-generation students, can be provided in a distributed environment (Allen, 2006). Another caution rests in the comparative completion rates between online and classroom delivery. If intended economic and social transformations are to be realized, access must be examined at more than just the point of entry.

The promise that economies of scale will make education more affordable is perhaps even less persuasive to most academics. That "proprietary institutions are likely to enter the market by contracting with the best professors to provide video-based courses with exclusive rights to their distribution and use" was a vision of higher education in the 1990s (Hooker, 1997, p. 8). Obviously, the proponents of such models have missed the significance of interactive technologies. Providing more efficient delivery of "lectures by famous faculty" would recreate in cyberspace the "world of the passive listener and single speaker that has marked much of what passes for higher education" (Lairson, 1999, p. 188). Despite the growing popularity of pod-casting on campuses, making the doubtful system of mass lectures more efficient does not appear to be much of an advancement over the correspondence school's traditional course-in-a-box. Another tension emanates from the fact that the bulk of what is delivered in the online environment consists of discrete training modules directed to particular job skills or competencies. While there seems to be slippage between what is articulated in the realm of learning outcomes (the skills we expect graduates to demonstrate) and our expectations around the values associated with the liberal arts, it is fair to say that higher education aims should be broader than the goals of the corporate training sector.

Critics such as David Noble (2001) present almost apocalyptic views on the incursion of educational technologies into the classroom. The Web's "dark side" is depicted as the "rapidly growing trend of university corporatism" and the exploitation of knowledge workers (Kompf, 2001). Challenges from the for-profit sector, the influence of corporate training agendas, and "the 'rush to serve' different clienteles"are described as jeopardizing the position of the post-secondary sector as the "source of objective analysis of the society in which it exists" (Crow, 2000, p. 2). Acting as the conscience of civil society speaks to a much broader purpose than meeting the immediate training needs of corporations. If this ideal is taken seriously, then one should expect that faculty would lead the debate from a perspective broader than their own protectionist instincts.

An alternative vision of democratic ideals in the digital age would have education enabling "people to learn about, with, and beyond technology" to open the "doors of economic, educational, and personal empowerment" (Milliron & Miles, 2000, p. 61). However, the reconceptualization of higher education should be done by – not to – the academy. Establishing the terms through which to assess online education should not be left to either the marketplace or to self-perpetuating bureaucracies. Taking back some of the momentum will be a challenge, since the articulation of regulator standards and consumer focused best practices are well underway. Attempts to transform codes of practice into benchmarking tools, which may provide frameworks more compatible to academic traditions of self-reflection and collegial review, have inherited many elements from these early efforts but are, as yet, largely unproven.

STANDARDS FROM FOUR JURISDICTIONS

The formulation of quality assurance systems for online education, while most frequently regulated at a regional or national level, has in recent years been driven by international developments. The global reach of the Internet and the lack of ways to regulate transnational commercial activities allow fraudulent operators to spring up. One possible approach is to promote consumer education through online directories or consortiums. Another possibility is free-lance course reviews from former students, similar to the book reviews found on the sites of online booksellers such as Amazon.com (Carnevale, 2000). This possibility was echoed in the findings of the symposium sponsored by the Pew Charitable Trust, which observed deficits in consumer-focused information, especially at the course level (Twigg, 2001). Student dialogues in *facebook.com* and the growth of sites like *ratemyprofessor.com*, along with the development of "viral marketing" campaigns, all point to the demand for information. Not surprisingly, the appetite is not large for allowing the marketplace to determine outcomes in a wide-open, for-profit model. Simply stated, it does not seem either ethical or efficient to leave students to bear the full risks for product testing various online-education ventures.

In the past two decades, there has been a marked increase in the size and influence of the cadre of higher-education, quality-assurance technologists working directly for government or in semi-autonomous agencies. Various quality assurance agencies are engaging in international discussions aimed toward at least equitable, if not reciprocal, recognition of accreditation processes. For example, the potential of harmonizing systems of higher education in Europe under the Bologna Declaration (European Ministers of Education, 1999) provided impetus for commission-supported projects sponsored by the European Quality Observatory (see http://www.eqo.info) and its parent organization, the European Foundation for Quality in e-Learning (EFQUEL). These projects include advocating for a federated approach to establish a European Quality Mark, to address an obvious "lack of credibility" with potential consumers of e-learning (EFQUEL, 2007, p.1). The UNESCO/OECD joint statement on cross-border delivery is another example of the intentions for international cooperation that would reduce the potential for abuses left open by regulatory gaps (UNESCO/OECD, 2005). Even with these international aspirations, however, the regulation of higher education, like the selection processes of most potential students, is a much more localized matter.

Responses from national and local quality assurance interests have varied. Some of the differences rest in the degree to which state-sponsored quality-auditing procedures have become entrenched in the past decade; others reflect the suspicions or traditions associated with distance education in general. The elaborate state licensing approach has been depicted as excessive and a sign of the erosion of the autonomy of higher education. To some, these measures demonstrate the drive to "harness the universities to perceived economic priorities" (Greatrix, 2001, p.12). In that light, it is interesting that the criteria of the state licensing agency have largely subsumed standards first developed for a peer review model of accreditation. In other locales, it appears that efforts have been made to use quality assurance standards to inform "buyer's guides."

The legislative and accountability frameworks for universities in Australia are confounded by the federal governance structure and the changes in funding sources. Under the Australian constitution, education is a matter within the jurisdiction of the states/territories, but the universities established through their own state's enabling legislation are directly funded by the Commonwealth (DEST, 2002a, p.5). The split in legislative authority and oversight, and the increase in non-governmental sources of revenues provided an impetus for the joint Ministerial Council on Education, Employment, Training and Youth Affairs to endorse protocols for state approval processes and to establish the Australian Universities Quality Agency, with the power to audit universities over a five-year cycle, using institutional self-assessment and visits from expert panels. The rationale for the development of the national system was explicitly framed in terms of competitive challenges, domestic and international, and of policies that have encouraged the universities to "align themselves more closely with industry needs" (DETYA, 2000, p.1). Under the revised regime, creditable quality assurance systems, providing evidence of the quality of service and skills of graduates, were explicitly intended to make the universities more attractive to business investors. The systems include national qualification frameworks to communicate expected standards for each level of post-secondary achievement.

The use of the term "university" in Australia is restricted by state or territorial legislation, and in order to be "self-accrediting," universities must demonstrate that they have appropriate quality assurance procedures in place. Within this framework, "universities are expected to engage in a pro-active, rigorous and ongoing process of planning and self-assessment which will enable them to ensure the quality outcomes expected by their students and the wider community" (DETYA, 2000, p.17). The Australian government policy framework has been presented as a marketing tool to address the advantages that global competitors enjoy by having "centralised, separate, and highly visible" bodies responsible for quality assurance (Vidovich, 2001, p. 258). Yet only two years after the Australian Universities Quality Agency was established, a more broadly framed review of the higher education system was initiated. Concerns expressed about the quality assurance system included "too much emphasis on institutional quality assurance and not enough on learning outcomes," and deficits in both the presentation and form of data (DEST, 2002b, p. ix-x). Concerns raised about e-learning initiatives included the introduction of a new range of costs, along with what appear to be the standard questions of "equity of access, cost-effectiveness, the quality of courses, the impact on learning outcomes and the impact on academic work" (DEST 2002b, p. 6). The results of these consultations and the intentions to simultaneously increase diversity in the range of recognized providers and improve the clarity and effectiveness of standards have met with mixed reviews (King, 2006; Nunan, 2005).

The selected examples of quality assurance frameworks from the United Kingdom centre on open and distance learning, with e-learning issues as acknowledged variables within a spectrum of delivery mechanisms. Three different external approaches to assessing the offerings by individual institutions include licensing procedures under the auspices of a government agency, a voluntary accreditation association, and a scheme for certification through quality marks. Again, much of the drive to enhance quality assurance schemes has been presented in the context of potential regional and global competition. Each of these examples also demonstrate ongoing tensions between external regulatory approaches and internal aspirations for improvement. It should be noted that the full network of subject-based auditing includes benchmark information linked to the national frameworks for higher education qualifications.

It has been suggested that the Quality Assurance Framework in the United Kingdom is not just comprehensive; it is "the most complex anywhere in the world" (Brown, 2000, p.335). The Quality Assurance Agency for Higher Education (QAA) was incorporated in 1997, with the aim of reducing some of the reporting burdens created by a combination of external assessments by funding agencies and quality assurance processes driven by peer review. Its mission is to "promote public confidence that the quality of provision and standards of awards in higher education are being safeguarded and enhanced" (QAA, 2000, p.1). While the purpose of reviews has remained the same, the 2004 revision of the handbook describes the features of academic review as

- a focus on the students' learning experience;
- peer review;
- flexibility of process to minimise disruption to the college;
- a process conducted in an atmosphere of mutual trust; the reviewers do not normally expect to find areas for improvement that the college has not identified in the self-evaluation;
- an emphasis on the maintenance and enhancement of academic standards and the engagement with the academic infrastructure;
- use of self-evaluation as the key document; this should have a reflective and evaluative focus;
- an onus on the college to provide all relevant information; any material identified in the self-evaluation should be readily available to reviewers; and
- evidence-based judgements. (QAA, 2004b, p. 3)

While the less proscriptive tone of these statements would seem to signal more recognition for the expertise of academic institutions, it may not appease the vocal critiques of the "audit culture" (Shore & Wright, 2000).

Initiated in 1998 through 2001 with revisions starting in 2004, the QAA also developed Codes of Practice for ten areas: post-graduate research programs; collaborative provision and flexible and distributed learning (including e-learning); students with disabilities; external examining; assessment of students; program approval, monitoring and review; career education, information and guidance; placement learning; recruitment; and admissions (QAA, n.d.a). The first iteration of the guidelines for distance learning included five system design elements, six elements for academic standards, program design and approval, three on the management of delivery, one on student development and support, three on student communication and representation, and five on student assessment. The main thrust of the original guidelines for distance learning was the integration between distance delivery and the general quality standards for teaching and learning activities expressed in the other codes of practice. The 2004 revision to the code of practice encompasses what were deemed to be good practices for a wide variation of delivery options which in "general do not require the student to attend particular classes or events at particular times and particular locations (QAA, 2004a, p. 3).

The QAA distance learning guidelines reference the work of the voluntary accreditation association in the United Kingdom's distance education sector, citing the Open and Distance Learning Quality Council (ODLQC) standards. The ODLQC (2005) accreditation standards, first established in 1999, revised in 2000, and again in 2005, are organized in six sections: outcomes (9 standards); resources (4 standards); support (7 standards); selling (9 standards); providers (10 standards); and collaborative provision (5 standards). While the detailed accreditation standards tilt toward institutional and process issues, the quality council also produced a succinct *Buyers Guide to Distance Learning*, listing questions that prospective students should ask of providers and of themselves. The list of questions on courses begins, "Can you look at the course first? Is the course right for you? How much support does it offer? Is there face-to-face training? Can you talk to former students? Have previous learners been successful? Can you compare courses?" The outcomes questions are, "What do you want to achieve? Is this the right qualification? Will there be an exam at the end? Are there restrictions?" The cost questions are, "How much will it cost? Is financial support available? When can you get your money back? Finally, for quality, "Is the provider independently inspected/accredited?" This last element carries a warning about other quality marks or schemes like ISO which "may suggest that the distance learning provision is of good quality, but do not guarantee it" (ODLQC, 2003, p.1). The statement points to the competitive nature of the quality assurance agencies and the presence of alternate quality markers, like those advocated by the British Association for Open Learning (BAOL), that explicitly reference the European Foundation for Quality Management (BAOL, 2002). The momentum behind such projects appears to be shifting, however, with amalgamation of BAOL and the Forum for Technology in Training into the British Learning Association (BLA, 2005).

With such an array of quality assurance prospects, it is noteworthy that in their study of "borderless education," higher education agencies in the UK have acknowledged that public accountability arrangements and elements of the credentialing or qualification schemes have been challenged by developments in for-profit, virtual, and corporate providers in the domestic and international higher education market. They propose that the quality frameworks addressing these developments would include

> currency and security of qualifications; audit of the system for design and approval of curricula or appropriate learning con-tracts; an internationally recognized system of educational credit; licensing of staff; security of assessment; adequate and accurate public information about learning opportunities; approved guid-ance and complaints systems for learners; transparent quality management processes for each agent in the educational supply chain; access to learning resources assured by the provider; and publication of guidance relevant to different modes of provision. (CVCP, 2000, p. 30)

It has also been suggested that the thinking on quality assurance will have to shift dramatically, from external compliance-based approaches toward comparative benchmarking and mutual recognition arrange-ments for international quality standards. Attempts to integrate an array of international standards have been made in other jurisdictions.

In Canada, the responsibility for education rests at the provincial, not the national, level. Each province has its own quality assurance frame-work or approach to determining whether post-secondary programs are eligible for student funding or to receive public money. The degree to which a province might regulate, or even provide, subsidies to private or for-profit educational institutions varies widely. It is fitting, then, that the Canadian example of quality guidelines originates with a private corporation sponsored by community and government-funded agencies (Barker, 2002a).

The *Canadian Recommended e-Learning Guidelines* (Barker, 2002a) bill themselves as "consumer-oriented, consensus-based, comprehensive, futuristic, distinctively Canadian, adaptable, and flexible." The latter feature admits that "not all guidelines will apply to all circumstances" (p. 2). This qualification is only realistic, as the list is exhaustive. The 138 recommendations are organized into three distinct sections: Quality Outcomes from e-Learning Products and Services, that includes 15 items related to how students acquire content skills, knowledge, and learning skills; Quality Processes and Practices, that includes 20 items on the management of students and the delivery and management of learning, using appropriate technologies; and Quality Inputs and Resources, that includes the remaining 103 items, which range through intended learning outcomes, curriculum content, teaching and learning materials, product and service information, learning technologies, technical design, personnel, learning resources, comprehensive courses packages, routine evaluation, program plans and budgets, and advertising, recruitment, and admissions information. A more succinct adaptation issued under the same initiative is the *Consumer's Guide to e-Learning* (Barker, 2002b), which structures 34 questions into basic, discerning, and detailed levels. These questions are paraphrased in Tables 1 to 3 of Appendix A to allow for comparison with the other frameworks, but the instructions to consumers provided with the *Consumer's Guide* are more telling.

Before you sign up for an e-learning course or program, you are to ask yourself:
- What is my purpose for taking this course? Do I know what I want or need to learn?
- Do I need a credit or certificate when I finish . . . or do I just want to know more?
- How much can I afford to spend? How much time can I invest?
- What hardware and software do I have, and is it enough?
- Where will I access the Internet, what will it cost, and how convenient will it be?
- Are my computer and Internet skills good enough for the course I have in mind? Will I need technical help? (Barker, 2002b)

Institutions intending to adapt their offerings to the online teaching and learning environment would be well advised to rephrase these questions along the following lines:
- What is our purpose for offering this course?
- Do we know what we expect students to learn?
- Do we have the technological infrastructure to support our students? Is it up-to-date?
- How skilled are our course developers and instructors in the online environment?
- What technical assistance do we have available?

Such questions are at the heart of the two models proposed in the United States.

In an analysis of the impact of electronically delivered distance education, undertaken for the American Council of Education, Judith Eaton (2002) suggests that the emergence of electronically delivered degrees, programs, courses, and services has the potential to undo the delicate balance between "accreditation to assure quality in higher education, the self-regulation of higher education institutions, and the availability of federal money to colleges and universities" (p. 1). Although U.S. higher education institutions are subject to state funding and regulatory bodies, and although the systems of accountability may vary from state to state, the federal government relies on accredited status to signal that institutions and programs are of sufficient quality to allow the release of federal funds in the forms of student grants and loans, research grants, and other federal program funds. Under traditional approaches to accreditation, the focus was on the verification of site-based resources contributing to a learning environment (e.g., the number of volumes in the library). To address some of the concerns raised by electronic delivery, the eight regional accrediting commissions in the United States developed the "Statement of Commitment for the Evaluation of Electronically Offered Degree and Certificate Programs," which declares the resolve of the commissions to sustain the following values:

- That education is best experienced within a community of learning where competent professionals are actively and cooperatively involved with creating, providing, and improving the instructional program;
- That learning is dynamic and interactive, regardless of the setting in which it occurs;
- That instructional programs leading to degrees having integrity are organized around substantive and coherent curricula which define expected learning outcomes;
- That institutions accept the obligation to address student needs related to, and to provide the resources necessary for, their academic success;
- That institutions are responsible for the education provided in their name;
- That institutions undertake the assessment and improvement of their quality, giving particular emphasis to student learning;
- That institutions voluntarily subject themselves to peer review. (reprinted in Eaton, 2002, p. 26)

The regional commissions also committed themselves to a common statement, "Best Practices for Electronically Offered Degree and Certificate Programs," which was developed by the Western Cooperative for Educational Telecommunications (Howell and Baker, 2006). The statement is organized into five discrete sections: institutional context and commitment; curriculum and instruction; faculty support; student support; and evaluation and assessment (WCET, n.d). Taken together, the Statement of Commitment and the Best Practices propose a consistent framework for developing quality standards. How those standards might translate into benchmarks was the subject of a study prepared by the Institute of Higher Education Policy (Phipps & Merisotis, 2000).

For "Quality on the Line," Phipps and Merisotis (2000) surveyed the literature to compile a list of 45 possible benchmarks. They then determined whether those benchmarks were recognized at various institutions delivering online courses, and examined the importance of each benchmark to administrators, staff, faculty, and students at those institutions. The result is a list of 24 benchmarks that should be considered "essential to ensure the quality in Internet-based distance education" (p. 2). The elements (see Table 4 in Appendix A) include institutional support, course development, teaching and learning, course structure, student support, faculty support, and evaluation and assessment benchmarks. The similarities between these benchmarks and the proposals from the accrediting agencies clearly demonstrate a common conceptualization of distance education in the United States. Where they diverge is in the degree to which the actual curriculum elements are prescribed, and in the relative weights given to institutional structures.

Both sets of standards are designed more for traditional face-to-face institutions introducing distance education programs than for distance education providers updating their mode of delivery. The currency of these standards within the accreditation community was confirmed by a U.S. Department of Education study, which observed that despite difference in their standard and means of assessment, "there was remarkable consistency" in how reviewers "evaluated distance education programs, and in what they considered to be most important indicators" (U.S. Department of Education, 2006, p. 2). The provider focus remains a strong orientation under both schemes and, unlike the accreditation standard for open and distance learning in the UK, neither U.S. scheme speaks to the importance of encouraging learners to take responsibility for their own learning.

PROCESS VERSUS OUTCOMES

One of the first principles in all of the quality assurance schemes considered here is guaranteeing consistency in the product's results. In the view of Total Quality Management advocates, "many quality management initiatives, especially in service industries, die because we fail in measurement of the outcomes" (Widrick et al., 2002, p. 130). The dangers of presenting higher education outcomes as strictly utilitarian competencies are familiar features in the debate about quality assurance activities (Gerard, 2002). Even if outcomes could be framed in wider terms, however, there is also a hazard of sliding into what has been aptly described as a variation on the "naming fallacy" – that is, assuming that "explicitness about standards" somehow provides assurance that the standards have been or can be achieved (Greatrix, 2001).

Major efforts have been directed to identifying "quality in under-graduate education," but according to Ernest Pascarella (2001), some of these efforts are "based on a naive understanding of just how difficult it is to accomplish in a valid manner" (p. 19). Most notably, he argues that institutional reputation and resources, and student or alumni outcomes are "potentially quite misleading," and that results based on either of these common approaches are more likely to be driven by inputs than by effective educational practices (pp. 19-21). The solution to this problem should rest in careful measures that address the integrity of the teaching and learning processes within institutions. The seemingly insatiable appetite for comparable measures, regardless of their validity, is a dimension of the operating environments of most post-secondary institutions. While it is clear that the rhetoric of accountability and the bureaucratic systems it has spawned are not likely to disappear, it may be possible to present a framework for quality online teaching and learning that attends to more than short-term transactional or monetary values.

Externally defined and inspected standards can lead to compliance-oriented responses in institutions. Benchmarking frameworks have been proposed in some jurisdictions as an antidote to mechanistic audit cultures. In keeping with the self-accrediting and international focus of Australian universities, the council on open, distance, and e-learning (ACODE), constituted in 2002, is open to accredited universities in Australasia – of which Australia, New Zealand, Papua New Guinea, and the South West Pacific are entitled to be members (see www.acode.edu.au). Beginning with a survey in 2002-03, the initiative followed up with a collaborative pilot project between the Universities of Melbourne and Tasmania to develop a trial framework with the following components: institutional context, purpose, scope, principles of service delivery, benchmarking priorities, indicators for priority areas, self-assessment/ranking, comparative matrix of strengths and weaknesses against indicators, and finally, an action plan for self-improvement (Bridgland & Goodacre, 2005). The full articulation of benchmarks includes scoping statements, a good-practice statement, performance indicators, and performance measures (ratings) in eight areas:

1) Institutional policy and governance for technology supported learning and teaching;
2) Planning for, and quality improvement of the integration of technologies for learning and teaching;
3) Information technology infrastructure to support learning and teaching;
4) Pedagogical application of information and communication technology;
5) Professional/staff development for the effective use of technologies for learning and teaching;
6) Staff support for the use of technologies for learning and teaching;
7) Student training for the effective use of technologies for learning;
8) Student support for the use of technologies for learning. (ACODE, 2007)

The process of benchmarking in this instance involved scoring the stages of planning, development, and implementation across different elements within each of the eight areas listed above. Other approaches to benchmarking reflect the interoperability questions, and try to apply software development principles and suggest finer levels of granularity. The areas investigated in a New Zealand project included scoring five process levels (delivery, planning, definition, management, and optimization) against 35 standards. The domains under investigation included ten factors for processes with impacts on learning; seven factors on the development of e-learning resources; six factors related to student and operational support; three factors related to evaluation and quality controls; and nine factors related to institutional planning and management (Marshall, 2006). An example which bridges two jurisdictions (The Open University in the UK and the University of Sydney in Australia) emphasizes the importance of the relationship between institutions and the prospective approaches which benchmarking might provide (Ellis & Moore, 2006).

RESHAPING THE DEBATE

Whether or not the demands of stakeholder groups (however ill-defined), the threat of fraud, or the intensification of competition from local or international providers are behind the current impulses for elaborating quality assurance mechanisms, a dual challenge is being presented to the providers of online teaching and learning. The common thread across quality assurance schemes in the four jurisdictions is the need to address the concerns from both inside and outside the academy. Even if online and distance delivery institutions have been made scapegoats for a wide range of changes, not the least of which is the erosion of higher education institutions' power to regulate themselves, there may still be an opportunity to address some of the concerns presented by colleagues in more traditional institutions. It follows that an overarching principle of any proposal to address quality assurance in online teaching and learning environments must recognize the integrity of higher education – no matter how it is delivered. The rhetoric of both the Australian and British qualification frameworks suggests just such an integrated approach, but the regulatory burdens they have spawned do little to reassure those who value the independence of higher education.

While institutional and regulatory sectors have debated appropriate consumer input tools, the Web has offered an array of solutions. Various directories proffer advice on how to select an institution with revenues tied to referrals or "pay-for-click." One of the more explicit rating schemes from the United States can be found at the Online Education Database (OEDb, n.d.), which ranks institutions that are accredited by the Distance Education and Training Council; found in other listings like *eLearners.com* or the U.S. News & World Report *E-learning Guide*. Much of the institution descriptions and rating factors used by OEDb relies upon the U.S. Department of Education's *College Opportunities Online Locator* (COOL, n.d.). For institutions which offer at least 50% of their degree programs online, the Department of Education OEDb digests the available data on acceptance rates, financial aid, retention and graduation rates. Other consumer-focused metrics selected by OEDb are peer web citations based on Yahoo's link domain search, scholarly citations based on Google Scholar, and the student-faculty ratio and years accredited as reported in *Peterson's College Search* (OEDb, n.d.). Established online programs are also making their way into discipline-based league tables like the business school ratings from the *Financial Times*. Similarly, for all the professional debates over the degree of asynchronous or blended experiences, on *ratemyprofessors.com*, students do not seem inclined to distinguish between face-to-face and online courses.

In the process of taking back some of the momentum in the debate, the academy must provide clear statements of educational goals.

Such goals need not be restricted to technical mastery in specific subjects. Moreover, the opportunity to pursue ideas beyond the needs of corporate sponsors should not be ignored. The measure of the effectiveness of the articulation of the educational goals should be the ways that a course, program, and institution's goals align with one another. Demonstrating a consistency of purpose should be persuasive to internal and external stakeholders alike, but should not presuppose that students are responsible for seeking their own learning outcomes. This suggestion returns to the essential need for quality to be constructed through consensus building among a range of institutional stakeholders, who must, at the same time, not promise, or be promised, more than can be delivered.

A second theme running through all of the frameworks presented here is the need for sustained institutional commitment to support distance learners. The precise nature of that support would be determined by the nature of the programs and by what students need in order to have a reasonable chance of attaining their aspirations in a given program. All too often, online delivery of courses and programs has been presented in an experimental mode, without long-term, planned infrastructure development. Whether it involves investing in technical systems, or in-training for support and instructional staff, the process of developing robust online teaching and learning environments should not be attempted as "one-offs." Some observers have gone so far as to suggest that digital technology may hamper rather than promote educational change, because investment focuses on short life-cycle technologies rather than the longer view needed for effective education (Ehrmann, n.d.). An institutional commitment to supporting learners will go a long way to satisfying other stakeholders without displacing the fundamental project of scholarship. This commitment can only be true, however, if students and educators are engaging in a collaborative process of discovery; that is, if academics are not simply dispensers or interpreters of content for passive students.

Learning technologies can promote powerful connections to content, context, and community. Unfortunately, they can also offer broad access to poorly designed and executed courseware. There are deliberate choices to be made in how to accommodate a generation of students who expect independent investigation, collaboration, and peer contacts to be facilitated in an online environment.

The threats to traditional delivery, and most especially the disaggregation of tasks associated with teaching in higher education, are providing new opportunities for exploring the constructions of community and knowledge, teaching and learning. In generating documented evidence of interactions with content and with others, the structure of the online environment lends itself to new kinds of exploration. Eventually, the goal of such inquiries should be to point to ways to improve the teaching and learning environment. Ultimately, online programs should be able to mobilize recent theory and research into how people learn, and enhance learning by "enabling the identified characteristics of effective learning environments and ensuring that they are present and accessible" (Herrington, Herrington, Oliver, Stoney, & Willis, 2001, p. 266). From that perspective, the pursuit of quality online teaching and learning environments may become as much an exercise in scholarship as it has been in market positioning or state control.

REFERENCES

ACODE. (2007). ACODE benchmarks for e-learning in universities and guidelines for use. *Australasian Council on Open, Distance, and e-Learning (ACODE) web site.* Retrieved August, 14, 2007, from http://www.acode.edu.au/aboutus/acodebenchmkwksp/ acodebmguideline0607.pdf

Adams, J., & DeFleur, M. (2006). The acceptability of online degrees earned as a credential for obtaining employment. *Communication Education, 55*(1), 32–45.

Allen, I. E., & Seaman, J. (2006). *Making the grade: Online education in the United States, 2006.* Sloan Consortium. Retrieved September 13, 2007, from http://www.sloan-c.org/publications/survey/pdf/making_the_grade.pdf

Allen, T. (2006). Is the rush to provide on-line instruction setting our students up for failure? *Communication Education, 55*(1), 122–126.

Arthur, L., Beecher, B., Elliot, R., & Newman, L. (2006). E-learning: Do our students want it and do we care? *Proceedings, 23rd annual ASCILITE Conference,* Sydney, Australia, Retrieved August 14, 2007, from http://www.ascilite.org.au/conferences/sydney06/ proceeding/pdf_papers/p192.pdf

Banta, T. W. & Associates (2002). *Building a scholarship of assessment.* San Francisco: Jossey-Bass.

BAOL. (2002). The development, implementation and use of the BAOL Quality Mark: A report to the Department for Education and Skills.

British Association for Open Learning (BAOL) web site. Retrieved July 29, 2003, from http://www.baol.co.uk/PDF/ qmrepdfes.pdf

Barker, K. (2002a, January). Canadian recommended e-learning guidelines (CanREGS). *LICEF Research Centre web site.* Retrieved July 29, 2003, from http://www.licef.teluq .uquebec.ca/fr/pdf/CanREGs%20Eng.pdf

Barker, K. (2002b, January). Consumer's guide to e-learning. *LICEF Research Centre web site.* Retrieved July 29, 2003, from http://www.licef. teluq.uquebec.ca/eng/pdf/ ConGuide%20Eng%20CD.pdf

Birnbaum, R. (2001). *Management fads in higher education: Where they come from, what they do, why they fail.* San Francisco: John Wiley & Sons.

BLA. (2005). Origins of the British Learning Association. *British Learning Association web site.* Retrieved August 15, 2007, from http://www.british-learning.org/about/origins.htm

Bok, D. (2003). *Universities in the marketplace: The commercialization of higher education.* Princeton, NJ: Princeton University Press.

Brennan, J., & Shah, T. (2000). *Managing quality in higher education: An international perspective on institutional assessment and change.* Buckingham: Open University Press.

Bridgland, A., & Goodacre, C. (2005). Benchmarking in higher education: A framework for benchmarking for quality improvement purposes. In *Proceedings EDUCAUSE Australasia,* Auckland, New Zealand. Retrieved August 5, 2007, from http://eprints.infodiv.unimelb.edu.au/archive/00000891/

Brown, R. (2000). The new UK quality framework. *Higher Education Quarterly, 54*(4), 323–342.

Carnevale, D. (2000, February). Assessing the quality of online courses remains a challenge, educators agree. *The Chronicle of Higher Education, 46(24).* Retrieved September, 13, 2007 from http://chronicle.com/weekly/v46/i24/24a05901.htm

Carnevale, D. (2002, May). Accreditors offer views on distance programs. *Chronicle of Higher Education, 48*(37), A36.

Caudron, S. (2001). Evaluating e-degrees. *Workforce, 80*(2), 44-48.

Cleary, T. S. (2001). Indicators of quality. *Planning for Higher Education, 29*(3), 19-28.

COOL. (n.d.). College opportunities online locator (COOL). *Institute of Education Sciences; U.S. Department of Education web site.* Retrieved September 13, 2007, from http://165.224.221.98/ipeds/cool/

Crow, S. (2000, January/February). Accreditation of online institutions. *Technology Source Archives at the University of North Carolina web site.*

Retrieved September 13, 2007, from http://ts.mivu.org/default.asp?
show=article&id=663

CVCP. (2000) Committee of Vice Chancellors and Principals and Higher
Education Funding Council for England (HEFCE). (2000, March).
The business of borderless education: UK perspectives, summary report.
Retrieved July 30, 2003, from http://www.universitiesuk.ac.uk/bookshop/
downloads/BorderlessSummary.pdf

DEST. (2002a). Meeting the challenges: The governance and management of universities. *Commonwealth of Australia, Department of Education,
Science & Training (DEST) web site.* Retrieved August 2, 2007, from
http://www.backingaustraliasfuture.gov.au/pubs.htm

DEST. (2002b). Striving for quality: Learning, teaching and scholarship.
*Commonwealth of Australia, Department of Education, Science & Training
(DEST) web site.* Retrieved August 2, 2007, from http://www.backing
australiasfuture.gov.au/pubs.htm

DETYA. (2000). *The higher education quality assurance framework.* Commonwealth of Australia, Department of Education, Training and Youth
Affairs (DETYA). Retrieved July 29, 2007 from http://www.dest.gov.
au/archive/highered/occpaper/00g/00g.pdf

Dolence, M. G., & Norris, D. M. (1995). *Transforming higher education: A
vision for learning in the 21st Century.* Ann Arbor, MI: Society for College
and University Planning.

Eaton, J. S. (2002). *Maintaining the delicate balance: Distance learning, higher
education accreditation, and the politics of self-regulation.* Retrieved July 29,
2003, from http://www.acenet.edu/bookstore/pdf/distributed-learning/
distributed-learning-02.pdf

EFQUEL. (2007). *Quality assurance and accreditation for European eLearning: The case for a European Quality Mark initiative.* Brussels: European
Foundation for Quality in eLearning (Green Paper No.4). Retrieved
July 15, 2007, from http://cms.eun.org/ shared/data/pdf/efquel_
quality_mark.pdf

Ehrmann, S. C. (n.d.). Technology changes quickly but education changes
slowly: A counter-intuitive strategy for using IT to improve the outcomes
of higher education. *TLT Group Web.* Retrieved July 30, 2003, from
http://www.tltgroup.org/resources/ Visions/Outcomes.html

eLearners.com. (n.d.). *eLearners.com web site.* Retrieved September 13,
2007, from http://www.elearners.com/

Ellis, R., & Moore, R. (2006). Learning through benchmarking: Developing a relational, prospective approach to benchmarking ICT in learning
and teaching. *Higher Education, 51,* 351–371.

European Ministers of Education. (1999). *The European higher education area: Joint declaration of the European ministers of education.* Convened in Bologna on June 19, 1999. Retrieved September 13, 2007, from http://www.cepes.ro/information_services/ sources/on_line/bologna.pdf

Gerard, D. (2002). The governance of universities: What is the role of the university in the knowledge society? *Canadian Journal of Sociology, 27*(2), 185–194.

Greatrix, P. (2001). Quality assurance into the 21st Century: Command and control or enlightened accountability? *Perspectives, 5*(1), 12–16.

Harvey, L. (2005). A history and critique of quality evaluation in the UK. *Quality Assurance in Education, 13*(4), 263–276.

Herrington, A., Herrington, J., Oliver, R., Stoney, S., & Willis, J. (2001). Quality guidelines for online courses: The development of an instrument to audit online units. In G. Kennedy, M. Keppell, C. McNaught, & T. Petrovic (Eds.), *Meeting at the crossroads: Proceedings of ASCILITE 2001,* pp. 263–270. Melbourne: University of Melbourne. Retrieved July 29, 2003, from http://elrond.scam.ecu.edu.au/oliver/2001/qowg.pdf

Hooker, M. (1997). The transformation of higher education. In Diana Oblinger & Sean C. Rush (Eds.), *The learning revolution.* Boston, MA: Anker Publishing Company Inc. Retrieved July 30, 2003, from http://horizon.unc.edu/projects/seminars/Hooker.asp

Howell, Scott L. and Baker, K. (2006). Good (Best) practices for electronically offered degree and certificate programs: A 10-year retrospect. *Distance Learning, 3* **(1), 41-47.**

King, R. (2006). Globalization, institutional aspirations and regulation: The Australian national protocols. *Observatory on borderless higher education strategic information service report.* Retrieved February 3, 2006, from http://www.obhe.ac.uk/products/reports/

Kompf, M. (2001, September). ICT could be the death knell of professoriate as we know it. *CAUT-ACPPU Bulletin Online.* Retrieved July 30, 2003, from http://www.caut.ca/ english/bulletin/2001_sep/commentary.asp

Lairson, T. D. (1999). Rethinking the 'course' in an online world. *Campuswide Information Systems, 16*(5). Retrieved July 30, 2003, from http://fox.rollins.edu/~tlairson/online.html

Larreamendy-Joerns, J., & Leinhart, G. (2006). Going the distance with online education. *Review of Educational Research. 76*(4), 567–605.

Marshall, S. (2006). E-learning maturity model version two: New Zealand tertiary institution e-learning architectural change and development, project report. Document on the *University of Victoria, Wellington*

University web site. Retrieved August 5, 2007, from http://www.utdc.vuw. ac.nz/research/emm/documents/versiontwo/ 20060726TeLRFReport.pdf

Milliron, M. D., & Miles, C. L. (2000, November/December). Education in a digital democracy: Leading the charge for learning about, with and beyond technology. *EDUCAUSE Review,* 50–62. Retrieved July 30, 2003, from http://www.educause.edu/pub/er/erm00/articles006/ erm0064.pdf

Moore, J. C. (2005). *The Sloan consortium quality framework and the five pillars.* The Sloan Consortium. Retrieved July 15, 2007, from http:// www.aln.org/publications/ books/qualityframework.pdf

Morrison, D., Mayes, T., & Gule, E. (2006). Benchmarking e-learning in UK higher education. *Proceeding of the 23rd annual ASCILITE Conference,* Sydney, Australia. Retrieved August 5, 2007, from http://www.ascilite. org.au/conferences/sydney06/proceeding/pdf_papers/p96.pdf

Noble, D. F. (2001). *Digital diploma mills: The automation of higher education.* New York: Monthly Review Press.

Nunan, T. (2005). Markets, distance education, and Australian higher education. *International Review of Research in Open and Distance Learning,* 6(1). Retrieved September 13, 2007, from http://www.irrodl.org/index. php/irrodl/article/view/223/306

ODLQC. (2003). A buyer's guide to distance learning: Finding the course you want. *Open and Distance Learning Quality Council web site.* Retrieved August 14, 2007, from http://www.odlqc.org.uk/documents/bg2003. pdf

ODLQC. (2005). Standards in Open and Distance Learning. *Open and Distance Learning Quality Council web site.* Retrieved August 14, 2007, from http://www.odlqc.org.uk/standard.htm

OEDb. (n.d.). *Online Education Database web site.* Retrieved September 13, 2007, from http://oedb.org/

Pascarella, E.T. (2001, May/June). Identifying excellence in undergraduate education: Are we even close? *Change,* 19–23.

Phipps, R. A., & Merisotis, J. P. (2000). Quality on the line: Benchmarks for success in Internet-based education. *The Institute for Higher Education Policy web site.* Retrieved September 13, 2007, from http://www. ihep.com/Pubs/PDF/Quality.pdf

Pond, W. K. (2002). Distributed education in the 21st Century: Implications for quality assurance. *Online Journal of Distance Learning Administration,* 5(2). Retrieved September 13, 2007, from http://www.westga. edu/%7Edistance/ojdla/ summer52/pond52.html

QAA. (2000). Handbook for academic review. *Quality Assurance Agency for Higher Education (UK) web site.* Retrieved July 29, 2007, from http://www.qaa.ac.uk/reviews /academicReview/handbook2000/acrevhbook.pdf

QAA. (2004a). Code of practice for the assurance of academic quality and standards in higher education. *Quality Assurance Agency for Higher Education UK web site.* Retrieved July 29, 2007, from http://www.qaa.ac.uk/academicinfrastructure/codeOfPractice/section2/collab2004.pdf

QAA. (2004b). Handbook for academic review: England, 2004. Review of directly funded higher education in further education colleges. *Quality Assurance Agency for Higher Education UK web site.* Retrieved July 29, 2007, from http://www.qaa.ac.uk/reviews/academicReview/acrevhbook2004/HandbookAcademicReview.pdf

QAA. (n.d.a). Code of practice for the assurance of academic quality and standards in higher education. *Quality Assurance Agency for Higher Education (UK) web site.* Retrieved July 29, 2007 from http://www.qaa.ac.uk/academicinfrastructure/codeOfPractice

QAA. (n.d.b). Guidelines on the quality assurance of distance learning. *Quality Assurance Agency for Higher Education (UK) web site.* Retrieved July 29, 2003, from http://www.qaa.ac.uk/public/dlg/dlg_textonly.htm

Quinn, J. B. (2001, July-August). Services and technology: Revolutionizing higher education. *EDUCAUSE,* pp. 28–37. Retrieved July 30, 2003, from http://www.educause.edu/ir/library/pdf/erm0141.pdf

Reid, I. (2005). Quality assurance, open and distance learning, and Australian universities. *The International Review of Research in Open and Distance Learning,* 6(1). Retrieved September 13, 2007, from http://www.irrodl.org/index.php/irrodl/article/view/222/305

Shore, C., & Wright, S. (2000). Audit culture and anthropology: Neoliberalism in British higher education. *Journal of the Royal Anthropological Institute,* 5(4), 557–575.

Sims, R., Dobbs, G., & Hand, T. (2002). Enhancing quality in online learning: Scaffolding planning and design through proactive evaluation. *Distance Education,* 23(2), 135–148.

Spahn, K. (2000, May). Baldridge and institutional research: Quality measures for the next millennium. Paper presented at the *40th Annual Association of Institutional Research Forum,* Cincinnati, OH.

Twigg, C. (2001) *Quality assurance for whom? Providers and consumers in today's distributed learning environment.* Retrieved August 5, 2007, from http://center.rpi.edu/ Monographs/Mono3.pdf

UNESCO/OECD. (2005). *Guidelines for quality provision in cross-border higher education.* Retrieved February 20, 2007, from http://www.oecd.org/dataoecd/27/51/35779480.pdf

U.S. Department of Education. (2006, March). *Evidence of quality in distance education programs drawn from interviews with the accreditation community.* Office of Postsecondary Education document. Retrieved July 15, 2007, from http://www.itcnetwork.org/Accreditation-Evidenceof QualityinDEPrograms.pdf

Vidovich, L. (2001). That chameleon 'quality': The multiple and contradictory discourses of 'quality' policy in Australian higher education. *Discourse: Studies in the cultural politics of education, 22*(2), 249–261.

WCET. (n.d.). Best practices for electronically offered degree and certificate programs. *Western Cooperative for Educational Telecommunications website* retrieved July 15, 2007 from http://wcet.info/resources/accreditation/Accrediting%20-%20Best%20Practices.pdf. Also available at http://wiche.edu/attachment_library/Accrediting_BestPractices.pdf and at http://www.neasc.org/cihe/best_practices_electronically_offered_degree.htm

Widrick, S. M., Mergen, E., & Grant, D. (2002). Measuring the dimensions of quality in higher education. *Total Quality Management, 13*(1), 123–131.

Zemsky, R. (2007, January 26). The rise and fall of the Spellings commission. *Chronicle of Higher Education, 53*(21), B6.

APPENDIX A

Tables 1 through 3 summarize the recommendations presented in the *Consumers Guide to E-learning* for post-secondary and adult education levels, which was produced by the Canadian Association of Community Education (Barker 2002b). The first level in the guide defines basic information needs. These guidelines anticipate that potential suppliers of all e-learning products will provide *written* advice to their students on these matters.

---

1. What are the intended learning outcomes, and what entry-level knowledge or skill is necessary for a reasonable chance of success?

2. What recognition will be awarded upon successful completion (e.g., transferable credits, degree, professional designation, etc.)?

3. What are the necessary learning skills needed for success (e.g., the ability to write, to manage time, to take examinations, etc.)?

4. What types of material are to be covered, and what are the sources and the relevance of this content?

5. What is the format for instruction and assignments (i.e., group or individual)?

6. Who will be teaching and assessing the students?

7. What is the nature of the assessments, and what are the criteria for success?

8. How long can the course can be expected to take, including mandatory or flexible timelines?

9. What are the minimum computer and operational system requirements, and what options exist, if any?

10. What technical skills will be required to access the course materials?

11. What are the total costs, including tuition, books and materials, equipment, and other fees?

12. How credible is the product? What are the qualifications of the design and delivery personnel, and how objective are the evaluation reports?

13. How does one get started? What are the complete registration procedures and services?

14. How does one get help? Who does one contact for technical assistance and content expertise?

15. What are the policies for withdrawal and refunds?

TABLE 1. Consumer's Guide to e-Learning recommendations

The second level, designed to help potential students distinguish among programs meeting all of the preceding criteria, is considered evidence of good e-design and e-delivery. The second-level recommendations are summarized below.

---

1. Systems work consistently for the learner.

2. Navigation is logical and well organized.

3. Content is relevant, well organized and presented in an interesting manner.

4. Materials are updated on a regular basis.

5. Access is provided to the learning resources, and advice is given on how to access institutional services.

6. Learning packages allow options for individuals to personalize the course.

7. Scheduled expectations (e.g., synchronous instruction and communication) are present for a reason.

8. What learners need to succeed is easily accessible to them online.

9. There are ways to connect to the instructor and to other students.

10. Assessment of learning takes a variety of forms, and is conducted against clear, achievable criteria.

TABLE 2. *Consumer's Guide to e-Learning* recommendations

The final level presents more detailed evidence of good e-design and e-delivery.

---

1. Individuals are made to feel like valued customers.

2. Scheduling of when to register, learn, and be assessed is flexible.

3. Materials are interesting and motivating.

4. Approaches and materials are free of cultural, racial, class, age, and gender bias.

5. Students are given opportunities to demonstrate current skills and knowledge for advanced credit or a shortened program.

6. The program provides a statement of acquired skills and knowledge, not just a completion certificate.

7. Various approaches are offered to appeal to different learning styles.

8. The institution provides access to objective evaluation reports on all delivery components: instructors, curriculum, student success, processes, and resources.

9. Courses and programs demonstrate a favourable comparison of benefits to costs.

TABLE 3. *Consumer's Guide to e-Learning* recommendations

Two documents recommending standards for quality distance education delivery have been widely circulated in the United States. As reported in Phipps and Merisotis (2000), the National Education Association (NEA), in conjunction with *Blackboard®*, validated 24 proposed benchmarks. The Western Cooperative for Educational Telecommunications (WCET) first developed a draft best-practices document in 1995 to inform regional accreditation agencies (Howell and Baker, 2006). The *Best Practices for Electronically Offered Degree and Certification Programs* were subsequently published by the Council for Regional Accrediting Commissions in 2001 (WCET, n.d.). The elements of these documents are presented in Table 4; the order in which the paraphrased WCET elements have been presented has been altered to facilitate comparisons.

NEA – 2000	WCET – BEST PRACTICES
Institutional support	**Institutional context and commitment**
1. A documented technology plan is in place that includes electronic security measures.	Each program is consistent with the institution's mission.
2. Reliable delivery systems are in place.	Each program is compliant with the statement of accreditation, and with the regulatory environments in which it operates.
3. Centralized support is available for building and maintaining the distance education infrastructure.	The institutional plan and budget demonstrates commitment to distance students and program sustainability. Sufficient infrastructure is available, and staffing is appropriate. The organization of the institution supports the process of program design and approval, and coordinates student services for distance students. Articulation and transfer agreements are consistent with the guidelines. Technical systems and training programs are in place for staff, faculty, and students. Technical requirements and the availability of support are communicated clearly. There is an explicit match between the technology used and the program requirements.
Course development	**Curriculum and instruction**
4. Guidelines are in place for minimum course design standards where learning outcomes (not technology) drive the content.	Academic rigour and breadth are assured through evidence from the approval processes, and by having academically qualified people define outcomes, develop curriculum, and determine assessment criteria.

TABLE 4. NEA 2000 and WCET benchmarks and best practices (per Phipps and Merisotis, 2000; and WCET, n.d.)

5. Instructional materials are reviewed periodically to ensure they meet program standards.	In programs, presentation, management, and assessment are the responsibility of people with appropriate academic qualifications.
6. Courses are designed to require students to engage in analysis, synthesis and evaluation.	
Teaching/learning	
7. Student interaction with faculty and other students is facilitated in a variety of ways.	Appropriate student-to-student, and student and instructor interactions are demonstrated and evaluated to inform the delivery design.
8. Feedback on student assignments and questions is constructive and provided in a timely manner.	
9. Students are instructed in proper methods of effective research.	
Course structure	
10. Before starting, students are advised about the program so that they can determine if they have the motivation and commitment to learn at a distance, and the technology required by the course design.	Program requirements are communicated, including technical, financial, and time commitments. Career opportunities and certification parameters are communicated, clearly and honestly.
11. Students are provided with supplemental course information that outlines the course objectives, concepts, and ideas; and learning outcomes for each course are summarized in a clear, straightforward written statement.	Where consortium agreement exist, performance expectations, appropriate oversight, training, and benefits are specified, and conform to regulatory and quality assurance standards.
12. Students have sufficient access to library resources.	
13. Faculty and students agree on expectations about times for student assignment completion and faculty response.	

TABLE 4. (continued)

Student support	Student support (IV)
14. Students receive information about programs, including admission requirements, tuition and fees, books and supplies, technical and proctoring requirements, and student support services.	Programs are designed to meet the needs of specific student populations. Program plans, communications, and infrastructure demonstrate ongoing commitment.
15. Students are provided with hands-on training and information to aid them in securing material through electronic databases (and other sources).	Admission, technical, and financial requirements are communicated clearly prior to admission to the program, along with information on timeframes, the criteria of assessment, the availability of advisory and support services, and technical help.
16. Technical assistance is available throughout the course or program, including practice sessions prior to the beginning of the course and access to technical support staff.	Students can access appropriate support services without coming to the physical campus.
17. Questions directed to student support service personnel are answered accurately and quickly, and structured systems are in place to address student complaints.	Distance students are demonstrably part of the academic community.
Faculty support	**Faculty support (III)**
18. Technical assistance in course development is available to faculty.	Workload and compensation policies are consistent. Faculty are aware of intellectual property issues.
19. Faculty members are assisted in the transition from classroom teaching to online instruction, and are assessed during the process.	Technical design and production support are provided for faculty, including design and instructional support services.
20. Instructor training and assistance, including peer mentoring, continues through the online course.	Faculty orientation and training are provided as needed; support for ongoing development and course management is demonstrated.

TABLE 4. (continued)

21. Faculty members are provided with written resources to deal with issues arising from student use of electronically accessed data.	Support is available for those providing direct services to students, including training and mentoring.
Evaluation and assessment	**Evaluation and assessment**
22. Each program's educational effectiveness and teaching/learning process is assessed through an evaluation process that uses several methods and applies specific standards.	As a component of the institution's overall assessment activities, documented assessment of student achievement is conducted in each course and at the completion of the program by comparing student performance to the intended outcomes.
23. Data on enrolment, costs, and successful or innovative uses of technology are used to evaluate program effectiveness.	When examinations are employed, they are written in circumstances that include firm measures for student identification.
24. Intended learning outcomes are reviewed regularly to ensure clarity, utility, and appropriateness.	Procedures are in place to secure personal information. Overall program effectiveness is measured.

TABLE 4. (continued)

ABOUT THE AUTHOR

Nancy Parker (nancyp@athabascau.ca) is the Director of Institutional Studies at Athabasca University and is actively engaged in a wide range of quality assurance and accreditation activities, including serving on Alberta Learning's Performance Measurement and Management Information Committee, and as Athabasca's institutional liaison officer to the Middles States Commission on Higher Education.

PART IV

DELIVERY, QUALITY CONTROL, AND STUDENT SUPPORT OF ONLINE COURSES

CHAPTER 14

TEACHING IN
AN ONLINE LEARNING CONTEXT

TERRY ANDERSON
Athabasca University

INTRODUCTION

This chapter focuses on the role of the teacher or tutor in an online learning context. It uses the theoretical model developed by Garrison, Anderson, and Archer (2000) that views the creation of an effective online educational community as involving three critical components: cognitive presence, social presence, and teaching presence. This model was developed and validated through content analysis and by other qualitative and quantitative measures. The work has been referenced by hundreds of scholars and is arguably the most popular model used for both the research and practice of online learning (Arbaugh, 2007). The original papers describing and validating the model, as well as links to more current work, are available at http://www.atl.ualberta.ca/cmc.

In many ways, learning and teaching in an online environment are much like teaching and learning in any other formal educational context: learners' needs are assessed, content is negotiated or prescribed, learning activities are orchestrated, and learning is assessed. The pervasive effect of the online medium, however, creates a unique environment for teaching and learning. The most compelling feature of this context is the capacity for shifting the time and place of the educational interaction. Next comes the ability to support content encapsulated in many formats, including multimedia, immersive environments, video, and text, which gives access to learning content that exploits all media attributes. Third, the capacity of the Net to access huge repositories of content on every conceivable subject – including content created by the teacher and fellow students – creates learning and study resources previously available only in the largest research libraries, but now accessible in almost every home and workplace. Finally, the capacity to support human and machine interaction in a variety of formats (i.e., text, speech, video, and so on), in both asynchronous and synchronous modalities, creates a communications-rich learning context.

To provide a mental schema for thinking about learning and teaching in this context, Garrison, Anderson, and Archer (2000) developed a conceptual model of online learning that they refer to as a "community of inquiry" model. This model (see Figure 1) postulates that deep and meaningful learning results when there are sufficient levels of three component "presences." The first is providing a sufficient degree of *cognitive presence*, such that serious learning can take place in an environment that supports the development and growth of critical thinking skills. Cognitive presence is grounded in and defined by the study of a particular content; thus, it works within the epistemological, cultural, and social expression of the content in an approach that supports the development of critical thinking skills (McPeck,1990; Garrison, 1991). The second, *social presence*, relates to establishing a supportive environment such that students feel the necessary degree of comfort and safety to express their ideas in a collaborative context, and to present themselves as real and functional human beings. The absence of social presence leads to students' inability to express disagreements, share viewpoints, explore differences, and accept support and confirmation from peers and teachers. Finally, in formal education, as opposed to informal learning opportunities, *teaching presence* is critical, for a variety of reasons that create the rationale for this chapter.

Anderson, Rourke, Archer, and Garrison (2001) delineate three critical roles that a teacher performs in the process of creating an effective teaching presence. First, teachers design and organize the learning experience that takes place, both before the establishment of the

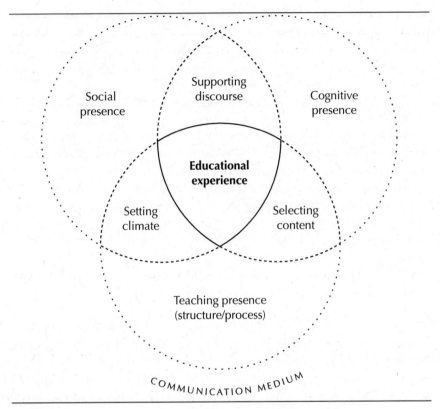

FIGURE 1. Community of Inquiry

learning community and during its operation. Second, teaching involves devising and implementing activities to encourage discourse between and among students, between the teacher and the student, and between individual students, groups of students, and content resources (Anderson, 2003b). Third, the teaching role goes beyond moderating the learning experiences when the teacher adds subject-matter expertise through a variety of forms of direct instruction. The creation of teaching presence is not always the sole task of the formal teacher. In many contexts, especially when teaching at senior levels, teaching presence is delegated to or assumed by students as they contribute their own skills and knowledge to the developing learning community.

In addition to these tasks, in formal education the institution and its teacher employees are usually fulfilling a critical credentialing role that involves the assessment and certification of student learning. This chapter focuses on these component parts of teaching presence, by defining and illustrating techniques to enhance this presence and providing suggestions for effective teacher practice in an online learning context.

DESIGNING AND ORGANIZING THE ONLINE LEARNING CONTEXT

The design and construction of the course content, learning activities, and assessment framework constitute the first opportunity for teachers to develop their teacher presence. The role the teacher plays in creating and maintaining the course contents varies from a tutor working with materials and an instructional design created by others, to a "lone ranger" or teacher who creates all of the content. Regardless of the formal role of the teacher, online learning creates an opportunity for flexibility and revision of content *in situ* that was not provided by older forms of mediated teaching and learning. The vast educational and content resources of the Net, and its capacity to support many different forms of interaction, allow for negotiation of content and activity, and a corresponding increase in autonomy and control (Garrison & Baynton, 1987). Teachers are no longer confined to the construction of monolithic packages that cannot be easily modified in response to students' needs. Rather, the design and organization of activities within the learning community can proceed while the course is in progress. Of course, such flexibility is not without cost, as customization of any product is more expensive than mass production of a standardized product. Thus, the effective online learning teacher makes provision for negotiation of activities, or even content, to satisfy unique learning needs. As they become more informed participants and consumers of formal education, learners are also demanding increased input into the control of their learning (Dron, 2007). Within this flexibility and negotiation of control, however, the need to stimulate, guide, and support learning remains. These tasks include the design of a series of learning activities that encourage independent study and community building, that deeply explore content knowledge, that provide frequent and diverse forms of formative assessment, and that respond to common and unique student needs and aspirations (see Anderson, "Towards a Theory of Online Learning," in this volume).

The design of e-learning courses is covered in greater detail in earlier chapters of this book, but this process provides opportunities for teachers to instill their own teaching presence by establishing a personalized tone within the course content. This presence is created by allowing students to see the personal excitement and appeal that inspires the teacher's interest in the subject. Borge Holmberg (1989) first wrote about a style of expression, "guided didactic interaction," that presents content in a conversational – as opposed to academic – style. This writing style helps the learner to identify, in a personalized way, with the teacher. Techniques, such as illustration of content issues with personal reflections, anecdotes, and discussions of the teacher's own struggles and successes as they have gained mastery of the content, have been inspirational and motivating to students.

Activities in this category of teaching presence include building curriculum materials. The cost of creating high quality, interactive learning resources has led to renewed interest in reusing content which is encapsulated and formally described using metadata and often referred to as "learning objects" (Wiley, 2000; McGreal, 2004). These resources are then made accessible in repositories such as the Multimedia Educational Resource for Learning and Online Teaching (MERLOT: see http://www.merlot.org/merlot/index.htm), or retrieved from the open Internet through the use of search engines. We have also seen an explosion in the availability of whole courses, a phenomenon that was ignited by the Massachusetts Institute of Technology (MIT), which with support from two large foundations, made a commitment to put components from all of that institution's courses online by 2008, freely available for download by anyone in the world. This challenge has led to the establishment of numerous open courseware sites and indices, linking and providing search services across institutional courseware repositories (see http://www .ocwconsortium.org/).

Creating or "repurposing" materials, such as lecture notes, to provide online teacher commentaries, mini-lectures, personal insights, and other customized views of course content, is another common activity that we assign to the category of teaching presence. We anticipate that work on educational standards for describing, storing, and sequencing of educational content, and for formally modelling the way in which learning activities are designed, will significantly change the design role of many teachers from content creation to customization, application, and contextualization of learning sequences (Koper, 2004). Finally, this design category of teaching presence also includes the processes through which the instructor negotiates timelines for group activities and student project work, a critical coordinating and motivating function of formal online course design and development, and a primary means of setting and maintaining teaching presence.

GETTING THE MIX RIGHT

The modern Web supports a number of media, each of which can be incorporated into the design of an online learning course. Getting the mix right between opportunities for synchronous and asynchronous interaction and group and independent study activities remains a challenge, however (Daniel & Marquis, 1988; Anderson, 2003a). There are two competing models of online learning, each of which has strong adherents and a growing body of research and theoretical rationales for its effective application. The first, the *community of learning model,* uses real-time synchronous or asynchronous communication technologies to create virtual classrooms that are often modelled, both pedagogically and structurally, on the campus classroom. This model evolved from telephone-based audio (and later video and web) conferencing. Its evolution to the Net has allowed for delivery directly to the learner's office and home, bypassing expensive remote learning centres that were a feature of the older virtual classroom models.

Web-based computer conferencing systems allow for asynchronous collaboration among and between student and teachers. The synchronous virtual classroom model has advantages, in that it is a familiar educational model with a great deal of similarity to teaching and learning in campus-based classrooms. It provides increased access by spanning geographic distance; however, it constrains participants in terms of a single time that learners and teachers must be present. This problem is compounded when a class spans many time zones. The asynchronous version of the virtual classroom overcomes the temporal limitations, but can result in a shortage of coordination and reduce opportunities for students to feel "in sync" with the class (Burge & Howard, 1994). Designing effective online courses will increasingly involve judicious selection of combinations of media and formats that balance the differential capacities of media to support the creation of social and cognitive presence with the educational need for variety, the special communications characteristics demanded of particular content, and the cost, access, and training requirements of the media.

The second model of online learning involves independent learners who work by themselves and at their own pace through the course of instruction. This model maximizes flexibility, but challenges the institution's and teacher's capacity to facilitate group, social, or collaborative learning activities. The *independent study model* is almost always selected in online learning models to allow for continuous enrolment or "just-in-time" access to educational content. It is very challenging to create collaborative learning or social activities when students are at very different places in the curriculum. The recent development of social software (Bryant, 2006; Dalsgaard, 2006), however, has inspired some us to begin thinking of ways in which "unpaced" learners can find each other, engage in short-term cooperative projects, and otherwise develop supportive networks and study-buddy relationships, even when their formal programming is unpaced (Anderson, 2005).

Fortunately, it is possible to combine synchronous, asynchronous, and independent study activities in a single course. In my own discussions with online students over the years, I have noticed a deep division between those who yearn for the immediacy of real-time communication, and those who are adamant that they have chosen online learning alternatives to avoid the time constraints imposed by synchronous or paced learning activities. Thus, many institutions, including Athabasca University, are developing both paced and unpaced models of delivery to accommodate student learning preferences and needs. Within a single class, it is possible to offer optional synchronous activities, and I usually build real-time Net-based audio-graphic sessions into the beginning section of my classes. These sessions allow me to quickly get to know the students from both a personal and professional viewpoint, explore their aspirations for the course, outline my own interests in the subject, discuss assessment activities, and provide an opportunity for students to ask pressing questions. Synchronous activities are also useful for guest interviews, for special activities such as debates and presentations, and of course, for holding the end-of-class social gathering – parties held in asynchronous time never seem to work! However, these activities can be "canned" and streamed for viewing by students in independent study mode.

Even if one's course design or the available technology precludes synchronous interaction, there are still opportunities to inject more than text-based lectures and discussions into the course. Online learning provides an opportunity for the teacher to build in video or audio presentations of themselves to enhance their presence to distributed learners. I have created two five-minute video productions that I link to my courses. The first provides an introduction to me and focuses on my professional growth within the discipline that I teach. The second discusses my own research agenda, and not only helps establish my academic credentials, but also, I hope, conveys my excitement for the research process within my discipline.

Thus, the challenge for teachers designing and organizing the online learning context is to create a mix of learning activities that are appropriate to student needs, teacher skills and style, learning objectives of the program of study, and institutional technical capacity. Doing so within the ever-present financial constraints of formal education systems is a challenge that will direct online learning design and implementation for the foreseeable future.

FACILITATING DISCOURSE

The second component of teacher presence is the critical task of facilitating discourse. We use the term *discourse* rather than discussion, as it conveys the meaning of relating to the "the process or power of reasoning" (Pickett, et al., 2007), rather than the more social connotation of conversation. Discourse not only facilitates the creation of the community of inquiry, but also the means by which learners develop their own thought processes, through the necessity of articulating their ideas to others. Discourse also helps students to uncover misconceptions in their own thinking, or disagreements with the teacher or other students. Such conflict provides opportunity for exposure to cognitive dissonance which, from a "Piagetian" perspective, is critical to intellectual growth. In fulfilling this component of teaching presence, the teacher regularly reads and responds to student contributions and concerns, and constantly searches for ways to support understanding in the individual student, and the development of the learning community as a whole.

The first task for the e-learning teacher is to develop a sense of trust and safety within the electronic community. In the absence of this trust, learners will feel uncomfortable and constrained in posting their thoughts and comments. We usually facilitate this "trust formation" by having students post a series of introductory comments about themselves. It is useful to request specific information, and to model an answer to the response request yourself. For example, the e-teacher may request that students articulate their reasons for enrolling in the course or their interest in the subject matter. I have seen this technique successfully extended at the beginning of regular online synchronous sessions by asking each student to respond spontaneously to a content-related "question of the week" that sets the tone for the growth of both social and cognitive presence. Other ideas for stimulating development of social presence, such as "icebreakers" (Dixon, Crooks, & Henry, 2007) and other activities borrowed from face-to-face adult education and training activities, can be very effective in breaking down inhibitors to free and open discourse.

Many online courses rely extensively on a model of discourse where the teacher posts questions or discussion items relevant to the readings or the other forms of content dissemination. I have found that overreliance on this form of discourse soon becomes boring, and allows much of the learning to be focused on responding to teacher-initiated items, rather than challenging students to formulate their own questions and comments about course content. We have seen much greater levels of participation, motivation, and student satisfaction when discussion groups are led by student moderators (Rourke & Anderson, 2002). It cannot be assumed, however, that students have the necessary skills to undertake successful moderation of class discussion, so role modelling by the teacher for the initial discussions is usually helpful. Finally, in an insightful critique of discourse in asynchronous computer conferencing, Rourke and Kanuka (2007) note the barriers felt by learners in developing critical discourse and recommend the need for "well-structured learning activities with clearly defined roles for teachers and students, and a method of assessing students' participation that reflects the time and effort required to engage in critical discourse" (p. 105).

Since the first issue of this text, a variety of social software tools have been demonstrated in both blended and online courses. Perhaps most popular has been "web logs" or "blogs" (Richardson, 2006). While it is unclear to what degree these new tools will hold advantages over older, threaded discussion groups that dominated the early forms of e-learning, there is little doubt that these new blog forms of discourse have generated renewed interest in reflective forms of writing to support learning (Cameron & Anderson, 2006).

ASSESSMENT IN ONLINE LEARNING

No element of course design concerns students in a formal educational context more assessment. Effective teaching presence demands explicit and detailed discussion of the criteria by which student learning will be assessed. A teacher who cultivates a presence of flexibility, concern, and empathy will reflect these characteristics in the style and format of assessment. In an earlier work (Garrison & Anderson,2003), my colleague Randy Garrison and I discuss assessment in online learning in greater detail. Here, I summarize the main features of assessment, and provide two examples of frameworks for the challenging task of assessing contributions to the online learning community.

We know from research on assessment that timely and detailed feedback provided throughout, and as near in time as possible to the performance of the assessed behaviour, is the most effective in providing motivation, shaping behaviour, and developing mental constructs (Shepard, 2000). For this reason, machine evaluations, such as those provided in online multiple-choice test questions or in simulations, can be very effective learning devices (Prensky, 2001). Most models of online learning, however, also stress the capacity for direct communication and feedback from the teacher to the student (Laurillard, 1997). This feedback is an integral part of the online teacher's function of facilitating discourse.

A commonly used component of student assessment in formal online education is to require students to post comments. The usefulness and efficacy of this practice, however, has been hotly debated on discussion lists about online learning. Jiang and Ting (2000) report that college students studying online perceived that learning was significantly correlated to the percentage of grade weight assigned to participation and their resulting participation in discussion. For some, however, the practice of marking for participation seems only to recall the onerous practice of attendance marking that rewards the quantity, and not the quality, of participation (Campbell, 2002). Others counter that in the absence of incentive for participation, a community will not be created. For instance, Palloff and Pratt (1999) argue that, given the emphasis on the process of learning in a social context that defines much constructivist-based learning design, participation in the process must be evaluated and appropriately rewarded. Most online students are practical adults facing much competition for their time; thus, they are less likely to participate in activities that are marginalized or viewed as supplemental to the course goals and assessment schema. Many courses I have reviewed have assessed participation in online activities as a component of the final mark, usually with a weighting of between ten and twenty-five percent.

Student assessment of any kind requires that the teacher be explicit, fair, consistent, and as objective as possible. The following examples illustrate how two experienced online learning teachers assess participation and thereby enhance their own teaching presence.

ASSESSMENT FRAMEWORKS

Susan Levine (2002) has developed a very clear set of instructions that she has used in graduate-level education courses to describe her expectations for student contributions to asynchronous online learning courses. She posts the following message to her students:

1. The instructor will start each discussion by posting one or more questions at the beginning of each week (Sunday or Monday). The discussion will continue until the following Sunday night, at which time the discussion board will close for that week.
2. Please focus on the questions posted. But do bring in related thoughts and material, other readings, or questions that occur to you from the ongoing discussion.
3. You are expected to post at least two substantive messages for each discussion question. Your postings should reflect an understanding of the course material.
4. Your postings should advance the group's negotiation of ideas and meanings about the material; that is, your contributions should go beyond a "ditto." Some ways you can further the discussion include
   - expressing opinions or observations. These should be offered in depth and supported by more than personal opinion;
   - making a connection between the current discussion and previous discussions, a personal experience, or concepts from the readings;
   - commenting on or asking for clarification of another student's statement;
   - synthesizing other students' responses; or
   - posing a substantive question aimed at furthering the group's understanding. (Levine, 2002)

Notice how Levine's instructions guide students on both the quantity ("two substantive postings" per discussion question) and the quality of contributions expected. Levine then goes on to describe qualitative aspects of a substantive posting. Notice also that from this posting of requirements, Levine reveals her teaching presence as structured and explicit, yet appreciative of qualitative outcomes associated with deep learning and critical thinking.

Nada Dabbagh (2000), from George Mason University, offers a slightly more prescriptive set of recommendations for posting:

- Postings should be evenly distributed during the discussion period (not concentrated all on one day or at the beginning and/or end of the period).
- Postings should be a minimum of one short paragraph and a maximum of two paragraphs.
- Avoid postings that are limited to "I agree" or "great idea," etc. If you agree (or disagree) with a posting then say why you agree by supporting your statement with concepts from the readings or by bringing in a related example or experience
- Address the questions as much as possible (don't let the discussion stray)
- Try to use quotes from the articles that support your postings. Include page numbers when you do that
- Build on others' responses to create threads
- Bring in related prior knowledge (work experience, prior coursework, readings, etc.)
- Use proper etiquette (proper language, typing, etc.)

Table 1 shows Dabbagh's sample framework for assessing messages on a weekly basis. Note that one of the protocols is the use of proper etiquette, including language, typing, and, I assume, spelling. The imposition of a requirement to adhere to particular protocols or standards is a hotly contested question among e-learning teachers. Some suggest that new forms of expression, grammar, and even spelling are arising in this medium, and that the lack of common tools (such as spell checkers) that plague many conferencing systems should allow for a much more relaxed form of expression. Others argue that requiring a high standard of written communication helps students learn to communicate effectively in the online learning academic context. Given my own problems with spelling and the growing number of online learning students whose first language is not their language of instruction, I tend to be much more tolerant of language informalities in postings than I do when marking formal academic papers for term assignments.

Notice how Dabbagh requires more frequent postings than Levine, and further stipulates that the messages should be spread through the

CRITERION	EXCELLENT	GOOD	AVERAGE	POOR
Timely discussion contributions	5-6 postings well distributed throughout the week	4-6 postings distributed throughout the week	3-6 postings somewhat distributed	2-6 not distributed throughout the week
Responsiveness to discussion and demonstration of knowledge and understanding gained from assigned reading	very clear that readings were understood and incorporated well into responses	readings were understood and incorporated into responses	postings have questionable relationship to reading material	not evident that readings were understood and/or not incorporated into discussion
Adherence to online protocols	all online protocols followed	1 online protocol not adhered to	2-3 online protocols not adhered to	4 or more online protocols not adhered to
Points	9-10	8	6-7	5 or less

TABLE 1. Evaluation Criteria for Facilitating an Online/Class Discussion (Dabbagh, 2000)

week. The second set of criteria (responsiveness and demonstration of understanding) illustrates the way the online discussion is used to motivate students to complete the weekly readings. Finally, compelling the learners' adherence to a list of online protocol categories links their grading explicitly to quantitatively measurable behaviours.

Both of the above instruction and marking schemes provide extremely valuable guidance to learners, and make clear and explicit the requirements of the teacher. But what are the costs of such evaluation? Assuming 20-30 students participate in an online learning class, the weekly assessment proscribed by Dabbagh could be a very time consuming activity. The amount of time required for assessment depends, in part, on the tools available to the online teacher. A good online learning system facilitates the display of the weekly postings by each student. An exemplary system would incorporate a number of active teacher agents that would

- scan the postings for spelling and grammatical errors.
- total the number of words.
- allow the display of preceding or subsequent postings and the location of the posting in its thread to help assess "responsiveness."

- graph the posting dates to allow quick visual identification of the timeliness of each contribution.
- present a grade book for easy entry of weekly scores.
- when appropriate, provide assistance for the teacher to create and automatically mark a variety of multiple-choice, matching, and fill-in-the-blank-type questions for student self-assessment.
- automatically alert students when a grade has been posted or altered.

Finally, it should be noted that creating teaching presence is a challenging and rewarding task – but should not be a life-consuming one! Research on assessment in distance education shows that rapid feedback is important for both understanding and motivation to complete courses (Rekkedal, 1983). The instantaneous nature of online learning, however, can lead to an unrealistic expectation by learners that teachers will provide instant feedback and assessment on submitted assignments. The virtual teacher has to lead a real life, so setting and adhering to appropriate timelines helps students to hold realistic expectations and relieves teachers of the unrealistic expectation of providing instantaneous, 24/7 feedback. In addition, online teachers must become ruthless time managers, guarding against the tendency to check online activity constantly, and to do everything to support the learners that can be done, rather than everything that can reasonably be done within the constraints of a busy professional and personal life.

Some online teachers, especially those teaching at graduate levels, may be uncomfortable with the prescriptive nature of the guidelines presented above. These teachers are often more comfortable with subjective assessments of students' contributions to the online community and with demonstrations of their individual learning. This type of assessment presents challenges to both students and teachers, due to the subjective nature of the assessment and the time required to review all contributions made during a course before assigning a grade. For these reasons, a number of authors have written about ways in which the students' own postings can be used as the basis for student assessment (Davie, 1989; Paulsen, 1995). Typically, these self-reflective assessments require students at the end of the course to illustrate both their contributions and evidence of learning by composing a "reflection piece," in which they quote from their own posting to the course. They should be given guidance to help them extract quotations that illustrate their contributions. Obviously, students who have not participated will not be able to provide any transcript references from their previous postings, and thus will generally receive lower evaluation scores on this project. Alternatively, a vicariously participating student (i.e., a lurker) may still be able to show learning by selective extraction of relevant postings from other students.

The increasing use of blog forms of discourse has resulted in the production of new rubrics for assessment. Bowling Green State University (n.d.), for example, provides links to 16 examples of such rubrics at http://facultydevelopmentbgsu.blogspot.com/2005/11/rubrics-to-evaluate-classroom-blogging.html. They are similar to the rubrics above, but perhaps pay greater attention to the reflective nature of learning that defined blogs from their origin as online diaries.

In summary, giving directions for modelling effective online discourse is a critical component of creating effective teaching presence. Assigning a portion of the assessment for class participation is a common practice in online learning courses. If participation is a formal and assessed requirement of the course, then developing and implementing an explicit assessment framework is an essential, but potentially time-consuming, teaching task. Some online learning teachers make this assessment into a more reflective exercise by assigning students the task of using their postings in the class conference, or their blogs, as evidence of their understanding the content concepts and their intellectual growth during the class. This type of assessed learning activity forces students to make quality contributions and then to reflect on them. Such a strategy moves the locus of responsibility from the teacher to the student, a solution that can save teacher time while contributing to students' understanding and metacognition.

PROVISION OF DIRECT INSTRUCTION

In this final category, teachers provide intellectual and scholarly leadership, and share their subject matter knowledge with students. The online teacher must be able to set and communicate the intellectual climate of the course, and model the qualities of a scholar, including sensitivity, integrity, and commitment to the unrelenting pursuit of truth. The students and the teacher often have expectations that the teacher will communicate content information directly. Ideally, this knowledge is enhanced by the teacher's personal interest, excitement, and in-depth understanding of the content and its application, in the context of formal study. The cognitive apprenticeship model espoused by Collins,

Brown, and Newman (1989), Rogoff's (1990) model of "apprenticeship in thinking," and Vygotsky's (1978) scaffolding analogies illustrate a helping role for teachers, from their position of greater content knowledge, in providing instructional support to students. Although many authors recommend a "guide-on-the-side" approach to teaching in e-learning settings, this type of laissez-faire approach diminishes a fundamental component of teaching and learning in formal education. A key feature of social cognition and constructivist learning models is the participation of an adult, expert, or more skilled peer who, in turn, "scaffolds" a novice's learning. This direct instruction makes use of the subject matter and pedagogical expertise of the teacher. Some theorists argue that online teaching is unlike classroom-based teaching, in that "the teacher must adopt the role of facilitator, not content provider" (Mason & Romiszowski, 1996, p. 447). This arbitrary distinction between facilitator and content provider is troublesome. Garrison (1998), in a lively exchange, focuses on differentiating so-called teacher-centred and student-centred instruction, and makes the point that "the self-directed assumption of andragogy suggests a high degree of independence that is often inappropriate from a support perspective and which also ignores issues of what is worthwhile or what qualifies as an educational experience" (p. 124).

Gilly Salmon (2000) describes the role and functions of an "e-moderator." In this model, the teacher's role in online conferencing is to facilitate learning. Her description suggests that the e-moderator does not require extensive subject matter expertise; instead, she writes, "they need a qualification at least at the same level and in the same topic as the course for which they are moderating" (p. 41). Such minimal subject-level competency seems to be less than that expected by learners and peers in higher education settings, however. Anderson, Garrison, Archer, and Rourke (2001) write:

> We believe that there are many fields of knowledge, as well as attitudes and skills, that are best learned in forms of higher education that require the active participation of a subject matter expert in the critical discourse. This subject matter expert is expected to provide direct instruction by interjecting comments, referring students to information resources, and organizing activities that allow the students to construct the content in their own minds and personal contexts.

Often, students hold misconceptions that impair their capacity to build more correct conceptions and mental schemata. The design of effective learning activities leads to opportunities for students themselves to uncover these misconceptions, but the teacher's comments and questions as direct instruction are also invaluable.

Although teaching presence is most commonly set in synchronous or asynchronous activities of the virtual classroom, it can also be set through fixed formats such as access to frequently-asked-questions databases or audio-, video-, or text-based presentations. Direct instruction can also be provided through an instructor's annotations of the scholarly work of others, including reviews of articles, textbooks, or web sites. These annotations can easily be shared by the class (and optionally by the whole Net) through social bookmarking tools such as Del.icio.us (see http://del.icio.us/) and Diigo (http://www.diigo.com/). Finally, the teacher may be asked to provide direct instruction on technical questions about access to net-based resources, manipulation of the networking software, operation of other tools or resources, and other technical concerns related to effective use of subject related resources.

THE PROCESS OF BUILDING TEACHING PRESENCE

Salmon (2000) has developed a model for e-moderators that demarcates the progression of tasks which the online teacher moves through in the process of effectively moderating an online course. The process begins by providing students with access and motivation. In this stage, any technical or social issues that inhibit participation are addressed, and students are encouraged to share information about themselves to create a virtual presence, as described above. In the second stage, Salmon suggests that the e-moderator continue to develop online socialization by "building bridges between cultural, social, and learning environments" (p. 26). In the third stage, the "information exchange," Salmon suggests that the teaching task moves to facilitating learning tasks, moderating content-based discussions, and bringing to light student misconceptions and misunderstandings. In the fourth stage, "knowledge construction," students focus on creating knowledge artefacts and projects that collaboratively and individually illustrate their understanding of course content and approaches. In the final "development" stage, learners become responsible for their own and their group's learning by creating final projects, working on summative assignments, and demonstrating the achievement of learning outcomes.

Salmon's model provides a useful guide and planning tool for online learning teachers; however, it should not be considered prescriptive. For example, students may be entering the online class with a great deal of technical and social experience with the online learning environment. In such cases, technical and social issues may have been resolved some time ago. Alternatively, a heterogeneous group may have some very sophisticated net-savvy students and some novices new to the online learning environment. Busy adult students may be anxious to avoid what they perceive as unproductive icebreakers associated with Stages 1 and 2, and desire to proceed to the more content-rich and potentially more meaningful learning activities associated with later stages. Thus, Salmon's model must be customized to the unique needs of each online learning community.

QUALITIES OF THE E-TEACHER

This chapter concludes with a discussion of the three sets of qualities that define an excellent e-teacher. First and primarily, an excellent e-teacher is an excellent teacher. Excellent teachers like dealing with learners; they have sufficient knowledge of their subject domain; they can convey enthusiasm both for the subject and for their task as a learning motivator; they are equipped with a pedagogical (or andragogical) understanding of the learning process, and have a set of learning activities at their disposal by which to orchestrate, motivate, and assess effective learning.

Beyond these generic teaching skills is a second set of technical skills. One does not have to be a technical expert to be an effective online teacher. One must, however, have sufficient technical skill to navigate and contribute effectively within the online learning context, have access to necessary hardware, and have sufficient Internet efficacy (Eastin & LaRose, 2000) to function within the inevitable technical challenges of these new environments. Internet efficacy is a personal sense of competence and comfort in the environment, such that the need for basic troubleshooting skills does not send the teacher into terror-filled incapacity. Finally, during this period of creation and adoption of new learning contexts and tools, the effective online learning teacher must have the type of resilience, innovativeness, and perseverance typical of all pioneers in unfamiliar terrain.

CONCLUSION

This chapter has outlined the three major components of teacher presence, and provided suggestions and guidelines for maximizing the effectiveness of the teaching function in online learning. I have not provided a lengthy list of "do's and don'ts" for online teaching in a cookbook fashion; rather, I have attempted to provide a broad theoretical model, focusing on the three main tasks of the online teacher.

The context of online learning is still very much in a fluid and changing state. The Web itself, and the technologies that underlie it, are evolving rapidly to create a second web – the "Semantic Web" (Berners-Lee, 1999), and a social web which is often called "Web 2.0" (O'Reilly, 2005). The development of teacher and student agents, the structuring of content into learning objects (Wiley, 2000), the social construction and annotation of content by learners, teachers, and practitioners, and the formal expression of learning interactions (Koper, 2001) are creating a second-generation web that provides new capabilities and challenges for online teachers and learners. As yet, we are at the early stages in the technological and pedagogical development of online learning. The fundamental characteristics of teaching and learning, however, and the three critical components of teaching presence – design and organization, facilitating discourse, and direct instruction – will continue to be critical components of teaching effectiveness in both online learning and classroom instruction.

REFERENCES

Anderson, T. (2003a). Getting the mix right again: An updated and theoretical rationale for interaction. *International Review of Research in Open and Distance Learning, 4*(2). Retrieved August 24, 2007, from http://www.irrodl.org/index.php/ irrodl/article/view/149/230

Anderson, T. (2003b). Modes of interaction in distance education: Recent developments and research questions. In M. Moore & W. Anderson (Eds.), *Handbook of Distance Education,* (pp. 129–144). Mahwah, NJ: Lawrence Erlbaum.

Anderson, T. (2005). Distance learning – Social software's killer app? In *Proceedings of the Open & Distance Learning Association of Australia,* Adelaide: ODLAA. Retrieved August 21, 2007, from http://www.unisa.

edu.au/odlaaconference/PPDF2s/13%20odlaa%20-%20Anderson. pdf

Anderson, T. (2008). Towards a theory of online learning. In T. Anderson (Ed.), *Theory and Practice of Online Learning*, 2nd ed. (pp. 45–74). Edmonton, AB: AU Press.

Anderson, T., Rourke, L., Archer, W., & Garrison, R. (2001). Assessing teaching presence in computer conferencing transcripts. *Journal of the Asynchronous Learning Network, 5*(2). Retrieved January 2008 from http://www.aln.org/publications/jaln/v5n2/v5n2_anderson.asp

Arbaugh, J. B. (2007). An empirical verification of the community of inquiry framework. *Journal of Asynchronous Learning Networks, 11*(1). Retrieved August 21, 2007, from http://www.sloan-c.org/publications/jaln/v11n1/

Berners-Lee, T. (1999). *Weaving the Web: The original design and ultimate destiny of the World Wide Web by its inventor.* San Francisco: Harper.

Bowling Green State University (n.d.). *Rubrics for enhancing and teaching @ BGSU.* Retrieved August 24, 2007, from http://facultydevelopment-bgsu.blogspot.com/ 2005/11/rubrics-to-evaluate-classroom-blogging. html

Burge, E. & Howard, J. (1994). Audio-conferencing in graduate education: A case study. *American Journal of Distance Education 4*(2), 3–15.

Bryant, T. (2006). Social software in academia. *EDUCAUSE Quarterly, 2.* Retrieved August 21, 2007, from https://www.educause.edu/ir/library/pdf/eqm0627.pdf

Cameron, D., & Anderson, T. (2006). Comparing weblogs to threaded discussion tools in online educational contexts. *International Journal of Instructional Technology and Distance Learning, 2*(11). Retrieved August 24, 2007, from http://www.itdl.org/Journal/Nov_06/article01.htm

Campbell, K. (2002). Power, voice and democratization: Feminist pedagogy and assessment in CMC. *Educational Technology and Society, 5*(3). Retrieved August 24, 2007, from http://www.ifets.info/journals/5_3/campbell.html

Collins, A., Brown, J. S., & Newman, S. E. (1989). Cognitive apprenticeship: Teaching the crafts of reading, writing, and mathematics. In L.B. Resnick (Ed.), *Knowing, learning, and instruction: Essays in honor of Robert Glaser,* (pp. 453494). Hillsdale, NJ: Lawrence Erlbaum.

Dabbagh, N. (2000). *Online-protocols.* Retrieved March 2008 from http://mason.gmu.edu/~ndabbagh/wblg/online-protocol.html

Dalsgaard, C. (2006). Social software: E-learning beyond learning management systems. *European Journal of Open, Distance and E-Learning, 2.*

Retrieved August 24, 2007, from http://www.eurodl.org/materials/contrib/2006/ Christian_Dalsgaard.htm

Daniel, J., & Marquis, C. (1988). Interaction and independence: Getting the mix right. In D. Sewart, D. Keegan, & B. Holmberg (Eds.), *Distance education: International perspectives* (pp. 339–359). London: Routledge.

Davie, L. (1989). Facilitation techniques for the online tutor. In R. Mason & A. Kaye (Eds.), *MindWeave* (pp. 74–85). Oxford: Pergamon Press.

Dixon, J., Crooks, H., & Henry, K. (2007). Breaking the ice: Supporting collaboration and the development of community online. *Canadian Journal of Learning and Technology, 32*(2). Retrieved August 24, 2007, from http://www.cjlt.ca/content/ vol32.2/dixon.html

Dron, J. (2007). *Control and constraint in e-learning: Choosing when to choose.* Hershey, PA: Information Science Pub.

Eastin, M., & LaRose, R. (2000). Internet self-efficacy and the psychology of the digital divide. *Journal of Computer Mediated Communications, 6*(1). Retrieved August 24, 2007, from http://jcmc.indiana.edu/vol6/issue1/eastin.html

Garrison, D. R. (1991). Critical thinking in adult education: A conceptual model for developing critical thinking in adult learners. *International Journal of Lifelong Education, 10*(4), 287–303.

Garrison, D. R. (1998). Andragogy, learner-centeredness, and the educational transaction at a distance. *Journal of Distance Education, 3*(2), 123–127.

Garrison, D. R., & Anderson, T. (2003). *E-Learning in the 21st century.* London: Routledge.

Garrison, D. R., & Baynton, M. (1987). Beyond independence in distance education: The concept of control. *American Journal of Distance Education, 1*(3), 3–15.

Garrison, R., Anderson, T., & Archer, W. (2000). Critical inquiry in text-based environment: Computer conferencing in higher education. *The Internet and Higher Education, 2*(2–3), 87–105.

Holmberg, B. (1989). *Theory and practice of distance education.* London: Routledge.

Jiang, M., & Ting, E. (2000). A study of factors influencing students' perceived learning in a web-based course environment. *International Journal of Educational Telecommunications, 6*(4), 317–338.

Koper, R. (2001). *Modeling units of study from a pedagogical perspective: The pedagogical meta-model behind EML Heerlen. Open University of the Netherlands.* Retrieved May 1, 2007, from dspace.ou.nl/bitstream/1820/36/1/Pedagogical+metamodel+behind+EMLv2.pdf

Koper, R. (2004). Use of the Semantic Web to solve some basic problems in education: Increase flexible, distributed lifelong learning, decrease teacher's workload. *Journal of Interactive Media in Education, 6.* Retrieved August 24, 2007, from http://www-jime.open.ac.uk/2004/6

Laurillard, D. (1997) (Ed.) *Rethinking university teaching: A framework for the effective use of educational technology.* London: Routledge.

Levine, S. (2002). Replacement myth. *IT Forum.* Retrieved March 2008 from http://www.listserv.uga.edu/cgi-bin/wa?A2=ind0208&L=itforum &P =R7059&X=60858A07F2C0090FD4

Mason, R., & Romiszowski, A. J. (1996). Computer-mediated communication. In D. Jonassen (Ed.), *The handbook of research for educational communications and technology.* (pp. 438–456). New York: Simon & Schuster Macmillan.

McGreal, R. (2004). *Online education using learning objects.* London: Routledge Falmer.

McPeck, J. (1990). *Teaching critical thinking.* New York: Routledge.

O'Reilly, T. (2005). *What is Web 2.0? Design patterns and business models for the next generation of software.* Retrieved August 24, 2007, from http://www.oreillynet.com/pub/a/oreilly/tim/news/2005/09/30/what-is-web-20.html

Palloff, R., & Pratt, K. (1999). *Building learning communities in cyberspace.* San Francisco: Jossey-Bass.

Paulsen, M. (1995). Moderating educational computer conferences. In Z. Berge & M. Collins (Eds.), *Computer mediated communication and the online classroom* (pp. 81–90). Cresskill, NJ: Hampton Press.

Pickett, J. P., et al. (2007) *The American heritage dictionary of the English language: Fourth edition.* Retrieved August 24, 2007, from http://www.bartleby.com/cgi-bin/texis/webinator/ahdsearch?search_type=enty&query=Discourse&db=ahd&Submit=Search

Prensky, M. (2001). *Digital game-based learning.* New York: McGraw Hill.

Rekkedal, T. (1983). The written assignments in correspondence education: Effects of reducing turn-around time. *Distance Education, 4*(2), 231–250.

Richardson, W. (2006). *Blogs, wikis, podcasts and other powerful web tools for classrooms.* Thousand Oaks, CA: Corwin Press.

Rogoff, B. (1990). *Apprenticeship in thinking: Cognitive development in social context.* New York: Oxford University Press.

Rourke, L., & Kanuka, H. (2007). Barriers to online critical discourse. *International Journal of Computer-Supported Collaborative Learning, 2*(1),

105–126. Retrieved August 24, 2007, from http://www.springerlink. com/content/r3243740340t0847/

Rourke, L., & Anderson, T. (2002). Using peer teams to lead online discussions. *Journal of Interactive Media in Education, 1.* Retrieved August 27, 2007, from http://www-jime.open.ac.uk/2002/1/

Salmon, G. (2000). *E-moderating: The key to teaching and learning online.* London: Kogan Page.

Shepard, L. A. (2000). The role of assessment in a learning culture. *Educational Researcher, 29*(7), 4–14. Retrieved August 24, 2007, from http://www.jstor.org/view/0013189x/ap040287/04a00020/0

Vygotsky, L. (1978). *Mind in society: The development of higher psychological processes.* Cambridge: Harvard University Press.

Wiley, D. (2000). Connecting learning objects to instructional design theory: A definition, a metaphor, and a taxonomy. In D. A. Wiley (Ed.), *The instructional use of learning objects: Online version.* Retrieved August 24, 2007, from http://www.reusability.org/read/chapters/wiley.doc

CHAPTER 15

CALL CENTRES
IN DISTANCE EDUCATION

ALEX Z. KONDRA, COLLEEN HUBER,
KERRI MICHALCZUK & ANDREW WOUDSTRA
Athabasca University

INTRODUCTION

In the past decade, call centres and contact centres have evolved to become the front line for customer interaction in many types of organizations. As such, they have a critical importance in the implementation of organizational strategy (Evanson, Harker, & Frei, 1998). Call centres have applications in many industries which offer customer service, as they can provide customers with a single access point to diverse services; they can also be critical in the management of an organization's relationship with its customers. While many organizations use call centres to solicit clients or customers for new sales or donations, they are also used to accomplish surveys of customer satisfaction or public opinion and provide services to customers. Despite their growing ubiquity, call centres have been subject to severe criticism as poor places to work (Taylor & Bain, 1999). Nonetheless, not all call centres are subject to the common criticisms of being highly Tayloristic and unrewarding places to work (Holman, 2002).

In education, call centres can be useful to an educational institution in many ways, ranging from simple provision of information to prospective students, to fundraising, collection of survey data, and even provision of instructional services (Hitch & MacBrayne, 2003). In distance education in particular, the call centre concept can be an effective communication tool, enabling the institution to provide and improve service to students in many areas, including instruction (Adria & Woudstra, 2001; Kondra & Michalczuk, 2007). When coupled with customer relationship management (CRM) software, a call centre can become a powerful tool in the development and maintenance of the student-university relationship, and provide a critical link to the university for an often isolated learner (Kondra & Michalczuk, 2007). CRM software can also provide for quality control in student interaction and even help in instructional design. At Athabasca University, call centres are used in a number of contexts and show the potential for expansion and consolidation, to take advantage of economies of scale.

ORGANIZATIONAL STRATEGY AND CALL CENTRES

Strategy and strategic decision-making have long been areas of active academic and practitioner inquiry. Chandler (1962) studied the development of American corporations in the early twentieth century, and postulated that corporate structure was designed to implement strategy; in other words, structure followed strategy. Much recent work (Eisenhardt, 1999; Kim & Mauborgne, 1999; Markides, 1999; Pascale, 1999) suggests that strategy is a dynamic that emerges from the competitive environment, evaluates that environment in an ongoing manner, and flexibly adjusts the corporate course when necessary. Organizations compete on the edge, adjusting their deployment of employees and other resources as necessary strategic changes are made (Hamel & Prahalad, 1994).

Over the past 20 to 25 years, experience has shown that information technology is an increasingly important potential contributor to an organization's productivity, and that organizations experience maximum value when information technology investments are strategically driven. Davenport and Short (1990) studied the relationship between information technology and business process redesign, and postulate an enabling link between, on the one hand, the development of strategic vision and process objectives, and on the other, successful, information-technology-driven process redesign.

Call centres provide an example of the application of these concepts. Call centre design has been enabled by the use of telecommunications technology and its ongoing integration with information technology. Call centre concepts are becoming integral to the redesign of business processes (particularly informational processes as distinguished from those focused on physical objects), and where call centre implementations are strategically driven and aligned, their value to the organization increases.

It is important that the objectives established for a call centre support and enhance the organization's strategic direction. For example, a call centre focused on routing telephone calls to the appropriate staff member or department has a relatively narrow task; it will be suited to an organization that needs to give short, concise answers to a high call volume. An inbound telemarketing call centre focused on sales will allow longer calls, focusing on minimizing waiting times and maximizing sales impact. If the organization as a whole is strategically focused on the creation of customer loyalty, however, the call centre would be a primary means to achieve that goal, and both of the examples above would fall short in contributing to this corporate strategy (Holt, 2000).

Many call centre managers are looking for ways to build cost-effective, competitive operations using industry benchmark information:

> We've become obsessed in this industry with mass comparison. We survey and benchmark and publish averages, quartiles and percentages. These numbers get proclaimed as 'industry standards' that your call centre should aspire to match. (Cleveland & Hopton, 2002)

As these authors go on to note, however, the surveys reveal that, overall, customers were not happy with the service. Call centres are in a chronic state of balancing productivity and quality (Kantsperger & Kunz, 2005), and balancing this inherent tension between call centre standardization and customization will always be a concern (Frenkel, Tam, Korczynski, & Shire, 1998).

Given the diversity of mission and function in call centres, it is likely that what fits one will not fit all. It is much better to examine what the organization is trying to achieve, and to build processes and systems that help to achieve these goals in effective and efficient ways. Call centres can be a sound strategic asset for an organization, because they can strengthen customer relationships, and enable the organization to learn more about customers, to serve them better. Adria and Chowdhury (2002) make a strong case for using call centres to improve an organization's ability to serve its customers. They argue for the empowerment of call centre managers and employees to enhance customer service, and they note that the main responsibility for workers in a call centre operation is to maintain and enhance the reputation of the organization. That is, the organization's carefully developed customer service culture is at risk during each customer interaction.

As universities deal with a more competitive environment, they are adopting a student-as-customer strategy (Driscoll & Wicks, 1998). Integrating a call centre into an overall strategic plan can separate one distance education provider from another. Given that the competition for students in the distance education environment is increasing, careful strategic positioning of the distance education provider is essential.

One of the strategic decisions that must be made by an organization is whether or not to outsource a call centre. A call centre can outsource as much or as little of the technology and services as they choose. By outsourcing, companies aim to benefit quickly from the fast and efficient resources from an outside source. The complexity of managing outsourcing relationships and gaining an accurate picture of results, however, is proving to be very difficult and costly. Outsourcing call centres in the education arena could prove to be even more difficult as customer service representatives (CSRs) are an important part of the overall teaching team and relationship management, thereby increasing the risk associated with outsourcing.

CALL CENTRES IN ORGANIZATIONS

Traditionally, call centres have been implemented in businesses to improve cost effectiveness and the delivery of customer services, as well as to generate additional revenue. While their popularity has been growing, they have a bad reputation and have been described as a "modern form of 'Taylorism'" (Zapf, Isic, Bechtoldt, & Blau, 2003, p. 311), and even as "satanic mills" (Kinnie, Hutchinson, & Purcell, 2000, p. 967). Criticisms of call centres include Batt & Moynihan (2002):
- Low skilled work
- Poor working conditions
- Fast, machine pacing of work
- Routine, standardized, and boring tasks

- High stress
- Short, fast job cycles
- Poor job security
- Low pay, possibly piece rate
- Extreme employee monitoring

These criticisms are associated with the mass-production, high-volume, low-value-added examples particularly associated with surveying and telemarketing, which are the most visible examples of call centres. Despite these criticisms, alternative models do exist that ameliorate these problems (Batt & Moynihan, 2002). Call centres can help streamline and enrich customer service, and provide customers and staff with a knowledge base through technology that complements labour, rather than replaces it, and does not create a frenetic pace of work. Some call centres have been designed in a manner that requires highly skilled workers with associated job security, high pay, task variety, and worker satisfaction (Batt, 2002). It is also possible to design enriched jobs by mixing administrative and other work to improve task variety, and by introducing high-commitment human resource management practices to increase overall job and user satisfaction (Houlihan, 2002).

The professional service and mass customization models are two high value-added call centre models that attempt to overcome many of the standard criticisms of call centres (Batt & Moynihan, 2002). In the professional service model, technology does not replace labour but complements it; employees need to be educated and highly skilled. Collaborative decision making with elements of discretion in decision making and teamwork are essential. Individuals develop substantial firm-specific social capital that hinges on trust among professionals. The mass customization model is a hybrid between the professional service model and the mass production model. This hybrid model attempts to keep costs down while providing a quality, customized service. Automation and process reengineering are essential to help keep costs down while trying to provide a high quality interactive experience. The hybrid model also requires CSRs to exercise a high degree of discretion and skill, as they are usually expected to deal with relatively complex user interactions.

In both of these high-involvement models, technology is intended to complement rather than replace labour; work is highly skilled, discretion is involved, and collaborative work is essential. Collaborative structures generally provide better call centre service (Batt & Moynihan, 2002), and both models are consistent with high-commitment human resource management practices that should improve overall job and user satisfaction.

Call centres have particular significance in three areas: customer service and retention, direct marketing, and information sources for management and customer feedback (Friedman, 2001).

- *Customer/student service and retention:* In business operations, call centres have become the primary contact point with customers, and serve as the means by which the organization creates a long-term relationship with individual customers and maintains customer satisfaction. Customer satisfaction will generally lead to retention and to word-of-mouth recommendations. In distance education, call centres can help create the same type of relationship. In the context of a university's service standards for processing applications, marking assignments, or answering calls and messages, call centre staff are the consistent point of contact with the student, and can even become their advocates.

- *Direct marketing:* The support provided by a call centre is increasingly seen as a service that customers expect to find integrated with product offerings, and available by phone and on the Internet. This contact with the customer (who, in the case of online or distance education, is a student) may result in opportunities to help the student choose additional products (programs or courses) and services (e.g., advising, counselling, tutoring), or may be used to prompt students to complete courses or programs.

- *Management information and student/customer feedback:* A call centre with good software accumulates a great deal of information about customers or students and courses. This information is collected by analysing call documentation data, or by directly presenting questions to the customer or student. The information can range from simple to complex, from student's opinions about university policies or problems with courses, to aiding in the design of web sites and even course design. Distance education institutions should make the collection and analysis of information a major call centre goal, particularly given that the distributed nature of this work makes the collection of such information difficult.

CUSTOMER/STUDENT SERVICE AND RETENTION

The help desk first emerged to help customers and staff of organizations deal with technical problems associated with computer use. Noel Bruton (2002), a well-known information technology (IT) consultant in Great

Britain, notes that the IT help desk took on its current form in the mid-1980s. The call centre concept used today came later, in the 1990s, to deal with issues and queries not related to technology. According to Bruton, a key difference between a help desk and a call centre lies in how the two functions deal with knowledge management. He contends that help desks, while they do impart prepared or pre-manufactured information, also require diagnostic skills from their staff. In addition, we exist in an information society where people desire immediate answers to questions, and the distance education environment is no different (Howell, Williams & Lindsay, 2003). Many colleges and universities support multiple software and hardware platforms. With increasing offerings in online distance education, students will not only be calling with questions related to course content; they will also require technical assistance. Good service to students requires a single contact point for both technical- and content-related questions.

Call centre services to students engaged in e-learning require that call centre staff have diagnostic skills. These skills enable them to work with students to determine the nature of, and solutions to, their course content queries (tutoring), and to work through program issues (advising). To deliver a one-stop shop for students engaged in e-learning, it is important that the diagnostic skills offered by help desk personnel are combined with the directive and prepared services of a typical call centre. In a consolidated call centre/help desk, the use of a knowledge base is important for both functions; however, with diagnostic situations, the bigger issue is usually trying to deduce the actual problem. The knowledge base built up for many course-related, program-related, and technical questions can be straightforward, comprised of simple questions and answers. The knowledge base for diagnostic questions must also include a step-by-step guide for asking questions to determine the nature of the problem, followed by steps for solving the problem. Learning to deduce the actual problem is a unique skill set and takes time to learn.

The staff of an online learning call centre must incorporate skills from both call centre and help desk environments, and have specialists available to deal with particularly complex issues. Good skills within an environment such as this usually include strong communication skills, student (or customer) service experience, and an ability to adapt to new situations. A good set of Frequently Asked Questions (FAQs), complete with step-by-step solutions, should be made available to call centre staff. And, as with course content queries, technical expertise should be available for more complex issues.

Brandt (2002) notes that only 14% of all help desk calls involve new problems that require serious attention, while the remaining 86% could all be resolved automatically, without human intervention, via web-based features. It has also been shown that if end-users are equipped with better documentation or automated self-help web-based facilities, calls to the call centre or help desk can be greatly reduced (Brandt, 2002; Jordan 2003; Lawlor, 2001). Lawlor further points to surveys showing that organizations that reduced the number of help desk/call centre calls by creating self-help options had a higher level of user satisfaction.

Doherty (2001) points out that help desks are typically organized in layers or tiers. Tiers can start at web-based self-help, which Lawlor (2001) designates as *Tier 0*, and move up in the hierarchy to the front-line facilitator, *Tier 1*, through the desktop analyst, *Tier 2*, to the network specialist, *Tier 3*. A consolidated call centre/help desk in education would likewise be layered in tiers. Where possible, web-based self-help (Tier 0) should be developed, providing extensive FAQ files, bulletin boards, and conference and chat areas. These are the least expensive solutions, and provide an immediate source of information. Call centre staff that are the first contact with students are Tier 1, technical experts to whom questions are referred are Tier 2, and the academics serve as Tier 3.

Direct Marketing Opportunities

Early uses of call centres included marketing and promotion, as well as the provision of technical assistance. There are two primary operating modes for these functions. The first is to field calls from current customers wishing to place more orders or discuss products, and from new customers directed to the call centre number by advertising and promotional materials. This is the function that increasingly involves the Internet. The second operating mode for a call centre is the outgoing cold call. A possible customer is identified by region, income, or some other factor, and is called at home with an offer of the organization's product, a solicitation of a donation, etc. A carefully prepared script is provided for the call centre staff to use in their contacts. This is a popular function of a call centre for charities and long-distance phone companies. Call centres are also used to carry out surveys (Coen, 2001; Hitch & MacBrayne, 2003).

In education, the primary use of call-centre technology in marketing and promotion is to field incoming calls from students who have learned of the educational institution through advertising, word-of-mouth referral, Internet search, or other means (Hitch & MacBrayne,

2003). Many institutions accept volumes of queries from prospective students and their parents, for which they provide information about their programs, both educational and extracurricular. Often, large numbers of attendants are only needed during peak recruiting seasons. In distance education, where students are not on campus, there is additional pressure to fill the information needs of current students on a day-to-day basis, typically by answering questions about course availability, helping a student get information about their performance, and so on. Finally, the student advising function, wherein an advisor works through program planning issues with a prospective or current student, is also an ideal candidate for applying the technologies and organizational format found in call centres. The question of cold calling to solicit customers or students is more questionable, but should perhaps not be dismissed out-of-hand. Cold calls could be used to remind students of impending course deadlines, possibly increasing completion rates and future enrolments, or to (re)inform them of potential new course or program opportunities. The structure of such calls and the criteria for initiation would require careful consideration.

Management Information and Student/Customer Feedback

Knowledge management (KM), rather than information management, can be a source of competitive advantage for an organization. A centralized call centre, when coupled with appropriate software, is now a key element of successful organizational strategy. Good knowledge management consists of more than collecting and disseminating information – it includes organizing and analyzing information to provide the maximum benefit for the organization and its customer:

> Customer service organizations require easy access to accurate, consistent information in order to answer customers' questions. KM provides the process to capture relevant information and make it readily accessible by agents and customers via self-service. (Jordan, 2003, p. 44)

Greater accumulation of knowledge and good management of that knowledge can allow CSRs to engage in a wider variety of tasks, allowing for greater economies of scales (Mitchell, 2001), and increasing task variety has benefits in terms of user and job satisfaction (discussed below). Good management of data is also important if CSRs are to locate and disseminate information quickly and accurately. It can also increase the efficiency of the overall operation by increasing CSRs' ability to resolve issues on first contact. rather than requiring a call-back or escalation to another level (Kotwal, 2004).

One of the significant advantages for instructional designers and academics is that CRM software enables tracking of all contacts to a call centre. CRM data can provide information on the nature of all inquiries about a course, and whether they are related to administrative matters or academic content which, in turn, can be mined by faculty or instructional designers. This tracking can identify instructional design issues related to a course and/or identify subject matter that could require supplemental material or remedial exercises to improve student success. Ideally, academics and instructional designers should provide self-service help for distance students. Given that they increasingly want instant access to information (Howell, et al., 2003), this specialized service would be the ideal solution. Also, in distance education, it is typical that one person designs a course while many deliver it; and as enrolments increase, an increasing number of people are involved in course delivery. As a result, KM becomes particularly important in situations of added-course delivery complexity. Collecting relevant feedback from a large group of individuals who deliver a course and from a large number of students enrolled in a course can be improved through CRM software that can track inquires by course. This provides for a systematic collection of information, and does not suffer from the so-called "recency effect," meaning that people tend to recall the most recent events, or recall errors. Clearly, this software can be particularly useful in the distributed work environment common in distance education. CRM software can help to overcome some of the communication problems associated with distributed work environments by being a central collection point for a myriad of information.

Call Centre Consolidation

It is not uncommon for an organization to have more than one call centre, each one focusing on a specific function. Nonetheless, call centre consolidation makes sense for a number of reasons, including the rapid progression in technological advances enabling better access to organizational information for call centre agents and customers (through KM), and improved employee satisfaction through increasing task variety and skill levels. When there are similarities in the tasks performed and overlap in the services provided by separate call centres, there is potential for economies of scale. An agent in a large group can handle more calls at a given service level than they can in a small group. Mitchell (2001) points out that "efficiencies" can be achieved up to a call-centre size of approximately 50 agents. After this point, incremental gains are minimal, if they occur at all. While many call centres contain many more than 50 agents, the maximum optimal size for their subunits or teams is 50. Other motivators for call centre consolidation include reduced equipment costs, simplified implementation of new technologies, better control over service quality, reduced management staff requirements, and consolidated KM.

In the past, call centres segmented calls on the basis of skills. Consolidation can also occur within a call centre by rationalizing the segmentation of some agent groups. For example, in a bank, commercial loans require different skills than personal loans. In other settings, technical help requires different skills than service, which requires different skills than sales. According to Mitchell (2001), knowledge management, process management, just-in-time training, and CRM all contribute to the tearing down of skills barriers to service. Mitchell notes that

> Today's segmentation strategies no longer look to agent skills as the basis for routing calls, but instead focus on client value to determine what services to provide through what media. Low value customers get routed to self-service technologies. High value customers get high-touch service. No matter who or what the customer ends up interacting with, the agent, human or computer, has all of the services, corporate knowledge and process flows needed to handle the customer requests. (p. 26)

In an educational environment, the concepts of "low value" and "high value" customers have no place; however, the concept of segmentation is potentially useful. Such segmentation could be based on student characteristics (graduate versus undergraduate, area of study, and so on), as well as the type of query. Many queries may be routed to self-service areas and others are routed to specialized agents. Data collected within the call centre through CRM software will inform the segmentation. Improving KM will allow each agent to handle more diverse and more difficult calls, and as more knowledge becomes incorporated into knowledge systems, training becomes more an exercise in teaching agents the "how to's" of developing customer relationships than focusing on each product or service offered. This can increase task variety and the skills and training required by CSRs that, in turn, can have a significant influence on employees' job satisfaction, absenteeism, and retention (discussed below). The integration of call centres also encourages the integration of knowledge management systems that, in turn, increases the consistency of messages from the organization to the customer and provides the organization with a "single face" (Kotwal, 2004). Integration can also lead to increased customer satisfaction, by having one person deal with different inquiries in a single customer contact, rather than requiring customers to make numerous contacts with an organization.

CRITICAL SUCCESS FACTORS FOR CALL CENTRES

Distance education shares the trends affecting many firms in financial service, telecommunication, and technology industries. A dominant trend is the increasing distance from the customer (or student). Phone companies, utility providers, and banks once operated many small outlets scattered throughout cities and were present in every small community; now, however, there are a few large facilities (and increasingly, online services) are backed up by call centres. For call centres to be successful and productive in any field, including distance education, a number of critical success factors must be in place. Successful call-centre implementation requires the development of effective processes and policies, the implementation of appropriate technology, and the adoption of effective human resource management processes (Evanson et al., 1998).

Processes and Policy

Once a call centre business strategy has been developed, and the processes required to carry out the designated objectives have been adopted, it is crucial that those processes be evaluated. A key part of this evaluation involves looking at the types of contacts the call centre is receiving, how contacts are routed, and how contact processes are managed. The call centre should also establish polices and standardized operational procedures. Most importantly, quality monitoring and reporting processes must be in place so that the call centre can continue to meet established objectives.

Call centres had their genesis and have been particularly effective in organizations that received large volumes of calls from customers who experienced uncertain results in seeking the right individual or department to deal with their specific issue. Staff in such organizations were also frustrated and not utilized effectively, as they forwarded calls or tried to help in areas outside their experience. Now, the direction of calls to one area allows call centre agents to handle queries in volume. Only calls requiring additional expertise not available in the call centre are referred to other areas of the organization. Call centres become a collection point for organizational information as databases are created to allow agents to handle a wider range of queries. Thus, over time, the expertise and information available to a call centre is expanded, so it can handle more incoming calls without resorting to referrals and call-backs.

A call centre concept can also be used to allocate and distribute workload in the organization. Without such a centre, highly paid professionals are often used to handle tasks that underutilize their expertise. A call centre with good call-routing processes can distribute calls to the individuals or automated agents most qualified to handle them. Ideally, all relevant information about a customer and their issues is documented and available to all agents within a call centre using CRM software. In addition, with collaborative systems, several agents can simultaneously work on a particularly difficult issue with a customer, with each staff member contributing their particular expertise in resolving the problem.

Customer-focused organizations use call centres most successfully (Evanson et al., 1998). Many firms seeking to become more customer-oriented purchase and install elaborate CRM software suites that track and record service transactions. If this installation occurs without significant planning, however, and especially if managers are dazzled by the "promises of the technology," the implementation often fails. Rigby, Reichheld, and Dawson (2003) emphasize that CRM installations work best if the organization starts with a customer strategy, then realigns its structure and processes to fit the strategy, and finally selects the technology that is appropriate for the chosen strategy and processes. Whether implementing CRM technology, call centre technology, or both, the organization must first ensure that its strategy is appropriately customer-focused, and that the technology under consideration fits with that strategy (Hitt, Frei, & Harker, 1998; Rigby et al.).

CRM products have helped call centres to organize some of their customer contact processes, and increase efficiencies and quality of service. According to Kiska (2002), a new approach must be added to follow up on CRM processes. Customer experience management (CEM) is emerging as a means to retain valued customers. It is widely known that retention of current customers is cost effective and highly profitable for an organization (Reichheld, 1996). This can also be true for a distance education organization that benefits from program or long-term students. A CEM process begins by identifying key measures for customer satisfaction and retention. The statistics it gathers can help organizations make sound decisions when it comes to call centre operations and policies (Kiska). Holt (2000) holds opinions similar to Kiska's, indicating that customer loyalty and satisfaction are closely linked to the success of the organization and call centre:

> If call centre operators used customer contact to understand attitudes to the company, to assess brand perceptions, to research responses to marketing activity, and to begin to unlock the secrets of long-term loyalty and advocacy, the value of that call centre operation would increase immeasurably. It will enable other parts of the organisation to assess the relevant issues and take the necessary action. (p. 11)

Technology

Information technology is increasingly important to a wide range of firms, and is the "enabling platform" for call centres, the Internet, and other innovations. Earlier in this chapter, we noted work by Davenport and Short (1990) on the relationship between information technology and business process redesign. Hitt and colleagues (1998) investigated the adoption of technology in the financial industry. They note that research has found IT investment to be a substantial contributor to productivity and productivity growth.

In the last 15 years, various call-centre technologies have become available to the market, including voice-over-Internet protocol (VoIP), customer-relationship-integration tools, and Internet and web communication tools and products. In their study of call centres in the financial services industry, Evanson and colleagues (1998) note that call centres need to ensure their technology is effective or appropriate for its strategy. Krol (2002) indicates that while excesses in the adoption of technology were common in the technology bubble, organizations are now returning to basics. That is to say, call centres are more interested in products that provide mission-critical services. Customer loyalty and service objectives should drive call centre technology investments.

Technology is transforming the traditional call centre, allowing staff to be in contact with customers in a number of different ways, including, but not limited to, email, chat, web browsing, and voicemail.

Finding the right technology is not an easy task, but the first steps must be to determine the organization's needs and to link customers with the information and services they require quickly. Knowledge databases, CRM or customer tracking, CEM or customer follow-up and retention, and handling of multiple contact media must be integrated into a system that is easily accessible to front-line staff, or to customers directly. Automated systems can match customers with call centre staff, based on the customer's profile and the staff member's knowledge focus. The banking industry is experimenting with such "intelligent routing," to direct calls from the bank's best customers to particular representatives (Knowledge at Wharton, 2002).

The first generation of call centres focused on answering telephone calls from customers (students). As the Internet has become more widely used, call centres have made use of it as well. Internet technology allows feedback to customers or students to occur through either of these two channels, and the more flexible Internet media provide a variety of tools, including web chat, asynchronous conferencing, video conferencing, and web call-backs.

Recently, call centres have also begun to make use of web sites to provide their customers with more information. There has been a push to provide customers with Frequently Asked Questions (FAQ) pages, where customers can look up and provide answers to their own questions, while intelligent question-and-answer systems can look up answers for clients automatically (Brandt, 2002). For example, Athabasca University has developed such a tool, called AskAU (see http://www.askau.ca).

When considering any of the web-based tools for use with a call centre, it is important to consider their positive and negative aspects, and how they will affect call-centre operations. Since the Internet gives customers (or students) the power to seek out answers on their own, organizations are challenged to develop integrated systems to allow delivery of services that are better and operate faster than those that customers can find for themselves. In addition, people tend to like "multi-channel" services, meaning they may use the web site, but also have direct contact with CSRs. These channels should be viewed as complementary, not competitive.

The Internet is capable of providing vast amounts of information for call centre staff, as well as for current and potential customers or students. Developing user interfaces that make this information quickly available, in a format that satisfies the diverse needs of users, is an ongoing challenge, however. A major impact of the new Internet-based technologies is that the "service bar" is being raised. If routine issues are handled on the Web through automatic agents, call centres must be in a position to handle more sophisticated calls.

Human Resources

Human, not financial, capital must now be the starting point and foundation for a successful strategy. Financial capital and also technology are increasingly being commodified, and each is found in abundant supply (Bartlett & Ghoshal, 2002). As a result, the skills, knowledge, and ability of an organization's staff to innovate will increasingly be the distinguishing factors for successful strategy implementation and value creation (Pfeffer, 1994).

Customer service studies show that when something goes right, customers give credit to the individual employee dealing with the problem; when something goes wrong, customers usually blame the organization itself. This makes it crucial for any organization to have the right number of people with the right skills, at the right place and the right time, ready to answer customer demands (Krol, 2002).

Given that personnel costs consume 60% of budgets in call centres (Batt, 2002), recruitment and hiring of front-line and call-centre managers, training and coaching of staff, and ongoing performance management are of critical importance to a call centre's success. Call-centre staff are the front-line human element for the customer. To promote the reputation of the organization, they need to feel they are a vital part of the organization. Selection of staff with customer service skills, such as excellent communication skills, writing skills, and a positive attitude, is extremely important. It is also important to recruit personnel with appropriate experience and educational background, to ensure they are capable of providing quality services to customers or students.

Training and ongoing coaching is also extremely important, as call-centre environments, technologies, and processes tend to change rapidly. Staff members must be involved in the changes, buy into the new processes, and have the information they need to be able to carry them out.

Assessment and performance checks are essential. What are the employee satisfaction levels? What are your customers saying about the service they are receiving? Retention of staff is as important as retention of customers, so that loyalty to service is maintained. Rigby and colleagues (2003) note that the prime driver of customer loyalty is the loyalty of the organization's employees. Creating a positive and healthy environment for employees and empowering employees reduces turnover. Institutions with higher employee empowerment tend to have higher overall employee retention (Evanson et al., 1998).

Adria and Chowdhury (2002) argue that call centres can and should allow employees to upgrade their skills, make more and better decisions, and participate in a team-based organizational culture. Skills training leads to higher employee satisfaction and higher productivity. Frontline staff should be corporate ambassadors for the organization. They also argue that organizations should pursue decentralization and team building: frontline employees are more productive if they are empowered to make decisions and provide input into the operation of the call centre; and customer service is more effective if employees feel they are part of the common effort to achieve excellence.

All of these factors lead to the conclusion that distance education providers need to develop high value-added call centres, coupled with high-commitment management techniques. These techniques include such things as increasing CSRs' discretion, high task variety, reduced surveillance, intensive training, self-directed team-oriented work structures, and the like (Houlihan, 2002; Kinnie et. al, 2000). It is hoped that by increasing CSRs' work satisfaction and retention, customer service will improve.

CALL CENTRES AT ATHABASCA UNIVERSITY

Athabasca University serves more than 32,000 students annually. Courses are offered primarily through independent study, which gives students the flexibility to set their own schedules in terms of time and place and, in effect, to pursue part-time studies and a full-time career if they wish. The university strives to remove the barriers of time, space, past educational experience and, to some degree, level of income. Athabasca University's mission and mode of operation make effective methods of communicating with students and prospective students of central importance. Using the call-centre model to build student satisfaction is an attractive alternative for Athabasca University.

Over the past 15 years, Athabasca University has developed three unique call centres:
- *The Information Centre*, the call centre operating as a "first point of contact," was established in 1995. Information Centre staff field all incoming calls not directed to a private line or to one of the

other call centres, and determine the purpose of the call. Information Centre attendants are well informed about the university's services, programs, and courses, and have access to a wide range of information. Many calls to the Information Centre are redirected to student advisors, to the Office of the Registrar, the Computing Services Help Desk, the School of Business Call Centre, or to course assistants. Prior to 1995, incoming calls came to a single telephone number in the Office of the Registrar, and many calls were lost. In addition, students expressed frustration with their experience in finding the right person in the institution to deal with their particular problem. Since 1995, many of these problems have been resolved, and the volume of calls and students served has increased exponentially. In the past five years, the volume of email queries has also risen rapidly, and an automated information system, *AskAU* (see http://www.askau.ca), has been added for students to obtain answers to questions without the intervention of a staff member.

- *The Computing Services Help Desk,* established in 1994, provides technical assistance primarily to help university staff obtain information and support for university computing resources; it helps staff to resolve problems with their Athabasca University equipment and supported software. The Help Desk does provide some assistance to students in computing science and psychology courses, but students are generally referred to appropriate academic units for courseware support.

- *The School of Business Call Centre* was created in 1994 as a pilot project to investigate the feasibility of alternative tutoring methods. It has grown to include almost all School of Business undergraduate courses, which account for approximately 18,000 registrations, or almost 30% of the university's undergraduate course registrations. The Call Centre is the central focus of student support in the undergraduate School of Business, and is integrated with its online course delivery platform, described in detail below.

Call Centres in Distance Education and Distributed Learning

Can a call centre be used as a vehicle for academic coaching and advising? In distance and online education, instructors and students are separated by eliminating the classroom. The historical practice in distance education has been to prepare detailed and thorough learning packages to guide students in their study, and to provide tutorial support by mail and telephone. The traditional tutor at Athabasca University is the focal point for student/institution contact, with the tutor answering many administrative queries, relaying marks, and directly helping in an instructional role.

In the early 1990s, the business faculty at Athabasca University developed a call-centre model as a "one-window" approach for its instructional tutoring (Adria & Woudstra, 2001). The key to its success has been the development of a groupware, "call-back conference" (an electronic bulletin board), to which call centre staff (referred to as undergraduate student advisors) post student subject-matter queries they cannot answer, and requests by students to speak to the course academic. In this way, academics field only substantive, course-related questions or problematic administrative issues. This system helps ensure that someone quickly responds who can answer students' questions and discuss the subject matter in depth.

The model also allows for the separation of the tutoring and marking roles, which are combined in the traditional tutor model at Athabasca University, and which can form a bottleneck in the effectiveness and efficiency of the instructional function by preventing the use of economies of scale, in both marking and handling administrative queries. In the traditional Athabasca University model, a tutor is responsible for all academic contacts for an assigned group of 28 to 40 students, and marks all assignments for this group. Tutors, who are paid regardless of whether they have contact with students, are typically available by telephone in three-hour blocks, once per week. Unfortunately, tutors are generally underutilized during this time by students. In the call-centre model, because students in any given course are not broken into groups, administrative questions are answered by the undergraduate student advisors, who form Tier 1 of the model; an academic expert role exists purely for answering students' academic content queries; and a specialist marker role has been created to handle marking duties.

Under the School of Business call-centre model, students in any course can call a toll-free 1-800 telephone number, five afternoons and six evenings per week. This call centre now provides students with about 60 hours of access to telephone and email assistance each week, and deals with approximately 80% of the calls directed to it (Adria & Woudstra, 2001), thus referring only 20% of the calls to academic support (academics and tutors). Course academics over a broad range of courses are thus freed from 80% of the calls that they (or their tutors) would otherwise receive. Moreover, students' queries are answered more quickly, rather than once per week during an academic's telephone contact hours. It is anticipated that the knowledge available to and level of expertise expected of selected staff will increase to allow direct answers to more of the 20% of the queries now referred to academic experts.

Prior to the implementation of the call-centre model, payments to telephone tutors were one of the School of Business's largest expenses. Each academic advisor now handles calls from about three times as many students per week as an average telephone tutor previously did. As a result, student support costs have dropped by approximately 25% in the School of Business undergraduate independent study courses, allowing resources to be deployed elsewhere. In addition, through the use of groupware, an online course-development and delivery system incorporating the call centre was developed for most School of Business undergraduate courses. Online course materials are continually developed and improved, allowing students to access course help through their course web sites, as well as to interact with call centre staff and academics via the Web, using chat or discussion boards.

The call-back conference database enables undergraduate student advisors and academics to track and resolve student queries online. However, the tracking in the call-back conference only accounted for approximately 20% of the student contacts that could not directly be answered by the undergraduate student advisors (Adria & Woudstra, 2001). Beginning in the 2002–2003 academic year, a comprehensive student tracking system has tracked all queries to the call centre, including those handled by the call-back conference, whether by email or telephone. This system is web-enabled and allows academics and other university staff to access the database from virtually anywhere, using a standard web browser. The database can produce reports and statistics on student contacts for use, among other things, in improving courseware. Reports such as these, and tracking information received from call-centre databanks, inform decisions about how services can most effectively be distributed to students.

There are numerous other advantages in addition to the ones already mentioned (i.e., improved data gathering, faster access to information, and reduced costs). When a contact centre is teamed with a central electronic bulletin board for posting academic student inquiries and a collaborative teaching environment (multiple academics and/or tutors assigned to a single course), it allows for the seamless handing-off of student inquiries from one academic/tutor to another, and the monitoring of service standards – factors that reduce the potential for litigation.

When student requests for academic support are posted centrally, an academic administrator can assign and re-assign the academic/tutor contact with the student accordingly. Academics/tutors are thus assigned by the time of day or day of the week that students are available, thereby meeting students' learning needs. Given that Canada spans six time zones, this level of flexibility is of particular importance. Also, in a continuous-enrolment (non-semester) environment, such a system is of great use. When an academic or tutor goes on leave, vacation, or is unavailable (i.e., illness, separation, or negligence), an academic administrator can immediately re-assign academic inquiries to another qualified person. It also allows for monitoring of student inquiries to determine if their queries are being dealt with in a timely manner and in compliance with service standards. Problems quickly come to light in the call-centre environment. This system can be compared to the long delays typical of the direct student-to-tutor model, which is hard to monitor and flag problem areas. Finally, CSRs are continually trained and updated in university policies, procedures, and programs. Under a direct-tutor model, the tutor is often the first line of contact for the student on matters beyond the academic (i.e., administrative). On occasion, academics and tutors have provided erroneous advice on administrative matters, leaving the institution open to litigation; this situation has created more work for administrators, who must then resolve resulting problems. Students are becoming increasingly litigious. As a result, it is in the best interest of the institution to have those with the most up-to-date knowledge – CSRs – provide administrative support to students.

Potential Developments in Athabasca University Call Centres

The Information Centre has operated as an inbound call centre and does not make outward calls, except to return messages. It has been effective in provision of information, which, in turn, supports and facilitates the recruitment process. In the future, there is no reason why the Information Centre could not expand its role to also make outgoing calls to potential students (i.e., high school and college graduates), informing them of opportunities at Athabasca University (should the university decide to pursue such a recruitment strategy). Of course, it would be necessary to balance the drive for efficient outgoing call practices with the need for customer focus. When call-centre staff have time, they could make outgoing calls, but clearly their main focus must be customer-retention calls (Evanson et al., 1998). For example, the School of Business Call Centre contacts students when they appear to be behind in their course work, and inquires if any support is needed, to encourage them to complete their course(s).

At Athabasca University, there is potential to consolidate the three call centre groups into a single organizational structure; together, they have less than 50 staff and some areas of service overlap. Organizational efficiencies are available. Even without consolidation of functions that involve direct student contact, significant quality improvements could be obtained by centralizing operations, such as centre design, staff planning, network design and management, ongoing standards reporting, IT liaison, contact automation, quality assurance, and training. Consolidation could also simplify disaster-recovery issues, as well as increase the CSR's task variety that, in turn, could improve job satisfaction, retention, and customer service. The integration of call-centre databases could provide a consistency of message and a single face, to help the university build solid relationships with its students.

The three call centres have enough overlap to make the economies of scale attractive. Achievement of such economies would logically involve widening the call-centre service to include all of the university's academic units. Many of the calls handled by the Information Centre deal with academic administration, and thus mirror calls handled by the call centre. The call-centre concept could also be extended to include functions served by the course assistants, who also answer student queries, relay mark and assignment information, and so forth. As more of these functions and those handled by staff from the Office of the Registrar are placed online, the group of services eligible for call-centre service will expand.

OVERCOMING BARRIERS TO CALL CENTRE IMPLEMENTATION IN DELIVERY

It is likely that there will be some resistance to implementing call centres in distance education, particularly with respect to course delivery. In part, using a customer-service model when dealing with students is not universally accepted and the use of the word "customer" when referring to students is in itself controversial. Nonetheless, although distance education providers are increasingly accepted in the mainstream, they are sensitive to criticisms around the commercialization of education and the use of a call centre in the delivery of education. Further, distance education providers are already criticized for their lack of personal interaction with students (Noble, 2001); implementing a call centre could further distance the learner from the academic, and depersonalize the learning experience even more. As a result, any potential implementation of a call centre on the delivery side of distance education must be strategically considered and carefully framed, so as not to be viewed as another example of universities relying on business models.

Rogers (1995, p. 36) posits that "the characteristics of an innovation, as perceived by the members of the social system, determine its rate of adoption." Major change requires that changes be framed properly in order for them to be accepted (Garvin & Roberto, 2005; Reger, Mullane, Gustafson, & DeMarie, 1994). When attempting to implement a call centre, senior administration must demonstrate how its implementation is (a) consistent with the culture and values of the organization, (b) consistent with academics' professional values, and (c) in the best interest of the students and organization.

Distance education "should be built on two foundations: the *needs of the intended students,* and the *learning outcomes of the course or program*" (italics original, Davis, Little & Stewart, 2008), and shifts the education model from the standard campus-centric model to a student-centred model (Yick, Patrick, & Costin, 2005). These are fundamental values of distance education. In addition, students typically want immediate answers to their inquires, most of which can be accommodated by the call centre. When combined with team teaching and an electronic bulletin board, calls centres can more easily meet the demands of students who require flexibility. Students are also more apt to receive the timely academic support they need, simply because their inquiries are being handled quickly, efficiently, and by the right person. Nonetheless, academics must be reassured about the nature of the inquiries that will be handled by the call centre, and those that will be passed along to academics and tutors.

In short, there needs to be a clear understanding of what is and is not an academic inquiry, so that academics and tutors do not feel threatened. By making a clear distinction between what is and what is not an academic inquiry, the integrity of the educational experience is maintained. The elimination of tedious administrative inquiries, for which academics and tutors typically have little or no interest and/or training, should also be appealing. Indeed, academics and tutors tend to be more interested in having thoughtful interactions with students, not dealing with routine administrative matters. If one can take the savings gained from implementing a call centre, and encourage course designs that increase meaningful interaction with students, such a model should be particularly appealing. The addition of more meaningful interaction adds to the value of the course and helps negate criticisms of distance education, specifically that it is an industrial model of education with little or no student-academic interaction. It would both improve the quality of students' learning experience and academics' teaching experience. CRM software could provide academics with valuable insights by gathering student inquiries on certain courses into a single location for analysis, a feature that could be valuable for course re-writes. When many people develop and deliver a course in a distributed work environment, CRM software could be particularly helpful.

Distance education students often feel isolated, as they tend to lack a community of learners upon which to rely. Having a single, instant source of support can reduce student frustration in attempting to gain information. Students in distance education are less able to rely on other students to gain information needed to navigate educational and institutional issues. A single, instant source of support can also help build the relationship between the student and the institution. The improved level of service to the student, in terms of obtaining timely academic assistance, may improve completion rates and increase student retention, both tangible benefits to students and the institution. The institution also benefits by being able to more proactively manage the student relationship, ensuring that their learning needs are met in a timely manner. The student, on the other hand, benefits from the provision of instant and accurate administrative information.

CONCLUSION

There are viable opportunities for the use of call centres in distance education. Call centres can provide a strategic opportunity for an institution facing dramatic increases in student numbers. Call centres hold the potential to reduce costs, improve student retention, improve student service, and possibly even improve student success. Nonetheless, those contemplating implementing a call centre in distance education must be cognizant of the criticisms associated with call centres, and thus should strive to develop a value-added call-centre model. By utilizing high-involvement human-resource practices, meaningful and engaging jobs can be designed that hold the potential to improve user satisfaction and reduce employee absenteeism and turnover.

Over time, the roles and responsibilities of a call centre could expand, and with sufficient economies of scale, might even be able to provide direct academic support, rather than just provide for the escalation of academic inquiries beyond the call centre. The advantages of a call centre are numerous; however, attempts to implement a call centre in distance education will likely meet some resistance. As a result, carefully framing the issue in terms of fundamental organizational and professional values, and clearly outlining these advantages to students, academics, and the institution, will be essential in order for call centre implementation to be successful.

REFERENCES

Adria, M., & Chowdhury, S. D. (2002). Making room for the call centre. *Information Systems Management, 19,* 71–80.

Adria, M., & Woudstra, A. (2001). Who's on the line? Managing student interactions in distance education using a one-window approach. *Open Learning, 16*(3), 249–261.

Bartlett, C. A., & Ghoshal, S. (2002). Building competitive advantage through people. *Sloan Management Review, 43*(2), 34–41.

Batt, R. (2002). Managing customer services: Human resource practices, quit rates, and sales growth. *Academy of Management Journal, 45*(3), 587–597.

Batt, R., & Moynihan, L. (2002). The viability of alternative call centre production models. *Human Resource Management Journal, 12*(4), 14–34.

Brandt, D. S. (2002). Automating your IT help desk. *Computers in Libraries, 22*(3), 52.

Bruton, N. (2002). Help desks and call centres – a comparison. Retrieved October 23, 2003, from http://www.bruton.win-uk.net/articles/hdcc.htm

Chandler, A. D., Jr. (1962). *Strategy and structure: Chapters in the history of the American industrial enterprise.* Cambridge, MA: MIT Press.

Cleveland, B., & Hopton, T. (2002, Oct. 5). Industry standards cannot replace sound decisions. *Call Centre Magazine.* Retrieved September 15, 2007, from http://www.callcentremagazine.com/article/CCM2002 1005S0002

Coen, D. (2001). Building a powerful telephone sales presentation. *Direct Marketing, 64*(7), 52–53.

Davenport, T. H., & Short, J. E. (1990). The new industrial engineering: Information technology and business policy redesign. *Sloan Management Review, 31*(4), 11–27.

Davis, A., Little, P., & Stewart, B. (2008). Developing an infrastructure for online learning. In T. Anderson (Ed.) *Theory and practice of online learning.* (pp. 121–142) Edmonton, AB: AU Press.

Driscoll, C., & Wicks, D. (1998). The customer-driven approach in business education: A possible danger? *Journal of Education for Business, 74*(1), 58–61.

Doherty, S. (2001). Help desk salvation. *Network Computing, 12*(7), 42–48.

Eisenhardt, K. M. (1999). Strategy as strategic decision making. *Sloan Management Review, 40* (3), 65–72.

Evanson, A., Harker, P. T., & Frei, F. X. (1998). *Effective call centre management: Evidence from financial services.* Retrieved September 15, 2007, from http://www.hbs.edu/research/facpubs/workingpapers/papers2/9899/99-110.pdf

Frenkel, S. J., Tam, M., Korczynski, M., & Shire, K. (1998). Beyond bureaucracy? Work organization in call centres. *The International Journal of Human Resource Management, 9*(6), 957–979.

Friedman, T. (2001). Call centre management: Balancing the numbers. *Industrial Management, 43*(1), 6–10.

Garvin, D. A., & Roberto, M. A. (2005). Change through persuasion. *Harvard Business Review, 83*(2), 104–112.

Hamel, G., & Prahalad, C. K. (1994). *Competing for the future.* Boston: Harvard Business School Press.

Hitch, L. P., & MacBrayne, P. (2003). *A model for effectively supporting e-learning.* Retrieved October 23, 2003, from http://ts.mivu.org/default.asp?show=article&id=1016

Hitt, L. M., Frei, F. X., & Harker, P, T. (1998). *How financial firms decide on technology.* Retrieved October 23, 2003, from http://grace.wharton.upenn.edu/~lhitt/itdec.pdf

Holman, D. (2002). Employee wellbeing in call centres. *Human Resource Management Journal, 12*(4), 35–50.

Holt, B. (2000). Calling out for the human touch. *Customer Loyalty Today, 8*(1), 11.

Houlihan, M. (2002). Tensions and variations in call centre management strategies. *Human Resource Management Journal, 12*(4), 67–85.

Howell, S. L., Williams, P. B., & Lindsay, N. K. (2003). Thirty-two trends affecting distance education: An informed foundation for strategic planning, *Online Journal of Distance Education Administration, 6*(3). Retrieved September 15, 2007, from http://www.westga.edu/~distance/ojdla/fall63/howell63.html

Jordan, J. (2003). Knowledge management: From nebulous to necessary for customer service. *Customer Inter@ction Solutions, 21*(10), 44–48.

Kantsperger, R., & Kunz, W. H. (2005). Managing overall service quality in customer care centres: Empirical findings of a multi-perspective approach. *International Journal of Service Industry Management, 16*(2), 135–151.

Kim, W. C., & Mauborgne, R. (1999). Strategy, value innovation, and the knowledge economy. *Sloan Management Review, 40*(3), 41–54.

Kinnie, N., Hutchinson, S., & Purcell, J. (2000). Fun and surveillance: The paradox of high commitment management in call centres. *International Journal of Human Resource Management, 11*(5), 967–985.

Kiska, J. (2002). Customer experience management. *CMA Management, 76*(7), 28–30.

Knowledge at Wharton (2002). *Web based call centres transform customer service.* Retrieved September 15, 2007, from http://knowledge.wharton.upenn.edu/article.cfm?articleid=129

Kondra, A., & Michalczuk, K. (2007). Implementing call centres in distance education: Overcoming organizational resistance. Paper presented at the *39ᵗʰ Annual Administrative Sciences Association Conference, Management Education Division,* Ottawa.

Kotwal, A. (2004). Contact centre knowledge management. *Customer Inter@ction Solutions, 23*(2), 40–42.

Krol, C. (2002). Firms stick to basics with call centre tools. *B to B Chicago, 87*(10), 22.

Lawlor, T. (2001, February 1). The people factor. *Computer Weekly.com.* Retrieved September 15, 2007, from http://www.computerweekly.com/Articles/2001/02/01/178224/the-people-factor.htm

Markides, C. C. (1999). A dynamic view of strategy. *Sloan Management Review, 40*(3), 55–63.

Mitchell, I. (2001). Call centre consolidation – does it still make sense? *Business Communications Review, 31*(12), 24–28.

Noble, D. F. (2001). *Digital diploma mills.* New York: Monthly Review Press.

Pascale, R. T. (1999). Surfing the edge of chaos. *Sloan Management Review, 40*(3), 83–94.

Pfeffer, J. (1994). *Competitive advantage through people.* Boston: Harvard Business Press.

Reger, R. K., Mullane, J. V., Gustafson, L. T., & DeMarie, S. M. (1994). Creating earthquakes to change organizational mindsets. *Academy of Management Executive, 8*(4), 31–43.

Reichheld, F. F. (1996). *The loyalty effect.* Boston: Harvard Business School Press.

Rigby, D. K., Reichheld, F., & Dawson, C. (2003, March/April). Winning customer loyalty is the key to a winning CRM strategy. *Ivey Business Journal.* Retrieved September 15, 2007, from http://www.iveybusiness-journal.com/article.asp?intArticle_ID=409

Rogers, E. M. (1995). *Diffusion of innovations.* New York: The Free Press.

Taylor, P., & Bain, P. (1999). An assembly line in the head: Work and employee relations in the call centre. *Industrial Relations Journal, 30*(2), 101–117.

Yick, A. G., Patrick, P., & Costin, A. (2005). Navigating distance and traditional higher education: Online faculty experiences. *The International Review of Research in Open and Distance Learning, 6*(2). Retrieved September 15, 2007, from http://www.irrodl.org/index.php/irrodl/article/view/235/320

Zapf, D., Isic, A, Bechtoldt, M., & Blau, P. (2003). What is typical for call centre jobs? Job characteristics, and service interaction in different call centres. *European Journal of Work and Organizational Psychology, 12*(4), 311–340.

ABOUT THE AUTHORS

Alex Z. Kondra (alexk@athabascau.ca) is the executive director of Athabasca University's MBA program in the Centre for Innovative Management in St. Albert, Alberta. He obtained a PhD in Industrial Relations from the University of Alberta in 1995. Previously, he was on faculty at the Fred C. Manning School of Business of Acadia University in Wolfville, Nova Scotia. At Athabasca University, he has taught organization theory, managing change, and administrative principles. His current research interests focus on changing organizational and industry structures and organizational culture. He has published in the journals *Organization Studies, Journal of Labor Research, Journal of Individual Employment Rights,* and the *Journal of Collective Negotiations in the Public Sector.* He also serves as an academic reviewer for numerous academic journals and conferences and has chaired the organizational theory division of the Administrative Sciences Association of Canada Conference.

Colleen Huber joined Athabasca University in 1994, when she became the first facilitator in the School of Business Call Centre. At the time of writing, she held the position of Learning Systems Manager, responsible for the systems used to deliver courses and manage information, as well as training staff on their use. Since 2003, she has worked as a consultant in the area of e-learning.

Kerri Michalczuk has been with Athabasca University since 1984. For the last five years, as Course Production and Delivery Manager, she has managed the day-to-day operation of the School of Business tutorial Call Centre, the first point of contact for students registered in business courses. Kerri also manages the production processes for developing online and print-based learning materials, including coordinating the work of production staff, such as editors, instructional designers, typesetters, and copyright personnel. Kerri has extensive knowledge of Athabasca University's administrative andproduction systems, and she sits on many committees that review, plan, and implement University systems.

Andrew Woudstra, MBA, CMA, is Professor Emeritus in the School of Business at Athabasca University, where he worked for the past 24 years before retiring in January, 2006. In addition to his teaching duties, he also served the University in various administrative capacities including Centre Chair; Associate Dean; Acting Dean; and Acting Vice President, Finance and Administration. Andrew has been involved in a number of innovative process changes in the School of Business, including the development of e-learning and the School of Business Call Centre, and has published in a variety of distance education journals and books.

CHAPTER 16

LIBRARY SUPPORT FOR E-LEARNERS: E-RESOURCES, E-SERVICES, AND THE HUMAN FACTORS

KAY JOHNSON, HOUDA TRABELSI
& ELAINE FABBRO
Athabasca University

INTRODUCTION

The growth of e-learning or online learning, in which education is delivered and supported through computer networks, is transforming academic libraries. E-learners and traditional learners have access to a universe of digital information, which frequently removes the need to visit a physical library. New information and communications technologies, as well as new educational models, require librarians to re-evaluate the way they develop, manage, and deliver resources and services.

Historically, librarians have provided services to distance learners that are equivalent to those available to on-campus learners (Slade & Kascus, 1998); this aspiration is grounded in the philosophical frameworks of the Canadian Library Association's *Guidelines for Library Support of Distance and Distributed Learning in Canada* (2000) (see http://www.cla.ca/about/distance.htm) and the Association of College and Research Libraries' *Guidelines for Distance Learning Library Services* (2004) (see

http://www.ala.org/ala/acrl/acrlstandards/guidelinesdistancelearning.
htm). Both the Canadian and American *Guidelines* recognize that distance learners frequently do not have direct access to the full range of
library services and materials, and that this necessitates equitable services that are more personalized than might be expected on campus.
The library literature provides a rich record of service models and best
practices; as such, there has been an explosion of publications as librarians consider ways to support learners in a networked environment
(Slade, 2000).

What do e-learners need from librarians? Suggestions advocating
changes to librarians' roles, in support of distance learning in the information age, appear throughout the literature. Librarians "must assert
themselves as key players in the learning process thereby changing their
roles from information providers to educators" (Cooper & Dempsey,
1998); they have become providers of technical support (Hulshof, 1999);
and they have been transformed from "information gatekeepers" to
"information gateways" (Haricombe, 1998). Lippincott (2002) advocates
librarian involvement, as teachers and learners, in learning communities:
"The librarian can shift the focus from explaining library resources to
meeting the ongoing information needs of the students in the broad
information environment" (p. 192).

In responding to the need to provide ongoing online library
support, librarians have worked at translating what they do in a traditional library into virtual or digital environments, while customizing
their services and resources for e-learners. Traditionally, libraries offer
circulation services, interlibrary loans, course reserves, an information
desk, a reference desk, and library instruction. To serve learners connected to their institutional library primarily through a computer
network, librarians provide remote access to, and electronic delivery of,
library resources, and use communication technologies to deliver
electronic reference services and instructional support.

When we speak of providing support to e-learners, we are referring to a wider community of learners than the term "student" suggests.
An academic library's learners may include students, faculty, staff,
researchers, and others. The library is seen as a source of training and
guidance to a community of learners concerned with navigating the
complexities of locating and using digital resources and services.
Moreover, the move toward an online environment has resulted in a
shift from the systematic one-to-one information flow of the past to a
new model in which the users and the providers of information are able

to relate in a many-to-many, dynamic relationship. For example, in the traditional model, a librarian provides a bridge between learners and information providers by selecting and cataloguing resources and by providing assistance with these resources. In the new model, the librarian serves as a facilitator by offering ongoing support which enables learners to interact and exchange knowledge with others, to communicate directly with the publishers and vendors of information resources, and to participate in a collaborative endeavour to make available rich collections of online scholarly information resources.

This chapter examines how libraries are responding to the challenges of delivering core services and library resources to e-learners. We look at library practices and technologies being applied in the development and maintenance of virtual libraries. We also consider the challenges and opportunities that virtual libraries bring to the support of e-learners, as well as the importance of providing support within a collaborative environment which stresses human factors, such as communication and interaction.

DEFINING THE VIRTUAL LIBRARY

Gapen (1993) defines the virtual library as

> the concept of remote access to the contents and services of libraries and other information resources, combining an on-site collection of current and heavily used materials in both print and electronic form, with an electronic network which provides access to, and delivery from, external worldwide library and commercial information and knowledge sources. (p. 1)

Additional terms for the virtual library include the digital library, the electronic library, and the library without walls. Many libraries are hybrids, providing virtual access to electronic resources and services, while maintaining and supporting the use of a physical collection housed in a library building.

With the tremendous growth of the Internet, e-learners have access to an overwhelming range of information sources, available at the click of a mouse, including library and academic resources, the sites of governments, non-governmental organizations, corporations and professionals, mainstream and alternative news, and an immense blogosphere. Librarians have traditionally selected and organized limited collections of resources with great care and provided assistance and instruction to their patrons in accessing and using these collections. Their task in the information age is to rescue e-learners from information overload, and to foster the competencies and critical reflection required to navigate an information environment characterized not by scarcity but by abundance and a multiplicity of formats and voices. A virtual library links e-learners to library catalogues, licensed journal databases, electronic book collections, selected Internet resources, electronic course reserves, tutorials, and to opportunities for communication and interaction with librarians. The virtual library permits e-learners to access and use library and networked resources and services anytime and anywhere that an Internet connection and computing equipment are available.

THE LANDSCAPE OF LIBRARY RESOURCES

Technology offers opportunities to be innovative, as the following discussion of electronic resources and services demonstrates, but it is important to bear in mind inequalities such as access to computing equipment, the availability, speed, and stability of Internet connections, and the information skills required to make optimum use of virtual libraries. Access to print-based library materials continues to be important, because not all of the information resources that e-learners need are available in electronic format; many of our most valuable research materials are still print-based.

Although there has been a shift away from purchasing print materials to be housed in a physical building, and toward providing access to licensed digital resources made available over a computer network, librarians continue to work to resolve issues pertaining to distance delivery of resources that are unavailable in digital format. Online catalogues, indexing, and abstracting systems provide e-learners with convenient access to bibliographic information about valuable scholarly documents. When those documents are not available in full-text form online, demand is generated for delivery from a library's print collection or from the collections of other libraries through interlibrary loans. Typical solutions for delivery of non-digital formats include the use of mail and courier services, the establishment of collections at designated sites, and the negotiation of agreements with other libraries through consortia.

Given that a growing number of learners are accessing library collections online, librarians are working to develop an integrated approach to providing access to electronic resources that facilitates retrieval and reduces confusion. A library web site can function as an information portal and an entry point to a range of online resources, with the library catalogue and journal databases as key components. Most online catalogues permit the integration of electronic books and electronic journals, enabling users to locate items from digital and physical collections with one search. User services – such as the ability to check due dates, renew materials, and request materials online – are also provided.

A number of electronic tools have come into play recently in the provision of distance library services. Federated search tools such as *WebFeat* (see http://www.webfeat.com/home/index.cfm); *dbWiz* (see http://dbwiz.lib.sfu.ca/dbwiz/), an open-source product created at Simon Fraser University Library (n.d.); and *Google Scholar* (see http://scholar.google.com) allow users to search a number of electronic resources simultaneously, using one interface. Libraries have the capability to customize the federated-search tool so that it searches a given set of electronic resources. Federated-search solutions offer e-learners a faster and easier way to search multiple resources, but they can also be a good starting point for researching a topic, in that they can help to identify the most suitable databases (McCaskie, 2004), a task which is often extremely challenging in the world of ever-expanding digital resources.

Google Scholar searches for scholarly articles, books, and other resources. Indexed items come from a variety of sources, including "academic publishers, pre-print societies, universities and other scholarly organizations" (Google Scholar, 2007). These items may be available online, or they may only be available in print. While having the ability to search for multiple resource types in one place is beneficial to the user, what makes *Google Scholar* so important is that it allows users to choose which libraries they want to search. *Google Scholar*'s Library Links program allows libraries that use *link-resolving software* to make their library holdings available in *Google Scholar*'s results lists. An e-learner, wishing to access a particular article, clicks on the link to the library to retrieve a list of databases that hold the article; the e-learner must then provide identifying information to enter the database via the library's authentication process in order to access the article. *Google Scholar*'s Library Links program also makes it possible to search library catalogues for items held by local libraries. Through a partnership with Online

Computer Library Center (OCLC)'s Open WorldCat project (http://www.worldcat .org/whatis/default.jsp), it is possible to search the collections of libraries whose holdings are in OCLC. A more recent addition is the ability to search AMICUS, the catalogue of Libraries and Archives Canada (see http://www .collectionscanada.ca/amicus/).

Link-resolving software products, such as *SFX* from *ExLibris* (see http://www.exlibrisgroup.com/sfx.htm), and *WebBridge* from *Innovative Interfaces Inc.* (see http://www.iii.com), allow users to *link out* from one database to another to retrieve full-text articles. Link resolvers or *link servers* work with open URL-compliant databases, and pass the user's library authentication information from one database to another, thereby allowing seamless access to full-text content without requiring the user to log in again. If an item is not available from an open URL-compliant database, link resolvers can direct users to search other library resources, including library catalogues and A-Z serials lists. All learners benefit from these products because they allow greater access to full-text materials without needing to search a number of databases; however, for online learners – and in particular those who are internationally based – the immediacy of retrieval is especially important. Providing easy online access and reducing the need to request print copies of articles enables libraries to provide better service to e-learners, and increases the e-learners' sense of connectedness to their library.

Personalized digital libraries have become another way to increase the connectedness of e-learners. While the tools mentioned above provide e-learners with greater access to resources, personalized digital libraries "streamline access to frequently used resources and create a friendlier online environment by permitting users to build their own digital collections in a personal workspace" (Johnson & Magusin, 2005, p. 129). One of the earliest instances of a personalized digital library was *MyLibrary@NCState,* which was released in 1998 as a way to combat the information overload that learners were facing, due to the library's recent expenditures on electronic resources (Morgan & Reade, 2000). The system requires learners to choose an area of academic interest during the account creation process (Morgan, 1999) and was developed in a way that can assist librarians in making collection management decisions, as it is possible to study the usage patterns of subscribers. The Open University of the UK has developed a pilot project called *MyOpenLibrary* (see http://myopenlibrary.open.ac.uk/), a personalized environment for their learners that uses the *MyLibrary@NCState* software, which was made public in 2000. According to the web site, *MyOpenLibrary* is "a personal library page, which knows who you are, what you are studying and presents the relevant electronic library resources...selected from Open Library" (Open University Library, 2005). It allows learners to select their own resources, as well as having resources supplied to them, based on the courses which they are registered in. Other examples include *MyCybrary* at the University of Winnipeg Library (see http://cybrary.uwinnipeg.ca/myCybrary/index.cfm), which offers learners opportunities to check their library account, keep up to date on new resources, and manage personal information services.

Librarians have become increasingly creative in enhancing their web sites. Because not all e-learners have physical access to reference tools – quick fact-finding tools that are the staple of library collections – libraries can perform a valuable service by providing learners with pointers to online versions. Athabasca University Library's Digital Reference Centre (see http://library.athabascau.ca/drc/), for example, offers a digital version of an academic library's reference collection, including almanacs and directories, atlases and maps, data and statistics, and dictionaries and encyclopedias. Librarians select quality Internet resources to help e-learners navigate the Web. For example, the Open University Library's *ROUTES* database (1999; 2004) contains quality-assessed, course-related Internet resources (see http://routes.open.ac.uk/).

It is impossible to ignore the phenomenon called "Web 2.0." There has been an explosion in the number of web users who are creating social content through weblogs, wikis, social bookmarking, podcasting, and other means (see Anderson, Chapter 12 in this volume). Librarians are increasingly cognizant of these tools, and have been investigating how they can be used within the library to provide services and instruction to learners, as "Library 2.0."

Weblogs are used by librarians in a number of ways. Blogs, such as *The Distant Librarian* (see http://distlib.blogs.com/distlib/) and *The Shifted Librarian* (see http://www.theshiftedlibrarian.com/), are designed as professional development tools for librarians. In other instances, blogs are used by librarians to keep patrons up to date on issues in the library, and to answer frequently asked questions. An example is *Frequently Asked Questions* (see http://frequanq.blogspot.com/), a blog maintained by the distance education librarian at Southern Connecticut State University. Weblogs can also be used for instructional purposes. Georgia State University Library (see http://www.library .gsu.edu/news/) has created subject-specific blogs that provide information about new resources in particular subject areas.

Social bookmarking, or social tagging, is a way for users to classify and share resources with others. Users assign tags, or keywords, to the sites that they bookmark, and these tags are then used in finding materials. This *folksonomy*, or informal classification, has exploded in popularity on the Web. A number of different social bookmarking sites are available, including del.icio.us (see http://del.icio.us/), CiteULike (see http://www.citeulike.org) and FURL (see http://www.furl.net). Some scholars and librarians are choosing to use these tools as a way to classify materials in their area of interest. Social tagging is used in academic libraries as a way to allow users to add content to the library web site. These resources may be in the form of web sites, bibliographies in specific content areas, or other items. The University of Pennsylvania Libraries created *PennTags* (see http://tags.library.upenn.edu/), a service that can be used by members of the University of Pennsylvania community. In addition to allowing users to tag web sites, *PennTags* allows users to tag resources from library catalogues, magazines, journals, and newspapers. It is possible to annotate resources, which can increase the pedagogical benefits associated with the use of social bookmarking. Integrated library system vendors are also beginning to explore the possibilities created by social tagging. For example, Innovative Interfaces Inc. is in the process of developing a new product called *Encore* (see http://www.iii.com/encore/main_index2.html), which allows librarians and patrons to tag resources found in library catalogues, including e-resources.

As libraries work to enhance their presence on the Web, a growing number have incorporated electronic course reserves (*e-reserves*). The traditional course reserves desk of an academic library, with its limited copies, short loan periods, and high late fines, can be a considerable source of frustration for students. In the e-reserves model, the library makes available, through the Web, items that faculty have selected and "placed on reserve" for students in a particular course. San Diego State University (SDSU) pioneered e-reserves in the early 1990s (see http://ecr. sdsu.edu/). SDSU uses *Docutek ERes* (2000-2007), a system that provides access to course readings, chat rooms, and bulletin boards. Many other libraries have initiated their own projects, using commercially available products or systems developed in-house. The library literature points to a diversity of approaches (Calvert, 2000; Lowe & Rumery, 2000; Algenio, 2002; Wilson, 2002; Warner, 2006).

Athabasca University Library's Digital Reading Room (DRR) (see http://library.athabascau.ca/drr/) is an e-reserves system developed in-house at Athabasca University, using open-source software. Scanning and mounting hardcopy materials is time consuming and requires securing of copyright permissions. The DRR encourages optimizing the value available from the library's electronic subscriptions through direct, persistent linking to content from the subscribed databases. Each course in the DRR has a *digital reading file.* The licensed contents, such as journal database articles, require authentication through the library's proxy server, permitting only Athabasca University's community of users to access them; non-licensed resources, such as web sites, are freely available to the public. A search engine permits e-learners to search across courses, providing a multidisciplinary approach to course reserves. By encouraging the inclusion of resources in a variety of digital formats, such as video, audio, and simulations, the DRR supports a wide range of learning objectives and styles.

Managing the remote access and authentication issues involved in making digital resources available has become a significant area of support to users of virtual libraries (Hulshof, 1999). Librarians may be called upon to respond to questions concerning login and password information, browser configuration, software installation, and a range of troubleshooting needs. Access problems are hugely frustrating for e-learners and must be resolved quickly. Ensuring that front-line library staff is adequately trained, providing clear instructions on the library's web site, and coordinating support activities with computing services personnel can contribute to effective technical support. E-learners also benefit from having a variety of means to contact the library, including email, web forms, and a toll-free telephone number.

LIBRARY SERVICES: CHALLENGES AND OPPORTUNITIES

The provision of appropriate and meaningful reference and instructional services to e-learners is fraught with both challenges and opportunities.

Reference

E-learners require more than access to e-resources. Traditionally, a reference librarian acts as an additional resource, someone who can be counted upon to provide expertise in making sense of library systems and research tools, and to offer a helping hand along that often slippery path known as the research process. Virtual library users face additional challenges in mining relevant information out of a computer system that "obstinately" returns zero hits in response to a query that does not match the character strings in its database files.

The most common means of providing electronic reference services to remote users has been email, the advantages and disadvantages of which have been well documented in the literature (Slade, 2000). The around-the-clock and around-the-world accessibility of email enables e-learners to connect with librarians beyond the walls of library buildings and outside the usual hours of operation. Email provides a written record of requests and responses, permits the electronic transmission of search results, and allows librarians time to reflect on requests. One of the most serious concerns about email reference services is their impact on traditional face-to-face reference interviews, particularly the absence of verbal and non-verbal cues, which typically assist a librarian in effectively responding to a question.

A well designed reference web form, such as that provided on the Athabasca University Library's "Ask about a Research Topic" web page (see http://library.athabascau.ca/about/contacts.php), encourages e-learners to include full identifying and course information. This web page encourages users to clearly describe their research problem and search terminology, and to state the parameters of their assignment. The feature also clarifies requests for librarians and reduces the need for email (Sloan, 1998). Automated email replies sent out in response to the receipt of a message reassure e-learners that their messages have been received and lets them know what to expect in terms of service.

Email reference service can be enhanced and supplemented with additional technologies that raise the level of interaction via real-time communication. Chat technology allows e-learners and librarians to send text messages back and forth instantly, using a form of communication that is familiar to most Internet users. A number of issues surround the use of chat in the provision of reference services to remote users. Choosing the appropriate program for the library's specific needs and resources is essential if the virtual reference initiative is to be successful. Available programs range from vendor-based systems that offer features such as "co-browsing, patron queuing, sharing files, and the ability to keep more extensive statistics" (Ward & Kern, 2006, p. 417-418), to instant messaging programs, which are freely available. Some chat programs require downloads on the part of users, which can be problematic and may also discourage e-learners from using the service. In an effort to reach more e-learners, some libraries have begun using instant messaging programs such as AOL's *AIM* product, MSN's *Messenger*, and *Yahoo!*

Messenger, primarily because many e-learners are already using these systems. More recently, libraries have begun experimenting with programs such as *Trillian* (see http://www.ceruleanstudios.com/) and *Pidgin* (formerly Gaim; see http://www.pidgin.im), which log into a number of instant messaging accounts simultaneously and allow librarians the flexibility to respond to instant messaging questions coming into the library, no matter which system the e-learner is using. This reduces the need to monitor several different instant messaging programs at the same time.

Virtual reference consortia have the potential to expand the library's abilities to serve its community of users effectively. Libraries in the consortia answer questions from e-learners in other parts of the consortium service area. Traditionally, chat reference services are only available during specified hours, so virtual reference consortia are beneficial for e-learners in different time zones than their home institution, because they increase the likelihood of a librarian being available to answer questions immediately. Even if the initial reference transaction is received through chat, however, it may ultimately prove difficult to provide a complete answer using this method. If a user requires assistance in learning how to use a particular library resource, it may be possible to provide a complete response via chat. However, if the user is requesting assistance to find information on a complex topic, the librarian may need time to determine appropriate search strategies before responding. In these cases, the follow-up response is often done by email. Providing e-learners with a toll-free telephone number remains an effective and convenient reference services strategy, particularly for intricate inquiries. The telephone reference interview works best when both librarian and e-learner are working in front of computers connected to the Internet.

Instruction

E-learners are frequently silent and invisible as they search and explore a library's online resources, and they do not have the same access that on-campus learners have to formal library instruction sessions. With the array of digital resources available to them, the many different interfaces and search tools, and the need for evaluation and critical thinking when using the Internet for research, information literacy skills are essential. Information literacy has been defined in relation to competencies, with information sources in a variety of formats. According to the Association of College and Research Libraries (2000), an information-literate student

1. determines the nature and extent of the information needed.
2. accesses needed information effectively and efficiently.

3. evaluates information and its sources critically and incorporates selected information into his or her knowledge base and value system.
4. individually, or as a member of a group, uses information effectively to accomplish a specific purpose.
5. understands many of the economic, legal, and social issues surrounding the use of information, and accesses and uses information ethically and legally.

Supporting the integration of information literacy skills training into the core curriculum has become an important issue for libraries (Slade, 2000). A discussion is also emerging around the need to promote critical reflection in relation to information and knowledge, to conceptualize a *critical information literacy* that goes beyond a focus on competencies. Critical information literacy draws on scholarship in critical theory and critical education to provide librarians with a theoretical framework that acknowledges their responsibility to help students see that knowledge is not neutral but socially constructed and contested (Luke & Kapitzke, 1999; Simmons, 2005; Elmborg, 2006). Teaching the value of incorporating peer-reviewed journals in research papers, for example, need not preclude a discussion about how alternative voices may be silenced by the peer-review process and how to find alternative literature.

As an extension of their traditional role in providing library instruction sessions and developing instructional materials, librarians design online tutorials and courses that promote information literacy and encourage active learning. Particularly fine examples are the University of Texas System Digital Library's (1998-2004) TILT – Texas Information Literacy Tutorial (see http://tilt.lib.utsystem.edu/); and Utah Academic Library Consortium's (2001) Internet Navigator (see http://medlib.med.utah.edu/navigator/), a multi-institutional online course developed by a team of librarians and web developers. The Open University Library created SAFARI (2001) (see http://www .open.ac. uk/safari), a freely available interactive tutorial, as well as an information literacy course called Making Sense of Information in the Connected Age or, more commonly, MOSAIC (Needham, Parker, & Baker, 2001). Athabasca University offers the undergraduate course, Information Systems 200: Accessing Information (see http://www.athabascau.ca/courses/infs/200/).

Many libraries provide instruction to e-learners by making information available on their web pages, including research guides and "how-to" pages. See, for example, Athabasca University Library's Help

Centre (see http://library.athabascau.ca/help.php). An awareness of the importance of context-specific help has grown and it is quite common to find links to tutorials at the point of need. Software packages for developing animated tutorials, such as ViewletBuilder (see http://www.qarbon.com/), Camtasia (see http://www.techsmith.com/camtasia.asp), and Captivate (see http://www.adobe.com/products/captivate/) enable librarians to demonstrate effective database searching techniques asynchronously. Brief tutorials that incorporate voice-over and demonstrate database features within the context of real searches are particularly effective. Joining an existing, collaborative initiative reduces workload and removes the need to "reinvent the wheel." The Council of Prairie and Pacific University Libraries (COPPUL), a consortium of twenty university libraries located in Manitoba, Saskatchewan, Alberta, and British Columbia, is responsible for the *Animated Tutorial Sharing Project* (*ANTS*). Participating libraries, including libraries outside of COPPUL, access a wiki where they can adapt databases for tutorial development, upload tutorials, and download tutorials developed by other libraries (see http://www.brandonu.ca/Library/COPPUL/).

Online tutorials usually operate on a model in which the e-learner interacts in isolation with a computer. Their effectiveness can be enhanced by the addition of more interactive forms of instruction. The librarians at the Florida Distance Learning Reference and Referral Center, for example, have experimented with chat software to simulate a virtual classroom and open a "live" group instruction to e-learners (Viggiano & Ault, 2001). Librarians can be incorporated through the learning management system, participating in online courses as teaching assistants, co-instructors, or co-designers. This 'embedded librarian' approach increases learner awareness of the value of the library in research and scholarship, and improves access to the expertise of librarians within the context of course needs and assignments (Matthew & Schroeder, 2006; Ramsay & Kinnie, 2006).

In addition, podcasting and video clips have become a popular choice in the delivery of instructional materials to remote users, as libraries recognize the popularity of mobile devices such as the *iPod®*. According to a Pew Internet and American Life survey, "more than 22 million American adults own iPods® or MP3 players, and 29% of them have downloaded podcasts" (2005, p.1). These methods allow e-learners to access the materials "anytime, anywhere," while still providing them with the type of instruction that their on-campus counterparts may receive. Tutorials range from a simple orientation to the library and its services to more in-depth tutorials on the research process or searching specific databases. For example, Mount Allison University Library (2006) makes audio *libcasts* available (see http://www.mta.ca/library/libcasts. html). These libcasts can be downloaded or subscribed to and listened to, using *iTunes*® or a similar product.

THE SUCCESSFUL VIRTUAL LIBRARY: PARTNERSHIP AND COLLABORATION

In reviewing definitions of the virtual library, Sloan (1998) identifies an emphasis on the technological and informational building blocks, and a neglect of the human components, such as the service tradition and human interaction. The continuing changes in technology have been truly astonishing, and the scope for building new information services and new ways of representing content seem unlimited. Although technology is the key infrastructure of the virtual library – a tool used to support library goals – human factors are the most important determinant of the success of the virtual library. As noted by Colgate, Buchanan-Oliver, and Elmsly (2005), technology could cause problems in building relationships because of the difficulty in developing a successful rapport between people via remote contact. One of the major challenges that virtual libraries face is the lack of opportunity for face-to-face reference service and communication. Combine this with a lack of awareness of library services (Nicholas & Tomeo, 2005) and the end result is poor communication between library staff and e-learners.

The digital library serves mainly as a facilitator in organizing and providing knowledge and resources to its users. Sharing knowledge and information among library staff, researchers, faculty, students, and other departments within the institution encourages them to work together, develop their skills, and form strong and trusting relationships. One method which can be effective in the development of strong relationships with faculty is the librarian-liaison role, where a librarian liaises with specific departments regarding resources, library services, and the provision of instructional support for students in those departments (Glynn & Wu, 2003). When the liaison focuses on building effective channels of communication and understands the effects of technology on communication, it becomes easier to share knowledge and information among institutional stakeholders. In addition, the focus on collaboration between the library and the faculty promotes a responsive approach to course design and supports teaching and learning objectives, particularly when this collaboration incorporates student contributions and feedback. This approach considers the library as an active partner of the learning community, helping e-learners to become "information literates" by integrating information literacy skills into the curriculum. The library can help e-learners to think critically about information, offer reference and instructional support, mentor their work by offering one-to-one communication and interaction, and work collaboratively with them to achieve a deeper level of understanding of what e-learners need.

A number of models can be involved in creating an environment that is responsive to the scholarly information needs of a diverse group of e-learners. Librarians select, describe, and ensure access to quality digital resources, providing e-learners with content from a wide range of resources and publications, including peer-reviewed journals. Within this framework, the library works with faculty, researchers, scholarly societies, and publishers to develop and manage a collection of enriched online scholarly resources. Such a partnership enables researchers to interact with others, exchange experiences, and publish their works online. The library role is thus transformed from simply providing library resources to meeting the ongoing support needs of the parties involved. The library also fosters research skills by encouraging e-learners to search, investigate, discover, and take advantage of these valuable online resources.

Further, senior management support and involvement is as much a key to success in developing the virtual library as in any other project. They need to work closely with the library staff to understand the nature of services, values, and support the library should be offering, and to adopt successful communication and interaction strategies. An institution providing distance and online education has an ethical obligation to ensure that its learners have access to appropriate library support. The Canadian Library Association *Guidelines* (2000) categorize responsibilities in terms of funding, administration, personnel, facilities, resources, services, publicity, and professional development of librarians. The *Guidelines* note as essential advance planning by the library in consultation with faculty, program administrators, and other appropriate campus personnel, and with librarians at unaffiliated libraries. The *Guidelines* also advocate that leadership should come from all levels of the institutional administration, but particularly from the library.

All staff involved in providing library support to e-learners must be included in the partnership. Technological changes have been the dominant force reshaping library services. Instilling a culture of sharing, motivation, equity, and active partnering encourages library staff to respond positively to the changing roles, responsibilities, and skills that the integration and use of technology requires. A well-designed, ongoing training program enables library staff to upgrade their skills to their new assignments, and helps them to understand and control fear of change.

The home institution has primary responsibility for library support, but can benefit from external partnerships, collaborative efforts, and consortia in supporting e-learners. Within Canada, university libraries extend in-person borrowing privileges to students, faculty, and staff from across the country, through the *Canadian University Reciprocal Borrowing Agreement* (Council of Prairie and Pacific University Libraries, et al., n.d.; see http://www.coppul.ca/rb/rbindex.html). There are also initiatives to share virtual reference desks, such as the Library and Archives Canada's Virtual Reference Canada (see http://www.collectionscanada.ca/vrc-rvc/index.html), through which e-learners benefit from the range of information resources and staff expertise available at a variety of participating institutions. Consortia approaches to database subscriptions enable libraries to expand the scope of the electronic resources they are able to offer their e-learners in a time of shrinking budgets and escalating journal costs. *The Lois Hole Campus Alberta Digital Library (LHCADL)* initiative, through funding provided by the Government of Alberta, provides participating post-secondary institutions in Alberta with digital information resources for teaching, learning, and research (The Alberta Library, 2006; see http://www.thealbertalibrary.ab.ca/viewChannel.asp?channelID=3). *LHCADL* includes an information literacy and awareness component dedicated to sharing expertise and training resources with participating libraries.

CONCLUSION

In summary, library services are an essential component of a quality online learning experience. As access to online courses grows, an increasing number of e-learners are dispersed around the globe, often in parts of the world where physical access to the collections of large academic and research libraries is impossible or severely limited. These learners are largely dependent on the quality and academic usefulness of services that the library can offer electronically. The strength of virtual libraries and digital collections depends on the relationships libraries develop and maintain with the creators, publishers, and aggregators of e-resources, as well as with those who use, learn from, and evaluate these resources. Providing ongoing technical, reference, and instructional support to e-learners requires that libraries redefine their values and services, collaborate with their users and other partners, and approach their tasks creatively.

REFERENCES

Algenio, E. R. (2002). The virtual reserve room: Extending library services off-campus. In P. B. Mahoney (Ed.), *The tenth off-campus library services conference proceedings* (pp. 11–18). Mount Pleasant, MI: Central Michigan University.

AMICUS. (n.d.). Libraries and Archives Canada. Retrieved September 1, 2007, from http://www.collectionscanada.ca/amicus/

Anderson, T. (2008). Towards a theory of online learning. In T. Anderson (Ed.), *Theory and practice of online learning*, 2nd ed. (pp. 45-74). Edmonton, AB: AU Press.

Association of College and Research Libraries. (2000). *Information literacy competency standards for higher education*. Retrieved May 21, 2007, from http://www.ala.org/ala/acrl/acrlstandards/informationliteracy competency.htm

Association of College and Research Libraries. (2004). *Guidelines for distance learning library services*. Retrieved May, 21, 2007, from http://www. ala.org/ala/acrl/ acrlstandards/guidelinesdistancelearning.htm

Athabasca University Library. (n.d.). *Ask about a research topic*. Retrieved May 21, 2007, from http://library.athabascau.ca/about/contacts.php

Athabasca University Library. (n.d.). *Digital Reading Room*. Retrieved May 21, 2007, from http://library.athabascau.ca/drr/

Athabasca University Library. (n.d.). *Digital Reference Centre*. Retrieved May 21, 2007, from http://library.athabascau.ca/drc/

Athabasca University Library. (n.d.). *Help Centre*. Retrieved May 21, 2007, from http://library.athabascau.ca/help.php

Athabasca University. (n.d.). *Information systems 200: Accessing information*. Retrieved May 21, 2007, from http://www.athabascau.ca/courses/infs/ 200/

Calvert, H. M. (2000). Document delivery options for distance education students and electronic reserve service at Ball State University Libraries.

In P. S. Thomas (Ed.), *The ninth off-campus library services conference proceedings* (pp. 73–82). Mount Pleasant, MI: Central Michigan University.

Canadian Library Association. (2000). *Guidelines for library support of distance and distributed learning in Canada.* Retrieved May 21, 2007, from http://www.cla.ca/about/distance.htm

CiteUlike. (n.d.). *CiteUlike.org home page.* Retrieved May 27, 2007, from http://www.citeulike.org/

Colgate, M., Buchanan-Oliver, M., & Elmsly, R. (2005). Relationship benefits in an Internet environment. *Managing Service Quarterly, 15*(5), 426–436.

Cooper, R., & Dempsey, P. R. (1998). Remote library users – needs and expectations. *Library Trends, 47*(1), 42–64.

Council of Prairie and Pacific University Libraries. (n.d.). *ANTS: Animated tutorial sharing project.* Retrieved May 22, 2007, from http://www.brandonu.ca/Library/COPPUL/

Council of Prairie and Pacific University Libraries, Council of Atlantic University Libraries, Ontario Council of University Libraries, & Conférence des Recteurs et des Principaux des Universités du Québec. (n.d.). *Canadian university reciprocal borrowing agreement.* Retrieved May 21, 2007, from http://www.coppul.ca/rb/ rbindex.html

The Distant Librarian. (2008). Retrieved March 24, 2008, from http://distlib .blogs.com/distlib/

Elmborg, J. (2006). Critical information literacy: Implications for instructional practice. *The Journal of Academic Librarianship, 32*(2), 192–199.

FURL. (n.d.). *FURL: Your personal web file home page.* Retrieved May 27, 2007, from http://www.furl.net/

Gapen, D. K. (1993). The virtual library: Knowledge, society, and the librarian. In L. M. Saunders (Ed.), *The virtual library: Visions and realities* (pp. 1–14). Westport, CT: Meckler.

Georgia State University Library. (n.d.). *Library news and subject blogs.* Retrieved June 7, 2007, from http://www.library.gsu.edu/news/

Glynn, T., & Wu, C. (2003). New roles and opportunities for academic library liaisons: A survey and recommendations. *References Services Review, 31*(2), 122–128.

Google Scholar (2007). *About Google Scholar.* Retrieved May 24, 2007 from http://scholar.google.ca/intl/en/scholar/about.html

Haricombe, L. J. (1998). Introduction. *Library Trends, 47*(1), 1–5.

Hulshof, R. (1999). Providing services to virtual patrons. *Information Outlook, 3*(1), 20–23.

Innovative Interfaces. (n.d.). *Encore product home page*. Retrieved May 27, 2007, from http://www.iii.com/encore/main_index2.html

Innovative Interfaces. (n.d.). *Innovative Interfaces.com home page*. Retrieved May 27, 2007, from http://www.iii.com/

Johnson, K., & Magusin, E. (2005). *Exploring the digital library: A guide for online teaching and learning*. San Francisco: Jossey-Bass.

Library and Archives Canada. (n.d.). *Virtual Reference Canada*. Retrieved June 7, 2007, from http://www.collectionscanada.ca/vrc-rvc/index.html

Lippincott, J. K. (2002). Developing collaborative relationships: Librarians, students, and faculty creating learning communities. *College & Research Libraries News, 63*(3), 190–192.

Lowe, S., & Rumery, J. (2000). Service to distance learners: Planning for e-reserves and copyright. In P. S. Thomas (Ed.), *The ninth off-campus library services conference proceedings* (pp. 213–220). Mount Pleasant, MI: Central Michigan University.

Luke, A. & Kapitzke, C. (1999). Literacies and libraries: Archives and cybraries.

Pedagogy, Culture and Society, 7(3), 467–491.

Matthew, V. & Schroeder, A. (2006). The embedded librarian program. *EDUCAUSE Quarterly, 29*(4). Retrieved May 22, 2007, from http://www.educause.edu/apps/eq/eqm06/eqm06410.asp

McCaskie, L. (2004). *What are the implications for information literacy training in higher education with the introduction of federated search tools?* Sheffield, UK: University of Sheffield. Retrieved May 24, 2007, from http://dagda.shef.ac.uk/dissertations/2003-04/External/McCaskie_Lucy_MALib.pdf

Morgan, E. L. (1999). *MyLibrary@NCState*. Retrieved May 27, 2007, from http://www.infomotions.com/musings/sigir-99/

Morgan, K., & Reade, T. (2000). Pioneering portals: MyLibrary@NCState. *Information Technology and Libraries, 19*(4), 191–198.

Mount Allison University Libraries. (2006). *Libcasts*. Retrieved June 7, 2007, from http://www.mta.ca/library/libcasts.html

Needham, G., Parker, J., & Baker, K. (2001). Skills for lifelong learning at a distance: Information literacy at the Open University. *The New Review of Libraries and Lifelong Learning, 2*, 67–77.

Nicholas, M., & Tomeo, M. (2005). Can you hear me now? Communicating library services to distance education students and faculty. *Online Journal of Distance Learning Administration, 8*(2). Retrieved May 7, 2007, from http://www .westga.edu/%7Edistance/ojdla/summer82/nicholas82.htm

Open University Library. (1999; 2004). *ROUTES* (*Resources for Open University Teachers and Students*). Retrieved May 21, 2007, from http://routes.open.ac.uk/

Open University Library. (2001). *Safari* (*Skills in Accessing, Finding, and Reviewing Information*). Retrieved May 21, 2007, from http://www.open.ac.uk/safari

Open University Library. (2005). *MyOpenLibrary.* Retrieved May 24, 2007, from http://myopenlibrary.open.ac.uk/

Open WorldCat. (2008). *What is WorldCat?* Retrieved March 24, 2008, from http://www.worldcat.org/whatis/default.jsp

Pew Internet and American Life. (2005). *Reports: Online activities & pursuits: Podcasting.* Retrieved May 24, 2007, from http://www.pewInternet.org/pdfs/PIP_podcasting2005.pdf

Ramsay, K. M., & Kinnie, J. (2006). The embedded librarian. *Library Journal, 131*(6), 34–35.

San Diego State University. (2000–2007). *Docutek ERes. Ereserves Home.* Retrieved May 21, 2007, from http://ecr.sdsu.edu/

SFX.com. (n.d.) *SFX.com home page: Context sensitive linking.* Retrieved May 27, 2007, from http://www.exlibrisgroup.com/sfx.htm

The Shifted Librarian. (2008). Retrieved March 24, 2008, from http://www.theshiftedlibrarian.com/

Simmons, M. H. (2005). Librarians as disciplinary discourse mediators: Using genre theory to move toward critical information literacy. *portal: Libraries and the Academy, 5*(3), 297–311.

Simon Fraser University Library. (n.d.). *dbWiz – database selection wizard.* Retrieved May 27, 2007, from http://dbwiz.lib.sfu.ca/dbwiz/

Slade, A. (2000). Keynote address – International trends and issues in library services for distance learning: Present and future. In P. Brophy, S. Fisher & Z. Clarke (Eds.), *Libraries without walls 3: The delivery of library services to distant users.* London: Library Association Publishing.

Slade, A., & Kascus, M. (1998). An international comparison of library services for distance learning. In P. S. Thomas & M. Jones (Eds.), *The eighth off-campus library services conference proceedings* (pp. 259–297). Mount Pleasant, MI: Central Michigan University.

Sloan, B. (1998). Service perspectives for the digital library remote reference services. *Library Trends, 47*(1), 117–144.

The Alberta Library. (2006). *The Lois Hole Campus Alberta Digital Library.* Retrieved May 21, 2007, from http://www.thealbertalibrary.ab.ca/viewChannel.asp?channelID=3

University of Pennsylvania Libraries. (n.d.). *The University of Pennsylvania Library's PennTag's web page.* Retrieved May 27, 2007, from http://tags. library.upenn.edu/

University of Texas System Digital Library. (1998–2004). *TILT—Texas Information Literacy Tutorial.* Retrieved May 21, 2007, from http://tilt. lib.utsystem.edu/

University of Winnipeg Library. (n.d.). *MyCybrary.* Retrieved June 7, 2007, from http://cybrary.uwinnipeg.ca/myCybrary/index.cfm

Utah Academic Library Consortium. (2001). *Internet Navigator.* Retrieved May 21, 2007, from http://medlib.med.utah.edu/navigator/

Viggiano, R., & Ault, M. (2001). Online library instruction for online students. *Information Technology and Libraries, 20*(3), 135–138.

Ward, D., & Kern, M. K. (2006). Combining IM and vendor-based chat: A report from the frontlines of an integrated service. *portal: Libraries and the Academy, 6*(4), 417–429.

Warner, D. (2006). Electronic reserves: A changed landscape. *Journal of Interlibrary Loan, Document Supply & Electronic Reserves, 16*(4), 125–133.

Wilson, P. (2002). The ins and outs of providing electronic reserves for distance learning classes. In P. B. Mahoney (Ed.), *The tenth off-campus library services conference proceedings* (pp. 413–422). Mount Pleasant, MI: Central Michigan University.

ABOUT THE AUTHORS

Kay Johnson (kayj@athabascau.ca) is a tutor and course author with Athabasca University. During her seven years of service with AU Library, she specialized in the delivery of reference, instruction, and circulation services to distance learners. Kay received her BA (English) and BA Honours (History) from the University of Ottawa, and her Master of Library and Information Studies from McGill University. Kay is co-author of *Exploring the Digital Library: A Guide for Online Teaching and Learning* (Jossey-Bass, 2005).

Houda Trabelsi (houdat@athabascau.ca) is an e-Commerce course coordinator at Athabasca University. She received a M.Sc. in business administration from Sherbrooke University and a M.Sc.(Information Technology) from Moncton University. Her research interests include electronic commerce, business models, e-learning, strategy, customer relationships management, trust and privacy in electronic commerce, World Wide Web navigation, and interface design.

Elaine Fabbro (elainef@athabascau.ca) is Head, Information Literacy & Public Services at Athabasca University Library. Elaine received her BA (Music) from the University of British Columbia and her Master of Library and Information Science from the University of Western Ontario. Her primary responsibilities are the provision of instructional and reference services to the AU community. She also tutors the AU course *INFS 200: Accessing Information*. Elaine is co-author of *Exploring the Digital Library: A Guide for Online Teaching and Learning* (Jossey-Bass, 2005).

CHAPTER 17

SUPPORTING THE ONLINE LEARNER

SUSAN D. MOISEY & JUDITH A. HUGHES
Athabasca University

INTRODUCTION

Creating a supportive learning environment for online learners is crucial for ensuring success, promoting persistence, and avoiding drop-out. The ideal learning environment aims to develop the learner's independence and facilitate the learning process by providing supports that are flexible, accessible, and readily available when needed. Certainly strong academic and tutorial support is necessary, and the special considerations in the case of online learning are the subject of earlier chapters. This chapter, however, deals with non-academic supports for the online learner and the important role they play in promoting a successful learning experience. In addition, practical advice is offered, as well as examples of the way such supports are provided in a variety of online learning contexts.

The ability and potential of online learning to enhance access to education, particularly higher education, is well recognized and evidenced by the way it has grown and expanded. Increasing numbers of learners are finding that online courses best meet their needs. At the same time, increasing numbers of distance education organizations are finding that online learning best meets the diverse needs of their students.

The types of organizations that provide online learning vary and each has particular characteristics and ways of providing support to their online learners. One type is what Daniel (1996) refers to as the "mega-university" – distance-teaching universities with 100,000 or more students. Indira Gandhi National Open University, with an enrolment of 750,000 students, is one example, as is the Open University of Hong Kong, with more than 400,000 students. The 68 online universities in China, with a total enrolment of 2.1 million students (Qui, 2006), have recently joined this category as well. Due to the high concentration of students in geographic areas, these universities typically rely on a network of local learning centres to provide student support, tutorials, and other services as an adjunct to the distance and online courses they offer. While these centres continue to be used, there is increasing availability of online support services as well.

Another type is the distance education organization that serves a population of learners spread over a wide geographical area. Athabasca University – Canada's Open University – is an example of this type of institution, with a current population of nearly 34,000 students worldwide (Athabasca University, 2006). Online student support is essential for serving students over such a great area. Athabasca University relies primarily on web-based information and resources, complemented by email, to provide learner supports, although telephone communications are used as well, especially with students located in Canada.

Still another type of organization providing online learning is the *dual-mode* institution, which provides face-to-face, classroom-based programs in addition to its online offerings. Such institutions are plentiful and their numbers are growing as traditional educational institutions embrace distance and online learning. These organizations, however, commonly face particular challenges associated with having to provide student support to two very different groups of learners – one onsite and the other at a distance – and often with very different needs. Thoughtful planning and significant financial commitment is often required to ensure high-quality student support for both groups.

Regardless of the context, student support is essential for successful online learning. Although supports may be provided in a variety of ways, the overall goal is to provide a learner-support-services system "where students feel at home, where they feel valued, and which they find manageable" (Tait, 2000, p. 289). Supports should be flexible, continuously available, easily accessible, and also genuinely useful. Learners have clearly told us that they need to see the value added by a resource; otherwise, they will not use it. They have also asked that supports be available, but not intrusive. With these caveats in mind, a constellation of learner supports is discussed in the sections that follow.

SUPPORTS FOR PROSPECTIVE STUDENTS

We can identify support needs best when we know our learners well. Each learner brings a unique set of skills, experiences, and expectations to the learning environment. As students' characteristics and needs are diverse, so too are their needs for supports and services. Therefore, we should ask questions about areas such as the prospective learner's readiness for online learning, access to and familiarity with the technology required, proficiency in the language of instruction, individual learning style or learning preference, and educational goals. These are things we need to know about our learners, and also things that learners need to know about themselves, in order to receive the greatest benefit from the learning experience.

With this information at hand, we can determine what supports are most critical for learners and establish priorities to ensure that resources, which are always limited, are directed to the most useful supports. When doing so, we must keep in mind that some learners will require more support than others, and that sometimes learners need more help at one point in their educational career than at others. Throughout the process, the focus should be on self-assessment to encourage independence in the learner, although counselling backup should be available when needed.

Making an informed decision to pursue online learning is the first step to a successful educational experience. The following section outlines resources that can assist potential online learners to a) assess their readiness for this form of learning; b) determine if they have adequate computing and connectivity requirements; and c) obtain advice for making specific program and career-related decisions.

Learner Readiness

The list below provides a series of questions for learners thinking about taking an online post-secondary program of studies, and identifies self-assessment tools that are available to help answer these questions.

- *Am I ready for university (or college)?* This online resource allows prospective learners to determine their readiness, from academic, financial, family support, and time perspectives. Prospective students are provided with a series of questions to help them examine their expectations and readiness; the process serves to highlight areas that might need special attention. Once the self-assessment is complete, follow-up email counselling concludes the process. For an example of such a self-assessment tool, see the "Am I Ready" web site (Athabasca University, 2007) at http://amiready. athabascau.ca/.
- *Am I ready for studies in the English language (or other language of instruction)?* This online resource assists the learner to determine if their command of the language is sufficient to allow for success, and places the learner in specific language course levels. The learner may be directed to online remedial resources, and should always have the option of contacting an advisor. For an example of such a resource, see the Online Resources at http://www. athabascau .ca/main/studserv.htm.
- *Am I ready for university-level mathematics?* Proficiency in mathematics has proven to be a significant success factor for certain courses, particularly for adult learners returning to the educational environment after some time away. Assisting prospective learners to identify their strengths and weaknesses in mathematics, and making remediation available, can avoid difficulties and promote success. Online self-assessment tools can help learners to determine their readiness for particular mathematics courses, to recommend a mathematics course appropriate to the learner's level, and to identify remediation resources. For an example of such a tool, see the Online Resources at http://www.athabascau.ca/main/ studserv.htm.
- *Do I have the skills to be successful in my chosen program?* This online resource outlines what skills are needed for particular areas of study. The resource should be program-specific and refer the student to online tutorials if needed. For an example of a resource that assists the learner to make program choices, see "Study at the OU" at the Open University (UK) web site at http://www.open.ac.uk.

Minimum Computer Requirements

At its most basic level, information should be provided so potential learners can determine if they have (or have access to) the necessary hardware, software, and connectivity to study online. Additional resources may be provided to help prospective students gauge their comfort with an online learning environment; for example, short sample experiences can be described to show students what they can expect, such as those provided in Deakin University's (2003) Learning Toolkit web site at http://www .deakin.edu.au/dlt2007/.

Career-Planning Resources

Potential learners often seek out online learning opportunities to initiate, further, or enhance their careers. Indeed, most learners will experience several career changes – some of them quite significant – throughout their working lives. As such, viewing the educational experience within the context of career development is important.

Online resources that assist learners to determine their interests and skills and that provide a career map aligned with educational programs are valuable. For example, see the United Kingdom's Open University (2007) web site at http://www.open.ac.uk, which focuses on the learner's need to contemplate the future in making educational choices, or "Mapping Your Future" on Athabasca University's (2007) Services to Students web site at http://amiready.athabascau.ca/. Resources such as these provide learners with a means of exploring career clusters and the credentials required to pursue them. After an initial exploration, learners may wish to communicate (via email and/or telephone) with a counsellor or program advisor to refine their career goals. Once this is achieved, electronic program plans may be designed, which take career goals as well as prior learning into account. In this process, it is important to have the learner explore first, and then to have the counsellor or advisor provide assistance as needed.

Program Advising

Distance and online learners frequently extend their learning over a number of years. As such, they require program planning that will help them achieve their educational goals in the most expedient manner possible. Moreover, learners often transfer between institutions and jurisdictions, increasingly so in our global learning environment, and as such require a means of coordinating their studies and ensuring transferability of courses when necessary. Proper academic advising is essential to meet the diverse needs of these online learners.

The role of the program advisor is to help learners understand program requirements, to take into account any courses being transferred into a program, and then to plan the remainder of their program accordingly. Moreover, as learners frequently change career and educational goals during the process of completing a program, academic advisors need to be readily available and have access to all program and transfer information in order to accommodate changes in students' program plans throughout their period of study.

SUPPORTING THE LEARNER

By assisting potential learners to make an informed decision to pursue online learning, we have enhanced their chances for success. Once a student has enrolled in a course, however, quite different support is required. Learners need to know what kinds of support they can expect and from whom, how to interact with the institution, what is expected of them, and how to know when they need assistance. As educators, we must anticipate an array of needs, and then plan accordingly to ensure that learners have what they require throughout their educational programs.

Learners require support in a variety of areas, such as administrative and logistic support, information and technological support, and assistance with studying, exam-taking, and writing skills. For learners with disabilities or other limiting conditions, specific supports may also be necessary. Some learners find that peer support or the availability of a learning community adds significantly to their educational experience. In addition, a students' union and an alumni association, as well as opportunities to participate in institutional governance, can be invaluable for promoting a successful and meaningful educational experience.

ADMINISTRATIVE AND LOGISTIC SUPPORT

Daniel (2000) points out that a key component of supported open learning is effective administration and logistics. Institutions engaged in distance and online education know that smooth administrative processes can be as much a factor in learner satisfaction and success as the design of learning resources, and learners themselves report that flexibility of access and smooth administrative support are important to creating a supportive learning environment.

As online learning has grown and evolved, so too have online administrative supports and services. Institutions that provide online learning report that students express a preference for having the control that online administrative processes afford. Online functions, such as course registrations, examination requests, or purchasing textbooks and course materials have become commonplace. Still, there are particular considerations in the provision of these services to online learners, such as those discussed below.

- Course registration and the maintenance of student records for dual-mode institutions may pose particular challenges, especially for organizations that offer continuous enrolment for online learners, as well as semester- or term-based enrolment for on-site students. Maintaining two forms of course registration may prove problematic and create redundancy and parallel systems along with commensurate high costs for maintaining them.

- Even though much of the course content may be provided online in a web-based course, there is usually still a need for print-based course materials, such as textbooks or readers. Students may obtain these materials in a number of ways. For example, some institutions provide these through their own course materials distribution system; however, factors such as warehousing, inventory control, and materials distribution must also be considered in this arrangement. Other institutions are choosing to use commercial online booksellers to fill students' textbook orders. Dual-mode institutions often "piggyback" an online ordering component to their existing bookstore operation to serve the needs of their online learners.

- Increasingly, publishers are offering online resources to supplement their textbooks as well as electronic versions of texts for students who may prefer these over-bound versions. Also, customized publishing is offered by many publishers.

- Some institutions provide printed versions of online learning materials for students who do not wish to read online, or to reduce their need for printing materials themselves. Some materials may be made available on CD-ROM or other storage media to reduce the need for lengthy downloads. These materials may be included as part of the course package or may be available on demand, perhaps for an additional charge.

- In addition to books and printed course materials, students may purchase some additional products at an online bookstore. Students often wish to purchase memorabilia or "logo-wear" as a symbol of belonging to the university or college. Computer software may be also sold at reduced student rates.

Above all, learners need to know what services they can expect to receive from the institution and how they will be provided. *Service standards*, such as those implicit in the following questions, should be clear and easily available: How long should it take to receive confirmation of a course registration? How much time does it take to receive an examination grade or feedback on an assignment? How quickly should a response be expected to an email message? How long does it take to receive a requested book from the library? These standards should be readily available to students and should serve as benchmarks for service units within the institution.

INFORMATION AND TECHNOLOGICAL SUPPORT

Drawing the line between academic support on the one hand and students' needs for information and technological support on the other is often a challenge, and these types of support must be coordinated carefully. There are three common formats for providing information and technological support:

1. An information centre, which provides institutional and program information;
2. A computing helpdesk, which troubleshoots students' technological difficulties and provides information; and
3. A call centre, which fields students' questions and requests, typically in a particular program area.

All three can work together to support the online learning process. Ideally, each should have the following characteristics:

- Reliable networks;
- Asynchronous access (e.g., email) with "24/7" availability;
- Synchronous access (e.g., toll-free telephone) at clearly identified times;
- Quick response, with acknowledgement and follow-up;
- Follow-through to resolution of issues or difficulties that students encounter;
- Simple, clear instructions;
- Access by attendants to all critical databases and expertise; and
- Ability to identify problems with policies, procedures, or systems, and to suggest change.

Portals

Increasingly, portals are used to provide learners with easy access to their online courses, as well as to a variety of web-based functions. Online learning is often accompanied by a plethora of different web sites to access, and multiple sign-on procedures and passwords. Portals can alleviate this situation by individualizing and integrating online interactions, thus enhancing the learner's experience by making access easier and more efficient.

METACOGNITIVE SUPPORTS

Some online learners are returning to learning after some time away, others may be new to post-secondary study altogether, and many may not have experienced online learning before and do not know how best to approach this new mode of study. By providing metacognitive supports like the ones described in this section, we can help online learners develop more effective and successful learning processes.

Metacognitive skills are those associated with "learning how to learn." For online learners, these kinds of supports enhance their ability to study online and facilitate their access to and retention of knowledge. Providing such supports can increase students' confidence, reduce stress, and enhance their learning experience. Resources to enhance the metacognitive skills of online learners include the following:

- Web-based resources that assist in the development of time management strategies and study schedules and that help students balance educational pursuits with other life demands;
- Online strategies and exercises to reduce exam anxiety;
- Resources that teach how to become a successful online learner;
- Online services and web-based resources that assist students in writing papers;
- Intellectual property-related resources that teach students how to use appropriate referencing, make correct citations, and avoid plagiarism;
- Library resources that teach students how to search online databases, critically analyze information from online publications, and so forth;
- Community-building tools and social software for facilitating learner interactions, such as making "study-buddy" connections for peer assistance.

Learning How to Learn Online

Learning online is different than learning in a conventional classroom-based setting. The pedagogical approach underlying online learning is commonly based on constructivism, where learners actively create knowledge in a personally relevant and meaningful manner. This mode of learning lies in stark contrast to the passive, receptive mode typical of traditional face-to-face instructional settings. To make the transition to online learning, Wang (2005) describes a "whole person" campaign aimed at transforming passive, receptive students into competent, self-directed, active learners (a description of this campaign is provided in *Mandarin* (http://www.beiwaionline.com/degree/zx/daohang/t200409 24_1110.htm). However, the need for learners to become more independent, involved, and dynamic – actively seeking and using online information and supports – is certainly not restricted to China. Such resources are no doubt useful for distance learners worldwide, particularly those for whom online learning is a new experience.

Writing Resources

Good writing skills are a mainstay of successful learning. The ability to produce well-written assignments, cogent reports, and clear presentations is facilitated by providing online learners with resources to assist with improving their writing skills. Online resources, such as the *Paradigm Online Writing Assistant* (http://powa.org/my/), provide instruction in a variety of different types of writing. Online support services are also useful. For example, Athabasca University's *Write Site* (http://www.athabascau.ca/html/services/write-site/), allows students to submit a draft of an academic assignment and receive feedback about organization, mechanics, grammar, and style before submitting it for marking.

Intellectual-Property-Related Resources

Traditions regarding what constitutes intellectual property and what is generally accepted common knowledge are not universal concepts, nor are they always understood. Cultural views about ownership of knowledge vary. Students do not always understand the concept of plagiarism, much less how to avoid it.

Institutions should ensure that intellectual honesty expectations are readily available to online learners and referred to frequently. Reminders in directions for assignments, links to approved style guides, links to anti-plagiarism services (see, for example, www.turnitin.com), and online tutorials on correct attribution of scholarly material and bibliographic citations reduce the chance that learners will fail to provide proper scholarly acknowledgement in their assignments and research. For example, the University of Puget Sound (2003) has designed an excellent resource that provides learners with exercises to enhance their understanding of the concept of plagiarism and to assist them in avoiding it (see http://library.ups.edu/research/guides/plagrsm.htm).

Community-Building Tools

As online learning has grown and evolved, so too has recognition of the importance of student interaction and the role it plays in peer support and the creation of an online or virtual community of "groups of people who share a concern, a set of problems, or a passion about a topic, and who deepen their knowledge and expertise in this area by interacting on an ongoing basis" (Wenger, McDermott, & Snyder, 2002, p. 4). Indeed, Lentell and O'Rourke (2004) include "supporting self-directed learner groups" and "supporting discussions" (online or face-to-face) that build "communities of practice" as a promising means of providing learner support for institutions with large numbers of students, especially those with limited resources in underdeveloped countries.

Tools to support interaction among online learners include asynchronous computer-mediated conferencing (electronic bulletin boards), text-based chat, synchronous audio conferencing, blogs, and wikis, among others. New forms of social software are constantly being developed with the aim of fostering student interaction, supporting individual and collective learning, and promoting a sense of belonging and mutual support.

While most online student interaction typically takes place within the course environment, usually in asynchronous conferences moderated by instructors or facilitators, there are also opportunities for students to join together informally outside of the courses in which they are enrolled. For example, program web sites may include an interactive "meet-and-greet" area where students can introduce themselves or discuss shared interests and concerns. At Athabasca University (2008), the Student Union offers clubs and groups, study buddies, mentoring, and discussion forums and chat through their web site at http://www.ausu.org/.

LIBRARY RESOURCES

In the early years of distance education, providing library support to learners was a challenge. Courses were developed in print format and comprehensive course packages were sent to each learner. The library typically provided a collection that was made available to the learner on request, either by mail or fax. Online sources of information, however, have transformed libraries in distance education. Where libraries once focused on holdings, they now focus on access; where they once were information repositories, they now are gateways to information. This transformation has allowed the library to become better integrated within courses and more actively involved in the overall learning process. Online learners require resources and support to make full use of the digital library that has evolved, and to use it effectively in their studies and written work. Moreover, as distance education institutions expand into offering post-graduate programs, there is increasing need for the library to be involved in facilitating student research, providing web-based information on topics such as searching online journals or conducting literature reviews.

ONLINE EDUCATIONAL COUNSELLING

Well-prepared resources can be provided online, but counselling assistance, both synchronous and asynchronous, is required as well, particularly for learners who are experiencing difficulty. In the online environment, learners can "fall through the cracks" if assistance is not readily available. From time to-time, a learner may need someone to assist in keeping a positive outlook and determining if an intervention is needed. Learners need to know that help is there if they need it. The institution should provide this resource and all institutional staff should be trained to identify when a learner might benefit from a session with a counsellor. It is important to remember, however, that while referrals can be made, the decision to pursue them belongs to the learner.

The work of the counsellor in an online learning environment has three aspects. The first is to be involved in the development of online resources that help learners to identify and address barriers to reaching their educational goals. The second is to interact with the learners when an intervention is required. The third is to work with other institutional staff to ensure that processes and procedures support and enhance learning.

While educational and career counselling are well suited to the online environment, personal counselling is less so. Generally speaking, personal counselling should be limited to immediate crisis resolution and referral. As such, counselling staff need information about local community resources, in a variety of locations, to which they can refer students in need.

STUDENT RIGHTS AND OMBUDS SERVICES

Online learners have as much need of clearly articulated rights as do learners in traditional educational settings. An advocacy process designed for online learners is one in which the learner is made aware of student rights and responsibilities. An institution can fulfill its basic legal responsibility by making a student code of conduct available online and in print upon request. A prudent institution, however, will go well beyond this demonstration of due diligence, particularly with regard to intellectual property and plagiarism, as discussed earlier.

All efforts to provide smooth interactions between the learner and the institution notwithstanding, there will be situations in which the learner becomes ensnared and does not know where to turn. A highly visible ombuds office should be available. Moreover, from an institutional perspective, the ombuds office can assist in identifying policy and procedure problems that require attention within the institution. Information about the Ombud's Office at Athabasca University can be found at http://www.athabascau.ca/ombuds/index.php.

Institutional Governance and the Students' Union

Institutions involved in distance and online learning may wish to provide opportunities for students to participate in institutional governance, as online learners can make valuable contributions and contribute unique insights in policy, planning, and similar matters. Including student representatives on the Board of Governors and on senior-level administrative and academic committees helps to ensure that student perspectives are considered and results in more informed decision-making. Involving students in such capacities also sends an important message – that students are valued, respected, and contributing members of the organization with a legitimate role to play in how the organization is governed.

Student government in the form of a student union is also possible in such institutions, although administration may need to make special arrangements to facilitate the process. In many ways, a student union faces the same issues as the institution to keep in touch with its constituency. Both are vying for the attention of learners, who are often juggling learning with many other life demands. Still, it is in the institution's best interests to have a healthy student union and to work together to meet the needs of the learners. Some means by which to achieve these goals include

- making networks available to the student union;
- providing one main institutional contact with whom student union representatives can interact;
- assisting in collecting student union fees;
- making information available, within confidentiality provisions;
- including student representatives on governing and decision-making bodies;
- having decision-making bodies meet through electronic means (e.g., teleconference, online conference) to maximize participation of students;
- keeping the student union and student representatives apprised of significant events, initiatives, and issues (e.g., strategic planning, budgeting, tuition fee increases);
- engaging in shared initiatives with the student union (e.g., including student union representatives in convocation, co-publishing newsletters);
- seeking advice from the student union on important issues; and
- demonstrating appreciation for the work of the student union.

Resources for Alumni

After graduation, students often wish to maintain contact with the institution and with fellow students. The educational institution, either on its own or through the student union, may wish to provide resources for alumni. Including a section for alumni on the institution's web site is one way to keep former students involved and informed. In addition, opportunities for fundraising and planned giving may be included. Some institutions have established an alumni association to maintain contact with former students.

RESOURCES FOR ONLINE LEARNERS WITH DISABILITIES

Increasing numbers of students with disabilities are recognizing the benefits of distance education and realizing the enhanced access it provides to post-secondary educational opportunities. Flexibility in the location of study, scheduling, and delivery of distance and online programs provide many students with disabilities with what may be their first real access to higher education (Paist, 1995; Kim-Rupnow, Dowrick, & Burke, 2001). On the other hand, distance learners with disabilities also face numerous barriers to success, including factors related to learner characteristics, life circumstances, workload, social integration, locus of control, study-time management, organization, satisfaction, motivation, and interaction with the instructor and other students.

Online learning presents additional challenges, especially for students with physical, sensory, and learning disabilities (Burgstahler, 2001; Fichten, Asuncion, Barile, Fossey, & De Simone, 2000). For example,

- keyboarding is difficult (or impossible) for learners with fine-motor problems or conditions such as Carpal Tunnel Syndrome;
- learners with hearing impairments are unable to comprehend uncaptioned video presentations;
- learners with hearing impairments or communication disorders (e.g., aphasia, severe stuttering) are unable to participate in audio-conferences;
- accessible web pages are a must for learners with visual impairments who use screen-reading software;
- the text-based nature of distance and online learning materials presents difficulties to students for whom the written word is a barrier, such as those with certain learning disabilities or reading comprehension problems.

These are but some of the challenges that online learning presents to the diverse population of learners with disabilities. To overcome barriers and achieve success, these online learners require appropriate, individualized, disability-specific support services and, when required, suitable assistive technology, as discussed in the case below.

DISABILITY SERVICES AT ATHABASCA UNIVERSITY

In April 1998, the Office for Access to Students with Disabilities (ASD) at Athabasca University was established (see http://www.athabascau.ca/asd/). Two years later, in November 2000, the *Policy for Students with Disabilities* was adopted. This policy defines students with disabilities as "those individuals who are disadvantaged by reason of any verifiable and persistent physical, learning, cognitive, sensory, psychological, neurological, or temporary impairment that may affect their academic progress" (Athabasca University, 2000). The policy further states that students with disabilities will receive the following services:

- Information
- Assessment of academic and technological accommodations and support requirements
- Educational and career counselling as it pertains to the disability
- Referrals to additional services or agencies
- Program planning as it pertains to the student's disability
- Time-management assistance (respective to the disability)
- Monitoring of progress in course work
- Registration assistance
- Information and assistance with applications for funding
- Assistance to obtain alternate format materials if materials cannot be produced on campus
- Support service arrangements (e.g., tutoring, academic strategist, interpreting, aide, reader, scribe)
- Exam accommodations
- Time extensions for courses
- Advocacy
- Liaison with departments and faculties
- Available volunteer assistance, including note taking, exam-writing assistance, mobility assistance, taping of readings, library research help, study help, tutoring, special project help.

The list above reflects the broad nature of services required by distance and online learners with disabilities. Certainly, not all of these learners require extensive services, but some do. Also, like any student, some learners with disabilities require more support at certain times in their program of studies than at others. This is especially true for prospective students. We have found that taking a proactive approach and planning disability-specific supports prior to enrolment is important in order to initiate a supportive environment that will promote successful learning and avoid many problems encountered after studies have commenced. As the statistics below show, prospective students make up a significant number of the total students receiving disability services at Athabasca University.

Students Receiving Disability Services

Since its inception, the number of students receiving services from the Office for Access to Students with Disabilities (ASD) has grown steadily.

In the five-year period between 2002 and 2007, numbers nearly doubled (see Figure 1). In April 2002, 709 active students and an additional one hundred prospective students received services through the ASD office; in April 2007, there were 1,584 active students and 193 prospective students receiving services.

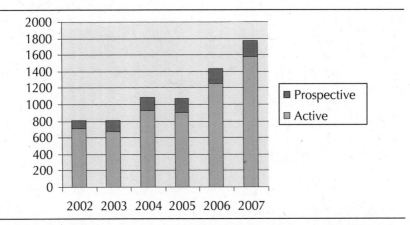

FIGURE 1. Students Receiving Disability-Specific Services at Athabasca University (Source: Athabasca University, Office for Access for Students with Disabilities, 2007)

To obtain a greater understanding of the nature of students with disabilities at Athabasca University and the services they receive, an exploratory study (Moisey, 2004) was conducted to coincide with the first three years of the operation of the ASD office (1998–2001). A total of 604 undergraduate students with disabilities were enrolled during this period. More than half (52%) had a physical disability, 20% had a learning disability, 20% had a psychological disability, and 7% had some form of sensory (hearing or vision) impairment. Their overall course completion rate – 45.9%, including early withdrawals – was somewhat lower than the general Athabasca University population – 52.5% when early withdrawals were included; and 59.5% when early withdrawals were excluded.

The study also found that students who received disability-specific services tended to have more success in terms of course completions. This finding is further supported by a more recent study, as yet unpublished, involving undergraduate students with disabilities ($n = 652$)

enrolled between April 2003 and April 2005 at Athabasca University. Statistical analysis reveals that students who received disability-specific services had significantly higher course completion rates than students with disabilities who did not receive such services. In short, it appears that providing support for distance and online learners with disabilities is important for promoting success in the courses in which they are enrolled.

Services and Accommodations

Learners with disabilities at Athabasca University are identified in three ways: a) they indicate on the General Admissions Form that they have a disability; b) they self-refer, often after viewing the ASD web site (especially true for prospective learners); or c) they are referred by their tutor or instructor (usually after encountering difficulty in a course). Once the initial contact is made, the next step in determining the student's particular needs is assessment.

Determination of learner support begins with a comprehensive, detailed self-assessment, which ascertains the student's level of ability in a variety of functional areas. Following verification of the assessment, consultation takes place with a specially trained service coordinator to determine what services and accommodations may be required.

Course accommodations: The most common type of course accommodation involves adding one or more two-month extensions to the normal six-month contract time for completing a course. Another form of course accommodation involves providing alternative formats of course materials (e.g., electronic or recorded audio versions of textual material, transcripts of audio materials).

Exam accommodations: These learner supports involve four types of accommodation: a) accommodation to the timing of an examination (e.g., deferral, additional time to complete the examination, provision for breaks during the exam); b) assistance with presenting questions and recording answers (e.g., printing the exam in larger font, giving an oral exam instead of a written exam, use of a scribe to record answers); c) environmental changes involving the exam room (e.g., taking the examination alone; playing relaxing music); and d) using an alternative format for the examination (e.g., substituting multiple-choice test items with short-answer questions).

External support: This service involves the provision of support from outside the university (e.g., the use of an academic strategist, interpreter, note-taker, study aide, support worker).

Assistive technology: This service involves assessment of learner needs for special equipment or software to assist in the learning process. Assistive technology commonly includes using adaptive software, such as programs for text-to-speech conversion and word prediction, screen readers, voice input and optical character recognition, and screen enlargers. Assistive-input devices may also be recommended, such as large-key keyboards or special trackballs. Services also include procurement of equipment, liaison with funding sources, and training.

Depending on their circumstances, students may receive one-time, occasional, or ongoing support to attain their educational goals. Because the characteristics of students with disabilities are as diverse as those of the general student population, a variety of services and accommodations is required. Each student's situation is different, and each has a unique set of goals and abilities; therefore, each requires an individualized set of supports to maximize their learning and to achieve the highest possible level of success.

CONCLUSION

Creating a supportive environment in which the online learner can flourish is a complex task requiring careful analysis, thoughtful planning, and ongoing monitoring and revision to ensure that students' needs are truly met. A constellation of resources and array of services are required to support the online learner in a manner that acknowledges individual differences and addresses them in the design of learner support services. Depending on the nature of the organization – a mega-university, a dedicated distance learning institution, or a dual-mode institution – the manner in which services and supports are provided may vary. But the aim remains the same: to provide an ideal learning environment that promotes the learner's independence while facilitating the learning process with supports that are flexible, accessible, and readily available when needed.

REFERENCES

Athabasca University. (2000). *Policy on students with disabilities.* Retrieved May 22, 2007, from http://www.athabascau.ca/policy/studentservices/policyforstudentswithdisabilities.htm

Athabasca University. (2006). *Annual report.* Retrieved May 24, 2007, from http://www.athabascau.ca/report2006/report2006.pdf

Athabasca University. (2007). *Am I Ready? Student support web site.* Retrieved September 25, 2007, from http://amiready.athabascau.ca/

Athabasca University. (2008). *Athabasca University Students' Union web site.* Retrieved March 23, 2008, from http://www.ausu.org/

Burgstahler, S. (2001). *Real connections: Making distance learning accessible to everyone.* Seattle: Washington University. (ERIC Document Reproduction Service No. 475789). Retrieved May 26, 2007, from http://p-adl.ucf.edu/events/seminars/ resources/distancelearn_1_0.pdf

Daniel, J. S. (1996). *Mega-universities and the knowledge media: Technology strategies for higher education.* London: Kogan Page.

Daniel, J. S. (2000). At the end of now – Global trends and their regional impacts. In V. Reddy & S. Manjulika (Eds.), *The world of open and distance learning* (pp. 451–461). New Delhi: Viva Books.

Deakin University. (2003). *Deakin learning toolkit.* Retrieved May 11, 2007, from http://www.deakin.edu.au/dlt2007/

Fichten, C. S., Asuncion, J., Barile, M., Fossey, M., & De Simone, C. (2000). Access to educational and instructional computer technologies for post-secondary students with disabilities: Lessons from three empirical studies. *Journal of Educational Media, 25*(3), 179–201.

Kim-Rupnow, W. S., Dowrick, P. W., & Burke, S. L. (2001). Trends in distance education: Implications for improving access and outcomes for individuals with disabilities in post-secondary distance education. *The American Journal of Distance Education, 15*(1), 25–40.

Lentell, H., & O'Rourke, J. (2004). Tutoring large numbers: An unmet challenge. *The International Review of Research in Open and Distance Learning, 5*(1). Retrieved May 23, 2007, from http://www.irrodl.org/index.php/irrodl/article/view/171/253

Moisey, S. (2004). Students with disabilities in distance education: Characteristics, course enrolment and completion, and support services. *Journal of Distance Education, 19*(1), 73–91. Retrieved May 11, 2007, from http://cade.athabascau.ca/vol19.1/MOISEY_article.pdf

Open University (UK). (2007). *Home page.* Retrieved May 13, 2007, from http://www.open.ac.uk

Paist, E. (1995). Serving students with disabilities in distance education programs. *The American Journal of Distance Education, 9*(1), 61–70.

Qui, M. (2006). *China: The distance learning market in China.* U.S. Commercial Service, Department of Commerce. Retrieved May 20, 2007, from http://commercecan.ic.gc.ca/scdt/bizmap/interface2.nsf/vDownload/ISA_4866/$file/X_5694307.doc

Tait, A. (2000). Planning student support for open and distance learning. *Open Learning, 15*(3), 287–299.

University of Puget Sound, Collins Memorial Library. (2003). *Academic honesty: Recognizing plagiarism.* Retrieved May 10, 2007, from http://library.ups .edu/research/guides/plagrsm.htm

Wang, T. (2005). Tensions in learner support and tutor support in tertiary web-based English language education in China. *International Review of Research in Open and Distance Learning, 6*(3). Retrieved May 6, 2007, from http://www.irrodl.org/index.php/irrodl/article/view/266/425

Wenger, E., McDermott, R., & Snyder, W. (2002). *Cultivating communities of practice: A guide to managing knowledge.* Boston, MA: Harvard University Press.

ABOUT THE AUTHORS

Susan Moisey (susanh@athabascau.ca) is an associate professor in the Centre for Distance Education at Athabasca University, where she teaches courses in instructional design, learning theory, and systems analysis. Dr. Moisey's research interests include inclusive education, distance education for learners with disabilities and other marginalized groups, online community building, and alternative models for instructional design.

Judith Hughes retired from Athabasca University in 2005. Most recently, Dr. Hughes served as Vice-President, Academic; Vice-President, Student Services; and Vice-President, External Relations. Her history is rooted in adult education, teaching and research, and administration.

CHAPTER 18

DEVELOPING TEAM SKILLS AND ACCOMPLISHING TEAM PROJECTS ONLINE

DEBORAH HURST & JANICE THOMAS
Athabasca University

INTRODUCTION

Virtual teaming with members dispersed over geography, time zone, and functional roles has become commonplace as result of proliferating communication technologies (Tran & Latapie, 2007; Hawkrigg, 2007). Communication technologies in synchronous and asynchronous form are not only used within business teams but also increasingly to facilitate online learning in management education (Lee, Bonk, Magjuka, Su, & Liu, 2006; Kalliath & Laiken, 2006; Brewer & Klein, 2006; Clark & Gibb, 2006; Williams & Duray, 2006). Though many discuss virtual teaming, there does not appear to be a lot of empirical evidence discussing the effectiveness of this type of team or the processes used (Mihhailova, 2007).

Early critiques of online and distance learning at the MBA or professional education level suggest weakness in the teaching of team and other soft-skill and process areas of the curriculum. Some academics question the suitability of topics such as team dynamics, communications, or leadership as candidates for online learning, believing that such "soft" aspects of the curriculum cannot be adequately taught through distance means. Challenges associated with leadership of teams, recognizing member talent, creating and transferring knowledge, building and promoting trust, engaging members, and dealing with isolation all contribute to ongoing scepticism (Hawkrigg, 2007; Lawley, 2006; Brewer & Klein, 2006; Tran & Latapie, 2007). The argument behind such scepticism is that what occurs in typical team training programs often involves experiential forms of human interaction and skill building for conflict resolution, goal setting, trust building, and collaborating – all difficult to imagine happening without face-to-face interaction. While questions remain surrounding the ability to develop such soft skills online, and whether online methods allow for sufficient social interactive experience among learners, some evidence suggests that computer-mediated teaming interaction may in fact be deeper, long-term, and thus exceed those in face-to-face environments (Brewer & Klein, 2006; Kalliath & Laiken, 2006).

In this chapter, we present our experience with teaching about and developing soft team skills by exercising teaming skills within an online environment. Three examples illustrate online team training and building/practicing skills in action. These cases exemplify what is possible with respect to developing knowledge of team dynamics and communications, and accomplishing team project work. The chapter begins by describing the first case, a professional designation learning program known as the professional logistician (P. Log), delivered by the Canadian Professional Logistics Institute (CPLI), where team concepts and practice are delivered online and at a distance with mid-career professionals. In describing aspects of one of the courses within this program, the team dynamics and communication module (TDC), we highlight the unique value and capability of an online learning environment.

The second part of the paper elaborates further on ideas about online learning and working, through two more case studies. Case 2 examines the operation and characteristics of a highly successful online project team. Case 3 presents some collected experiences of MBA-level online learning teams. This section synthesizes lessons learned from all three cases. We highlight key benefits gained through structured interaction which incorporates solid project management and team development practices, specifically gaining agreement on how members will work together, assign accountability, manage flexibility, monitor progress, and incorporate social interaction. These areas, we believe, are the key ingredients for the successful use of online teaming in learning – or any other – environments. Two key topics arise from our experiences with developing and working with online teams, and are emphasized in a discussion of technology and trust. We make some summary comments on the impact and role of these two concepts as cross-cutting themes, and conclude with some practical recommendations about managing online learning teams.

Ultimately, we are interested in challenging the perceived barriers surrounding the ability of online learning to contribute to soft-skill and competency development. It is our view that this method of team development learning is not only effective in the development of soft skills and social interaction competency, but that online learning may in fact be the superior method. We hope that our experiences of what is possible in online learning environments provide some specific and practical guidance on what it takes to accomplish team development and training online.

DEVELOPING TEAM SKILLS ONLINE

In this section of the chapter, we discuss the online team dynamics and communication (TDC) module, part of the Canadian Professional Logistics Institute's (LI) professional logistician (P. Log) designation program. Our purpose in emphasizing this module is to provide concrete evidence of how one institution is providing effective soft-skill training online, through the creative use of technology and other distance tools.

The module described herein is part of an overall package that the LI created in response to the increasing development needs of emerging professionals within the logistics field.[1] In their early version of this program, the LI combined face-to-face with online learning methods within their program. Modules delivered online included team dynamics, integrated logistics networks, and logistics process diagnosis. Modules delivered in a face-to-face format included those on leading and managing change, supply-chain strategies, ethics, and leadership. In this hybrid-learning program, methods have blended in a unique way to develop "soft" and "hard" practical skills, and understanding with a heavier emphasis on soft skills than is typically provided in this field. Courses also seek to develop tacit understanding, insight, trust, and confidence in an online collaborative process for learning and working. Given the success of the hybrid-learning program, and building interest in moving to a global program and providing additional flexibility for learners, the LI took a further step. In 2006, in collaboration with Athabasca University's Centre for Innovative Management (AU-CIM), the LI developed a fully online pathway in their program for earning the P. Log. New online courses include ethics and decision making, strategic supply-chain management, and leading through change, running parallel with face-to-face courses of similar content. As a result of adding the fully online pathway, students have increased access to courses regardless of their global location, greatly increasing the diversity of the student body and of learner flexibility.

We focus on the TDC module delivered as part of this program online. The module content is similar to that delivered in face-to-face team-learning sessions, drawing in part on ideas from practitioner approaches to teaming such as Aranda et al. (1990). Learners are asked to build on insights and ideas taken from Katzenbach and Smith (1999), among others, to develop key success indicators of teams. The online delivery method is different, however, in that people connect only through collaborative technologies and do not meet face-to-face during the module. In the hybrid program, learners meet face-to-face in other modules, usually after they have completed the team dynamics module. With the introduction of the fully online pathway, however, learners typically only meet virtually. The online learning environment allows students and their employers to access courses and get beyond the significant challenges of cost, time, place, and risk imposed by more traditional forms of corporate training and university teaching. Using communication technologies to provide team training mirrors work completed in organizations, by developing the communication, coaching, teaming, and collaborative skills needed in highly complex and distributed corporate work environments (Clark & Gibb, 2006). Students develop soft skills online, such as the process skills highlighted, and gain grounded experiential learning that contributes to developing managerial-process-skill competence. The LI online program values and supports adult learners by providing them with a program that aligns with their daily business realities (Waight & Stewart, 2005).

The TDC module uses technology to support learning in two ways. The module is four weeks in duration and encompasses two phases: a stand-alone CD-based computer simulation that each student interacts with and completes independently, and student interaction with fellow learners that is facilitated pedagogically by an engaged and available academic facilitator, and the use of an asynchronous message board and synchronous chat tools. We describe both phases of the module in some detail, and explore the value of both the simulation and facilitated team work in providing important teachable moments from which both tacit and explicit learning derives.

THE TEAM DYNAMICS AND COMMUNICATIONS (TDC) MODULE – PHASE 1

The first part of the TDC module has learners engage in experiential individual learning through a simulation containing scenarios of typical team challenges. Research has shown that simulations and web-based games used in conveying specific aspects of course material can be a highly effective way to learn by doing (Chipman, 2007). In the TDC course, the learner is expected to interact with simulated team members (filmed scenarios and pre-recorded graphics) on a time-sensitive, critical mission, gathering information, and experiencing team and team-relevant issues as they progress through the various scenarios. Overall, the TDC simulation focuses on process skills needed for effective team dynamics and *online teaming*: team process discussions, role assignments, leadership, conflict resolution, decision making, and planning for goal success. Many of the scenarios crafted were taken from real experiences that highlighted the most salient issues of team development. Information on how different people store information and label organizational stories was used to construct the decision paths in each scene of the scenario. Cultural ideas around probable failures and interpretations of these failures were used to inform the scripting. The resulting scenarios were dramatic and interesting, and encouraged participation.

The setting for the simulation is a remote area where lightning has started a forest fire and damaged a telecommunications tower. The learner enters the online space and becomes part of an emergency response team that has been given the responsibility of repairing the tower. To ensure some team struggle at this stage of learning, participants are required to deal (online) with the challenges of travel by canoe, and must arrive within a set period of time. If the team functions poorly on the tasks and arrives late, the consequence presented is that telecommunications in the area will go down, and firefighters will not be able to prevent the forest fire from approaching a small nearby town. Every decision that learners make has been designed to have immediate consequences in the simulated world. The result is that the risk of failure is clearly conveyed.

Teachable Moments

Although an individual learner's poor decision or mistake may cause the team to lose valuable time on the "trip," mistakes create important *teachable moments*.[2] Failure on any task is considered to be a learning opportunity, by determining what went wrong. To facilitate learning at these moments, an online coach pops up within the simulated environment to provide just-in-time positive and negative feedback, depending on the learner's decisions. Learners therefore immediately face their mistakes, and are able to learn from them in a private and safe environment.

It is Schank's (1997) view that real learning occurs only when people are thrown into scenarios in this manner. Participants make decisions, solve problems, make mistakes, and have access to an expert as required, to answer questions and to give them advice. Because simulations are private, Schank believes that learners may be more willing to risk failure and use that experience for learning. By contrast, failure in organizations is more often negatively perceived, a fact that stifles creativity. In a simulation, people can fail privately with dignity rather than feel humiliated when failure occurs in a public way. Failure, like having fun and telling stories, is a powerful way to induce emotion and a powerful learning tool.

Emotions coupled with technology can produce a further positive situation. Computers store the learning that has occurred, and can retrieve it if similar patterns are observed later on, thus making learning more specific to individual needs. It is our view that learning facilitated by emotional drive and technological tools is very powerful. Underlying this statement is a key assumption that through this unique approach, individuals are provided with an opportunity to learn to *do* something extremely relevant to them (rather than simply learning *about* something), making the knowledge gained through experience both explicit and tacit (Schank, 1997; Stewart, 2001).

Scenarios come to life and require that learners interact with conceptual information built into the scenarios. Different conceptual aspects of team structure, culture, accountability, and politics are woven into the module design. Information is presented sequentially. Scripts were built in a way similar to a child's multiple-path story; the development of the story depends on the choices made. Learning becomes customized, allowing participants to spend greater amounts of time dealing with concepts and skills that are more unfamiliar or challenging. Storytelling is incorporated into the simulated environment as a means of relating content and experiences back to the workplace.

Getting beyond Technological Apprehension

In an earlier evaluation of this product, Hurst and Follows (2003) state that as participants entered the module for the first time, some learners experienced technical challenges and apprehension regarding the use of technology. The challenges were not only related to computer incompatibility, but also the degree to which participants were ready to engage in online learning environments. For many, there appeared to be an initial hesitancy and fear associated with learning in a technologically mediated environment. In the evaluation phase, many related their early experiences with the technology to their later impressions of the module. They found the module to be "fun, challenging...an overall good learning experience," but noted that it had been "quite different and a little scary in the beginning." For some, technical problems persisted.

It was interesting that, when probed, individuals remained worried that they would fail in a public way and as a result become embarrassed, because of their unfamiliarity with learning online. This finding highlights the need to do further work in making participants feel comfortable with, and trusting of, the online environment early in the process. Lawley (2006) describes trust and member-comfort level as foundational ingredients for effective teamwork and collaboration, regardless of how or where the team interactions take place. The strength of the apprehension surrounding the idea of failure prior to entry into the simulation and online discussion was very apparent, and provides clear evidence that Schank's (1997) claim about a learner's willingness to take risks and fail privately is of critical importance.

To deal with this learning barrier, further facilitation was introduced before learners used the simulation tool; the intent was to encourage a greater level of comfort and to minimize any emergent stress. Once the apprehension surrounding technical difficulties was dealt with in this manner, learners' evaluations of their online learning experience became much more positive. One participant noted that, "I thought that the interactive CD [simulation tool] was very well put together and a neat way to learn. I know I now have a better understanding of team building, conflict resolution, and the importance of communication."

Capturing and Building on the Learning

Learners are asked from time to time to make notes of what they are thinking and feeling about their experiences, so that they can use their insights later in online discussions. Self-evaluation tools concerned with communication preferences, leadership style, and conflict handling are built into the module to give learners an opportunity to focus on specific issues, and to develop and reflect on new skills and competencies. Self-reflective tools are intended to supplement the experience of the simulation through private assessment of personalized feedback. The feedback and record keeping both provide learners with input prior to entering the second portion of the module, where they engage in a more traditional teamwork situation with live team members, albeit facilitated online and at a distance.

TDC MODULE – PHASE 2

In the second phase of the TDC module, learners engage with a synchronous chat environment to attend weekly team meetings. They are assigned tasks during each meeting and expected to figure out how to work together over the course. Students use various technical tools such as chat, email, voice over Internet protocol (VoIP), and message boards to divide tasks, discuss ideas, and prepare summary documents. Participants are provided with an asynchronous message board for posting their documents and questions for review. During the initial chat meeting, teams are formed, and members are encouraged to introduce themselves to one another, discuss their impressions of the simulation experience, and practice brainstorming and consensus decision-making processes, by beginning with a minor task to come up with a team name. The new team is then asked to review their experiences of the first phase of the module, and state which aspects they find to be most important to their learning, and most helpful in early stages with forming the new team. Members are encouraged to discuss aspects of team structure, roles, processes, measures of success, accountability, and so forth. The new team is also asked to review a chat protocol, provided below, encouraging them to discuss conduct expectations and to provide additional information, based on their perception of the new team's needs.

Chat Protocol

- Allow each learner to complete his/her thought before responding – this means do not interrupt or intrude with your thought while another is speaking.
- Be patient – not everyone has advanced keyboard skills.
- Avoid having side conversations; it's rude not to pay attention.
- Signal when you've finished a statement [some use a happy face to signal they have completed their input J].
- Signal when you don't understand something; use a question mark to get the facilitator's attention.
- Signal your "reactions" by using an exclamation mark (!) for surprise, a sad face for disagreement L, or some combination of symbols.
- Do not shout [CAPITALS MEAN THAT YOU ARE SHOUTING].
- Do not leave your computer during a scheduled session; it is impossible to get your attention if you leave the room.
- Officially sign on and off so that everyone knows when you are present.
- Keep statements brief and to the point; the chat box has a limit of 256 characters per statement; you can keep talking, but in spurts.
- Prepare notes and key ideas ahead of time so that you can engage in the discussion without trying to figure out how to word your statements. (CPLI, 2000, p. 45)

Once the new virtual team establishes ground rules, it is assigned the task of creating a reverse logistics plan as a follow-up to their personal work with the simulation in Phase 1. This task provides continuity as well as additional time for social interaction, allowing participants to get to know one another and become comfortable with the facilitated online chat environment. During this initial stage, it is important for participants to establish and re-establish how their conversations will take place, who will speak, and in what order, to ensure full participation in the experience.

To launch the team task, members are presented with a scenario update, and advised that the fire is almost under control, and that the crew will be finished repairing the tower in approximately six hours. The team task is to work together to create a plan to get team members and the used and remaindered supplies back to the point of origin. They are given three possible options to discuss, as well as many contingencies to consider while coming up with a detailed reverse logistics plan. The facilitator emphasizes the importance of consensus decision making for the task, and reminds team members of lessons learned during the first part of the module.

The facilitator also works to introduce new constraints in an effort to surprise the team, and as a way of introducing potentially conflicting ideas, to get the team working through the developmental phases experientially as well as intellectually. Additional constraints imposed include transport route changes, modes of transportation, environmental conditions, presence of wildlife, handling and disposing of hazardous goods, and other options to challenge the team and to bring out different and creative points of view. The goal in this part of the module is to force differences among team members to the surface, with the hope of inciting conflict, so that participants have the opportunity to experience and work through new ideas, skills, and competencies in working with others in teams.

The second task assigned to the online team is the creation of a team-charter template, a tool for governing the team's work and social interaction. This is the core activity for the module. The completed team-charter template resembles a checklist, and represents the collective wisdom of what the team members believe to be the important issues to be addressed in creating and deploying an effective team as quickly as possible. The document contains ideas on how teams should be formed and structured; how their purpose should be defined; how team culture should be developed, and how the team should collaborate, ensure accountability, measure success, and achieve high performance. Learners are instructed first to respond individually to the questions posed, and then to work in their teams to synthesize the information and create one common document. Individuals attend weekly meetings in the chat room to discuss the work that is needed over the course of the week, as well as what should and should not be included in the document. Members volunteer for the roles of leader, scribe, and timekeeper – roles that are rotated among participants, to allow for skill development. By the time learners are given this assignment, they are typically comfortable with the online environment and appear to forget the lack of face-to face cues. The module steps are similar to the principles outlined by Clark and Gibb (2006) regarding the design of grounded experiential learning for virtual teams. The LI module provides for individuals to

- meet electronically and build rapport through exchange of personal information

- establish team name/identify
- set out rules for engagement, plan for work
- develop communication planning and coordination processes.

ENCOURAGING EXPLICIT AND TACIT LEARNING

In each offering of the module thus far, learners completing the task have spent most of their time discussing team structure and process issues. Interestingly, a parallel of explicit and tacit learning occurs; that is, as team members discuss pertinent team-development issues, participants also appear to experience the same issues. During a more recent offering of the module, a discussion took place around conflict resolution. There was mild disagreement among team members over how conflicts at an impasse should be resolved. While some argued that "troublemakers had the option to leave the team," others stressed that this was not an appropriate option. Their view was that "consensus must occur."

The discussion heated and circled for some time, until the similarities between the topic under discussion and the discussion itself were pointed out. This created a powerful learning moment, combining intellectual and experiential elements. Since participants had already discussed effective listening at length, they were able to recognize the value of the discussion, and moved forward with developing a process they could all live with. The learning opportunity or teachable moment was noted as one in which concepts were both discussed and experienced. The template task provided the opportunity for learners to crystallize their learning in the creation of the document itself, to take stock of what they had learned individually and collectively, and to consider where such learning could be recreated in future teams beyond the module.

Increasing Trust in Technology, the Process and Each Other

At the end of the module, participants seemed quite comfortable with the technologically mediated environment, with one another, and with the facilitator. The participant comfort level increased after the first chat meeting experience. One learner noted that, "I initially found it difficult to converse electronically with ten other people, although I see my children doing it all the time. Once I got the hang of it, it became enjoyable." People commented increasingly on the content of the module as they became more comfortable with the technology, and the use of it became tacit during Phase 2. Team members took control of the work, held additional meetings, assigned tasks to sub-group members, posted longer documents, and so on. They often used email and the message board for in-depth communications, and the chat tool for work planning or coming to final decisions. This type of technology use is consistent with other findings (Gareis, 2006). Phase 2 activities grounded the learner's new skills and knowledge in additional collaborative experiences. Individuals also had an opportunity to discuss their ideas with others in a facilitated environment.

Participants also suggested improvements; for example, they thought that the short introductions at the beginning of Phase 2 to break the ice should be extended, and should perhaps include personal auto-biographies, to allow for further confidence building, and comfort with the communications medium and with each other in social interaction. However, while many learners thought that the initial introductions were too brief and should be extended, it is interesting to note that when asked to provide those same introductions at the beginning of each module, they seemed guarded and reluctant to share personal informa-tion. It was only as team members became comfortable with one another, trusting other team members and the overall process, that sharing of personal information and humour surfaced.

Learners also provided feedback for how to improve team communications during each session. One idea was to develop a speak-er's order, so that all would have a chance to contribute fully to the conversation. When used, this approach appeared to generally improve the team's performance and interactions during the discussions, decision making, and collaborating in subsequent tasks.

Team adjournment activities asked learners to comment on what they found to be the most positive characteristics of the team experience of each team member. Interestingly, during the first pilot offering of the module, team members decided that they did not want to comment on each individual in the way requested, because they did not want to single out individuals – they were a team. They met offline to discuss this issue, and the team as a unit presented their revised version of the exercise to the facilitator, clearly demonstrating their commitment to the team and their internalization of the learning.

We can now take lessons from the online development module and apply them more broadly to further online teaming experiences. Important aspects of team development experience highlighted include an emphasis on member roles and competencies, such as autonomy, coordination, and collaboration. Here we must note, in particular, organizational factors, the use of technology, personal management, and interpersonal skills. Organizational factors include networking, knowing the organizational landscape, and maintaining guidelines. The use of technology in online teaming requires knowledge of when to communicate, coordinate, and collaborate, as well as how to communicate effectively and conform to expected communication etiquette. The personal management category includes the ability to prioritize work, set limits, create opportunities for learning and growth, collect and provide feedback, discuss strengths and weaknesses, manage boundaries, and understand cultural perspectives and how these differences can affect perception.

ACCOMPLISHING TEAM PROJECTS ONLINE: TWO FURTHER CASES

Building from our previous discussion of online team development, we use this section of the chapter to explore and compare the operation of a highly successful online project team and the operation of online learning teams used in an MBA program. In the MBA program, online teams are groups of task-driven individuals who behave as a temporary team, but who may be separated by geographic or temporal space, and who use network-based communication tools to bridge these spaces. By reviewing the experience of these teams, we hope to provide insights into the practices that facilitate collaboration and learning in an online world. Recommendations from these experiences may help others working in the online world or endeavouring to use online learning teams, and so may further develop online team learning programs in a distance education environment.

We explore experience with two different types of online teams: the first is an online research team that conducted a major, practitioner-sponsored research study in three phases over a three year term; the other is one of the online learning teams used in Athabasca University's (AU) MBA program.

Online Research Team – Case 1

The first case study of a real-life online project team provides a way to explore common assumptions and theories. The online team in question participated in a meaningful project under serious resource constraints and within a tight schedule. The project was completed slightly behind schedule and over budget, but to great critical acclaim.

At any one time, the project team was composed of between four to eight members. The core team was made up of four members over the course of the first phase. During the second and third phases, only three members participated throughout. All of the core team members were academics and researchers (students). Each team member took the lead on different project tasks; however, one member acted as the formal team lead on contract documents and in the majority of correspondence. The fourth core team member, who joined the team after the project had been initiated and only worked on the first phase of the project, tended to play a lesser role overall. While three of the four core team members actually lived in the same city, the team rarely met in person because of travel and work schedules.

At the end of Phase 1 of the project, the four core team members participated in a series of Jungian-based personality and team assessments. The tests were chosen for their simplicity, availability, and potential to provide interesting insights into the operation of the team; however, they are not represented as the best or most suitable tests. An earlier paper (Delisle, Thomas, Jugdev, & Buckle, 2001) presents the results of the State (behavioural – trust orientation, and team process) and Trait (personality) assessments, highlighting the traits and behaviours that contributed to the operation of this creative and successful online project team. Insights gained as a result of several assessments showed that the team as a whole was relatively balanced, with a slight proclivity towards introverted, sensing, thinking, and judging approaches to the world. All of the members tended to take a thinking stance, leading to a potential weakness on the feeling factors. In addition, all four team members had a relatively trusting orientation in general. Finally, team process assessments provided evidence of a highly effective team, approaching synergistic operation. Further discussion of the impacts of these differences and the usefulness of these tools can be found in Delisle et al (2001).

The team explicitly recognized its activities as a project and engaged in good project management practices. The team did not purposely set out to 'build an effective team' or pay attention to what the teaming literature would suggest to build effective teams.

MBA Online Learning Teams – Case 2

The MBA learning teams were made up from a student population with an average age of 40 years, and who typically worked full-time in middle management roles in a variety of industries and organizations of many different sizes. The students were randomly placed in learning teams at the beginning of each course. Most courses required that the team complete two or three major assignments (usually based on a Harvard-Business-School-type case assessment) over the eight-week-long semester. These cases were done in three stages. Two weeks were spent on preparing and analysing the case situation and providing recommendations in a report format. One week was devoted to critiquing another group's case report, and then responding to the critique of one's own case report. In addition, the students engaged in asynchronous text-based discussion of course materials.

In the first class of the MBA program, students were given an orientation to the online technology and appropriate ways of working in the online environment, along with a quick introduction to best practices in team development. Typically, they were assigned to learning groups with others they had never met before. As the program progressed, there were increasing chances that the teams could include a few members who had worked together before. This situation was a relatively accurate simulation of the work environment that individuals face in modern organizations. More often than not, a team must rapidly come together with individuals who may or may not know one another, and must quickly begin to perform assigned tasks.

Unlike the research project team, students in learning teams were encouraged to review and adopt good teaming practices early in each and every course. As in the TDC module discussed earlier, online learning groups were assigned at the outset, and given the task of developing of an operating team charter, intended to shape the way they would work together. This activity, however, was not graded, and was done with varying degrees of competence and intensity by each learning team.

Another key difference that the MBA learning team had from the research project team was the formal application of project management practices to the operations of each learning team. The research team consistently viewed their work as *project work*, and although the duration of various memberships within the actual team varied, all worked toward a common completion goal. On the other hand, the MBA teams tended to view their work as *process work*, toward an individual end result in a course or MBA program, rather than work on a specific project – an attitude that might have been due to lack of exposure to project management principles, and/or to the nature of the learning environment itself.

The contexts experienced by a team working on an assigned project for the sake of the project and a team of students working on a project for grades are quite different. In each case, however, we noticed important knowledge being transferred through explicit and tacit learning while the team members worked towards their goals. Several practices seemed to facilitate these learning processes. We turn now to a discussion of the practices that we believe support both learning and teaming in an online environment.

KEY PRACTICES IN SUCCESSFUL ONLINE TEAMING

Looking across the research project and MBA learning team experiences and drawing from our earlier discussion on teachable moments and tacit and explicit learning from the TDC module, we see a number of key attributes associated with the successful use of online teams emerging. It is our view that these key practices include agreement on how teams will work together, how accountability is assigned, how progress is monitored, and how social interaction is incorporated. We discuss each of these practices with examples from the three cases.

Agreement on How Teams Will Work Together

In the case of the highly successful online research project team, there was very little initial discussion of how the team would work together. The three initiating team members were driven over-achievers who were highly motivated by the task. All were known to each other. Two had worked on a small project together earlier, and so had already established a certain amount of trust and goodwill. This relationship and common understanding of the importance of meeting goals played a significant part in helping them to form and start working quickly. These team members understood the need to define deadlines and complete deliverables on time. The common focus on agreed-upon goals and timelines enabled team members to monitor their own personal goals to ensure alignment with the overall project goals.

The project began with almost impossible deadlines from the beginning. Whereas this reality could be a recipe for failure on any team, in this case, the common threat allowed the team to coalesce quickly and was the catalyst for many spin-off projects. As the project careened towards its first "drop-dead deadline" about two weeks after the project started, tempers were frayed and workloads heavy. Once the first deadline was met, there was a one-month period in which the team waited to see if the proposal would be accepted. During this time, the group exchanged numerous emails, sharing their situations and discussing their goals, objectives, and personal commitments for the period ahead.

By the time the proposal was accepted, the team had a much clearer idea of each member's individual commitments, and how difficult it would be to get this project successfully completed. One team member was working 80 hours a week on a high-pressure professional job. Another had a two-month-old baby, two other children, a full-time job, and a thesis to finish, in addition to this project. The third was halfway through a Ph.D. project and had a faltering marriage. They discussed how they would meet the upcoming deadlines and who would take the lead on various tasks. Sharing issues, life experiences, and challenges allowed the team to feel a greater sense of cohesion and cooperation, and ultimately to jump in and help each other out when necessary.

Slowly, and in an emergent rather than conscious fashion, an agreement on how the team would work solidified. It was never written down or formally agreed upon, but it seemed to involve the principles noted below.

- The deadlines must be met. This project was important to all.
- Whoever was best able to lead on a particular task would do so.
- Each member would contribute 150% to this project, and endeavour not to let the other team members down.
- Team members would raise a flag (let others know about tasks not likely to get done on time).
- Team members would pitch in to complete work as needed.

It seemed clear that this team would never have been able to make the progress they did if they had not had this one-month "breathing space" to figure out how they would work together. They learned these lessons experientially, by being thrown into the process, and the result was fortunately positive. If this team had clearly applied team-building approaches to their own work prior to commencement, rather than after the first deadline, they might have been able to tackle this task explicitly and incorporate some best practices earlier, and avoided some angst later on. Whatever the case, what is highlighted here is once again the unique marriage of explicit and tacit learning about team process. This team learned the importance of dealing with social interaction issues and established rules for working together as they stormed through their first real process issues, realizing the teachable moment.

Experience with MBA learning teams suggests, however, that explicit teaming might not have helped. Students in every offering of the project management course are encouraged to develop a formal team charter before starting to work on the learning exercise. Some individuals and some teams take this task very seriously and tease out the details of how they will work together before beginning their work; nonetheless, most do not appear to think this task important until after problems begin. This difference may be due to individual orientations toward working in teams in MBA courses (Williams & Duray, 2006). Tight timelines and task-driven individuals do push the teams into action, however, as in the case of the research team above. When conflicts began to brew or issues around collaboration become important, charters were worked out-on-the-fly, during the course of the first team assignment. Some teams were compelled to revisit this exercise; others failed completely on the first task before they recognized the need for and value of this process element. In any case, students' perceptions regarding what was needed to get teams on track and implications for not doing so became real (Williams & Duray).

The importance of this part of team process appears to be learned explicitly, but as highlighted by the case examples, does not become "real" until conflicts occur within the process and teams acquire knowledge experientially. It seems that once the importance of the charter becomes clear and the gap between theory and practice obvious, the teachable moment occurs. In some teams, this moment may be lost; however, it appears that in the experience of each online team to date, it was not. Within the learning module, the facilitator was able to use the moment to pull out or convey some important information. Within both actual teams, the members were able to go back to information provided, recognize the source of difficulty, and move on to develop a charter.

In our view, it is what occurs in the gap between failure and the recognized need for additional information or work to deal with the failure that builds capability. This moment is where we believe online development products are most powerful. What is also clear about this "gap experience" is that trust in technology, trust in process, and trust and cooperation between individuals are critical factors (Williams & Duray, 2006). Such aspects are built and supported through effective leadership and tools, such as the team charter. Team charters and chat protocols, as noted in first case with LI students, are some of the tangible tools that force teams to explore these issues in advance. Incorporating these products into any online teaming experience is likely to improve the ability of the team members to work together.

Assignment of Accountability and Building in Flexibility

Team charters also outline forms of accountability and flexibility for team-identified roles and responsibilities that are fundamental for high performance. In traditional team literature, the need for clearly defined roles is fairly well recognized. It is believed that it is absolutely essential that everyone clearly know who is doing what, particularly in online teams, where you may not be able to observe what others are working on. At the same time, online teams require a certain amount of flexibility to get the most out of their members. If one member of an online team has a time differential that is advantageous, it only makes sense for that person to take responsibility for certain tasks even though someone else may be accountable for them. Sometimes, given the asynchronous nature of much online teaming, this necessity can cause problems.

Lipnack and Stamps (1997) found that in online teams, team roles defy definition, because online teams focus on achieving tasks in a fluid and flexible manner. Shifts in leadership can also drive changes in team members' roles (Miller, Pons, & Naude, 1996). In online teams, leadership fluidly moves from one group member to another, from one geographic or temporal site to another, or both. In many cases, more than one team member possessed information vital to the overall team's functioning and well-being, and as a result accepted leadership status assigned by the team based on that expertise. Team members seemed willing to step into and out of the leadership role, careful not to step on one another's toes.

At times, roles and leadership may not be as clearly defined in the online environment. The literature suggests that the need for boundary spanning and communication may intensify as roles and objectives become more ambiguous (Eccles & Crane, 1987; Weick, 1982). Further, the amount of boundary spanning may vary over time, influencing communication patterns and the ability to shift roles easily (Burt, 1993; Weick, 1982; White, Boorman, & Breiger, 1976). Such ambiguity can prove uncomfortable for those used to working within traditional, rule-based organizations. Research suggests that teams who have met, or have first established face-to-face relationships, form bonds more easily and tend to be more comfortable when faced with shifting roles (Walther,

1996). This finding points to the need for some form of "kick-off event" for online teams. Indeed, face-to-face may be superior, but voice and online also work, as evidenced by the research team.

Sometimes the trick is simply to assign an initial responsibility and then trade it off as necessary. This was certainly the case in the online research team. Tasks were initially accepted or assigned to an individual, based on their availability or their inclination to take responsibility for the task. If there was some reason that deadlines could not be met, the task was reassigned or shared. Careful record keeping helped to know who was doing what and when. Such "tracking" facilitated the development of more ambiguous roles among team members by helping them to juggle responsibilities and maintain accountability for deliverables.

In the MBA teams, we have witnessed good use of role assignment in the beginning of most courses. Everyone signs up for a particular task. It sometimes falls down when individuals are assigned tasks for which they are not well suited, or when circumstances make it difficult for individuals to fulfill their assigned roles. Many do not adapt well to the fluid nature of work that is characteristic of asynchronous online teams. Because work is not done at the same time, it is important that people speak up and volunteer when they see that someone needs help. For people used to doing their own jobs and letting someone else worry about the big picture, this can be a difficult skill to master.

Teams who quickly come together and share details of their personal schedules, why they are only available at certain times, and when they may not be available, tend to work better. In the online research team, due to work commitments, one member could only work on the project early or very late in the day. Another "night owl" was productive between 10 p.m. and 4 a.m. The third and fourth members used flexible daytime schedules. Each member picked up and organized their work after another member stopped, to enable them to finish elements quickly and without delays.

The balance between accountability and flexibility introduces an ambiguity into the working relationship that many find difficult to deal with. Can I count on you or not? Do I need to monitor you or not? How do I know when to help? To make the process work, individuals must engage in self-monitoring, team process monitoring, and proactive commitment to the work of learning. Individuals whose goal is completion of the course or project task are the least likely to engage in this type of behaviour, and the most likely to exhibit free-loader tendencies. It is the commitment to the project, the learning, or to the individuals that fosters team members' ability to deal with the ambiguity of shifting roles and responsibilities. Without the necessary commitment and trust, a team will not be able to balance accountability with the flexibility needed to achieve true synergy.

Monitoring Progress

The research team used minutes, email, conference calls, and deadlines to monitor task progress. Weekly conference calls were boisterous, friendly events that each member looked forward to. While this team rarely met face-to-face, each individual's personal urgency and commitment to deliver on the commitments they made, and to check another item off their weekly list of deliverables, kept the team moving forward. When commitments could not be met, team members openly admitted the reason behind their tardiness and took steps to complete the task or accepted another's offer of help.

The research project team teleconferenced weekly for one hour. The first five minutes of each conference call was devoted to catching up on "social history." Approximately 45 minutes was reserved for detailed discussion of upcoming project deliverables and the status of outstanding tasks. Team members took turns chairing these meetings. The final 10 minutes of each meeting was used to report on team members' external commitments (i.e., thesis progress, work promotions, baby's first steps) and relevant personal issues.

The team members considered themselves to be quite introverted, so they marvelled at the extroverted nature of their interactions, both in email and conversations. One member stated that, "although we have three introverts, you'd never know it from our interactions. Feeling comfortable, trusting, and sharing with each other brings out the E in us" (Delisle et al., 2001). Conference calls allowed the team to stay on top of three critical elements of progress – social activities, project activities, and external activities – each of which added an important component to the interaction. Shared goals and open communication around objectives and limitations combined with trust to ensure future reciprocity and accountability.

In addition, the research project team submitted monthly status reports to the funding sponsor on their project activities and accomplishments. This formal requirement forced the research team to take stock on a regular basis of accomplishments and outstanding tasks. This "taking-stock" activity encouraged accountability and the meeting of deadlines. It also provided a formal arena for tackling outstanding issues and raising concerns that needed to be dealt with by all major stake-holders in the project.

The MBA learning teams worked on much shorter timelines, measured in weeks versus years. Their use of status reporting seemed to be much lower. Some teams did status checks during the course of the project, but most tended to set a plan and then try to work to that plan. As in any project, this is where many of the problems become apparent, as the team fails to manage the ambiguous and changing nature of the work environment.

With the Logistics Institute's TDC module, regularly scheduled weekly "chats" served a similar structuring function to the monthly status reports and weekly conference calls used by the research team. The requirement to engage with all members of the team at one time and be ready to make good use of the time served to facilitate regular progress monitoring and progress checking.

Competing demands and disparities in commitment and desired outcomes (pass vs. "A" students) created traps for many learning teams. Competing demands, however, are no different in the working world. Resolution rests with team members' open communication of goals and expectations, and working around each individual's peculiar demands and interests. Status reporting and regular discussions of process and feedback were catalysts for this type of sharing, and for ensuring that important issues were addressed on a timely basis.

Incorporation of Social Interaction

In general, the research team's social interaction occurred by email and in person, but most often by conference calls. They tended to be boister-ous, laughter-filled, productive, valued time. Conference calls can act as a welcome counterbalance to release pressure, meet stakeholder expec-tations, help team members deliver results on time and on budget, and work through the many obstacles that typically emerge. They create a supportive camaraderie that helps members manage their own substan-tial professional workloads above and beyond the online project activities (Delisle et al., 2001).

Hartman (2000) suggests that fun on projects is a substantial moti-vator, and contributes to a culture where work is accomplished without the same level of burnout as in other environments. In general, the research team did three things to explicitly to ensure that the project was fun for all involved:

- *Celebrate success:* The beginning of each conference call always included *kudos* to anyone having completed a task or reached some other milestone. E-cards were used judiciously to celebrate any success or other event. Status reports started with accomplishments for the period, even when the more critical part, remaining concerns or issues, had yet to be addressed.
- *Plan for interaction:* Some of the project's limited funds were set aside to support celebratory dinners or events when all the parties could be found in the same locale. One research conference a year was funded so the entire team could meet face-to-face. This face-time provided continuing benefits in keeping the team motivated and onside for the more tedious and grinding work.
- *Communicate about other than project activities:* The research team regularly made an effort to catch up on the social aspects of the various team members' lives. Knowing how every team member's life was going provided insight into what one could be expected to do, and where others might be able to help out. Socializing also allowed trust to grow on a number of levels. It is one thing to trust someone's competence; it is quite another to care about an individual and to trust that they will care about you.

Admittedly, the second of the above goals is difficult to accomplish or imagine in an online learning environment. It is surprising, however, how innovative students can be when given the opportunity. Since its inception, the Athabasca University MBA program has provided a non-graded workspace for students to use as they wish. This workspace is akin to the online water cooler or coffee house. It provides MBA students with "room" to get to know each other away from the pressure cooker of the team project workspace. Although the space is used to varying degrees, it works most effectively as a way of enhancing the learning environment. One student has very successfully run "Joe's Bar" in the roundtable workspace of every course, much to the delight of fellow students and of academics. Sharing jokes, humour, frustration, births, deaths, and other life occurrences in these informal settings allows students to get to know each other in ways that they would normally do over a cup of coffee or mug of beer outside of class time.

A variation of this phenomenon also began to occur in each offering of the TDC module. Participants appeared to regret the completion of the module, insofar as it meant losing access to the rich social interaction they'd experienced with their new team. We found that adjournment ceremonies and behaviours online and in the synchronous and asynchronous environments were quite similar to those experienced in the adjournment phase of a face-to-face team. MBA students often exhibited withdrawal at the end of the program in a similar fashion. The research team experienced similar "mourning" at the end of their project, as the unique circumstances of the project drove a fiercely supportive and productive working relationship that has been difficult to replicate since completion.

Further research on the effectiveness or contribution of these technologically enhanced social realms to the learning activity is needed. Lee and colleagues (2006) suggest that task, social, and technological dimensions need consideration as well. They also state that critical to the success of virtual teams is a "pedagogical transformation of teaching and learning skills ... [and] ... shifting mindsets from residential programs to online environments" (Lee et al., p. 507). It would be interesting to see if the number of team entries, such as jokes and other forms of socializing in the various learning programs, actually correlates with grades; effort or entries in the course or case work; student satisfaction; or other measures defined as team success. Some evidence also suggests that students use a variety of communication technologies for different social and intellectual tasks (Rourke, Anderson, Garrison & Archer, 2001).

CROSS-CUTTING THEMES

Across all the team experiences highlighted in this chapter, we note three important common themes with respect to using teams and teaching about teams in an online context. The first theme deals with the use of technology to enable online teaming. The second suggests that trust in the technology, the process, and the people is a prerequisite to both the learning and the functioning of the teams. Finally, developing and leading supportive cultures through instilling beliefs, values, and processes that facilitate open communication, support, and trust is important in realizing learning and teaming in this environment.

Technology as Enabler

Technology played two important roles in the online learning or teaming experience. First, apprehension and preconceived notions about technology-mediated discussion caused problems in getting teams started, as evidenced in the team module and reaffirmed in every run of the MBA courses. Second, technology failure in online teams could be a convenient excuse: "I didn't get that note." "I couldn't participate in the teamwork because my computer hard drive crashed." Or technology failure in teams could produce significant levels of frustration. In an eight-week course, having your hard drive go can take you down for a significant portion of the course, and make it very difficult to carry your end of the team commitment.

The Role of Trust

With respect to trust, we distinguish further between online and traditional teams in their situational awareness. Online teams function on an *intentional awareness*, because only specific characteristics of suitable resources or providers may be known (Chen, 1997). *Situational awareness* for online teams is contrasted to the *extensional awareness* more likely in face-to-face teams, where the specific resources or providers are known. This different kind of awareness plays a big role in how the team becomes an entity, as well as how it weaves together its skills sets, and how it builds trust.

It is our view that the level of trust among participants (perhaps from having members who had worked on other teams together, or from a shared level of trust in the experience through the culture of the program, or as a result of trust in the coach) determines how well people work together and how seriously the charter is taken. It was clear to the team members of the online research team that they would have had difficulty working together without a strong desire to do so, and without trust in the other team members' abilities. Thus, trust in competence, contract, commitment (Reina & Reina, 1999), and character (Marshall, 2000) are all significant in the initial stages of online team development. Lawley (2006) supports this by suggesting that trust is fundamental to effective teaming, and that the lack of trust will seriously hinder the team's work. Further, good leadership is essential for building and nurturing the cultural conditions that allow trusting relationships to flourish.

Weick (1996) states that people organize cooperatively on teams to learn and complete their work. There is a continuous mix of agency and communion that creates reciprocity between individuals, and that benefits both learning and team function. As highlighted in this chapter, trust is also required for meaningful cooperation, and is not clear in the early stages of relationship building.

The development of trust is not, nor can it be, a quick and easy task. There is a need to look behind learners' apprehension and fear, to listen to and capture individuals' hearts before trust can follow. Here is an interesting paradox when considering trust. On the one hand, we see that a team must be productive quickly, and that individuals need to trust and to be trusted within the team. On the other hand, few people on teams or in any relationship will trust immediately. Team members thrown together are more likely to distrust the motives of others at the outset. This has implications for development, early sharing of personal information, and hence, charter development, as found in our three cases. The cases also highlight the distance that people will go when they do trust, and how reluctant they are to let go of a team member once a trusting relationship is in place. Social interaction and trust are key attributes in any team and learning process.

We need to know more about how to discern trust levels early, and what we can do to build them rapidly. A team member's decision to trust other team members will likely show the degree of leeway or freedom members have to act without controls in place, the level of benevolence felt, the evidence of openness, and the degree of risk taking realized. When a high level of trust exists, fewer rules or controls may be necessary. Trust is a tricky concept and a necessary consideration in online teaming. If we can invoke a culture and process that encourages rapid development of trust, then this can only facilitate our learning and teaming processes.

IMPORTANCE OF LEARNING AND TEAMING CULTURE

Another point highlighted by our discussion of trust, trust building and the implications for team performance, is how we might create or transform a culture to allow meaningful, trusting relationships to develop. Marshall (2000) states that "to create a truly customer-driven, team-based, and trust-centered organization... require(s) a fundamental change in the organization system...." (p. 66). Transforming a business culture to become more team- and relationship-based, where trust would flourish, is challenging and likely requires agreements between management and others to spell out trade-offs between risk, skill, labour, rewards, and how people should treat each other. Such an agreement would have to deal with underlying beliefs about human nature, drivers of the business, and how management and other actors in the workplace will work together.

The examples described in this chapter may provide tools for developing a culture of trust, accountability, and transparency conducive to rapid trust development. The importance of establishing a team charter early on to focus the team is only one example of the importance of engineering the culture of teams. The establishment of the team charter and acknowledgement of culture was important in our three cases; in each case, team members ignored this fact until faced with situations of conflict. Support from Malhotra, Majchrzak, and Rosen (2007) indicates that educators and leaders must work to develop and nurture a culture that allows for trust between people to develop effective teaming. To this end, leaders should

- establish and maintain trust through use of communication technology.
- ensure diversity is understood and appreciated.
- manage work/life cycle.
- monitor team members' progress and enhance recognition of member contributions.
- enable members to benefit from the team. (p. 60)

CONCLUSIONS

This chapter sheds light on some of the challenges in teaching teams and using online teaming in distance education programs, by providing some insights into the operations of a team-building distance simulation, a successful online research project team, and the use of teams in a distance-based MBA program. Our experience in these and other online team teaching and working situations convince us that these skills are teachable and transferable to an online learning environment.

In multiple runs of the Logistics Institute's team-learning module, we found the CD simulation to be an effective way to introduce the concepts of, and process tools needed for, effective teamwork. Following up with online teamwork in an online facilitated setting, it appears that individuals are developing understanding and needed skills online.

Over the 14-year history of the distance MBA programs at Athabasca University, we have witnessed similar results. Our students develop not only an explicit understanding of online team dynamics, but also tacit skills to make it happen. Two of the primary skills developed in traditional MBA programs are networking and oral presentation of information. In our program, we work on these skills too, but the main skills our students develop as a result of the program are the ability to share information, insights, and criticism over the web, and to build and work very effectively in online teams.

The biggest problem for any team is the assumption that you can put people together to work on a task, and they will automatically become a team and know how to work together. This assumption is equally false in face-to-face and online team environments. In the online world, it may be even easier to ignore the human process side of teamwork, in the absence of physical clues revealing the psychological health (or lack of) in the team. The trick is to put the effort into the process side of teaming and teaching, even when it is less visible than in the face-to-face environment. We reiterate, however, that it can and must be done.

Project team learning in an online world has become a fact of life at work and in educational settings. The experience from the three cases described provides some suggestions for how to approach this activity in learning or work settings.

NOTES

1. Dr. Hurst worked with a team invited by the LI to develop learning modules for their millennium project. The invitation was based on her research interests and previous experience in the logistics field. The team dynamics and communications module was developed as a two-part learning program, the first part an individual experience of a simulation product intended to allow the participant to learn about concepts while interacting within a simulated team, and the second part an online learning environment allowing the participant to learn how to participate within a team or with real participants working at a distance. The real-team sessions are facilitated while students work through and apply concepts. Dr. Hurst has facilitated, evaluated, and revised the module on an ongoing basis. The experiences described here are drawn from her experiences in facilitating the module, with the permission of the students and the Logistics Institute.

2. *Teachable moment* is the precise point at which a learner makes a mistake and wants to correct it, or to learn alternative information with which to interpret questions or responses. It is a brief window where the learner is most receptive to new information that is focused, personalized, and in context. Schank (1997) adds that learners are emotionally aroused when making a mistake. If error occurs publicly, they close off from embarrassment; if failure is private, as in online learning, the moment of failure is when the learner is most

receptive to new information and learning. Teachable moments often begin with a question and an individual's personal curiosity (see Bennett, 2000).

REFERENCES

Aranda, E. K., Aranda, L. & Conlon, K. (1998). *Teams: Structure, process, culture and politics.* Upper Saddle River, NJ: Prentice Hall.

Bennett, C. (2000). Capturing the teachable moment: In-house staff development. *Oregon Library Association Quarterly, 5*(4). Retrieved October 18, 2003, from http://www.olaweb.org/quarterly/quar5-4/bennett.shtml

Brewer, S., & Klein, J. D. (2006). Type of positive interdependence and affiliation motive in an asynchronous, collaborative learning environment. *Educational Technology, Research and Development, 54*(4), 331–354.

Burt, R. (Ed.) (1993). *The social structure of competition in networks and organizations.* Boston, MA: Harvard Business School Press.

Canadian Professional Logistics Institute (2000). *Team dynamics and communications module.*

Toronto: CPLI.

Chen, L. L. J. (1997). *Modeling the Internet as cyberorganism: A living systems framework and investigative methodologies for online cooperative interaction.* Unpublished doctoral dissertation. University of Calgary.

Chipman, A. (2007, April 4). Game Teaches Business Skills by the Scoop. *Wall Street Journal,* B4B.

Clark, D. N., & Gibb, J. L. (2006). Virtual team learning: An introductory study team exercise. *Journal of Management Education, 30*(6), 765–787.

Delisle, C., Thomas, J., Jugdev, K., & Buckle, P. (2001, November). Virtual project teaming to bridge the distance: A case study. Paper presented at the 32nd annual Project Management Institute Seminars & Symposium, Nashville, TN.

Eccles, R.G., & Crane, D. B. (1987). Managing through networks in investment banking. *California Management Review, 30*(1), 176–195.

Gareis, E. (2006). Virtual teams: A comparison of online communication channels. *The Journal of Language for International Business, 27*(2), 6–21.

Hartman, F. (2000). *Don't park your brain outside.* Philadelphia: PMI Publications.

Hawkrigg, J. (2007, March 12). Virtual teams need human touch. *Canadian HR Reporter, 20*(5), 16.

Hurst, D., & Follows, S. (2003). Virtual team development building intellectual capital and cultural value change. In M. Beyerlein (Ed.), *The collaborative work systems fieldbook,* (pp. 543–560). Denton, TX: University of North Texas.

Kalliath, T. & Laiken, M. (2006). Use of teams in management education. *Journal of Management Education, 30*(6), 747–750.

Katzenbach, J. R., & Smith, D. K. (1999). *The wisdom of teams: Creating the high-performance organization.* New York: Harper Collins.

Lawley, D. (2006). Creating trust in virtual teams at Orange: Overcoming barriers to collaboration. *Knowledge Management Review, 9*(2), 12–17.

Lee, S. H., Bonk, C. J., Magjuka, R. J., Su, B., & Liu, X. (2006). Understanding the dimensions of virtual teams. *International Journal on eLearning, 5*(4), 507–523.

Lipnack, J., & Stamps, J. (1997). *Online teams: Reaching across space, time and organizations with technology.* New York: John Wiley and Sons.

Malhotra, A., Majchrzak, A. & Rosen, B. (2007). Leading virtual teams. *Academy of management executive perspectives, 21*(1), 60–70.

Marshall, E.M. (2000). *Building trust at the speed of change: The power of the relationship-based corporation.* New York: American Management Association.

Mihhailova, G. (2007, Summer). Virtual teams: Just a theoretical concept of a widely used practice: *The Business Review, Cambridge 7*(1), 186–192.

Miller, P., Pons, J. M. and Naude, P. (1996, June 14). Global Teams. *Financial Times Mastering Management Series,* p. 12.

Reina, D. S., & Reina, M. L. (1999). *Trust and betrayal in the workplace: Building effective relationships in your organization.* San Francisco: Berrett-Koehler.

Rourke, L., Anderson, T., Garrison R., & Archer, W. (2001). Assessing teaching presence in computer conferencing transcripts. *Journal of Asynchronous Learning Networks, 5*(2). Retrieved October 9, 2007, from http://www.sloan-c.org/publications/jaln/ v5n2/pdf/v5n2_anderson.pdf

Schank, R. (1997). *Online learning: A revolutionary approach to building a highly skilled workforce.* New York: McGraw-Hill.

Stewart, T. A. (2001). *The wealth of knowledge: Intellectual capital and the twenty-first century organization.* New York: Currency.

Tran, V. N., & Latapie, H. M. (2007, Summer). Developing virtual team problem-solving and learning capability using the case method. *The Business Review, Cambridge, 8*(1), 27–33.

Waight, C. S., & Stewart, B. L. (2005). Valuing the adult learner in e-learning: Part two – insights from four companies. *Journal of Workplace Learning, 17*(5/6), 398–414.

Walther, B. J. (1996). Computer-mediated communication: Impersonal, interpersonal, and hyper personal interaction. *Communication Research, 23*(1), 3–43.

Weick, K. E. (1982). Management of organizational change among loosely coupled elements. In P. S. Goodman (Ed.) *Change in organizations: New perspectives on theory, research and practice* (pp. 375–408). San Francisco: Jossey-Bass.

Weick, K. (1996). Enactment and the boundaryless career: Organizing as we work. In M. B. Aruther & D. M. Rousseau (Eds.), *The Boundaryless career: A new employment principle for a new organizational era* (pp. 40–57). New York: Oxford University Press.

White, H. C., Boorman, S. A., & Breiger, R. L. (1976). Social structure from multiple networks I – Block models of roles and positions. *American Journal of Sociology, 81*(4), 730–780.

Williams, E. A., & Duray, E. (2006). Teamwork orientation, group cohesiveness, and student learning: A study of the use of teams in online distance education. *Journal of Management Education, 30*(4), 592–616.

ABOUT THE AUTHORS

Deborah Hurst (deborahh@athabascau.ca) is an associate professor of Organizational Behaviour and an academic area manager for Work and Organization Studies at the Centre for Innovative Management, Athabasca University. Deborah's research contributions include dealing with teaming for knowledge transfer, cultural organization change, learning and knowledge management, building leadership capability through knowledge sharing and managing the contributions of contingent knowledge workers. In 2007, Deborah along with colleagues Kay Devine and Lindsay Redpath, received the Best Careers Papers award from the Western Academy of Management. Before coming to Athabasca University, Deborah was a faculty member at the School of Business at Acadia University. In addition, she worked in the private sector for several years, most notably with General Motors Canada.

Janice Thomas (janicet@athabascau.ca) is the program director for the Executive MBA in Project Management at the Centre for Innovative Management, Athabasca University. Dr. Thomas brings to her academic role 25 years' experience in the field of project management. Prior to becoming an academic, she spent 10 years as an information technology and organizational change project manager. Dr. Thomas is a scholarly researcher who actively presents and publishes her research for academic and practitioner audiences around the world. She also supervises masters and doctoral students. In 2006, Dr. Thomas was recognized by the PMNetwork as one of the 50 most influential women in project management.